Malaysian Cinema, Asian Film

Film Culture in Transition
General Editor: *Thomas Elsaesser*

Double Trouble: Chiem van Houweninge on Writing and Filming
Thomas Elsaesser, Robert Kievit and Jan Simons (eds.)

Writing for the Medium: Television in Transition
Thomas Elsaesser, Jan Simons and Lucette Bronk (eds.)

Between Stage and Screen: Ingmar Bergman Directs
Egil Törnqvist

The Film Spectator: From Sign to Mind
Warren Buckland (ed.)

Film and the First World War
Karel Dibbets and Bert Hogenkamp (eds.)

A Second Life: German Cinema's First Decades
Thomas Elsaesser (ed.)

Fassbinder's Germany: History Identity Subject
Thomas Elsaesser

Cinema Futures: Cain, Abel or Cable? The Screen Arts in the Digital Age
Thomas Elsaesser and Kay Hoffmann (eds.)

Audiovisions: Cinema and Television as Entr'Actes in History
Siegfried Zielinski

Joris Ivens and the Documentary Context
Kees Bakker (ed.)

Ibsen, Strindberg and the Intimate Theatre: Studies in TV Presentation
Egil Törnqvist

The Cinema Alone: Essays on the Work of Jean-Luc Godard 1985-2000
Michael Temple and James S. Williams (eds.)

Micropolitics of Media Culture: Reading the Rhizomes of Deleuze and Guattari
Patricia Pisters and Catherine M. Lord (eds.)

Malaysian Cinema, Asian Film

Border Crossings and National Cultures

William van der Heide

Amsterdam University Press

To Julia

Front cover illustration: Poster for Hang Tuah (1956)
Courtesy of the National Archives of Malaysia

Back cover illustration: Poster for XX Ray II (1995)
Courtesy of the National Film Development Corporation Malaysia (finas)

Cover design: Kok Korpershoek, Amsterdam
Lay-out: japes, Amsterdam

isbn 90 5356 580 9 (hardcover)
isbn 90 5356 519 1 (paperback)
nugi 922

© Amsterdam University Press, Amsterdam, 2002

All rights reserved. Without limiting the rights under copyright reserved above, no part of this book may be reproduced, stored in or introduced into a retrieval system, or transmitted, in any form or by any means (electronic, mechanical, photocopying, recording or otherwise) without the written permission of both the copyright owner and the author of the book.

Contents

Acknowledgments — 9

Introduction — 11
Panggung Wayang; Malaysian Cinema, Asian Film — 11
The Realities of Film Viewing — 12
The Scope of this Study — 21

Chapter 1: Border Crossings — 25
Introduction — 25
National Cinema and Genre — 27
Cross-cultural Analysis — 29
Transtextuality — 32
The Hamburger Western — 36
The Samurai Film and the Noodle Western — 38
The Samurai Film and the Hamburger Western — 39
The Sword Film and the Spaghetti Western — 41
The Spaghetti Western — 44
The Martial Arts Film and the Chop Suey Western — 47
The Stunt Film and the Curry Western — 51
Conclusion — 54

Chapter 2: Malaysian Society and Culture — 57
Introduction — 57
Identity — 58
National Identity and National Culture — 60
Malaysian Identity — 65
Pre-colonial Malaysia — 66
    Foundational Narratives — 71
Colonial Malaysia — 77
    Parsee Theatre and Bangsawan — 81
Postcolonial Malaysia — 87
    The National Cultural Policy and its Consequences — 95
Conclusion — 101

Chapter 3: Film in Malaysia — 105

Introduction — 105

National Cinema — 106
    National Cinema Texts — 109

The Film Industry and Film Culture in Malaysia — 116

Early Film-going in Malaya — 118

The British in Malaya — 119

Origins — 123
    Laila Majnun, India and Indonesia — 124
    Shaw Brothers — 129

The Golden Age — 132
    The Indian Connection — 133
    The Studio System — 134
    P. Ramlee — 138
    Indian Cinema — 141
    Hong Kong Cinema — 141
    Indonesian Cinema — 144

The Decline — 145

The Revival — 149
    Government Assistance and Controls — 150
    Hong Kong Cinema — 156
    Indian Cinema — 158

Conclusion — 159

Chapter 4: Malaysian Cinema — 161

Introduction — 161

The Indian Cinema of the 1950's — 162

Hujan Panas — 166

Penarik Beca — 170

Hang Tuah — 176

Semerah Padi — 183

Hang Jebat — 191

Ibu Mertua-ku — 198

Matinya Seorang Patriot — 205

Fenomena — 212

Selubung — 218

Perempuan, Isteri &...	225
Sembilu	233
Conclusion	240
Conclusion	241
Notes	249
Filmography	265
Bibliography	271
Index	293

Acknowledgments

Most of the research work for this project was undertaken in Malaysia in February-March 1994 and August-September 1994, when I was a Visiting Fellow at the Asian History Centre, Australian National University and on study leave from the University of Canberra. Some follow up work took place in Kuala Lumpur in May 2001, supported by a grant from the University of Newcastle.

I therefore thank the following persons (and their institutions): Dr. Satendra Nandan, University of Canberra; Dr. Ian Proudfoot, Asian History Centre, Australian National University; Dr. Samsudin Abd. Rahim, Communications Department, Universiti Kebangsaan Malaysia; Dr. R. Karthigesu, Communications Program, Universiti Sains Malaysia, Penang; Mr. Abdul Rahman, Mr. Norshah bin Thamby and Mr. Mohd. Zulkifli bin Ab. Wahab from the National Film Development Corporation Malaysia (FINAS); the film directors Dato' L. Krishnan, Jamil Sulong, Aziz Osman and Adman Salleh; the film producer, Ruhani Abdul Rahman; K. S. Maniam, novelist and academic at the Universiti Malaya; Hamsah Hussin, writer and critic; Baharudin Latif, film critic; and to Raja Ahmad Alauddin, film director and academic, for our stimulating conversations in Malaysia and Australia.

I particularly want to thank Raimy Ché-Ross for valuable assistance in translating the dialogue of the un-subtitled Malaysian films and for perceptive comments on the cultural significance of aspects of these films.

Finally, my gratitude to Professor Philip Bell, University of New South Wales, for the faith he retained in me over the many years that it took for my research project to assume its present form; furthermore, Professor Bell improved the arguments herein by his comments and questions.

I am grateful to Allen & Unwin for allowing me to use four diagrams from Wang Gungwu's *Community and Nation* in chapter 2. The photos for figures 5, 10 and 11 were taken by Julia van der Heide. The other illustrations have been provided courtesy of the National Film Corporation Malaysia (FINAS) and the National Archives of Malaysia.

The publication of this book would not have been possible without the very positive response to the manuscript by the series editor, Thomas Elsaesser, University of Amsterdam and the support of Jaap Wagenaar, from Amsterdam

University Press. The English Department, University of Newcastle generously contributed to the cost of publication.

An earlier version of chapter 1 was published as 'Boundary Riding: Cross-Cultural Analysis, National Cinema and Genre' in *Social Semiotics*, 5: 2, 1995, pp. 213-237; part of chapter 4 has been published as 'SEMERAH PADI: A Proposal for a New Nation' in *Asian Cinema*, 12: 1, 2001, pp. 3-13.

Introduction

'Di Mana Kan Ku Chari Ganti'
(Where can I find a replacement)
(the title of a P. Ramlee song in IBU MERTUA-KU, 1962).

Panggung Wayang; Malaysian Cinema, Asian Film

'Panggung Wayang' is a frequently used phrase for cinema and cinema-going in Malaysia. It is made up of two words: 'Panggung,' meaning a theater, a stage and even an audience, and 'Wayang,' which refers to the traditional shadow puppet theater of the Malay world.[1] Wayang is sometimes also combined with the word 'Gambar,' which means a picture, a drawing or a photograph, to signify a movie. It is reputed that P. Ramlee (of whom more below) constructed a word 'Pawagam,' made from the first few letters of *Pa*nggung, *Wa*yang and *Gam*bar, to designate the cinema (Ché-Ross, 1996), but it appears not to have caught on, although I did see an old Shaw Brothers cinema in Melaka called *Pawagam Rex*.[2] However, Panggung Wayang is a particularly appropriate conjunction, because it combines the two major influences on film in Malaysia: the 'Bangsawan' (Malay opera) theater tradition, which provided personnel and stories to the Malaysian cinema, and the shadow puppet theater, a proto-cinematic medium that has been so important in Malay culture, even though its influence on the cinema is quite indirect. Both of these theatrical forms will be elaborated upon in chapter 2.

The book's title, *Malaysian Cinema, Asian Film*, not only identifies the focus of interest of the argument, it also highlights an important distinction between cinema and film culture. The term cinema, in association with a 'qualifier' like Malaysian, Indian, Asian, Malay, Tamil, Cantonese or feminist, refers to a specific film production aggregate based on national, regional, ethnic, linguistic, gender or any other identity characteristic (the limitations of some of these categorizations are discussed in chapter 3). On the other hand, film culture or film refers to the collective film experience of a particular community both synchronically and diachronically. This book will thus consider not only films produced in Malaysia, but also (to a greater or lesser extent) all of the film activities that take place there. For example, Indian cinema will be relevant to the Malaysian film culture, but so will Indian film culture (as well as Indian culture more generally). Ultimately, the emphasis on film and film culture strives to ensure that any particular entity (e.g. Malay cinema) is never isolated from its social and cultural context and its intertextual relationships. Obviously, the argument has to define boundaries for itself, even if these are recognized as being quite fluid. The focus will be on the major forces of interaction as these impinge on the Malaysian film culture. This means that the Indian, Chinese (especially Hong Kong), Indonesian, American and European film cultures will be of importance to the argument, but in roughly descending order. More general influences from these cultures will also be considered, as will be those of Islam, the Arab world and the 'third world.' Nevertheless, the book's concern is film studies and primary attention will always be given to films as expressions of particular communities and shaped by broader social, economic and ideological forces. The methodologies employed in the argument will be a combination of close textual analysis and cultural analysis, both of which will be examined in some detail in chapter 1.

The Realities of Film Viewing

Film analysis, cross-cultural analysis and transtextuality will all be discussed in the next chapter in conceptual terms, but it must not be forgotten that these activities cannot be totally isolated from the actual experience of film viewing. When working within one's own film culture, familiarity and practice can often erase the distinction between the pleasures of viewing and more formal analytical activities. However, this is much more difficult to do in another culture. The social situations of film viewing are often different and, in the case of Malaysian cinema, most of the films were viewed without subtitles; only later was the dialogue translated with the assistance of a 'Bahasa Melayu' (Malay language) speaker. The following experiences are therefore included because they highlight the 'messiness' and 'riskiness' of watching some of these films before the whole process was 'tamed' through video copies of the films and the support of a guide to the language and the culture, acting like the 'dalang' (narrator/interpreter) at a Wayang performance.

ALI BABA BUJANG LAPOK[3]
On August 29, 1994, I was traveling on a bus from Kuala Lumpur to the Universiti Kebangsaan Malaysia (National University of Malaysia) in Bangi, about forty kilometers south of Kuala Lumpur. With all the traffic difficulties of a large metropolis like Kuala Lumpur, the journey took over an hour. The buses on this route are the long distance type and are fitted with the obligatory video playback system. On this morning, the bus was filled with university students who were obviously enjoying the film that was being shown on the

bus' television set, singing along with the songs and even joining in with some of the film's dialogue – a form of audience involvement quite normal in Indian cinema, but in the West confined to 'cult' films like THE ROCKY HORROR PICTURE SHOW (1975). They were watching a well-worn tape of a 1961 black-and-white comedy called ALI BABA BUJANG LAPOK (lit. Ali Baba Confirmed Bachelors),[4] directed by and starring P. Ramlee, together with S. Shamsuddin and Aziz Sattar, a threesome that had played 'confirmed bachelors' in a series of BUJANG LAPOK films going back to 1957.

Figure 1: ALI BABA BUJANG LAPOK advertisement

What surprised me most was that this 'old' film was genuinely loved by these young students; they were obviously very familiar with the film and were certainly not laughing at it. This does not mean that Malaysian young people love old films per se, but that they and most Malaysians (not just Malays, but also Indian and Chinese Malaysians) love P. Ramlee, who was and still is the most admired figure in contemporary Malaysian popular culture, despite the fact that he died in 1973 – an Indian equivalent to such a popular culture 'hero' would have to be a combination of Raj Kapoor (director/actor), Dilip Kumar (actor), S. D. Burman (composer) and Mohammed Rafi (playback singer). His stature is such that the title of one of his best-known songs (quoted at the head of this chapter) is indicative of the void he left behind. However, this certainly does not imply that all Malaysians like Malaysian-made films – the title of a recent book on Malaysian cinema: *Love Malaysian Films*[5] (Baharudin Latif (ed), 1989)[6] – is more of a plea than a reality. On the contrary, most Malaysians do not watch Malaysian films and those that do are almost all ethnically Malay – this problematic situation will be discussed more fully in chapter 3. There were certainly no barriers to the students' response to the film on the bus, despite the fact that it was over 30 years old and showed three middle-aged actors creating rather clichéd comedy routines out of the Ali Baba story.[7] I could admire this explosion of popular culture enthusiasm, but it was impossible for me to join in.

To Live

This sort of cultural exclusion was even more pronounced when I saw Zhang Yimou's To Live (1994) a week or so later in a large, dilapidated cinema in Melaka. The audience was quite small, but it responded to the film very favorably. Almost all of them were Chinese Malaysians. I enjoyed the film too, but I have never been more conscious of watching a *Chinese* film. For a start, I was very aware that some of the audience would have been profoundly, if indirectly, affected by the events depicted in the film: the defeat of the Nationalist armies by the Mao Zedong's Communists in 1949, the 1958 Great Leap Forward and the start of the Cultural Revolution in 1966. While I had a good understanding of these events, I lacked any experience in relation to them. Of greater significance was my relationship to the film's social and cultural domain. I hasten to add that this did not result from anything *in* the film or *about* the film – after all, I had read quite a lot about the film and was probably more knowledgeable about the work of Zhang Yimou and of Chinese cinema than anyone else in the audience. It was occasioned by my seeing the film in another country with an audience that, I felt, recognized the film's social rituals of gambling, eating, marriage arrangements and funeral ceremonies as 'local knowledge.' Suddenly, the film's 'Chineseness' became its dominant characteristic, engendering a powerful alienation effect that was only tempered for me by the main character's occupation: a shadow puppet performer. Because of my study of the Malaysian shadow puppet theater, this fact partially returned the film to culturally familiar territory. Nevertheless, no other viewing experience has so affected my response to what I had seen on the screen and highlighted my limitations as an analyst.

CHUNGKING EXPRESS

Watching Wong Kar-wai's 'avant-garde' thriller, CHUNGKING EXPRESS (1994), in a Kuala Lumpur cinema a few weeks earlier had elicited quite a different response. In the middle of the film, the phone rang. There is nothing particularly strange about this, except that it occurred during a chase scene in the back streets of Hong Kong, where a woman in a blonde wig was pursuing some double-crossing drug dealers. Even so, mobile phones had been around in Hong Kong longer than in most other places. However, the call was answered by a male Chinese voice directly *behind* me. Maybe this was an interactive movie, in which the spectator could communicate with the film by phone and so alter its plot direction! The reality was both more pedestrian and amazing. The voice behind me was answering a call from a friend or business associate – it was unlikely to have been from a double-crossing drug dealer (especially in Malaysia). Under the circumstances, I presumed he would propose to return the call after the film was finished. To my amazement, he proceeded to engage his caller in a long conversation, which, because of the exciting and noisy chase sequence that was taking place on screen, had to be carried out at a very high volume. Given my (fetishistic?) obsession for audience silence during a film screening, I wanted to turn around and tell him to keep his voice down, but I decided not to respond – after all he might have been the drug dealer! No one else in the cinema admonished him either. I thus presumed that this was not an uncommon occurrence. The man's use of the phone in this way seems to run counter to the purpose of that technology: the ability to have a private conversation with another person at a speaking volume that would not be heard by a person nearby.

CHUNGKING EXPRESS is itself littered with missed, diverted, regretted and treasured phone conversations: the plain-clothed policeman in the film's first story longs for one such call to be 'canned without an expiry date' (cans of food, expiry dates and specific times of the day are recurrent motifs). The film also deals with proximity and its relationship to intimacy, as well as with invasion of privacy: in the second story, a woman working in a fast-food shop obsessively returns to the uniformed policeman's apartment to reorganize its contents, while listening to *California Dreaming* at a very high volume. In these respects, the event *in* the cinema reverberated with those in the film, creating an imaginary relationship every bit as powerful as the Metzian Imaginary on the screen itself.

This whole situation also made me think about noise – in the communication sense of the word. The telephone conversation in the cinema was noise, because its presence as well as its volume level interfered with the attention I was giving to the film's soundtrack. It was also noise, because, while I could clearly hear the telephone user, I could not understand the Cantonese he was speaking. But, of course, the film was also 'speaking' Cantonese! Was its dialogue then also noise? After all, I had to *read* the English subtitles to make any sense of the dialogue. For him, the film's soundtrack was the noise. He may therefore have been reading the subtitles also (probably the Chinese rather than the English ones), since his own voice would have made it difficult for him to hear the dialogue. However, for a person proficient in reading Chinese, the dialogue is always partially redundant, because Hong Kong films always carry Chinese subtitles in order to accommodate those viewers who cannot understand the dialect in which the film's dialogue has been dubbed (typically Cantonese or Mandarin). On the other hand, the issue of noise or interference may well have been totally irrelevant for him. The competition between the soundtrack and the telephone conversation was certainly of great concern to me. However, especially given his behavior, he might have been quite comfortable with the coexistence of information sources without insisting on a hierarchical order. This postmodernist sense of de-canonization and performance echoed the film's own strategies: narrative fragmentation, multiple narrators, and an emphasis on style, including a radical use of slow and stop motion. Nevertheless, one could talk of a sort of breach of contract. We had both purchased an 'entitlement' to watch a film in a situation where the film's voice presumed or even demanded attention. This whole experience emphasized the social context and social contract in which we engage when going to the cinema, but it also highlighted the specificity of any viewing occasion and the resultant influence of that occasion on the interpretation of the film: the film's concerns with telephones, communication processes and the competition between music and dialogue were foregrounded for me due to this experience *in* the cinema. It furthermore suggests that technologies like the cinema or the telephone are constantly reassigned roles and meanings by social contexts and communication priorities.

Femina
Most Hong Kong films also have English subtitles, even if their spelling and grammar are sometimes quite incomprehensible. In Malaysia, Hong Kong films also carry Bahasa Melayu subtitles, so there are often three strips of written language cluttering up the lower half of the screen. Malaysian films, on the other hand, are rarely subtitled, since they have little currency (literally) outside of the country. In March 1994, I saw a film called Femina (1993) and would now like to discuss it in terms of my response to it at that time. Later I saw it on video with my translator, but these notes were written just after the un-subtitled viewing and raise the question of how I made sense of a film, in which the dialogue was largely unintelligible to me.

Figure 2: FEMINA poster

After watching the un-subtitled film in a Kuala Lumpur cinema, I felt that I had a pretty good idea of its primary plot elements: the increasingly antagonistic relationship between two women – the owner and the editor of a fashion magazine called FEMINA – and the eventually romantic relationship between the editor and a minibus driver, set in contemporary Kuala Lumpur. Such plots have fueled romantic comedies the world over and genre familiarity helped clarify the details of the plot. There was also a secondary plot about a prostitute. While I understood its function in the film, I was quite unclear about some of its details, e.g. whether the prostitute, her father and the pimp were illegal Indonesian immigrants and if/why the father allowed her to become a prostitute. (Interpolation: it is interesting that comprehension faltered in the sub-plot rather than in the main plot; perhaps these narrative units are more cryptic than the main plot and are quickly sketched out through dialogue, rather than elaborated by means of the whole range of verbal and non-verbal 'languages'). Nevertheless, the point of these scenes, as is the case with most sub-plots, was to parallel the main plot, with the prostitute being contrasted with the two women running the fashion magazine.

Let me try to identify what I knew about this film before watching it as this might have channeled my interpretation in certain directions:
- the director was Aziz Osman, whom I had met a week or so before; we did not talk about this film at all, but he identified himself as a thinking entertainer who wanted to deal with important social issues (Aziz Osman, 1994);
- I noted a reference to the film on a television program devoted to Malaysian cinema, RENTAK KARYA; there were some clips from the film that made little impression on me at the time;
- I saw a poster for the film at FINAS (National Film Development Corporation Malaysia), where I had interviewed Aziz Osman. The art work for the poster was also used in the newspaper advertisement for the film (and on the video cover): two women, one reading a book on feminism, were each holding a leg of a man suspended upside down between them and it suggested (reinforced by the film's title) a comedy about male/female relations, even something feminist with the women having power over the man. The statement above the image, which I translated as 'When women have power... !' warned of the consequences of women exercising power over men, thus contradicting or at least questioning the image's message. The poster made me think of American screwball comedies, especially films like I WAS A MALE WAR BRIDE (1949) and ADAM'S RIB (1949). I did not recognize the actors' names, although I recalled their faces once the film started – this was particularly the case with Erma Fatima who played the lead in FANTASI (Fantasy, 1994), a film I had seen the previous day;
- a number of people – the critic Baharudin Latif, Abdul Rahman of FINAS and Raja Ahmad Alauddin of Universiti Kebangsaan Malaysia – had talked to me about Aziz Osman and this undoubtedly set up certain expectations. There may have been other forms of pre-knowledge that were less specific such as the release of the film throughout the country on the eve of the Muslim feast days of 'Hari Raya Aidil Fitri,' celebrating the end of the fasting month of Ramadan. This was a sought after time to release a film, implying that the film was expected to be popular.

The other major influence on my interpretation of the film was my minimal comprehension of spoken Bahasa Melayu. This was further affected by the everyday speed of talking and the specificity of the dialect of middle-class Kuala Lumpur Malay young people. Consequently, my understanding was limited to specific words and phrases within conversations and to greetings and other discrete statements. Of course part of this Kuala Lumpur dialect is the frequent use of English and this was especially the case with the magazine owner, played by Susan Lankester (a Pan-Asian actor). However, the English was largely confined to phatic communications such as greetings and a range of comments that were peripheral to the plot. There were, however, a few statements that helped to clarify the narrative and reveal the tensions between the two women, e.g. the magazine owner's 'Remember Tina, that we are partners' (Tina was the magazine's editor, played by Erma Fatima).

In light of all of the above qualifications, it may seem surprising that I was confident that I had acquired a reasonable grasp of the film's plot and themes. Although a minibus was bombed, fights broke out and the police raided a brothel, this was not an action film, which would usually make it easier to follow (perhaps this is why action films, and not just those from America, are so popular the world over). There was, in fact, a lot of dialogue. This raised the question as to the relevance of the dialogue. The question has nothing to do with what the director/scriptwriter might have been thinking; for them, the dialogue was part of a 'seamless' audio-visual package. For someone in my situation however, it made me wonder about the status of this dialogue. Did it provide an extra layer of meaning, a set of nuances or elaborations? Or did the film's cultural specificity most potently reside in the dialogue?

Before continuing with these questions, I must acknowledge that the reactions of the audience in the cinema also affected my interpretation. To take one example, the male members of the audience laughed loudest when the driver was arguing his case, whereas the female viewers responded most enthusiastically when the two women had the advantage. This said something about the film's strategies, but also about gender polarization in the audience.

The film seemed to me to be totally comprehensible as an example of the Hollywood classical narrative as defined by David Bordwell (Bordwell, Staiger and Thompson, 1985: 12-59). The narrative trajectory, point-of-view and continuity system utilized by the film were drawn from what has become the dominant means of articulating stories in films and television programs. The primary and secondary characters functioned as the film's causal agents. The film also operated within the dominant forms of gender construction in terms of women's social role and general visual representation. While there seemed to be less fetishization of the characters' faces and bodies, this may be as much due to the absence of a star system in contemporary Malaysian cinema as to Muslim modesty or Islamic ideology (certainly, television commercials and the ubiquitous pop music programs stressed this fetishization more overtly than the movies did). The film was a typical example of the romantic comedy and the physicality of action and language (paradoxically, this was obvious from the *way* the language was spoken and thus less problematic than the meaning of the words) had strong screwball-comedy overtones.

It could be argued that the film was so 'transparent' (interpretatively) because the director, Aziz Osman, was an excellent visualizer, able to tell stories through the design and sequencing of images (a point made by Baharudin Latif, who likened Aziz Osman to Steven Spielberg). One must not forget the role of the other components of the soundtrack either. In fact, it seems likely that the incomprehensibility of much of the dialogue forced me to pay more attention to these other components, especially the music (although I found its muzak-like nature annoying). Of course, the difficulty with the dialogue also made me concentrate more on the visual track, looking there for clues unavailable elsewhere. It is very likely that the language problem made me work all the harder in trying to maintain a grip on the film than might otherwise have been the case.

The fact that the film was contemporary (rather than historical) and cosmopolitan (rather than set in a 'kampung', i.e. village) also aided my understanding (the city as an international/global text). Although it is just such a statement that, on reflection, worries me most. If the film had been set in 15th century Melaka, I would have been much more reticent about making statements such as those above. The bold assumption that a 'city film is a city film,' wherever it may be located, can lead to dangerous presumptions about sameness, because, as a generalization, we initially tend to orientate any experience towards the known and the familiar (and find solace and comfort in such 'recognition'), actively looking for universalities, whether of behaviors, customs or places, before then asserting difference or rather constructing an 'otherness' that oscillates between exoticism and condescension.[8] So perhaps I made the film 'mean' through a massive assumption on my part. Maybe the film was 'transparent' because I projected my cultural assumptions onto the film, in a way that was impossible for me to do when watching To Live.

It is remarkable how similar the above interpretation is to that which I and the translator developed much later. There were clarifications and corrections, such as the details of the sub-plot, but much else was confirmed. Even the film's ambivalent attitude to the role of women in Malaysian society was picked up at the first viewing. However, the main difference was the absence of what the anthropologist Clifford Geetz called 'thick description... a multiplicity of complex conceptual structures, many of them superimposed upon or knotted into one another' (Geetz, 1973: 10). The subsequent analysis of the film 'tracked' the changes in the male/female relationship in a more nuanced way. I now became aware of 'how' as well as 'what.' I was more conscious of cultural reverberations than I was capable of noticing when seeing the un-subtitled film in 1994. In retrospect, I do not believe that cultural specificity resides solely in the dialogue any more than it does in any other single element of the film's discourse. However, the spoken language and certain other social manifestations of culture (non-verbal behavior and customs come to mind) are often more difficult to identify than are narrative structures, genres and stylistic strategies.

These examples suggest a complexity of response that is not always possible to include in the detailed analysis of texts, which has a tendency to extract the text out of its social context and its reception. In return, however, a cross-cultural approach re-inserts the text into another set of complexities. An analysis of FEMINA might contemplate the film's 'moves' on western feminism, Malaysian/Malay cultural identity, Islamic propriety and gender roles, arguing that the film ultimately cannot (nor perhaps wants to) reconcile these tensions as it awkwardly tries to negotiate a middle course between enjoyable entertainment and social tract.

The Scope of this Study

This book argues that Malaysian film culture can only be satisfactorily understood using analytical approaches quite different from those that have typically been applied to national cinemas.

National cinema has tended to be conceptualized in overtly homogenous terms, with difference constructed primarily through formal categories such as authorship and genre. Cultural difference, on the other hand, is conventionally located on the boundaries of the national cinema by proposing that difference exists primarily between national cinemas, while simultaneously suppressing or erasing internal cultural heterogeneity, e.g. Brian McFarlane and Geoff Mayer's *New Australian Cinema* (1992). Since most analyses of national cinema have been of societies with entrenched, dominant cultural communities (and therefore are assumed to have relatively unproblematic and hegemonic cultural identities), this approach to national cinema is not surprising – Noel Burch (1979) defines Japanese society and Japanese cinema in just such terms.

An examination of film in Malaysia has to confront the complex ethnic, religious and social differences that lie so obviously at the heart of the country, and consequently any discussion based on homogeneity is untenable. Such a film culture should not be discussed in terms of coherence and common identity, but should acknowledge and actually propose a set of multiple, even contradictory, identities. Whereas Susan Hayward in a book on French cinema as *national* cinema (1993) is able to propose seven 'typologies' for an examination of French cinema (while at the same time qualifying the exclusiveness of these categories), I argue that such a typological approach is totally inappropriate to the study of film in Malaysia.

The continually negotiated and contested cultural identities in Malaysia instead suggest a form of analysis that stresses cross-cultural and transtextual interactions. This form of analysis does not reject the existence of the 'discourse of nation,' which, with respect to film in Malaysia, is frequently invoked in government film policy ('The film industry can play a major role in promoting national unity,' Malaysian Deputy Prime Minister, Abdul Ghafar bin Baba, 1989) and national(ist) rhetoric about cultural sovereignty and cultural imperialism ('The Western individuals controlling the media could also influence our thoughts, attitudes and culture. If we are not careful, we too can be influenced to destroy ourselves,' Malaysian Prime Minister, Dr. Mahathir Mohamad, quoted in *New Straits Times*, 1994a). Instead it focuses the debate onto one of the central tenets of 'nation': the border, which I discuss not as a line of separation between two distinct cultures, but as the site of interaction of cultural forces. Here, interaction is not just another term that invites comparisons between specific national cinemas; rather, it emphasizes relationships between and within particular cultural communities (which might be both larger and smaller than the nation). At a certain level, this reconfigures the borderline into a series of 'lines of connectedness' that might be the consequence of diasporic histories, e.g. Indian cinema and Indian film culture in Malaysia. On the other hand, these lines may also exist between quite different cultural communities, e.g. Indian cinema and Malay cinema. The border is still a valuable metaphor for the discussion of national cinema (at the very least as a strategy), but it needs to be accompanied by other concepts that open the border's resistance to difference.

This study of film in Malaysia details the characteristics and complexities of its film industry and film culture (Malaysia has hardly ever been mentioned in studies of national cinemas, regional cinemas, 'third world' cinemas or international cinema). This in turn leads to a re-conceptualization of the 'national cinema' paradigm away from its fixed categories and towards the application of a range of approaches to a particular film culture: Malaysia. In doing so, it forces a reconsideration of the general applicability of this paradigm (a particular conception that has come to be employed as a universal category), by suggesting that cultural difference is at the (invisible) center of all nationally-constituted cultures (if usually less obviously so than in Malaysia). An important contribution to this reassessment is the adoption of cross-cultural analysis as the primary methodology for this study. Cross-cultural analysis immediately foregrounds my own cultural location in relation to the study's subject matter, while also emphasizing the cross-cultural nature of all analysis (diachronically and synchronically). It also suggests that cultural practices such as film production occur in the context of a complex web of cultural forces that produces (in a given culture, at a given time) a specific set of expressions constructed from available cultural opportunities and resources.

The following chapters do not engage in any detailed audience analysis, other than to refer to some primary and secondary sources that comment on the complex nature of that audience when examined in terms of cultural difference. As indicated above, I employ a cross-cultural approach that places me at the center of the analysis and therefore consciously acknowledges that my interpretation is not undertaken from inside that culture, except to the extent that I 'lived' in that culture for a number of short periods of time. I do, however, argue that this culture is so constructed by difference that any use of the inside/outside dichotomy is inherently problematic.

In chapter 1, *Border Crossings*, I focus upon the relevance and applicability of cross-cultural analysis and transtextuality to this study and apply these concepts to a case study of the Western genre and its transformations through different film cultures, all of which are present in and continue to impact upon Malaysian film culture.

In chapter 2, *Malaysian Society and Culture*, the concept of cultural identity is examined and its relationship to national identity discourses is interrogated. I then go on to argue that due to geographic location and historical consequence, Malaysia is a society crossed by lines of voluntary and forced connectedness (migration, trade, colonialism) that are expressed politically, religiously, socially and culturally. Consequently, any understanding of Malaysian culture must acknowledge its pluralist nature and not attempt to suppress those cultural forces that militate against particular versions of the nation.

In chapter 3, *Film in Malaysia*, I analyze the conceptualizations of national cinema and examine some texts on the national cinemas of France, America, Japan and Australia for their elaboration of notions of homogeneity, difference and cultural specificity. I argue for the employment of the term 'Malaysian film culture' rather than 'Malaysian cinema' (the more usual way of describing this and most other national cinemas), because the Malaysian experience of film is much more encompassing than just those films actually produced in Malaysia. This leads to a discussion of Malaysian film culture as the interaction between Malaysian, Chinese, Indian, Indonesian and other film cultures. While there is some discussion of the Malaysian film industry, the chapter concentrates on historical and contemporary filmic and other cultural influences on film production, distribution and exhibition in Malaysia.

In chapter 4, *Malaysian Cinema*, I undertake detailed analyses of a selected number of films made in Malaysia from the 1950's to the 1990's; they are discussed chronologically to trace the continuity and discontinuity of ideas and strategies. All of the films are 'Malay' (although that identity marker will itself be questioned and qualified), but the analyses do not contain them within that label. Instead, I stress their location in the complexities of Malaysian film culture and Malaysian culture in general. Cross-cultural and transtextual approaches are adopted to argue that notions of national cinema discourse like coherence, homogeneity, uniqueness, and national identity are inappropriate categories, as the films (like all films) make connections both more centrifugal and more centripetal than national-cultural boundaries.

1 Border Crossings

'[The exotic is] when you travel the world as a foreigner, looking at each country as something exotic, then when you go back home, that becomes the most exotic place there is. It's a way of becoming foreign to yourself'
(Raul Ruiz, quoted in Romney, 1992: 15).

'The person who finds his homeland sweet is still a tender beginner; he to whom every soil is as his native one is already strong; but he is perfect to whom the entire world is as a foreign place. The tender soul has fixed his love on one spot in the world; the strong person has extended his love to all places; the perfect man has extinguished his'
(Hugo of St Victor – a twelfth-century Saxon monk, quoted in Said, 1993: 407).

'I'm a stranger here myself'
(quoted in JOHNNY GUITAR, 1954).

Introduction

This book is primarily concerned with the analysis of Malaysian film culture and films produced in Malaysia over the past fifty years. Prior to tackling the films themselves, it is necessary to examine some fundamental theoretical issues that are central to the argument, particularly cross-cultural analysis and transtextuality. There are certain other issues that also need discussing, but this will be done at the relevant stages of the overall argument: national and cultural analysis in the chapter on Malaysian society and culture (chapter 2) and national cinema in the chapter on film in Malaysia (chapter 3), while other, more specific issues will be raised during the textual analyses in the chapter on Malaysian cinema (chapter 4). Rather than dealing with cross-cultural analysis and transtextuality in abstract terms, this chapter strives to demonstrate their importance and relevance to the argument by applying them to a case study that starts off in 'familiar territory.'

One of the major challenges facing this book is the lack of familiarity with or interest in Malaysian film worldwide and even within Malaysia itself.[1] Furthermore, most of the films that will be analyzed are only available without subtitles. Consequently, this book will need to present material that would be assumed in the discussion of most other film cultures. For this reason, this chapter will introduce the Malaysian film culture by initially focusing on the cultural forces that have profoundly shaped that film culture. The case study will strategically commence at the so-called 'cultural imperialist' center of film culture – Hollywood – and travel to the border of Malaysian film culture via 'lines of connectedness' to European, Japanese, Chinese and Indian film cultures. These film cultures not only influence the films actually made in Malaysia, but they are also ever-present in Malaysian cinemas and on Malaysian television, especially in films from Hong Kong, India and America – the Tsui Hark film ONCE UPON A TIME IN CHINA II (1992) was the third most popular film shown in Malaysia in 1992 (Baharudin Latif, 1993a: 242). These major cultural and filmic influences are mentioned in the case study and will be elaborated upon in the chapter on film in Malaysia (chapter 3). The following case study examines a particular interaction between these film cultures by tracing the changing textual and social fate of the Western genre throughout them.

It is important to point out that there is no discernible presence of this genre in any of the Malaysian films that will be analyzed in detail. However, a 1962 P. Ramlee-directed comedy, LABU DAN LABI (Labu and Labi) does reference the Western. Labu (Mohd Zain) and Labi (P. Ramlee) are both servants of a rich, miserly Malay businessman and they engage in a series of fantasies about becoming rich (in order to marry the businessman's daughter). In one of these, Labu is Jesse Labu, Jesse James' brother, who saunters into a saloon and demands a glass of milk. The saloon door then opens to reveal Labi as the sheriff, who intends to capture Jesse Labu dead or alive for the reward money of $5000. Labi says he is Nat King Cole's brother. There follows a gunfight between the two until they return to reality. The fantasy is extremely playful, with the characters moving between their various personas. The scene does draw upon the Western genre (Jesse James, saloon stereotypes, iconography), but these are continually undercut (references to milk and Nat King Cole as well as the ever-present Malay physiognomies). Even so, the film does not particularly recontextualize the Western. The accentuation on Western iconography in the film's poster is massively out of proportion to its role in the film, since the above scene occupies no more than five minutes of film time. Perhaps the drawing power of P. Ramlee in a Western (he dominates the poster) was too tempting for the studio's advertising department to pass up.[2]

Nevertheless, characteristics of the *transformation* of the Western genre, especially in Indian and Hong Kong cinema are of crucial importance in Malaysian films. In particular, it will be argued that the Western changed the Indian stunt-film genre and social genre and the Chinese martial arts genre, all of which in turn shaped and changed the Malaysian cinema of the 1950's/60's and the 1980's/90's. Thus, while the example of the Western genre seems quite

Figure 3: LABU DAN LABI poster

tangential to the main thrust of this book, it is actually of central relevance; at the same time it represents a powerful example of the complexity of cultural transformation and fecundity. It also suggests that the Western influence (playing on the ambiguity of the term as both a particular culture and a genre) on other film cultures is more complex than the cultural imperialism argument allows for. The subject matter of the case study also highlights the cultural location of the analyst (an essential facet of cross-cultural analysis) – in fact, it travels the major 'lines of connectedness' taken by the author, before he himself became interested in Malaysian cinema.

National Cinema and Genre

National cinema and genre are two quite traditional means by which films have been categorized, studied and discussed. As critical constructs, they have been useful in identifying formal, thematic and cultural commonalities within their defined boundaries, but the persistent application of these categories has also limited the ways in which films are considered in relation to each other – whether outside of or across such categories. Unfortunately, or perhaps inevitably, national cinema and genre studies are rather myopic and tend to eschew difference because of the specific limits they place upon their subject.

National cinema is typically discussed using the nationalist discourse of cultural authenticity, while at the same time confronting the perceived external threats to national sovereignty through legal, economic, esthetic and cultural sanctions. Consequently, the films are commonly examined as expressions of unique cultural characteristics, squeezing out the essence of national identity. This leads to such films being called 'uniquely Australian' or 'uniquely Japanese,' although rarely 'uniquely American,' implying that the American cinema is usually not perceived as a national cinema. Studies of national cinema are frequently couched in diachronic terms, constructing narratives of origin, adversity, survival and triumph.

At first glance, genre would appear to be a transnational category, but in practice genre studies rarely deal with genre in this way. The term genre is most frequently applied to the American cinema and studies of particular genres are overwhelmingly devoted to American genre films. Where the genre is 'non-American,' it is usually given a national label: the Japanese samurai genre, the Chinese kung fu genre and the Indian stunt film. If a genre does cross national boundaries, this is often presented as a devaluation of the purity of the genre, as was the case with critical responses to the Italian Western.

The term 'Spaghetti Western' was first coined by American critics about Italian Westerns and was intended in a pejorative sense. It started a craze in the 1960's and 70's among film journalists of applying culinary labels to what they regarded as inauthentic, alien and derivative Westerns: Sauerkraut Westerns, Paella Westerns, Camembert Westerns, Chop Suey Westerns, Noodle Westerns, Borsch Westerns and Curry Westerns. No similar label was ever applied to the American Westerns, which might otherwise be called Hamburger Westerns (Frayling, 1981: xi). On one level, these labels represent harmless and amusing filmic versions of the diversity of ethnic cuisines – a particularly safe form of multiculturalism – but they really function as a threat to 'keep off my land.' Fortunately, the threat was not heeded.

Following a more theoretical discussion of cross-cultural analysis and transtextuality, this chapter traces some of the connections between these 'Westerns,' not in order to identify some overarching master narrative, but to acknowledge intertextual relations while also emphasizing local cultural characteristics. In this context, national cinema and genre are still useful categories, but they are more effectively approached through their interaction with each other than through their total separation or their virtual superimposition (the two analytical norms described above), with cross-cultural analysis being the most appropriate tool for such a reassessment.

Cross-cultural Analysis

The term cross-cultural is firstly useful for stressing the cross-cultural nature of *all* analysis, whether this occurs across or within cultures. However, its appropriateness is most apparent in its emphasis on the border as a site of interaction: a point of departure and arrival, a place of familiarity and difference, a zone of commingling and contestation. The border thus represents both a crossing and an intersection, while at the same time implying divergence and difference (Chambers, 1994: 122). This emphasis on the border runs counter to certain postmodernist proposals for the dissolution of all boundaries and categories, which would lead to the undifferentiated globalism of a 'cinema without walls.' Rather, borders are sites for analytical and creative activity informed by concepts such as hybridity and syncretism (terms that do not dissolve difference, but retain traces of that difference), which are constructed through processes such as translation, transformation and adaption – often grouped under the label of intertextuality, although Gérard Genette proposed the more encompassing term of transtextuality (Stam, 1992: 22-27). Cross-cultural analysis, like cultural studies in general, is an interdisciplinary practice, drawing on existing disciplines and methodologies and is therefore itself transtextual. Recent discussions on cultural studies have stressed the importance of avoiding its reduction to just another discipline, by proposing it as a 'conjunctual practice' (Hall, 1990: 11) and as a practice 'that exists in parenthesis [...] in abeyance, under erasure' (Chambers, 1994: 122), so that it might best be identified as ~~cultural studies~~.

The term cross-cultural analysis itself acknowledges the existence of a boundary between two or more cultures, discourses or histories. Consequently, it becomes important to conceptualize the relationship between these particular entities. Paul Willemen, utilizing the writings of Mikhail Bakhtin, discusses three possible relationships 'with other socio-cultural networks' (Willemen, 1994: 212-213): projective appropriation, ventriloquist identification and creative understanding.

Projective appropriation involves the analyst projecting his or her belief system and theoretical perspectives upon the texts of another culture at the expense of the specificity and the context of those texts. The subsequent erasure of difference is most frequently at work in the wholesale and unqualified application of American-European theory to the texts of other cultures. Criticism of such an approach has become more vocal in the last few decades as charges of Euro-centrism and Orientalism have become more frequent, not the least by analysts from the cultures that have been thus interpreted. An intriguing example is Vincent Crapanzano's critique of a renowned study by anthropologist Clifford Geetz of the Balinese cockfight; Crapanzano argues that Geetz articulates the cockfight through western cultural texts (*King Lear* and *Crime and Punishment*) and that Geetz locates himself 'behind and above the native, hidden but at the top of the hierarchy of understanding' (Crapanzano, 1986: 72, 74). However, the book in which Crapanzano's critique appears, a book that strives to redefine and indeed redeem ethnography, was subsequently charged with much the same crime. bell hooks, analyzing the cover of the book, found that it recycled the 'metaphors of colonialism, domination and racism' of much of the ethnography that the book itself intended to invalidate (hooks, 1991: 128). In film studies, similar criticism has been voiced by theorists such as Clyde Taylor and Teshome Gabriel (Taylor, 1987; Gabriel, 1986).

Ventriloquist identification has the analyst totally subordinating him or herself to the other culture, thereby intending (supposedly) to erase one's own cultural identity and cultural power. Perhaps the most interesting case is that of the 'cultural transvestite,' T. E. Lawrence, of whom Edward Said wrote, 'The Orientalist has become now the representative Oriental, unlike earlier participant observers... for whom the Orient was something kept carefully at bay' (Said, 1978: 242). Another well-known (if fictional) example is Kurtz, whether in Conrad's *Heart of Darkness* or Coppola's APOCALYPSE NOW (1979). Similarly, tourism encourages this type of identification with the 'other,' a form of participant-observation that Malcolm Crick suggests links tourists and anthropologists (Crick, 1991). In film studies, this relationship is quite rare, especially compared to the previous one. It is perhaps evident in some academic writing on popular culture, where the analyst locates him or herself uncritically within the domain that is being examined.

Creative understanding is obviously (befitting most triadic categorization) the favored approach, with its suggestion of dialogue, in which the analyst is conscious of his or her own cultural location when engaging in the analysis of cultural texts. This involves a *process* of 'othering' oneself, but not of becoming (or attempting to become) the 'other.' The analyst here works on the border, constantly and consciously being aware of the forces of interaction and conflict that inevitably operate there. Trinh T. Minh-ha refers to such a figure as 'necessarily look[ing] in from the outside while also looking out from the inside' (Trinh T. Minh-ha, 1989: 145). She also suggests that '[d]ifferences do not only exist between outsider and insider – two entities – they are also at work within the outsider or the insider – a single entity' (p. 147), so that the analyst is also constructed of conflictual and, perhaps, irreconcilable differences (much like her suggestion that the first world and the third world are not distinct entities, but that each incorporates the other). While not mentioned by Willemen, Bakhtin also emphasizes the importance of the state of 'outsidedness,' in which 'meaning only reveals its depth once it has encountered and come into contact with another, foreign meaning: they engage in a kind of dialogue, which surmounts the closedness and onesidedness of these particular meanings, these cultures' (Bakhtin, 1986: 7). Bakhtin here suggests that cross-cultural analysis represents the most productive form of cultural and textual engagement. This runs counter to critiques of cross-cultural analyses that represent them as inappropriate and unwelcome invasions into local cultural territory, implying that sense of 'keeping off my land' that was referred to earlier in relation to the transformation of the Western outside of the American cinema. This attitude is evident in an otherwise interesting article by Yingjin Zhang, in which writings on Chinese cinema by E. Ann Kaplan, Chris Berry and Esther Yau are criticized for their inappropriate application of western theoretical constructs to non-western texts (Zhang, 1994). Zhang argues that these analyses lack a thorough examination of the texts (if this is so, then the criticism should surely be one of scholarly incompetence), but his essay also contains an undercurrent of resentment that is only voiced in a footnote, which quotes Zhang Longxi to the effect that 'the Chinese experience is of utmost importance in [Chinese] literary scholarship' (p. 51). Certainly it is, but not to the exclusion of other experiences that may be brought to bear on it.

The employment of Willemen's third category as the preferred mode of cross-cultural analysis also recognizes that texts can be read in multiple ways and that particular readings occur because of the analyst's 'cultural opacity' in relation to the text or the culture in general. Analysts may well lack sufficient understanding of a culture's socio-historical specificity. On one level this can be self-evident, for example, when the analyst is only too aware of the difficulty of making sense of a particular text or an aspect of a text. When the border asserts itself so blatantly, there are ways of acquiring an intra-cultural interpretation (note that this is an interpretation and not an explanation) for the analyst to consider. A more difficult situation occurs when the analyst assumes familiarity and comprehension. This does not result in a 'misreading,' but in an interpretation that unconsciously adopts Willemen's projective appropriation relationship. The solution is not to jettison the ensuing analysis, but to compare other analyses to it, preferably from other cultural and ideological perspectives. Of greater concern is the situation where the analyst adopts an ethnographic persona by reading texts as culturally, socially and historically authentic, thereby interpreting social behavior and even the presence of artifacts and particular landscapes as culturally accurate. All texts, including those of the documentary genre, must be recognized as representations.

The above concerns intend to quarrel with singular, culturally approved readings of texts by 'insiders' and, to a lesser extent, by 'outsiders' given honorary insider status. Such a reductionist approach is questionable, especially when it is recalled that even within a particular cultural community, there exist multiple and competing readings of any particular text. These criticisms do not deny the importance of an awareness of cultural specificity or the need for sensitivity to the social and cultural aspects of the society, within which the particular text is produced (as the following textual analyses will attempt to demonstrate). More specifically in relation to film studies, this caveat also requires the rejection of the often-stated (and more often assumed) universality of film language and of particular textual strategies. In chapter 4, it will be argued that constructs such as the 'gaze,' the 'look' and the 'viewing subject' are often employed quite differently in Indian and Malaysian films than is the case in the majority of American films, upon which the theory of the 'gaze' has been constructed.

Transtextuality

There has been an increasing tendency to examine culture in all its forms in terms of texts and intertextual relations. Mikhail Bakhtin is again an important figure here – his work has influenced cultural studies to a remarkable extent. In media studies, this is most evident in the work of Robert Stam, who argues that '[w]ithin a Bakhtinian approach, there is no unitary text, no unitary producer, and no unitary spectator; rather, there is a conflictual heteroglossia ('manylanguagedness') pervading producer, text, context and reader/viewer. Each category is traversed by the centripetal and the centrifugal, the hegemonic and the oppositional' (Stam, 1989: 221). At this level, the intertextual refers as much to cultural communities as to the texts themselves, thus broadening the use of the term to encompass intra- and inter-cultural concerns. More textually focused, Roland Barthes discusses the text as a field of signification where many possible and often contradictory meanings converge: 'any text is an intertext; other texts are present in it, at varying levels, in more or less recognisable forms: the texts of the previous and surrounding culture' (Barthes, 1981: 39). Barthes' final comment again emphasizes the diachronic *and* synchronic nature of intertextuality. Gérard Genette defines transtextuality as 'all that which puts one text in relation, whether manifest or secret, with other texts' (quoted in Stam, 1992: 22-23) in order to extend the range of what is often included under the label of intertextuality. In fact, Genette limits intertextuality to the more explicit textual relations: quotations and allusions – obvious references to other texts or textual systems with the 'obviousness' undoubtedly varying according to the particular cultural community being addressed. Two of his further four categories are also of relevance to the following discussion: the metatextual, which proposes a critical and analytical relationship, and the hypertextual, where a posterior text transforms or adapts an anterior text or texts to a greater or lesser extent. The words 'anterior' and 'posterior' are particularly interesting here, as they implicitly reject the more commonly used terms 'original' and 'copy' with their overtones of duplication, violation and devaluation. Adaption (a term preferred to adaptation, which has become synonymous with a certain type of rigid textual transformation) therefore emphasizes the repositioning of existing material, unencumbered by and yet cognizant of the cultural location and the medium of the anterior text(s). Paul de Man, writing about translation, refers to the process as one of decanonization, involving a 'movement of fragmentation, a wandering […] a kind of permanent exile' (quoted in Bhabha, 1994: 228). This sense of movement and wandering is also applicable to the process of adaption itself, where texts can be said to migrate as well as to become exilic, once again underlining their cultural history and their subsequent cultural redefinition – what Homi Bhabha calls their 'newness' (Bhabha, 1994: 227).

The term 'newness' is actually taken from Salman Rushdie's novel *The Satanic Verses* in which a film producer says that his new film is 'about how newness enters the world' (Rushdie, 1989: 272). This phrase is central to Rushdie's own conception of his writing and it is also at the heart of transtextuality. Rushdie discusses it more analytically in an essay entitled 'In Good Faith,' which was his response to the many attacks on *The Satanic Verses*. In this essay, he argues the case for hybridity and transformation as the crucial cultural and textual inspiration for a writer like himself: '*Mélange*, hotchpotch, a bit of this and a bit of that is *how newness enters the world*. It is the great possibility that mass migration gives to the world...' (Rushdie, 1991: 394). Rushdie here links transtextuality (the movement and transformation of textual material) to the movement of peoples; a conjunction that is now often discussed within the framework of the term diaspora, which has strong associations with issues like border crossings, marginality and hybridity.

In much of the theorization of diaspora, there is an emphasis on origin and on the powerful links (sometimes broken, or at least frayed) to that 'anterior' society and culture. This is even the case in a complex and sophisticated paper by Vijay Mishra, 'The Diasporic Imaginary: Theorizing (the Indian) Diaspora' (Mishra, 1995). It is equally, if not more, important to consider the destination culture, the 'posterior' culture. Diaspora means to scatter and disperse and this is usually presented as the condition of those who leave (willingly or unwillingly) a particular place. However, it can also be applied to the place of arrival, with the social and cultural scattering and dispersal occurring with reference to the domiciled society and culture. In fact, Ashis Nandy goes so far as to suggest that '[t]he diaspora must work towards dismantling links with the mother-country and entering the political realm of their new country... one must not just develop cultural links, but also severances' (quoted in Papastergiadis, 1990: 105). Migrant communities and cultural texts are thus transformed by and within their new contexts. Yet they can retain an ambivalent and even reified relationship to their anterior society and culture. This might involve the maintenance of traditions in the domiciled society that have already changed or are in the process of changing in the anterior society, e.g. the practice of Hinduism in the diaspora being 'much more exclusive and homogenic' than in India itself (Nandy in Papastergiadis, 1990: 104). Similarly, the Fijian Indians were often so totally focused on foundational Indian cultural texts such as the *Mahabharata* and the *Ramayana*, that they did not look up to notice where they were and what was about to happen to them: the 1987 coup by Colonel Rabuka (Nandan, 1995). Thus, the call to cultural nostalgia that is often raised in relation to diasporas as well as the frequent charge of cultural imperialism (the reverse side of the coin, where the migrating culture is said to overwhelm and obliterate the resident culture) are best confronted by Rushdie's focus on 'how newness enters the world,' on the migration and local interaction of cultures and texts.

Edward Said describes the process by which such 'influence, creative borrowing, or wholesale appropriation' occurs in an essay entitled 'Traveling Theory' and he proposes that the movement of ideas and theories through space and time typically occur through a number of stages:

> 'First, there is a point of origin, or what seems like one, a set of initial circumstances in which the idea came into birth or entered discourse. Second, there is a distance traversed, a passage through the pressure of various contexts as the idea moves from an earlier point to another time and place where it will come into a new prominence. Third, there is a set of conditions – call them conditions of acceptance or, as an inevitable part of acceptance, resistances – which then confront the transplanted theory or idea, making possible its introduction or toleration, however alien it might appear to be. Fourth, the now full (or partly) accommodated (or incorporated) idea is to some extent transformed by its new uses, its new position in a new time and place' (Said, 1984: 226-227).

Despite the fact that the first stage seems to imply some essentialist notion of origin and source (whereas any 'original' idea or theory is always itself of diverse origins, a representation that is already 'trapped' in the condition of transtextuality), Said's sequence of events places equal emphasis on anterior and posterior cultures and texts, on their interaction and on their eventual location, whether this be conceived of in synchronic or diachronic terms. It also acknowledges that this movement is not one of undifferentiated absorption and assimilation. The 'new' idea, theory or text, like the concept of translation that Bhabha valorizes in Walter Benjamin's writings, shows the signs of resistance and the presence of difference (Bhabha, 1994: 224). The transformation of generic material in the films examined in this chapter exhibit many of these same characteristics.

In fact, the concept of transtextuality is particularly appropriate for genre studies, which proposes the non-uniqueness of texts and the consequent opportunity for their categorization. The term genre tends to conjure up images of boundaries and exclusions, but a concern with the historical, social and cultural aspects of genre can at least help counter the frequent recourse to the structuralist goal of 'discovering' deep structures and ahistorical essences, evident in a text of some relevance to this study: Will Wright's *Sixguns and Society*. Again, Bakhtin helps loosen the constraints of generic systematization by suggesting that formal properties are also social properties, with the relationship between the text and the world being based on ideology rather than mimesis, influenced by the 'here' and 'now,' but also inscribed in culture:

> 'Cultural [...] traditions [...] are preserved and continue to live not in the individual subjective memory of a single individual and not in some kind of collective 'psyche,' but rather in the objective forms that culture itself assumes [...] and in this sense they are inter-subjective and inter-individual (and consequently social); from there they enter literary works, sometimes almost completely bypassing the subjective individual memory of their creators' (Bakhtin, 1981: 249, note 17).

In film studies, this might lead to a fluid and interactive relationship between a film genre (emphasizing formal properties), a genre film (a specific social utterance in the context of the genre, but not necessarily consciously so) and a particular production system (Hollywood, Cinecitta, Toho, Shaw Brothers, Bombay/'Bollywood'). This chapter engages the Western genre as both an anterior and a posterior textual system, but then goes on to discuss it in transnational and transtextual terms in the process of which its formal and sociocultural concerns are quite radically transformed.

The Hamburger Western

The Western has been the most popular of American film genres: about a quarter of all Hollywood features between 1926 and 1967 were Westerns (Buscombe, 1993a: 35). In genre studies, the Western has always been the privileged genre and repeatedly labeled as the American genre par excellence. The American Western itself will not be discussed in any detail, but rather emphasis will be given to its interaction with the European Western as well as with certain other groups of films that seem to be tangential to the Western and fit more into the 'national' genre category referred to earlier: the Japanese samurai film, the Chinese martial arts film and the Indian stunt film. However, their generic labeling in the West as the Noodle Westerns, Chop Suey Westerns and Curry Westerns does imply a perceived association with the Western as a genre. The inter-relationship between all these 'Westerns' is best approached through transtextual transformations, which can range from overt quotations to more imperceptible and unconscious citations from the cultural 'pool.' Stories and styles are absorbed, adapted and transformed in the context of local cultural production practices, with the concepts of origin(ality) and authenticity fading in the face of such multidirectional cultural activity. Historically, this transtextuality of the Western genre occurred most prolifically in the 1960's at a time when the traditional film industry structures were starting to fragment and new production practices emerged. Phil Hardy, in an encyclopedia of the Western, refers to this period as one of the internationalization of the Western (Hardy, 1983: 274), a generalization that should be treated with considerable caution because of its implication of undifferentiation. However, Hardy does dispel the misconception that, until the 1960's, only American films were genre films.

In keeping with the already stated reluctance to rigidly define genre, the typical characteristics of the American Western are presented here through a number of frequently-cited critical texts on the genre (Buscombe, 1993a; Cawelti, n.d.; Hardy, 1983; Kitses, 1969; Wright, 1975): the historical period is 1865-1890 and covers the building of the railways, the coming of the settlers, the mining camps, the Indian wars, the cattle drives, the activities of the outlaws and the end of the Civil War; the geography is where the above took place, usually called the West and the American frontier; and the iconography includes particular landscapes, a specific cluster of characters, means of locomotion, technologies of communication and technologies of death. The ideological tensions of the Western are frequently presented in terms of the wilderness/civilization dichotomy and elaborated through a series of tensions: nature/culture, individual/community, West/East, male/female

(Kitses, 1969: 11). It has been pointed out that critical emphasis on this dichotomy has confined the analysis of the Western to an 'internal dialogue [...] blind to the presence of Chicanos' (Noriega, 1992: xv) and, by extension, to questions of race in general (Native American, African American, Chinese). Noriega's discussion of the repressed history of the classic Western in relation to Mexican and Chicano culture is interesting in the light of the Italian Western's almost obsessive concentration on that culture.³ The narrative intertexts of the American Western include 19th century American tales and novels, European conquest and imperialist novels as well as European chivalric romances going back to *The Iliad* and *The Odyssey*. Will Wright categorized Western plot structures in terms of the relationship of the protagonist(s) to society: integration (e.g. SHANE, 1953), disillusionment (e.g. HIGH NOON, 1952) and alienation. Wright called this last category the 'professional plot,' where the protagonists remain outside society and offer themselves as 'guns for hire' to enable one group in society to exact vengeance on another (Wright, 1975: 85-123). This plot structure became dominant in the Westerns of the 1960's and while revenge is a common plot motivator in films and narratives in general, it is particularly central to the films under discussion.

By the early 1960's, the Hollywood studio system had started to collapse and was gradually being replaced by the package-unit system, based on short-term arrangements and independent producers (Bordwell, Staiger and Thompson, 1985: 330). This transformation of Hollywood resulted in a drop in film production in general and Westerns in particular. In 1953, 92 Westerns were made in Hollywood (representing 27% of all films), whereas by 1963 the number had dropped to 11 (only 9% of total production) (Buscombe, 1993a: 48). As will be argued, this should not be interpreted as an indication of the death of the Western, so much as an opportunity for its displacement, interaction and transformation.

One of the consequences of the package-unit system was that independent production companies were more daring and more outward looking in the sort of project they were willing to fund than were the Hollywood studios (Schatz, 1983: 186-187). Independent American producers were now also more conscious of developments in European cinema, particularly the French New Wave, and the impact of the art cinema as evidenced by the flourishing European Film Festivals. During the 1950's, these festivals had also introduced Japanese cinema to the West and this led to the circulation of Japanese films in European and American art-house cinemas. One of the more successful of these was SEVEN SAMURAI (1954), which was shown in America in an 'RKO-butchered' edition under the title of THE MAGNIFICENT SEVEN (Richie, 1984: 108). The subsequent John Sturges Western of the same name thus very clearly asserted an intertextual relationship with the Japanese film.

The Samurai Film and the Noodle Western

Like Hollywood, the Japanese film industry was studio-based but it was driven by an even more rigid, generic categorization. This was further accompanied by the traditional Japanese system of school-based esthetics, with a master passing on the traditions to the pupil, who slowly moved up the creative ladder and tended to work within the master's genre (Desser, 1983: 4). This rigidity is apparent in the crucial distinction between period films ('jidai-geki') set in the time before the Meiji Restoration of 1868 and modern films ('gendai-geki') set after that date. Particular genres then exist within each of these categories.

The samurai genre resides in the period film category, and is historically located in the Tokugawa Period (1600-1868).[4] This is rather ironic since the samurai protagonist therefore existed in what was a period of virtual peace in Japan, making him obsolete as a warrior. The heroic elevation of the samurai developed out of the pre-Tokugawa wars of the 11th and 12th centuries and revolved around their code of behavior called 'bushido'. The primary tension within the code was between duty ('giri') to a lord or a cause, and human feeling ('ninjo') and the samurai film constantly confronts the irresolvable conflict inherent in this tension. The obsolescence of the samurai during the Tokugawa Period also led to low-ranking samurai and masterless samurai ('ronin') taking a more pragmatic outlook and selling themselves as mercenaries (Silver, 1975: 11). During this period, the samurai narratives, which had been traditionally maintained through oral storytelling, were written into Kabuki and Bunraku plays – a form of transtextuality that led to the plays of Chikamatsu Monzaemon and, eventually, to the samurai film genre.

The samurai film had been popular before World War II, but these films were relatively actionless as a result of the strong influence of the Kabuki samurai tradition, for example in films of Mizoguchi Kenji such as THE LOYAL 47 RONIN (1942). The genre reappeared only after the end of the American Occupation, during which time all films dealing with feudal loyalty were prohibited (Hirano, 1992: 44-45). The samurai film went on to become a prominent genre in the 1960's, only matched by the yakuza (gangster) genre. David Desser argues that a number of sub-genres developed during this post-war period; two of these are relevant here: the nostalgic samurai drama and the sword film. The nostalgic variant dealt with the wandering ronin, caught in the giri/ninjo dilemma and resigned to his own demise – SEVEN SAMURAI is considered the first example of this sub-genre. The sword film or 'chambara' has two characteristics similar to the American Western: the 'sword for hire' and powerful villains, whose presence inevitably leads to violent battles. The giri/ninjo conflict becomes irrelevant here with the emphasis being placed on greed and revenge – YOJIMBO (The Bodyguard, 1961) initiated this sub-genre (Desser, 1983: 32, 43).

SEVEN SAMURAI and YOJIMBO were both directed by Kurosawa Akira. While trained within the strict tradition of the Japanese apprenticeship system, Kurosawa eventually broke away from that tradition. His work during the American Occupation was of considerable importance in shaping his career: NO REGRETS FOR OUR YOUTH (1946) was considered an exemplary democratization film, 'a perfect response to requests from the occupation government to make films that would help democratize the Japanese mind' (Hirano, 1992: 180-181). Kurosawa's subsequent films have always incorporated western values and western cultural practices and he has tended to address his own society through western texts. He adapted canonical western texts by Shakespeare (THRONE OF BLOOD, 1957 and RAN, 1985), Dostoevsky (THE IDIOT, 1951) and Gorky (THE LOWER DEPTHS, 1957), popular fiction by Ed McBain (HIGH AND LOW, 1963) and film genres such as the Western and the gangster film. SEVEN SAMURAI, YOJIMBO and SANJURO (1962) all use the American Western's archetypal plot of a stranger or strangers coming across a problem, dealing with it and then departing. SEVEN SAMURAI actually looks like a Western in its use of landscape, the placement of the characters in the landscape and the interplay of movement and stasis. These characteristics identify that film as homage to the American Westerns of the 1940's and early 1950's.[5] Such similarities of plot and spectacle undoubtedly attracted the Mirisch Company to the film and helped determine the genre in which its adaption of SEVEN SAMURAI, called THE MAGNIFICENT SEVEN (1960), would be made. Edward Buscombe suggests that '[i]f a Western could be made from a Japanese movie with the plot virtually unchanged' (Buscombe, 1993a: 48), then the genre was not as culturally specific as had been supposed. However, while its generic location was almost inevitable, the differences between the two films are quite profound.

The Samurai Film and the Hamburger Western

Both SEVEN SAMURAI and THE MAGNIFICENT SEVEN highlight the relationship between the professionals (ronin/gunfighters) and the farmers, but they define that relationship quite differently. This is best illustrated by examining the endings of the two films. In SEVEN SAMURAI, after the grueling fight with the bandits, the three remaining samurai stand in reverence before the burial mound of their four comrades. A young woman, with whom the youngest samurai had earlier had a liaison, hurries past him with hardly a glance and joins the other village women and men in rice planting and singing. While the young samurai looks upon the farmers' absorption in their own affairs with sadness and maybe even envy, the two older samurai accept the villagers' response with resignation, acknowledging that the farmers are the winners and they are once again defeated. The social distance between the farmers and the samurai is stressed not just in the dialogue between the two samurai and the absence of communication between the two groups, but also in the cross-cutting between them, with most of the scene focusing upon the farmers working in their rice field. The film's pace has slowed down after the frenetic battle and a resigned sadness ('mono no aware') suffuses the images. The fate of the remaining samurai is clearly that already undergone by their comrades: death and oblivion. As is typical of the samurai genre, the film perceives the relationship between samurai and farmers in terms of class identity and hierarchy, in other words as an *intra*-cultural chasm.

At the end of THE MAGNIFICENT SEVEN, the village elder tells the three remaining gunfighters that only the farmers have won and that they remain like the land itself. As the gunfighters ride away from the village, they are viewed through the eyes of the young woman, who is attracted to the young gunfighter. The three stop at the edge of the village, continuing to be watched by the woman, who in effect becomes the narrating center of the scene. The gunfighter leader convinces the young man that he should remain in the village – he agrees and rides up to where the woman is husking corn and proceeds to unbuckle his gun belt, signifying his return to the land. Meanwhile, the gunfighter leader tells his remaining comrade that the old villager was right and that only the farmers won, whereas they (the gunfighters) lost, as they always do. Compared to the Japanese film, there is much greater interaction between the villagers and the gunfighters, both verbally and visually and at the same time much less emphasis on the farmers actually working the land. The young gunfighter, who was a farmer's son, returns to the land, while the older gunfighters philosophically accept their fate: not death, but their rootlessness, at least until they find another job elsewhere (as they do in the two sequels to this film). There is also no reference by the gunfighters to the deaths of their comrades; only the three village boys visit the graves of the four dead gunfighters. In contrast to the farmers' total lack of interest in the samurai, here the village elder, the girl and the three boys all show obvious gratitude and devotion to the gunfighters. The interaction is *inter*-cultural with the relationship defined in terms of ethnic difference: American/Mexican which translates into a clear superior/inferior hierarchy, with the farmers treated as children who cannot help themselves – the village elder describes the gunfighters being like the wind needed to rid the land of locusts. Buscombe also notes the presence of this condescension and suggests that the film's liberalism – helping the defenseless – depends on their inability to help themselves (Buscombe, 1993b). At the end of a review of the film, in which he engages in some vigorous Hollywood-bashing, Joseph L. Anderson, a renowned scholar of Japanese cinema, mentions that THE MAGNIFICENT SEVEN was commercially successful in Japan and that this had led a Japanese film studio to contemplate a remake (!) 'as one of the new Japanese Westerns' (Anderson, 1962: 58). Without further elaboration, he finishes his review with the statement that United Artists had announced a Western based on Kurosawa's YOJIMBO. THE MAGNIFICENT SEVEN was never remade as a Japanese Western, but YOJIMBO, as shall be seen, was reworked as a Western two years later but by an Italian not an American company – both instances indicate the strong desire to localize anterior texts rather than just import them.

While SEVEN SAMURAI was an important film in the transformation of the Western in the 1960's, its influence occurred only indirectly through THE MAGNIFICENT SEVEN. The American film was actually much more popular in Europe than in America itself. Interestingly, the French and Italian titles of the film translate as 'The Seven Mercenaries' (Frayling, 1981: 128), cruelly but more accurately indicating the film's conceit and also the European audiences' reading of the film. European enthusiasm for the film and for Westerns generally was to lead to a transatlantic move by the genre with Rome/Spain becoming the centers of its production for some years. This is quite contrary to the 'cultural imperialism' argument that asserts the unidirectionality of popular cultural flows. The Italian Western 'plundered' THE MAGNIFICENT SEVEN for the figure of the gunfighter (now quite unrelated to the cowboy) as a professional, a wanderer without ties, with an interest in weaponry bordering on fetishism, an emphasis on violence and its spectacularization and, most importantly, its Mexican setting. However, the Italians rejected the moralism of the American film and began altering the relationship between Americans and Mexicans/Chicanos in their films. They also brought a nihilism and cynicism to the genre that came from another source altogether: the Japanese sword film YOJIMBO.

The Sword Film and the Spaghetti Western

YOJIMBO is set in the period of turmoil at the end of the peaceful Tokugawa Period, when American and European pressure caused the Japanese to frantically engage in modernization. The film's boundary category is a feudal/modern one and the conflict is once again intra-cultural. The protagonist, Sanjuro, is an itinerant swordsman, a commoner and not even a ronin, who offers his services to the highest bidder – a true 'sword for hire.' He cynically plays the two factions within the town against each other for his own purposes. While Sanjuro might appear amoral, the film makes it clear that his behavior is positively exemplary compared to the deviousness and self-aggrandizement of the economic power bases in the town.

The story and structure of YOJIMBO became the basis for one of the most successful Italian Westerns: A FISTFUL OF DOLLARS (1964) – the change of title again foregrounds the mercenary character of the film's theme. A number of critics have described A FISTFUL OF DOLLARS as a shot-for-shot copy of Kurosawa's film (Cook, 1981: 433; Jameson, 1973: 8). If that is the case, the Italian film is an excellent example of the adage that to translate is always to transform. Robert C. Cumbow also talks in terms of a shot-for-shot remake, but then questions the 'originality' of the Japanese film by stating that YOJIMBO 'is reputedly based upon the Bud Boetticher-Randolph Scott film BUCHANAN RIDES ALONE (1958)' (Cumbow, 1987: 2), in which the Randolph Scott character takes advantage of an interfamilial conflict in a small town. On the other hand, Kurosawa himself says that '[t]he story is so ideally interesting that it's surprising no one else ever thought of it' (Richie, 1984: 147). Sergio Leone, the director of A FISTFUL OF DOLLARS, acknowledged his 'debt' to YOJIMBO,[6] but argued that both directors should really pay copyright to the 18th century Italian dramatist, Carlo Goldoni, who employed the basic plot in his play *The Servant of Two Masters* (Frayling, 1981: 147). Frayling also mentions the thriller *Red Harvest*, written in 1929 by Dashiel Hammett, as a more contemporary source for both films (Frayling, 1981: 150).[7] John Cawelti takes up Frayling's comment about *Red Harvest*'s Jacobean credentials by finding resemblances between the plots and protagonists of Italian Westerns (especially Leone's) and Jacobean and Spanish Renaissance revenge tragedies: both have 'heroes' that are 'marked by superior stratagems, unscrupulousness, and skill in violence. Their style [...] is one of supreme detachment and coolness' (Cawelti, 1974: 114). These descriptions could just as easily refer to the Sanjuro character in YOJIMBO. While one can keep referring to anterior texts in the presence of such textual 'shuttling,' any reference to an 'original' text does start to become untenable.[8]

Acknowledging the similarities between the two films, it is also important to deal with their differences. A good example of these intertextual relations is a scene that seems superficially to be very much the same in both films, yet illustrates some of the formal, thematic and cultural differences. The protagonist (The Man with No Name/Sanjuro) approaches one of the two power bases in the town (the Baxters/the silk merchant and his henchmen). In A FISTFUL OF DOLLARS, The Man with No Name walks up to the Baxters and demands that they apologize for what they did to his mule. As they laugh at him, The Man with No Name starts to draw his gun. The laughter stops and he unhesitatingly kills them all. He then sees a man running into the street who identifies himself as John Baxter and who nervously pulls a badge out of his pocket to prove that he is the town's sheriff. The Man with No Name is singularly unimpressed and walks away past the undertaker, telling him that he will need four coffins instead of the three he had initially ordered. The dialogue is self-conscious and ritualistic, while the conversation about the mule seems almost parodic, undercutting and trivializing the impending conflict and carnage. The gunfight is spatially fragmented, with all the major figures framed separately but in tight close-ups. The editing is functionally overextended and time is stretched well beyond the norm. The music is impudent rather than threatening and the 'natural' sounds are amplified so as to emphasize their constructedness. While iconographically the scene signifies a Western gunfight, its formal qualities indicate other concerns and a different esthetic, which will be further discussed in the analysis of ONCE UPON A TIME IN THE WEST (1968).

In YOJIMBO, Sanjuro walks up to the silk merchant's men and comments on their gentle faces. This offends them and they proudly divulge their evil pasts. They threaten to kill Sanjuro, who warns them that they will be hurt if they try and that they are all fools. As they draw their swords, Sanjuro cuts loose with his sword and immediately walks away, leaving dead bodies, a hand with a sword in it lying on the ground and men screaming with pain. He passes the undertaker and tells him that two coffins are needed; on looking back at the dead and injured, he suggests that the undertaker prepare three coffins instead. The formal aspects of this scene are totally different from those of the Italian film. Here the shots are photographed with a long lens, which flattens the perspective and tends to estheticize the images. Sanjuro is always in the same size shot as the gang ('plan américain' or medium long shot), so that the space is always coherent and never ambiguous. The scene is brief although the individual shots are quite extended; there is no build up of suspense, just a series of ridiculous gestures on the part of the gang members that are terminated by the swift and violent killing. Like the action, the dialogue is abrupt and understated. The economy of the scene is in great contrast to the elaborateness of the scene in the Italian film. YOJIMBO's representational system resides in the Japanese sword film, in Japanese cinema and in Japanese culture in general (Burch, 1979: 291ff).[9] This does not mean that its difference makes the film unintelligible to non-Japanese viewers; rather its difference is part of its intelligibility.

A FISTFUL OF DOLLARS is also thematically different from the American Western because of its engagement with Italian cultural concerns, particularly

Catholicism, social and gender codes of behavior and attitudes towards death. These characteristics make the frequent location of the stories in Mexico almost inevitable and also appropriate. The Italian Western found a context in Mexico's Hispanic culture that was close to the Italian tradition. Paul Smith argues that the Italian Western's concentration on the peon figure represented a more 'local' example of the 'other' than the figure of the Indian, who is almost totally absent from the Italian Western; he also suggests that it helped make the Italian Western more successful in 'third-worldish' markets (Smith, 1993: 1-17).

The Spaghetti Western

Rome's Cinecitta Studios, like Hollywood, had a tradition of making genre films, but the production process and the life cycles of genres operated in a much more concentrated fashion than in Hollywood, typical of a system where production costs are relatively low – the same approach is evident in Hong Kong. Genre production is based on the principle of saturation and replacement: if the genre is successful then a large number of such films are completed very quickly; when box office receipts fall, the genre is dropped in favor of a new genre. This is graphically demonstrated in the case of the Italian Western: more than 300 were released in Italy between 1963 and 1969 – 10 in 1963, 66 in 1966-67 and 7 in 1969 (Frayling, 1981: 256). This production approach had been active since the early 1950's and resulted in the ephemeral existence of genres like the sentimental 'weepie,' the farcical comedy, the sword and sandal epic, the horror film, the Mondo Cane genre and the James Bond spy genre (Frayling, 1981: 68-102).[10]

Italian film producers' interest in making Westerns was actually not due to the success of THE MAGNIFICENT SEVEN in Europe, but to the surprising popularity in Europe of the Winnetou series of German Westerns in 1963. The German influence on the Italian Western was purely financial and one of the major production companies of these Westerns went on to co-produce A FISTFUL OF DOLLARS. The themes of these German films were Rousseau-inspired, focusing on the noble Indian warrior and the idealized German immigrant in the USA; they were based on novels written by the German writer, Karl May, in the 1890's (Frayling, 1981: 108-110). This is in stark contrast to the more Hobbesian 'philosophy' of the Italian Western, which is best summed up in the opening title of FOR A FEW DOLLARS MORE (1965): 'Where life had no value, death, sometimes, had its price.'

The presence of Hollywood producers, directors, technicians and actors at Cinecitta must not be overlooked. The studio had been the production site of many American-produced Biblical and pseudo-Biblical epics in the 1950's and early 1960's, e.g. HELEN OF TROY (1954), BEN HUR (1959) and SODOM AND GOMORRAH (1961), on all of which Sergio Leone had worked. On one level, the production of Westerns in Italy by Italians might represent a riposte to Americans coming to Italy to make films on Italian and Roman subjects that had previously been the staple of popular Italian cinema since the 1910's. To camouflage these Westerns as American films, the Italians engaged some recognizable American actors from B Westerns and television Westerns, e.g. Lee Van Cleef and Clint Eastwood, while at the same time giving themselves English-sounding pseudonyms, e.g. Sergio Leone called himself Bob Robertson.

Of all the Italian film genre influences on the Italian Western, the most important was the sword and sandal epic or mythological genre. Many of the directors of the Italian Western had worked in these Greek and Roman spectaculars and brought characteristics of their European mythical archetypes like Ulysses, Achilles, Ajax, Hector and Perseus into the Western. Phil Hardy provides the cryptic equation: 'James Bond + Hercules = The Man with No Name' (Hardy, 1983: 274). Sergio Leone had himself directed a sword and sandal epic, THE COLOSSUS OF RHODES, in 1962, before going on to the Western. It is tempting to describe Jean-Luc Godard's two Italian films of the 1960's as metatextual versions of these two genres. CONTEMPT (1963) is a film about the filming of a sword and sandal epic based on Homer's *The Odyssey* and WIND FROM THE EAST (1969) critiques the Western in terms of American imperialism in the third world and casts the Italian Western actor, Gian Maria Volonte, as a racist cavalry officer. While Leone's Westerns were not overtly political, other films like A BULLET FOR THE GENERAL (1966), scripted by Franco Solinas, the scriptwriter of the political thriller BATTLE OF ALGIERS (1965), and KILL AND PRAY (1967), in which Pier Paolo Pasolini plays the role of a priest, made Mexico an ideological battleground for the presentation of anti-American and pro-revolutionary sentiments. It is as if the farmers from THE MAGNIFICENT SEVEN have taken up arms not against the bandits but against the American gunfighters. These 'border-crossings' between Italian popular cinema and art cinema highlight an inter-relationship between these two modes of production that is rarely commented upon in national cinema and genre studies.

Sergio Leone made ONCE UPON A TIME IN THE WEST in 1968 just after the peak of production of the Italian Western, and the film is its most baroque and self-conscious example. Whereas in his earlier films Leone shot the exteriors in Spain (as was the case with most Italian Westerns), here he went to the iconographic 'heart' of the American Western: Monument Valley. Based on a story by Leone, Bernardo Bertolucci and the Italian horror filmmaker Dario

Argento, the film is a complex reworking of Leone's previous films, American Westerns and aspects of the European art cinema that make the film as metatextual as any of Godard's films. Ennio Morricone's musical score is central to the mood and rhythm of the film to the extent that it was composed before shooting began and then played on the set during production. A critic has described the film as an opera 'in which the arias are not sung but stared' (Jameson, 1973: 11) and Martin Scorsese suggests that '[t]he music, the framing, the camera movement, the bigger-than-myth epic characters and story are opera' (quoted in Cumbow, 1987: 213). These comments about the film's 'Italianness' are further reinforced by Robert C. Cumbow, who devotes a whole chapter of his book on Leone to the links between his films and Italian opera, which was the great pre-cinematic European synthetic art form (Cumbow, 1987: 213-216). Like the plots of many Italian operas and many Italian Westerns, ONCE UPON A TIME IN THE WEST is a revenge story that once again recalls the Jacobean and Spanish Renaissance plays with their plots about power and corruption.

The scene in the film that precipitates the revenge is the massacre of the McBain family. Brett McBain is preparing to welcome his new wife to the ranch and his older son is to fetch her from the railway station in Flagstone. The focus is on the nuclear family, with the new wife reconstructing the family unit previously ruptured by the death of McBain's first wife. Suddenly shots break out and McBain, his older son and his daughter are killed. The younger son, Timmy, runs out of the house and watches in terror as four men in leather coats walk into the yard. The leader, Frank, smiles at the boy and then shoots him in cold blood, the gunshot dovetailing into the sound of the train's arrival in Flagstone. Scenes of settlers being killed outside their own homes are common to many Westerns, but, as in the scene's most direct influence, THE SEARCHERS (1956), such massacres are usually carried out by Indians. Not only are the killers here 'Americans' but the blue-eyed leader of the gang, Frank, is played by Henry Fonda – a major star of the American Western. This deconstruction of the American Western genre is accompanied by formal strategies that lay bare the parameters of the classical film itself: the frantic cutting from extreme close-up to long shot, the fragmentation and confusion of point-of-view (when McBain is trying to see what is wrong, the camera tracks with his turning head, which occupies the bulk of the image),[11] an eye line that has the characters looking almost directly into the camera and the long, slow preludes to action. Time is stretched, space is fragmented and abstracted, gestures are quoted in an almost Brechtian way and the music is operatic and emphasizes the inevitability of events. The film takes the strategies of Leone's previous Westerns to the stage where their similarity to the films of art directors like Michelangelo Antonioni became apparent: a concern with duration and 'temps mort' and a lack of interest in clear motivation and suspense. This apparent asceticism is however accompanied by a self-conscious, even over-elaborate visual and aural style more typical of Luchino Visconti, also frequently called an operatic filmmaker. To therefore label Leone's films as Westerns is both reasonable and at the same time totally misleading. Such category ambivalence also applies to a series of genres that do not even look like Westerns but are often labeled as such in the West. An examination of these genres that flourished far to the east of Rome promises an intertextual thicket that is superficially familiar but also more opaque.

The Martial Arts Film and the Chop Suey Western

Hong Kong production companies like Shaw Brothers developed an assembly-line production system that probably put even the Italians to shame. The range of genres was more limited, but their transformations were more rapid. In the 1960's, sword-fighting films like DRAGON GATE INN (1967) were extremely popular, but by the early 1970's these were replaced by the fist-fighting or kung fu film, various sub-genres of which quickly superseded each other: the costume kung fu film, the ghost kung fu film, the comedy kung fu film and the contemporary kung fu film (Frayling, 1981: 89). The commercial success of the Italian Westerns in Hong Kong led to their stories, plot structures and stylized violence being incorporated into the Hong Kong action films, especially the martial arts film genre, a broader category that includes both sword-fighting films and kung fu films. It also led to Hong Kong/Italian co-productions like the 1974 BLOOD MONEY (also known as THE STRANGER AND THE GUNFIGHTER) starring Lee Van Cleef and Lo Lieh that mixes kung fu and Italian Western elements (Hardy, 1983: 345).[12]

The Chinese martial arts film genre, 'wu xia pian' – 'wu' means fighting or combat and 'xia' means chivalry or valor (Ng Ho, 1981: 85) – was based on an oral and literary tradition of chivalrous tales with the knight-errant figure as the central protagonist. Like the samurai code of bushido, the knight-errant had a code of chivalry based on altruism, justice, courage, honor and generosity. Unlike the samurai (who was a pivotal figure in the maintenance of the feudal order in Japan), the knights-errant wandered the countryside and righted wrongs. They were Taoist in their anarchic individualism, representing a tendency towards non-conformism in traditional Chinese society that often goes un-remarked. By acting on universalist principles of justice, they rejected the Confucian links between obligation and duty to family and the hierarchical order (Liu, 1967: 7-13). Stylistically, the martial arts film was strongly influenced by Chinese opera, especially the military category with its stereotyped characters, elaborate ritual acts, costumes and musical accompaniment (Felheim, 1972: 326).

The Cantonese martial arts film was one of the dominant genres of the Hong Kong cinema in the 1950's and 1960's, only matched by the Cantonese opera film in popularity and vitality. Part of their success was due to expanding overseas markets, especially those of Singapore and Malaysia. These markets in turn helped finance the popular series of films featuring the 19th century kung fu master, Huang Feihong (Yu, 1981: 100-101) – by 1980, 85 feature films and a television series based on this character had been made. The 1960's saw many innovations take place in the martial arts films, including the introduction of the bounty hunter protagonist from the Italian Western and a new type of choreography influenced by Japanese films like YOJIMBO and the ZATOICHI samurai series (1962-1988) (Yu, 1981: 104). The heroes of these 1960's films were no longer the ideal knight-errant figures of old; they were now motivated by monetary gain, revenge, fame and personal power. These themes are reminiscent of those of the Italian Western. In fact, Vicki Ooi compares King Hu's martial arts films to the same theatrical genre as was applied by John Cawelti to the Italian Western – the 16th century Jacobean revenge tragedy (Ooi, 1980). In the second half of the 1960's, the Cantonese martial arts film was overtaken by the Mandarin version of the same genre as epitomized by the spectacular series of films of King Hu, e.g. DRAGON GATE INN and A TOUCH OF ZEN (1971). By the early 1970's, the kung fu sub-genre started to dominate the Mandarin martial arts film. On a production level this was occasioned by Raymond Chow leaving Shaw Brothers in 1970 and decentralizing his new production company, Golden Harvest, into semi-independent companies headed by stars and directors. The first successful example of this mode of production was the series of films made by Bruce Lee (Fore, 1994: 44-45).[13]

Bruce Lee had moved from Hong Kong to the USA in the 1960's and had worked rather unsuccessfully in the American film and television industries (events interestingly covered in the 1993 film, DRAGON: THE BRUCE LEE STORY). Nonetheless, the experience did teach him different ways of staging and filming confrontations and fights that he incorporated in his own films. He had also proposed to a Hollywood television executive that he (Lee) star in a television series about a Shaolin monk who had been forced to flee China in the 19th century and who wandered through the Wild West using only kung fu for protection. The idea was rejected, at least partly because the producer considered Lee too short and too Chinese (!), but it resurfaced as the TV series KUNG FU made from 1972-75 starring David Carradine as a Chinese-American. This rejection fueled Lee's anti-Americanism, which became a more generalized anti-Westernism and anti-foreignism in the films he made after returning to Hong

Kong. This is most evident in THE WAY OF THE DRAGON (1973), the only film Lee himself directed. The film is set in Rome, where Lee arrives from Hong Kong on an assignment to protect a Chinese restaurant from a local gang.[14] Lee's character has traits of the traditional knight-errant although any altruism is tempered by his single-minded obsession with kung fu – even the sexy restaurant owner does not interest him. However, the plot also resembles the Western's professional plot with its structure of arrival/involvement, accomplishment of mission and departure/disengagement. Part of Lee's agenda is to demonstrate the superiority of Chinese martial arts over all other forms of combat – even guns are ineffective in the face of kung fu. This is all summed up in the fight between Lee and Chuck Norris, who plays an American karate expert, in the Colosseum. The duel is won by Lee and it affirms his physical, moral and racial superiority over apparently dominant forces – this helps to explain Lee's popularity among overseas Chinese, Puerto Ricans and other immigrant groups (Cheng, 1984: 24). Earlier in the film, as Norris arrives by plane in Rome, the film 'quotes' (unaccredited) the musical theme associated with Henry Fonda's first appearance at the McBain ranch in ONCE UPON A TIME IN THE WEST. The music recurs when Norris turns up at the Colosseum.[15] This intertextual reference links Norris with the Fonda character as a serious threat and combatant. More generally, the Colosseum alludes to the sword and sandal epics, with Norris giving Lee the 'thumbs down' just as the Roman emperors condemned the early Christians to the lions. Equally, Rome as the center of traditional European culture is a fitting place for Lee to demonstrate his superiority. On the other hand, the gestures and rituals associated with the fight and its aftermath, dwelt on to an extent not seen in gunfights and sword fights, refer directly to the kung fu martial arts genre. THE WAY OF THE DRAGON is in fact an excellent example of a metatextual work, providing a critical perspective on western film and culture, Hong Kong film culture and even the previous two films in which Lee had starred: THE BIG BOSS (1971) and FIST OF FURY (1972).

This sense of generic continuity and intertextual transformation within the Hong Kong cinema is as noticeable today as it was in the 1970's. Films like ZU: WARRIORS FROM THE MAGIC MOUNTAIN (1983) and the CHINESE GHOST STORY series (1986-91) draw on the 'fantastique' and ghost martial arts films of the 1950's and 1960's. Similarly, Tsui Hark's 1990's series of films featuring Huang Feihong, which, in the context of the films discussed in this chapter, are appropriately called the ONCE UPON A TIME IN CHINA series (1991-94) in English, take up the ethnocentrism of the earlier series, but expand it to encompass the problematic role of 'the foreign' in 19th century China: European-American colonial forces, business people and missionaries; westernized Chinese men and women; and modern technology, particularly, and paradoxically, photographic and film technology. Finally, John Woo's contemporary gangster films such as the A BETTER TOMORROW series (1986-89) and THE KILLER (1989), with their themes of revenge, are almost literal re-workings of the traditional martial arts films.[16] In Wayne Wang's LIFE IS CHEAP... BUT TOILET PAPER IS EXPENSIVE (1989), a Chinese-American comes to Hong Kong in a cowboy hat and boots to the musical theme from THE MAGNIFICENT SEVEN and his arrival is inter-cut with fragments from the Marlboro cigarette commercial (which, of course, used that same theme). A 'stranger in town,' he talks of Hong Kong as the final frontier at the edge of China and the last outpost in the wild wild east.[17] Even the film's title echoes that statement at the beginning of FOR A FEW DOLLARS MORE (1965) that was referred to earlier: 'Where life had no value....' Wang's film is concerned with decapitations and amputations, and this refers as much to the satiric and parodic tone of the film as to the subject matter. In this context, the references to the American Western and the Italian Western enable the issue of post-1997 Hong Kong to be discussed in terms of the colony's defenselessness and the threats from the northern 'bandits.'

However, this intertextual fecundity is not confined to Hong Kong. Mainland Chinese cinema is now mostly identified with Fifth Generation directors like Chen Kaige and Zhang Yimou, but there has been a parallel commercial cinema since at least the mid-1980's. Much of this is directly influenced by Hong Kong cinema, but there are some films that have developed a more complex relationship to Chinese and other popular cinemas. The 1992 film THE SWORDSMAN IN DOUBLE-FLAG TOWN directed by He Ping is a wonderful example of such intertextuality. The film was produced by the Xi'an Studio, the former head of which had encouraged the making of Westerns at the studio (Rayns, 1992; Zhang and Xiao, 1998: 358). Wu Tianming was in fact talking about films set in Western China like YELLOW EARTH (1984) and RED SORGHUM (1987), but the reference to the American Western is not totally facetious. A book of short stories set in China's West and Northwest entitled *The Chinese Western* has the editor acknowledge the relationship between this 'genre' and the American Western (Zhu, 1988: viii).[18] Tony Rayns argues that RED SORGHUM also revived a Chinese film genre that had been popular in the late 1930's – the 'folk-tale movie,' where village stories became allegories for Chinese resistance to the Japanese invasion. Other examples of this genre include Chen Kaige's LIFE ON A STRING (1990) and THE SWORDSMAN IN DOUBLE-FLAG TOWN. All are set in the past, are rural, have rough, independent characters and use an off-screen narrator to locate the story (Rayns, 1992).

The plot of THE SWORDSMAN IN DOUBLE-FLAG TOWN has elements reminiscent of the other films already discussed: a stranger rides into town to find his promised bride and comes up against two brothers who control a gang that is terrorizing the community, which seems unable and unwilling to confront the bandits. The stranger, still a teenager, is forced to defend the town and kill the gang leaders, before being allowed to leave with his bride. While this plot may remind one of traditional American Westerns like HIGH NOON, the Chinese film takes an ironic approach to the American genre that is more typical of the Italian Western. The professional plot is located in the figure of Sandfly, a wandering swordsman, who is only willing to help the young hero for money. Sandfly eventually does arrive in the town but only after the final confrontation has taken place, but he still asks for money – his mercenary attitude defines him in negative and amoral terms, whereas it would not in the Italian Western. On the other hand, Haige, the young hero, draws on his own resources (including meditation) to deal with the leader of the gang. The final sword fight has many of the characteristics of the Leone Westerns with the long build-up using extreme close-ups and long shots, spatial fragmentation and the stretching of time. The town looks as dusty and desolate as that in any Italian Western. On the other hand, Haige's mystical powers over his swords align it with the fantastique sub-genre of the traditional martial arts film.

The Stunt Film and the Curry Western

The final example comes from the Indian commercial cinema. The Indian film industry is the largest in the world, producing around 800 films per year, of which about 20% are made in the Hindi language. These Hindi films are the most popular throughout India and the Indian diaspora, and this sector of the industry is usually referred to as Bollywood, although these films are by no means only produced in Bombay. Surprisingly for such a prolific industry, the production system is very fragmented and basically operates through one-picture contracts. This had been the case since the early 1940's when the studio system started to break down and even the 'one-big-family' studios had disappeared by the end of the 1940's (Barnouw and Krishnaswamy, 1980: 120-121) – the centrality and continuity of the family is as ever-present in the film industry as in politics and in the film texts themselves. The genre categories were determined in the 1930's and have not changed substantially since then, although they are so general that internal variation is possible and necessary: socials (films dealing with contemporary life), historicals (dealing with courtly life), mythologicals (primarily adaptions from the *Mahabharata* and the *Ramayana* – the two main traditional Indian epics, which are of fundamental importance to *all* Indian films), stunt films (dealing with 'dacoits,' i.e. bandits) and fantasy films (based on Persian stories such as *1001 Nights*) (Thomas, 1987: 304-305). However, all these genres have their own overarching form just as

Hollywood genres have their 'classical' form: loosely-structured digressive narratives, plots and stylistic elements that remind of the Hollywood melodrama, elaborate dialogues, a cornucopia of music, singing and dancing and a strong sense of spectacle. Thematically, they tend to concentrate on the family and 'the problem [of] genealogy' (Mishra, 1985: 137). Like the Indian epics, the films tend to be very long – the average film runs for at least two and a half hours.

In the early 1970's, the revenge theme emerged as a major concern in Hindi films, particularly in the socials and the stunt films. It has been argued that this theme was taken from imported action films like Italian Westerns, but most Indian critics also relate it to the changes in Indian society in the 1970's (Dissanayake and Sahai, 1992: 66; Basu, Kak and Krishen, 1980: 74). These films were extremely popular and dealt with a group of men – mercenaries, dacoits or police working outside the system – who were paid or forced to confront a gang of powerful villains. The most popular of these films was SHOLAY (Flames of the Sun) made in 1975. It is still one of the most popular Indian films, and dialogues from the film have been released on audiocassette (a frequent occurrence with Hindi films) and are still played at fairs, weddings and religious ceremonies (Dissanayake and Sahai, 1992: 54). While SHOLAY is frequently described as a Curry Western, other films with the revenge theme invoke different American genres, e.g. ZANJEER (The Chain, 1973) was based on DIRTY HARRY (1971), but in the Indian film, the policeman was located in the family melodrama tradition (Jain, 1990: 125).

In SHOLAY, the revenge theme is directly linked to the professional plot. Two prisoners are hired by a rural landlord (an ex-policeman) to destroy a group of dacoits, headed by Gabbar Singh. The two professionals and especially the one played by Amitabh Bachchan, the most popular Indian actor of the last thirty years and an icon of Indian cinema, could have come from the Italian Western, although their relations with the women in the film are quite different. Similarly, Gabbar Singh resembles the villain of FOR A FEW DOLLARS MORE, but he, rather than any of the film's 'positive' characters, became one of the most popular figures ever to have been created by the Indian cinema (Dissanayake and Sahai, 1992: 59). SHOLAY also resembles THE MAGNIFICENT SEVEN, but here the professionals function solely to provide support for the revenge-seeking landlord, whose arms had been amputated by Gabbar Singh – in fact the two professionals literally become his arms, his instruments for revenge, his 'guns.' There are also many scenes in the film that remind one more generally of the Western. Often such allusions are very self-conscious as when Amitabh Bachchan crouches inside a burnt-out merry-go-round in the landlord's estate and fires at the bandits like a Westerner inside a circled wagon train shooting at the Indians (a term that starts to run out of control here!).

However, the film's focus on the family, on the figure of the renouncer-hero, on the particular social context of the vengeance plus its employment of a 'local' narrative form situates it firmly and unambiguously within the traditions of the Indian cinema.

The massacre scene in SHOLAY occurs about half-way through the film and the events immediately and literally recall the massacre of the McBains in ONCE UPON A TIME IN THE WEST, as do other aspects of the scene such as the amplified 'natural' sounds, an echoing whine on the soundtrack reminiscent of Morricone's musical style and the merging of Gabbar Singh's gun-shot killing the boy with the train arriving at the station, which is here carrying the landlord coming home on leave (at this stage he is still a policeman). There are however stylistic differences, and the killing of the landlord's family is shown through a combination of freeze-frames and slow-motion shots reminiscent of countless Italian Westerns as well as SEVEN SAMURAI. Nevertheless, the major difference is that the Indian film emphasizes the cohesiveness of the landlord's extended family. Prior to the killing, the sons and daughters of the landlord talk of the effectiveness of the arranged marriages that have taken place in the family; this contrasts with the discussion between McBain and his daughter, which deals with their impending wealth. The optimism of the landlord's son about the family's future is tempered by shots of a bullock cart wheel, which comes to represent the wheel of fate ('chakra'), and by shots of another of the landlord's sons shooting at birds, suggesting the fateful consequences of taking any form of life – in the Italian film, Brett McBain's shooting of ducks carries no such overtones. The scene thus combines Indian cinema characteristics and those of the Italian Western. In the ensuing arrival of the landlord at his estate where he sees the laid-out bodies of his family, the Indian melodramatic tradition strongly reasserts itself with the music, spectacle, emotion and repetition contrasting radically with the similar scene in ONCE UPON A TIME IN THE WEST, where the mood is elegiac and restrained.

A film like SHOLAY mimics the Italian Western, particularly ONCE UPON A TIME IN THE WEST, more literally than do any of the other examples discussed in this chapter.[19] At the same time, the overall film is the least like any of the other films. This sort of intertextual tension is evident on the broader thematic level as well. In revenge films like SHOLAY, the family is under threat from the forces of darkness and can only find protection by employing avenging figures like the film's two professionals. Chidananda Das Gupta suggests that such 'solutions' represent a loss of faith in society's institutions and 'that in this corrupt age (Kaliyug), only the individual must make the heroic protest' (Das Gupta, 1991: 110). Mercenaries and vigilantes have remained the dominant protagonists of Indian popular cinema. In recent years this has extended to the figure of the avenging woman in films like ZAKHMI AURAT (Wounded Women,

1988), where a woman's rape and death leads a group of women to castrate the men responsible – such figures powerfully invoke the mythical archetypes of the goddesses Durga and Kali. The commercial Indian film director, N. Chandra is quoted as saying that '[i]n films as in life, we are moving from the *Ramayana* to the *Mahabharata*,' i.e. from a world of romance and faithfulness to one of violence and chaos (Chandra, 1994: 89), once again underlining the bonds between contemporary culture and society, and foundational texts. These thematic concerns are not confined to Indian cinema. In an interesting echo of the above comments on the rise of the vigilante, John Cawelti argues that the post-Leone American Westerns like CHISUM (1970) and BIG JAKE (1971) emphasize 'the failure of society to protect the innocent and [...] the need for the private leader and avenger' (Cawelti, 1974: 117). This is raised less out of a desire to engage in the dangerous practice of reading films as unmediated reflections of contemporary society than as another instance of intertextuality.

Conclusion

This chapter has attempted to demonstrate that the transformation of the Western is a complex process and that it has not occurred in one direction only. This is particularly interesting in a genre that is usually described as the most American of film genres. While it must be recognized that this transformation has not just happened since the 1960's, it has certainly accelerated since then and more importantly the transformation has taken place outside Hollywood. The Italian Western was created primarily because of a set of commercial opportunities, but it also deconstructed and reconstructed the genre sending it spinning in all directions. The Japanese samurai and Chinese martial arts films had for decades adapted traditional wanderer and knight-errant narratives and here the influences of the American and Italian Western tended to do no more than revitalize the existing genres by changing the character of the protagonist. In India, the form of the popular film is so fixed that the influence of the Western was both more obvious and literal and much less permanent, being overwhelmed by larger narrative and stylistic norms. It is also important to note that the American Western, and perhaps American cinema more generally, was forever changed by these 'foreign' transformations. This is particularly apparent in the films Clint Eastwood made when he 'returned' to America after the Leone trilogy, such as HIGH PLAINS DRIFTER (1972) and in the more recent UNFORGIVEN (1992) (dedicated to Leone and Don Siegel), in the Westerns of Sam Peckinpah of the late 1960's (especially THE WILD BUNCH, 1969), but also in most subsequent American-made Westerns.

The analyses of these films and genres finally need to be placed in the context of what Arjun Appadurai calls 'global cultural flows' (Appadurai, 1990: 6), which are multi-directional if also asymmetrical. These flows no longer originate in just a few centers of popular culture located in the West, from which 'cultural imperialism does its work.' It is strange that the term 'cultural imperialism' is invoked primarily in discourses around popular culture, with calls for cultural purity, authenticity and isolation whereas the matter rarely raises an eyebrow in the fields of science, art, literature and scholarship in general (Hannerz, 1989: 70-71). A more effective and productive strategy is to focus on the creative interaction between the transnational and the local and between the local and the local, which engages in the sort of intertextual tension referred to earlier. This is not a simple process to understand nor an easy one to analyze, for it requires an appreciation of the oscillation between homogenization and difference, loss and invention, and destruction and creation (Clifford, 1988: 17).

The Brazilian Modernists of the 1920's established a Cannibalist Movement, which proposed 'cultural anthropophagy as an anticolonialist artistic strategy, i.e. to devour what is useful in the foreign and excrete what is not' (Stam, 1992: 196). In a less aggressive tone, Amin Sweeney describes the Malay text, the *Hikayat Seri Rama*, not as a translation of the Hindu epic, the *Ramayana*, but as an adaption of that epic into a Muslim work for a Muslim audience 'that concerns the breaking of a contract mediated by the prophet Adam between a Muslim king, Rawana, and the Muslim God' (Sweeney, 1991: 26). In later chapters, it will be argued that Malaysian films are similarly grounded in the culture in which they are produced, whatever the many cross-cultural influences that are inevitably and creatively brought to bear on them. These examples support this chapter's argument against some overarching master narrative or master structure that produces texts through the never-ending elaboration of abstract principles of repetition and difference. They also recognize the activities of local cultural producers drawing upon available cultural repertoires for representations and situating these representations in the particularities of their own histories and cultural inflections. This suggests a de-centering of categories, including those of national cinema and genre, rather than a rigid adherence to or dissolution of such categories. The analyst therefore employs cross-cultural strategies to acknowledge the existence of the boundary, while constantly asserting that it is fluid, mobile, penetrable, contestable and creative.

> 'I learn to tread lightly along the limits of where I am speaking from – where there are limits there are also other voices, bodies and worlds on the other side, beyond my particular boundaries' (Chambers, 1994: 5).

2 Malaysian Society and Culture

'If cultures and civilizations are the tectonic plates of world history, frontiers are the places where they scrape against each other and cause convulsive change... For purposes of world history, the margins sometimes demand more attention than the metropolis... [but] peripheries have little history of their own: what gets recorded and transmitted is usually selected according to the centres' criteria of importance'
(Felipe Fernandez-Armesto, 1995: 8).

'Race has always been an issue in my country, even before Independence, but never has it been as serious and divisive as it is today. Almost every issue is seen from the perspective of race to the point where it is impossible to obtain a consensus of public opinion on **any** issue'
(Kee Thuan Chye, 1993: 145).

Introduction

In the previous chapter, the concept of transtextuality was used to trace the complex interaction and movement of filmic texts across cultures through a process of anterior and posterior textual relations. This chapter pursues similar 'lines of connectedness' and their involvement with notions of cultural and national identities. Once again it is useful to speak of 'anterior' and 'posterior' relationships, but in this context those relationships apply to societies and cultures and their participation in the voluntary and/or forced migration of peoples – appropriately encompassed in the concept of transmigration, which the *Shorter Oxford English Dictionary* defines as the passage from one country to another as well as the condition of transition and transformation.[1] This therefore applies both to emigration, with its emphasis on the anterior, departed culture and the 'mother-country,' and to immigration, with its focus on the posterior, arriving, domiciled or 'host' culture. As will become apparent, 'newness,' as referred to by Salman Rushdie and discussed in the previous chapter, is not solely the consequence of arrival and interaction (or lack of interaction); 'newness' also occurs as a result of leaving a society, and continues in the subsequent interaction between the departed and the domiciled society and, finally, 'newness' also affects the departed society as a consequence of emigration.

Malaysia is a country and society that because of geographic location and historical consequence is crisscrossed by lines of voluntary and forced connectedness as a result of trade, migration and colonialism. The outcomes of these interactions are manifest in Malaysia's political, religious, social and cultural configuration.

This chapter will not (and cannot) present a detailed analysis of these histories and structures. Instead, it will limit itself to examining certain aspects of Malaysia's society and culture that contribute to identifying the 'lines of connectedness' and their place in the construction of local identity, or rather, identities. The discussion is also only relevant to the extent that it helps to contextualize the arguments of the following two chapters. Before focusing on Malaysia's history and culture, it is important to make some comments on the concept of identity, particularly its cultural and national manifestations.

Identity

Identity is a complex and even confusing construct and any discussion of the topic is fraught with dangers. The emphasis here is on certain cultural meanings of the term. Even when the discussion is limited to 'cultural identity,' it is not always easy to distinguish between different uses of the term, especially the tension between 'descriptive' meanings and more 'ideological' ones, e.g. the distinction between self/others and self/other. Stuart Hall distinguishes between three conceptions of identity:
a) the Enlightenment subject, characterized by an unchanging, fixed notion of identity, one that is frequently criticized as essentialist or ontological;
b) the sociological subject, representing a less individualistic perspective and proposing a more interactive relationship between self and society, resulting in a notion of identity that is less certain or centered and more influenced by outside forces. These first two categories also represent the rather stereotypical dichotomy between western individualism and the Asian emphasis on community;
c) the postmodern subject, which rejects any sense of a fixed or essentialist identity; identity is instead perceived as being fluid, fragmented and even contradictory, so that it may well be preferable to speak of identities rather than identity (Hall, 1992: 275).

From the postmodern perspective, the Enlightenment 'project' is one that erased history by the transformation of the historical relations of self to others 'into an ontological relationship to the Other' (Morley and Robins, 1989: 17). In reaction to such an essentialist proposition, Jacques Derrida argues for a more complex relationship between self and other, where '... cultural identity presents itself... as the *irreplaceable* inscription of the universal in the singular, the *unique testimony* to the human essence...' (Derrida, 1992: 73), in which the two statements oscillate in emphasis between the 'singular,' the 'unique' and the 'universal,' the 'human essence,' i.e. between the self and the other, if one considers the other as all that is not the self. Derrida therefore suggests that the two are inseparably interconnected, not as hierarchy but as a form of symmetry or a mirror image.

As a consequence, identity formation involves the construction (and, in terms of the ontological argument, the fixation) of links between particular individuals and groups, based on commonalities *and* differences. Identity is therefore more persona-based than subject-based, with individuals defining themselves in terms of a range of 'identity markers' that result in affiliations based on ethnicity, religion, class, language, gender, sexuality, etc. An interesting example of the assumptions regarding the status of such categories occurs in an early sequence of NORTHERN CRESCENT, a 1991 Channel Four television feature in which a new primary school headmaster, Mr. West introduces himself at assembly to his students, most of whom are of Pakistani ethnicity. Mr. West asks the students to name the greatest storybook in the world. After replies (seriously given) such as *The Guinness Book of Records* and GHOSTBUSTERS, he tells them that it is *The Bible* – his own ethnicity is thus quite apparent. He proceeds to read them the story of Ruth as an example of people making their home in a new place and being welcomed there – he applies this to his own arrival at the school that morning, seemingly oblivious to its application to the Pakistani immigrants in this Yorkshire town (the film will go on to question whether any sense of 'welcomeness' is given to these people). The headmaster says he's not surprised to have received such a welcome, as it is part of the great tradition of this country and particularly of Yorkshire. He notes that of the 180 pupils in the school, 176 were born in Yorkshire. He then asks them whether they would say that they are Yorkshire boys and girls. Only four students (one of Pakistani ethnicity) put up their hands, leaving the headmaster looking surprised and perplexed. The sequence is an excellent example of identity presumption, in this case of place of birth as an unquestioned and fixed identity marker. Similarly, the reference to *The Bible* as the greatest book in the presence of so many presumably Muslim students indicates the headmaster's confident if naive ethnocentrism.

The teacher's coupling of a particular form of group-affiliation based on place and people ('Yorkshireness'/'Britishness') and that group's 'ownership' of a specific positive quality (welcomeness), which is in turn exemplified by reference to a foundational narrative (*The Bible*), represents some of the central elements of nationalism, which has over the last few centuries become the predominant definer and container of group identity. Despite the responses of the students, most people would identify themselves in terms of nationality and would assert that this is an essential part of their being. That this essentialism is very close to a genetic attribute is apparent in the process by which an 'alien' becomes a 'citizen' of a country – a process of naturalization where the migrant acquires attributes of the 'nature-born.' This involves and invokes a discourse in which the concepts of the 'natural' and the 'national' are linked.[2] Yet there remains a distinction between the naturalized migrant and the 'nature-born' citizen that is based on place of birth, a distinction that is frequently invoked in case of conflicts between the country of acquired citizenship and the country of birth. This distinction and the consequent mistrust in terms of loyalty extends to the locally-born offspring of such migrants as well – this was demonstrated by the treatment of people of Arab ethnicity in Australia during the Gulf War in 1991.

National Identity and National Culture

In an enormously influential book on national identity, Benedict Anderson argues that national cultures are 'imagined communities,' '*imagined* because the members of even the smallest nation will never know most of their fellow-members, meet them, or even hear of them, yet in the minds of each lives the image of their communion' (Anderson, 1991: 6). Here, Anderson is stressing the creativity involved in this process of imagining in contrast to what he regards as Ernest Gellner's judgmental attitude of equating invention with fabrication and falsity (Anderson, 1991: 6). Further, in contradistinction to Gellner's view that 'nationalism ... sometimes takes pre-existing cultures and turns them into nations, sometimes invents them, and often obliterates pre-existing cultures' (Gellner, 1983: 49), Anderson asserts that all communities, probably even those having total face-to-face contact, are 'imagined' (Anderson, 1991: 6). This is an important point for my purposes since it allows the argument to proceed on the basis of nations being imagined through a process of representation or meaning construction. As the subtitle of his book indicates, Anderson goes on to examine nationalism diachronically by locating its origin in 18th century Europe with the rise of capitalism, in particular print-capitalism and its manifestation in the commodified and mechanized production of books and newspapers, which 'made it possible for rapidly growing numbers of people to think about themselves, and relate themselves to others, in profoundly new ways' (Anderson, 1991: 36). While Anderson goes on to link nationalism to imperialism and colonialism, and to de-colonization, there is a strong sense of universalism about his perspective (or rather a Euro-centrism – paradoxical given his long-term commitment to Southeast Asian studies), which is noted by Partha Chatterjee in his book, *The Nation and its Fragments*. Chatterjee accepts much of Anderson's argument, but wants to qualify it by proposing that colonial (and postcolonial) societies 'fashion a "modern" national culture that is nevertheless not Western' (Chatterjee, 1993: 6). This decoupling of the West from the process of modernity is not sought to 'emphasize... an "Indian" (or an "Oriental") exceptionalism' but to act as 'a demonstration that the alleged exceptions actually inhere as forcibly suppressed elements even in the supposedly universal forms of the modern regime of power' (Chatterjee, 1993: 13). Such a perspective coincides with my argument that a national culture can only be analyzed in all its complexities by emphasizing these 'forcibly suppressed elements' in relation to, and in the face of, the powerful tendency to cultural centralism (or universalism).

Since the focus of this book is cultural, I want to move away from Anderson's more historical perspective and return to the question of representations as the means by which national cultures are constructed. These representations take the form of a wide range of cultural artifacts such as stories, songs, ceremonies and symbols like flags and colors, and they are narrativized and propagated through cultural institutions like the state, the education system, cultural bodies and community organizations. Stuart Hall identifies five primary means by which a national culture is constructed (Hall, 1992: 293-295):

1. The *narrative of a nation*: how the story of a nation is told in fictional and non-fictional accounts and forms. These become the touchstones of 'nationness' that construct the nation. It is important to note that this narrative encompasses *all* the stories of a nation, but that some of these stories, at a given time and in a given community, achieve dominance and even erase some of the other stories. Consequently there is always conflict, with different groups constructing different versions of the narrative of a nation. Alternatively the same narrative may well be interpreted in radically different ways by different communities, e.g. the foundational Indian epic, the *Ramayana* is regarded by the majority of Indians as embodying the ideals of Indianness in its representation of the god/hero, Rama, and his battle with the demon-king Ravana; however, in certain parts of India this same text is read as 'a thinly disguised historical account of how North Indians, led by Rama, subjugated South Indians, ruled by Ravana' (Richman, 1991b: 178).

2. The emphasis on *origins, continuity, tradition and timelessness*: national identity is therefore fixed from time immemorial, unaffected by historical change. This can be a troublesome characteristic, not just in colonial and postcolonial societies, but also where there has been a major shift in a society's social or cultural system, e.g. the status of traditional animistic beliefs in a society converted to Islam, such as Malaysia.

3. The *Invention of Tradition*: that resonant title of Hobsbawm and Ranger's book, is the means by which a society can overcome the problems referred to in the previous category by fixing 'certain values and norms of behavior by repetition, which automatically implies continuity with the past' (Hobsbawm, 1983: 1). The construction of Bangsawan theater as a Malay traditional practice is an excellent example, which will be discussed later in this chapter.
4. The *foundational myth*: often associated with specific oral and written texts that construct genealogies back to a 'time before time,' e.g. the prologue of the *Sejarah Melayu* (Malay Annals) discussed later in this chapter.
5. The idea of *a pure, original people or 'folk'*: a very powerful shaper of national identity and sovereignty. It is frequently used to assert 'ownership' and nationhood, as with the Malays in Malaysia employing the term 'bumiputera', meaning indigenous people or 'sons of the soil' (lit. prince of the soil), but this is very much a political assertion, particularly in the face of the continuing existence of the 'orang asli' (the aboriginal people of the Malay peninsula).

These aspects of national identity formation all function to create a contemporary sense of nationness, but, paradoxically, do so through a powerful call upon the past, which then shapes and defines that sense of nation. In that respect, national identity erases difference by imposing a set of attributes on all members of the nation – an unwillingness to accept all these attributes threatens identity and therefore threatens expulsion from that community. Similarly, national identity tends to erase all other identities. Slavoj Zizek makes this point quite graphically when he writes of the 'violent act of abstraction' involved in 'the preamble to every democratic proclamation "all people *without regard to* (race, sex, religion, wealth, social status)"' (Zizek, 1992: 163). In reality, of course, nations are crossed by those differences to which Zizek refers and it is the role of nationalism to contain and neutralize those differences, particularly when that nationalism is in contest with another nationalism. Thus national cultures are '"unified" only through the exercise of different forms of cultural power' (Hall, 1992: 297). One of the major rhetorical (and administrative/statistical) strategies employed in this ideological drive for a cohesive identity formation is to invoke constructs like race and ethnicity. Ethnicity, which literally means nation, has become confused with race, which has strong biological overtones; even though race has no status in biology, it has remained in the popular imagination as a social definition, including such terms as the human race. On the other hand, ethnicity is typically aligned with culture, but this is equally problematic as there are no discrete or distinct cultures in existence. So ethnicity has no fixed markers and the crucial issue is how it is constructed and for what purposes. Ethnicity has also been linked with minorities, and the term 'ethnic minorities' is frequently used in Australia. This is rather tautological since there is no reference to ethnic majorities or majority (although it is obviously implied, just as the term 'white' is an implied correlative of 'black'). Perhaps the way out of this problem is not to use the word 'ethnicity' at all, or to apply it to everyone, in the sense that we are all ethnically located. Such a view of ethnicity 'acknowledges the place of history, language and culture in the construction of subjectivity and identity' (Hall, 1988: 29), while at the same time recognizing that an individual or group is not contained or confined by that place nor is that place hierarchically superior (or inferior) in relation to another's putative ethnicity. This conception of ethnicity will operate throughout this book as a statement of principle, but it is also necessary to accept that the term is still often used interchangeably with the word race, particularly in countries like Malaysia, where a clear-cut and 'self-evident' ethnic division is said to exist. As will become clear, national cultures cannot erase differences, ethnic or otherwise, and one of the major functions of national identity formation is to bring a semblance of community ('to speak with one voice') to this potential fragmentation.

The tension between a tendency to uniformity and a tendency to hybridization (which can also be expressed as the conflict between the center and the margin) is at the heart of national culture and its various manifestations such as technologies of storytelling and language. Anderson linked the rise of the novel in Europe to the rise of nationalism, and Timothy Brennan (using Bakhtin's concept of 'heteroglossia') has examined this relationship in greater detail. 'The novel objecti[fies] the nation's composite nature: a hotch potch of the ostensibly separate "levels of style" corresponding to class: a jumble of poetry, drama, newspaper report, memoir and speech' (Brennan, 1990: 51). These involve different discourses but the form of the novel strives to contain them and represent a sort of harnessed heterogeneity. Similarly, modern technologies of communication, including film and television maintain an often-uneasy balance between heterogeneous elements and some form of cohesion – these in turn mimic the tensions in the broader culture. Language itself undergoes constant changes that check any tendency to homogeneity by a concurrent hybridization or creolization. Even English, which has been labeled the only 'supercentral language' (De Swaan, 1991: 316) because there are increasing numbers of bilingual speakers competent in this language, might well be better described as 'Englishes,' with the development of indigenous forms of English throughout the world. On the other hand, there are few if any monolingual countries (De Swaan, 1991: 320) and languages other than the 'national language' are often spoken at home and in local communities. This is particularly the case in Malaysia, where all school children learn Bahasa Melayu, yet take their cultural identity principally from the linguistic community to which they belong.

On a global level, there are similar tensions between homogenization and heterogeneity, the latter taking the form of either hybridity (where 'imagined communities' form and reform, independent of national boundaries) or local essentialism (where communities feel threatened or besieged by globalization or more regional forms of change and so reassert the community traditions Hall referred to above). In this context, it is often argued that national identity is in crisis in the face of the 'push-pull' forces of globalization and localism. There certainly seem to be powerful global cultural flows (Appadurai, 1990: 11) as well as local forces, both of which threaten to weaken, if not destroy, national cultural identity. Stuart Hall even suggests that there may well be a greater and somewhat ironic consequence: 'though powered in many ways by the West, globalization may turn out to be part of that slow and uneven but continuing story of the de-centring of the West' (Hall, 1992: 314).

It is nevertheless the case that the 'call to nation' remains one of the most powerful definers of individual and group identity. The rhetoric of nation is constantly proclaimed in politics, business, sports and culture as well as in debates about indigenous and immigrant peoples, where such rhetoric is a constant covert whisper that, every now and then, breaks out into a shout, a curse or a song. Nationalism may not be as strongly asserted as it once was, but the attitudes and emotions implicit in the term have certainly not disappeared – they are just voiced differently. This is clear in the exclusivity camouflaged by the use of words like 'we,' 'the Australian community' and 'the Australian people.' Suggesting that identity is more fractured than it once was does not mean that national identity is less important than say global or local identity. They represent different persona and affiliations to communities of interest, such as ethnicity, religion, the environment, sports, an academic discipline or internet/intranet interaction.

An intriguing example of the confusions of identity resulting from such 'reconfigurations' is the response of Malaysia to the Australian television series EMBASSY (1990-92). The program makers denied that the series was set in an actual country, but the Malaysian government concluded, through a nationalist discourse, that the country the series called Ragaan was in fact Malaysia. For the producers, Ragaan was an 'imagined geography' constructed from (Orientalist) conceptions of Asia. Malaysia's Prime Minister, Dr. Mahathir Mohamad, on the other hand, extrapolated from these cultural elements a particular set of characteristics that matched, and thus slighted his nation, *despite* the obvious differences between this 'nation' and Malaysia. Both parties therefore constructed a nation for their own specific purposes. Dr. Mahathir may well have been pleased with the opportunity this gave him to berate the Australian government (particularly when the *national* broadcaster was involved), but this event does underline the process of narrative construction involved in the defining of national identity.³

Malaysian Identity

In constructing and discussing versions of Malaysian identities, it is necessary to examine aspects of Malaysian social and cultural history in the context of the theoretical arguments proposed so far in this chapter. This will be undertaken in three main sections: pre-colonial, colonial and postcolonial Malaysia. The employment of the 'colonial' as the defining characteristic of Malaysian history accentuates the powerful legacy of European colonialism on that society, despite its relatively brief presence (about 450 years). At the same time, as will become apparent, the cultural influence of the pre-colonial Melakan state on contemporary national identity is partly due to its *pre*-colonial status.⁴ In other words, the discourse of national identity (which was activated well before independence) is strongly linked to the colonial issue.

Before proceeding with the historical and cultural discussion, it is necessary to distinguish between the terms Malay, Malayan and Malaysian. The distinctions are central to the argument that follows and so preliminary definitions are important at this stage. The first term, Malay, is cultural and is considered an ethnic description. In the *Historical Dictionary of Malaysia*, a Malay is identified as 'a person of the Malay race. In the Twelfth Schedule of the Federal Constitution, a Malay is defined as a person who: (i) habitually speaks the Malay language, (ii) professes the Muslim religion and (iii) conforms to Malay customs' (Kaur, 1993: 91). The other two terms are descriptions of national identity (although it may already be obvious that their relationship to the term Malay is not unproblematic). Malaya was inaugurated as a political entity in 1948 as the Federation of Malaya and was constituted from the nine Malay states (Perlis, Kedah, Perak, Selangor, Negeri Sembilan, Johor, Pahang, Trengganu and Kelantan) and the Strait Settlements of Penang and Melaka. This entity is now called West or Peninsular Malaysia. Independence was proclaimed in 1957. 'A Malayan was a citizen of the Federation of Malaya, irrespective of racial origin' (Kaur, 1993: 91). Malaysia was formed in 1963 and further included Sarawak and Sabah (together called East Malaysia) and Singapore (which then left again in 1965 to become an independent state). A Malaysian is a citizen of the Federation of Malaysia. I will maintain the distinction between the three terms, except in cases where a broad, generalized description is appropriate, in which case the term Malaysian will be used, irrespective of the historical moment (as in the next heading).

Pre-colonial Malaysia

The Malay Archipelago, which comprises what are now the countries of Malaysia, Singapore, Indonesia and Brunei, and is locally called Nusantara, has been aptly described as 'the lands below the winds' (the subtitle of Anthony Reid's 1988 book). This refers to the annual monsoon patterns in the region causing ships from the west and from the east to take shelter there, thus marking the Archipelago as 'the convergence of two major sea routes... [linking]... the great markets of India and China' (Andaya and Andaya, 1982: 10). The area became an important meeting place of traders and, inevitably, a place of constant cultural interaction. The resultant migration of peoples to and from the Archipelago was to represent one of the most distinctive features of the region over the centuries. Whether it was elite or mass migration, temporary or permanent migration, it played a major role in the shaping and constant reshaping of the political, social and cultural identity of the region.

While the interactions operated at all levels and from all directions, the dominant cultural flow was from India. The process was initially labeled as the 'Indianization' of the Archipelago, but more recently it has been referred to as 'self-Indianization,' to remove any connotation of colonialism and 'cultural imperialism' and to convey a sense of interaction resulting from movements of peoples in both directions. Indian traders and Brahmin priests visited and settled in the region while Malay traders traveled to the Indian subcontinent and returned with new ideas and customs as well as traded goods (Wang, 1992: 174). Through such processes, cultural activities were appropriated for local purposes. I. W. Mabbett suggests a more unidirectional flow, in which Indianization ought to be recognized as part of a larger 'Aryanization' and 'Sanskritization' that started in India itself centuries earlier and that later extended to Southeast Asia – its gradual spread also changed those influences as they came into contact with local elements (Mabbett, 1977). This applied particularly to the adoption of Hinduism and Buddhism as religious practices and as models for the conceptualization of kingship and the relation of the ruler to the ruled. The result was the transformation of the coastal trading centers into Indian-style city-states, in which the ruler was defined as God on earth, as the reincarnation of the Hindu Gods of Shiva or Vishnu (Ackerman and Lee, 1988: 16-17). The Hindu/Buddhist influences tended to be confined to the courts and the urban regions and had little effect on people in the Malay kampung, although over time some of the customs did permeate everyday life, such as the wedding rituals, which still involve the viewing of the bride and groom (called 'bersanding' in Bahasa Melayu, lit. 'side by side'), based on the Indian concept of 'darshan' or 'darsan' (lit. seeing), which will be of relevance to the film analyses in the following chapters.

Kampung culture was based on customary practices accompanied by animistic ritual. The Malay word for custom is 'adat' and it refers to the totality of 'concepts, rules and codes of behaviour considered as legitimate or right, appropriate or necessary' (Karim, 1992: 14). Its application ranges from the mundane sense of acting properly to the concept of Malay identity and cohesion, and covers the full range of economic, social and cultural practices. One of the most interesting aspects that Karim discusses in relation to adat is the concept of 'bi-laterality,' which provides women with equality and autonomy in traditional Malay society, where identity and status is more typically ranked by age and seniority, matrimony (irrespective of gender), socioeconomic position, personal attributes and morality (Karim, 1992: 5-7). In such a system, the young were positioned rather lowly in hierarchical terms, whether male or female. In an interesting description of sexual relations in 16th and 17th century Southeast Asia, Anthony Reid suggests that one of the consequences of women having such status was that 'the value of daughters was never questioned in Southeast Asia as it was in China, India, and the Middle East' (Reid, 1988: 146); he goes on to describe acceptable sexual relations to include premarital sex, monogamy and easy divorce (Reid, 1988: 156) – practices that would become problematic as the region came under the influence of Islam. The animistic religion of the Malays concentrated on their relationship with the natural world, with ritual functioning as the means by which malevolent and beneficent spirits were invoked by identified practitioners of magic, called 'bomoh' (Ackerman and Lee, 1988: 12-13).

Perhaps the most pervasive and influential cultural consequence of Indianization was the introduction and localization of stories from the two principal Indian epics, the *Mahabharata* and the *Ramayana*. It is impossible to overestimate the importance of these foundational texts in Indian culture. They are part of the Hindu religious tradition, but do not function as 'holy writ,' the way *The Torah*, *The Bible* and *The Qur'an* represent the 'religions of the book.' The Indian epics are esthetic, social, political and cultural texts as much as religious texts – in European terms, they are compared as much with *The Iliad* and *The Odyssey* as with *The Bible*. The epics were originally oral texts and therefore circulated in multiple versions. When they were eventually written down there were also quite a number of versions, some of which were consciously competing narratives, intending to contest previous interpretations – Richman's *Many Ramayanas* (1991a) details these matters extensively. Without disregarding the diversity and heterogeneity of the Mahabharata and Ramayana tradition, it is necessary to briefly (a term not easily applied to either epic!) outline their core narrative elements.

The *Mahabharata* is a very long work and the most referenced version is by Vyasa. The central conflict developed in the epic is that between two groups of cousins, the Pandavas and the Kauravas. The Pandava brothers are five in number: Yudhisthira, Bhima, Arjuna, Nakula and Sahadeva and they are all married to the same woman, Draupadi. The Kauravas number one hundred and are led by the eldest, Duryodhana. The Kauravas are presented as somewhat more malevolent than the Pandavas, the eldest of whom, Yudhisthira, loses everything to the Kauravas in a game of dice, including Draupadi, who is stripped naked and humiliated by the Kauravas, before being returned to her husbands. The Pandavas are exiled for twelve years in order to stop Yudhisthira from becoming king; a subsequent attempted reconciliation between the two parties fails. This results in a cataclysmic battle between the Pandavas and the Kauravas at Kuruksetra, with the Pandavas, and in particular Arjuna, being supported by Krishna, who acts as counselor and charioteer. There follows the segment of the epic best known outside India: the *Bhagavad Gita*, a treatise/poem in which Krishna speaks to Arjuna about doubt, action, love and the infinite. On the eighteenth day (the number is very significant: there are that number of books in the epic and the same number of chapters in the *Gita*) the Kauravas are totally annihilated (Blackburn, 1989). The *Mahabharata* has been called India's 'Doomsday Epic, a grand tale of a pyrrhic victory' (Lal, 1980: 6), although it is also interpreted as expressing 'the battle that constantly recurs in the human soul' (Nandan, 1995).

The *Ramayana* is a much shorter and more 'romantic' work and the most influential version is by Valmiki, although it is contested by a number of other versions. The central narrative starts in the city of Ayodhya, where the retiring king appoints his eldest son, Rama, as his successor. However, because of a promise made to his youngest queen, the king is forced to banish Rama, his wife Sita and his half-brother Laksmana to the forest. Ravana, the king of Lanka, hears of the beauty of Sita and, in disguise, lures Rama and Laksmana away from Sita, kidnaps her and takes her to his island kingdom. Rama enlists the help of a monkey, Hanuman, who locates Sita in Lanka. Hanuman is captured, but escapes, setting the city on fire. The monkeys build a bridge to Lanka and a devastating battle ensues between Rama and Ravana, and Ravana is eventually killed by Rama. Rama initially refuses to take Sita back since she has lived in another man's house. She undergoes a trial by fire to convince him of her chastity (until further rumors ultimately lead him to banish her – this part of the narrative is bracketed because the central myth of the epic is the pure and eternal love of Rama and Sita, with Sita embodying all the attributes of the perfect Indian wife) (Richman, 1991: 5-7).

The inclusion of these narratives in the cultures of the Archipelago was to take place over a long period of time and was constantly reworked in the context of prevailing norms. In general terms, they were incorporated in three different performance modes: the shadow-play or Wayang versions, the professional storyteller versions and the written versions like the *Hikayat Pandawa Jaya* (The Story of the Pandava Victory), *Hikayat Pandawa Lima* (The Story of the Five Pandavas) and the *Hikayat Seri Rama* (The Story of Rama) (Singaravelu, 1981: 131 and Singaravelu, 1983: 227). The Wayang versions, especially those based on the *Ramayana* and called the *Cherita Mahraja Wana*, will be discussed later in the chapter.

While Chinese traders were also involved in the activities of the trading centers in the Archipelago, the impact of Chinese culture was minimal compared with that of India, with which there appeared to be much greater affinity (Andaya and Andaya, 1982: 15). Later chapters will reconfirm a similar, skewed cultural impact in the Malaysian film industry. On the other hand, the arrival of Islam changed the region profoundly and its impact started to be felt from about the 11th and 12th century. In remaining sensitive to the complexity of all cultural interactions, it is important to note that Islam came to the Archipelago primarily via Indian Muslim traders, although Arab traders also visited the region, but often after stopovers at the Malabar and Coromandel Coasts of Southern India (Ackerman and Lee, 1988: 19). Partly because of this 'intermediate' Indian interaction, the Islam that eventually came to the Archipelago was itself influenced by Sufism, or Islamic mysticism. It has been argued that Sufism was able to 'syncretise Islamic ideas with existing local beliefs and religious notions' (Mohd. Taib Osman, 1984: 268) and thus build on animism and Hinduism rather than insist on their total repudiation. In this way, Islam had a powerful impact on the whole population and not just on the court culture, as was the case with Hinduism and Buddhism. However, the impact at the courts was not negligible as Islam reaffirmed the power of the ruler, but it was modified significantly from the Hindu concept of divine kingship to an Islamic one where the ruler is 'God's shadow on earth' (Mohd. Taib Osman, 1984: 266). While the distinction is important, it will be clear from a later examination of the power structure in the *Hikayat Hang Tuah* that the relationship between ruler and ruled was still absolutist.

The structure of this Malay state, the 'Kerajaan' (a term built around the Sanskrit word 'Raja,' meaning prince or ruler) can be represented in diagrammatic form (Wang, 1992: 230):

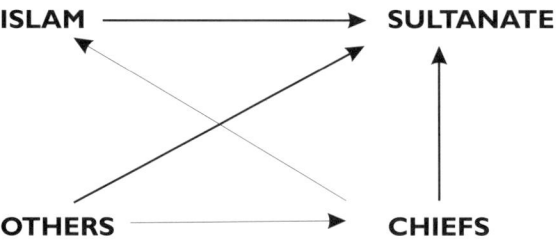

Figure 4: The Kerajaan model[5]

Wang Gungwu suggests that the introduction of the Islamic and Persian influence on the conception of the ruler (Raja or, the from now on more frequently used Arabic word, Sultan) provided the Sultan with religious authority over his subjects, although not at the expense of adat, evidenced by the Malay proverb: 'Let the child die but not adat.' The diagram illustrates the dominant position of the Sultanate, but also the challenge to it of Islam, which argues for the unimpeded relationship between the Islamic community and God. The Chiefs were the leaders of local tribes, while the fourth pole (Others) represents migrant or itinerant traders and settlers. The changing relationships between these power bases will be re-examined at other crucial stages of Malaysian history. Clive Kessler argues that Malay society is a profoundly political society and that the identity of the Malay people is defined through their subjecthood. Consequently, the Kerajaan 'is not only a ruler's domain but his subjects' sociocultural condition, that of having a raja' (Kessler, 1992: 136). This suggests an extremely strong bond between ruler and ruled, in which their roles are rigidly defined. Kessler identifies the model for this conception of Malay culture as residing in the Melakan Sultanate (Kessler, 1992: 146).

The Melakan Sultanate is widely regarded as representing the Golden Age of Malay culture and is still the reference point for the construction of Malay identity. Its importance is evidenced by constant references in popular discourse (newspapers, television programs, films and political debate) and within formal historiography. The Malaysian historian, Muhammad Yusoff Hashim, acknowledges that for many scholars 'the history of the nation should begin with Malacca' (I have preferred the Malay word Melaka), but he does stress that its traditions were inevitably 'a perpetuation of the political-cultural history of the Malay world' (Muhammad Yusoff Hashim, 1992: 255). Despite this caution, Melaka has become the idealization of all that Malay society represents, becoming a foundational myth in Stuart Hall's categorization of national culture and identity. Perhaps the fact that Melaka became the region's most powerful trading and cultural center at a time when Islam was making a major impact in the region also contributes to its pivotal role in Malay consciousness – it linked Islam and Malayness so intimately that one is unthinkable without the other. In that respect, all that came before Melaka was but a preparation for Melaka, which was the foundation of the Malay nation and Malay nationalism (in retrospect, of course).

The Sultanate lasted just over one hundred years, from about 1400 to 1511, when it was captured by the Portuguese, marking the commencement of European colonialism in the Malay Peninsula for the following four and a half centuries. Despite there being a debate among historians about the genealogy of the early Sultans of Melaka (Wang, 1992: 147-157, Muhammad Yusoff Hashim, 1992: 73-86), the origin of the Melakan Sultanate is frequently located in the arrival of a Malay prince, Paramesvara, from Palembang (the central city of the Srivijaya Empire, located in what is now southeastern Sumatra), who converted to Islam and changed his name to Iskandar Shah. This helped ensure continuing commercial alliances for the new trading port (Ackerman and Lee, 1988: 21-22). It also initiates a genealogy that, as will be seen, constructed an origin for the Sultanate in the 'time before time.'

Foundational Narratives

While some of the 'narratives of nation' emphasize the importance of Islam, others stress the cosmopolitan nature of the Sultanate. The 16th century Portuguese writer, Tomé Pires noted the way that Melaka acted as a hinge for the whole region by holding together 'the ethnic and religious solidarity that connected each foreign colony in the town to its mother country [and] the solidarity of neighborhood that bound them together under the local ruler and local law' (Thomaz, 1993: 79). Allegiances were therefore non-exclusive and almost conditional, creating a society of great tolerance and one that encouraged heterogeneity. Thomaz also suggests that there were a number of co-existing versions of the origin of the Sultanate, with one version linking the dynasty to a semi-divine Hindu king. This leads Thomaz to suggest that 'Even if this syncretism was not consciously designed, it fit[s] well with the pluralistic character of Melaka society' (Thomaz, 1993: 80). Muhammad Yusoff Hashim is less sanguine. After praising the tolerance and mutual respect that seemed to have existed at the time, he suggests that a closer examination of group relationships paints a less rosy picture, particularly in Malay-Tamil relations (many of the Tamils were also Muslims). His summary of the evidence accepts that Melaka was a great cosmopolitan society, but that it 'was no longer inhabited by Malays and other indigenous peoples alone, and accordingly gave birth to a society whose members had differing ambitions' (Muhammad Yusoff Hashim, 1992: 244, 253). This latter scenario does not announce the Golden Age so confidently and effusively, and seems to forecast the ethnic problems that would come to a crisis point in 1969.

However, there were more influential, contemporary and local accounts of the Sultanate, especially the *Sejarah Melayu* (Malay Annals) and the *Hikayat Hang Tuah* (The Story of Hang Tuah). While the former is described as being more historical than the latter, it is important to distinguish them from modern European historiography (Chatterjee, 1993: 77). As with the Indian epics, both were oral texts that were eventually written down. The *Sejarah Melayu* as it now exists in written form dates from the 18th century and is regarded as the most important Classical Malay work (Muhammad Yusoff Hashim, 1992: 15), admired as much for its literary qualities as for its construction of the history of the Malay world. It opens with a genealogy that links the Sultanate back to Palembang and then all the way back to Alexander the Great, who under the name of Iskandar Zulkarnain is identified as a great Muslim king (Andaya and Andaya, 1982: 33). While this may seem to be purely a means of legitimizing the sovereignty of the Melakan Sultans, it also and perhaps more importantly functions as ritualistic reverence for one's superiors, important in a culture that places such a high value on age and seniority. In fact, as the renowned Malaysian literary scholar Muhammad Haji Salleh (1991: 8-9) points out, the beginning of the prologue of the *Sejarah Melayu* gives praise to the qualities of Allah, and echoes 'a literary tradition that includes also the prologue of the *wayang kulit*' where the puppeteer or dalang invokes the genealogy of the spirit world. The *Sejarah Melayu* also 'introduces' the arguments for defining and shaping the relationship between the ruler and the ruled in the form of a story set in Palembang, i.e. earlier than the Sultanate and therefore legitimized through tradition and continuity (Andaya and Andaya, 1982: 33). The story deals with the negotiation of power relationships that remain central to Malay and Malaysian culture: 'Malays do and shall not rebel against their leaders,' which is met by a counterargument: 'Malays shall remain loyal to their rulers so long as their rulers rule over them with justice' (quoted in Kessler, 1992: 147). These pronouncements are also crucial to the political and ethical issues raised in the Hang Tuah story.

The *Sejarah Melayu* mentions the figure of Hang Tuah in passing, but he is the main character in the *Hikayat Hang Tuah*, which is in many respects the most important cultural text in Malay society. It occupies a similar position to *The Iliad* and *The Odyssey* in European culture and the *Mahabharata* and the *Ramayana* in Indian culture. However, unlike the heroes of those texts, Hang Tuah is an ordinary Malay, probably one of the sea people, who originally came to Melaka with Parameswara (Muhammad Yusoff Hashim, 1992: 208).

He became an important official at the Melakan court and epitomized all the qualities of the traditional Malay hero. Like these other epics, the *Hikayat Hang Tuah* was originally an oral narrative that was written down some time after the Portuguese capture of Melaka (Iskandar, 1970: 45). It therefore served as an elegy to a glorious Golden Age that had been cruelly cut short – thus the famous, defiant Malay saying from the *Hikayat Hang Tuah* that 'Malays and their culture shall not disappear from this world' (quoted in Kessler, 1992: 147). Surprisingly, the *Hikayat Hang Tuah* has not been translated into English although a short English-language version of the story was written by M. C. ff Sheppard in 1949 (this became the basis for the 1956 film HANG TUAH, which will be discussed in detail in chapter 4). Typical of a work that originated as an oral text, and thus another similarity with epics like the *Ramayana*, is the minimal concern with narrative causality. For example, the story refers to the antagonistic relationships between Melaka and Majapahit, clearly presenting them as cotemporaneous, when the central Javanese Majapahit Empire had already waned by the time Mansor Shah was the Sultan of Melaka and Hang Tuah one of his court officials (Kassim Ahmad, 1966: 4). Hang Tuah's many successful adventures in Majapahit therefore confirm the superiority of Melaka *even if* Majapahit had been at the zenith of its power at the same time as Melaka.

While the *Hikayat Hang Tuah* is a long and episodic narrative describing Hang Tuah's travels and adventures through many parts of the then known world, the most important story is the conflict between Hang Tuah and Hang Jebat in the context of their relationship to the Sultan. Tuah and Jebat were two of a group of five friends, who had known each other from childhood and who as a group became officials at the Melakan court. They are sometimes likened to the Three Musketeers, but a more significant comparison is with the five Pandava brothers. While the conflict in the *Mahabharata* (and in its localized version, the *Hikayat Pandawa Lima*) is familial and manifested in the war between the (five) Pandavas and the Kauravas, the conflict between Tuah and Jebat refers to the appropriate relations between the ruler and the subject. Tuah represents the first saying from the *Sejarah Melayu* quoted above: 'Malays do and shall not rebel against their rulers,' while Jebat questions such absolute loyalty by invoking the qualification inherent to the second saying: 'Malays shall remain loyal to their rulers so long as their rulers rule over them with justice.'

Because of jealousies and conflicts among officials at the Melakan court, Tuah is accused of treason ('derhaka,' the most serious and fatal of crimes) for alleged adultery with one of the Sultan's 'dayang' (palace women). The Sultan orders his immediate death, but the Bendahara (Chief Minister), aware of his innocence, secretly smuggles Tuah out of Melaka. Tuah undergoes and unquestioningly accepts a period of exile (exile is also a major narrative component of both the *Mahabharata* and the *Ramayana*). Jebat is given Tuah's position (that of admiral or 'Laksamana,' a name based on Rama's half-brother in the *Ramayana*)[6] at the court, but he becomes more and more incensed at the travesty of justice that has taken place. He ousts the Sultan from the palace and installs himself – this is outright rebellion. Eventually, the Bendahara tells the Sultan that Tuah is still alive and that the Sultan will need the abilities of a warrior like Tuah to remove Jebat. So Tuah is brought back to Melaka; he reaffirms his absolute loyalty to the Sultan despite his treatment and unconditionally agrees to kill Jebat for his treasonable behavior. After a protracted battle in the palace and some judicious cheating, Tuah mortally wounds Jebat, who then runs 'amuk'[7] for three days throughout Melaka killing thousands of people before dying himself. The summary of this episode of the story is derived from familiarity with a number of secondary sources (Kassim Ahmad, 1966; Nanney, 1988; Sheppard, 1949; and the 1956 film).

In this central episode of the *Hikayat Hang Tuah*, Tuah and Jebat represent two distinct and contradictory attitudes to the ruler. Tuah is unambiguously identified as having the appropriate relationship – he is the true Malay hero and embodies the highest values of Melakan tradition and culture. Jebat is a traitor and serves as a warning to all who contemplate disloyalty. It is perhaps useful to treat Tuah and Jebat as an interdependent relationship that is under constant tension, as a dichotomy in conflict. The issues raised by this linkage of differences are to reverberate throughout Malaysian culture from the 17th century onwards to the extent that 'to know what Malaysians are thinking, see how they interpret Hang Tuah and Hang Jebat' (Nanney, 1988: 173). The Tuah/Jebat story is a central narrative of nation, with its meanings constantly being reinterpreted and contested. As will be discussed later, in the 20th century, Tuah's star was to fall as Jebat's rose in line with the increasing nationalist aspirations of the Malays.

The Tuah/Jebat story was performed by storytellers (either from the oral tradition or from the written version) and also by the dalang in the Wayang, although it was by no means the predominant fare of the Wayang. Its primary stories were derived from the local versions of the Indian epics. Similarly, it is generally believed that the Wayang 'technology' – screen, leather puppets, light source, commentary and music – arrived in the Archipelago from South India (Sarkar, 1983: 213). The earliest form of Wayang from which all the other styles are said to have developed was the 'Wayang Beber': there was no screen, only a storyteller who unrolled sections of a long scroll while narrating the story to an audience (Reid, 1988: 206 and Brandon, 1993: 141). This form of Wayang recalls some of the pre-cinematic performance modes in Japan before the coming of the sound film (Anderson, 1992: 293), while the Wayang proper is itself a fascinating proto-cinematic technology – the Chinese name for cinema translating as 'electric shadows.'

Figure 5: Wayang exhibit, National Museum, Kuala Lumpur

A number of forms of the Wayang existed in the Archipelago, but the one of major importance in the Malay Peninsula was the Wayang Siam, which derived its material principally from the Rama cycle of stories. While most performed stories included elements of what Sweeney calls the 'Rama tree,' i.e. the story of the King of Lanka, Ravana, here called Wana, and the events surrounding Rama and Sita and known as the *Cherita Mahraja Wana*, most Wayang performances consist of 'twig, flower and leaf stories' that may have little to do with the Rama cycle of stories (Sweeney, 1972: 4, 8). This is indicative of the intense localization of the Rama stories, which, even in its most literal transformation, is a Malay narrative and not an Indian one, as Sweeney points out in the quotation cited near the end of the previous chapter. The localization of the *Ramayana* is also evidenced by the conviction of many dalang that the island Lanka actually refers to Langkawi, an island north of Penang (Singaravelu, 1981: 132). The performance itself recognizes two distinct and separate audiences: the visible audience and the real audience – the inhabitants of the spirit world, who are invoked at the beginning of the performance and hopefully appeased at its conclusion. At the very beginning of the performance, the dalang recites a spatial and temporal genealogy (Becker, 1979: 233, 237), somewhat similar to the beginning of the *Sejarah Melayu* and the *Hikayat Hang Tuah*. The Wayang represents an 'uneasy' amalgam of Malay animism, Hindu-derived narratives and hero figures, and Islamic prayers. This has led to Muslim disquiet over the pre-Islamic aspects of the Wayang, including that of the figure representation of the puppets themselves (Tan, 1989-90: 144-145), even though their stylization may have been influenced by Islamic objection to figural images (this concern was to spill over to a dislike of the image-based aspect of cinema itself). The Wayang has largely lost its cultural impact in Malaysia (except as a nationalist and tourist-driven discourse), especially in comparison with Indonesia, where it remains culturally and politically important (Sears, 1996: 219).[8]

Nevertheless, aspects of the Wayang are significant. While it is pre-Islamic, it remains a frequently invoked Malay cultural tradition. More importantly, its narrative structuring is still relevant. The author of the Wayang, its auteur, is the dalang or Wayang narrator. As well as manipulating the puppets and 'conducting' the percussion orchestra, the dalang tells the stories using narrative digressions, word repetition and rhythmic speech patterns – the title of Sweeney's 1994 book, *Malay Word Music*, thus seems a very apt description of the dalang's performance style, even though Sweeney is writing about a different genre of storytelling. In the context of Malay storytellers, it is appropriate to note that the Bahasa Melayu word is 'penglipur lara,' literally the 'soother of woes,' thus clearly identifying the social and cultural role of the storyteller (Muhammad Haji Salleh, 1991: 43). The dalang is the controller of the narrative and of the arrangement of events – an always-present if invisible narrator (although certain audience members may be able to watch the performance from 'behind' the screen). The dalang's oral, visual and musical control over the performance can be compared to that of the film director and particularly to a director/performer like P. Ramlee, who in the 1950's and 1960's had a similar overarching control over his films.

Perhaps of greater importance is the construction of narrative in the Wayang. Remembering that traditional performances last all night, the organization of narrative material, as in all oral performance, is based on fixed structures that the dalang draws upon using a mnemonic system of event recall. The performed story is based on an invariable sequence of places and events. A. L. Becker's important article on 'text-building' in the Wayang analyzes narrative construction in great detail, and what follows are some of his main conclusions (Becker, 1979). The plot typically starts in the palace or court, moves to the natural environment (forest, mountains, sea) to finally return to the court. It is therefore a journey out and back – mimicking the Wayang's overall invocations and appeasement of the spirits (p. 225). Coincidence and digression are the primary narrative devices. Interestingly, the Javanese and Bahasa Melayu word for coincidence ('kebetulan') means 'truth' (p. 225). Coincidence is also the motivational characteristic of melodrama in general, but coincidence is usually disparaged in western culture, which favors narrative causality as the appropriate and 'realistic' motivation for events and behavior. 'Truth' versus 'realism' – the difference surely is one of perspective and cultural norms rather than esthetic quality. Wayang narratives give great attention to place, but are not constrained by linear temporality (which is itself linked to causality), so that the story can range across times – coincidence is after all the striking conjunction of incidents (p. 226). Such 'coincidence' of different times similarly occurred in the Melaka/Majapahit episodes of the *Hikayat Hang Tuah* referred to earlier.

The pre-colonial Malay world is a complex history of economic, social, political and cultural interactions, strongly influenced by a number of waves of temporary and permanent migration. Its high point was the Melakan Sultanate, which has become the supreme touchstone of Malay and Malaysian identity, not so much as a historical phenomenon, but through the ways in which it has been narrativized in retrospect in both oral and written form. It therefore exhibits many of the characteristics of nation formation identified by Stuart Hall earlier in this chapter.

Colonial Malaysia

The pre-colonial migrations to the Archipelago cannot be called invasions and are therefore totally unlike the European penetrations into the region. The capture of Melaka by the Portuguese in 1511 initiated a 450 year period of colonial control over the Peninsula, with the Dutch in time replacing the Portuguese and the British taking over from the Dutch early in the 19th century. The objective of colonization was initially not very different from the previous interactions in the region: the trading of goods indigenous to the region or brought there by ship from both the east and the west. However, under colonialism, exchange and trade agreements were replaced by full-scale appropriation of lands and peoples. Trading activities were now undertaken between Europeans with local people providing the labor necessary to 'optimize' production output. In certain other respects, there were further similarities between the colonial powers and the earlier migration patterns. Once again religion accompanied the new arrivals, although Christianity in its various forms had almost no impact on the Malays – there was some very limited conversion of the Chinese and Indian laborers that were to arrive in the Peninsula during this period (Ackerman and Lee, 1988: 26-32). Another similarity was that India, although now colonized, was once again involved in the system of interactions in the Peninsula: the Portuguese came to the Archipelago via their territory of Goa in India and the British initially governed the Peninsula from their colonial offices in India. However, India was destined to play a much more direct role in the reshaping of the Malay Peninsula during colonial times.

The need for manpower by the European colonizers in Malaysia led them to import labor from countries such as China and India. The British considered the Malays lazy, whereas the poverty of the Chinese and the Indians made them a compliant labor force. Unlike the earlier migrations to the region, this mass migration was not based on mutual interaction and most were temporary migrants – this is the sojourner pattern of migration (Wang, 1992: 177-178), which also occurred in Australia in the 19th century. A brief study of one of the migration systems employed by the British illustrates the problems that were to result from this style of migration. The favored method of acquiring Indian laborers was the 'kangani' system; the kangani was a headman who recruited groups of people from his own village and caste, thus personalizing the whole process (Jain, 1993: 9). It was more popular and effective than the indentured system, where individuals were recruited by agencies in India (the method used in Fiji). These migrants worked and lived together on plantations and functioned as transplanted communities, retaining the same social ties and cultural traditions. However, there was also a sense of displacement as well as minimal interaction with other local communities – emotions and situations perceptively examined in K. S. Maniam's 1983 English-language play, *The Cord*, with the title conveying the social and cultural bonds that the community attempts to maintain internally and with the homeland, bonds that would also inevitably fray. This is further exacerbated by the phenomenon of 'kaala pani', the 'crossing over black waters,' which was believed to result in the loss of connection to the home society – this phenomenon has been contrasted to the Indian migration and trading activities of earlier centuries: 'Then the Hindus would sail to Sumatra and other islands... [n]ow the thought of a sea voyage strikes terror in the heart of a Hindu' (quoted from a 19th century Indian historian by Chatterjee, 1993: 97). The consequence of mass migration was the development of a series of distinct enclaves that remained inward looking and homogenous in terms of culture and occupation, whether Indians, Chinese or Malay. The migrant communities were also outward looking – to their 'motherland,' but not to the world in which they actually lived. The long-term consequences of this social and cultural separation are still apparent today, but such 'divide and rule' techniques served the British well in many of their colonies. The numbers involved in this mass migration were staggering and transformed the ethnic dynamics in the Peninsula. Between 1900 and 1940, a total of 16 million Chinese and Indians arrived there; typical of the sojourner pattern, most of them later returned to China and India, but a considerable number stayed. This meant that whereas in 1880, Malays represented 90% of the total population of one million, by 1957, Malays had dropped to 49.7% of a total population of 7.5 million (Ibrahim Saad, 1983: 60). Such a major demographic shift would have significant social and political consequences.

The developing nationalist movements in the countries, from which these (now) permanent migrants came meant that, for most of them, nationalism and national culture were concerns that related solely to their 'mother countries' and not to the place they were living in (Wang, 1992: 188). This is the diaspora scenario that confirms for Benedict Anderson that nationalism is still very much alive, where communities have powerful loyalties to a range of political causes in their motherlands, causes which they fund but otherwise have no direct involvement in or responsibility for (Anderson, 1992: 46). Malay nationalist interests were inhibited by the kerajaan political system in which loyalties were localized and enforced. Wang argues that it was precisely the motherland-directed nationalisms of the immigrants that created a common nationalist bond between Malays (Wang, 1992: 188), very conscious of being outnumbered in 'their' homeland, where they, as its 'original' people, were in danger of losing their identity.

This is the context in which the most recent colonial power arrived in the Malay Peninsula. Initially, the Japanese invasion of Malaya in 1941 was perceived as the triumphant defeat of colonialism, a view encouraged by the Japanese through their 'Greater East Asia Co-Prosperity Sphere' agenda (Goto, 1996: 164-166), which promoted Asian solidarity (while being a cover for Japanese imperialism). The Japanese encouraged the Malays with slogans such as 'Asia for Asians' and supported the Indian independence movement of Subbad Chandra Bose with its goal of driving the British out of India, but their attitude to the Chinese was more antagonistic (Wang, 1992: 189), no doubt a consequence of the war the Japanese had waged against the Chinese since the early 1930's. The Japanese 'divide and conquer' policy, echoing that of the British before them, served only to increase the tensions between the Malays and the Chinese.

However, it was the return of the British at the end of World War II that really fueled Malay nationalism. The British proposed the Malayan Union as a means of gaining more direct control over the Peninsula. 'The establishment of the Union would have eventually destroyed the foundations of the privileged position of the Malays... and they realized this quickly enough to react [to the proposal] in an uncharacteristically aggressive manner' (Wang, 1992: 189-190). While this consolidated Malay nationalism, the British Malayan Union proposal convinced the other communities that there were political and nationalist opportunities for them in Malaya itself and not just in their homelands. The situation was complicated by the fact that the Sultans approved of the British proposal (Andaya and Andaya, 1982: 255). In the face of such strong Malay opposition, the proposal was withdrawn and replaced by the Federation of Malaya in 1948, which confirmed the priority of the Malays while providing the other communities with permanent residence. All this strengthened the hand of the Malays, who were fully united in their resolve in contrast to the discord within the migrant communities, a discord based on ethnic, religious and political conflicts in their homelands: the Nationalist/Communist tension and the linguistic, clan and class divisions of the Chinese; the Hindu/Muslim and ethnic/class conflicts of the Indians (Wang, 1992: 191). Singapore was excluded from the Federation because the Malays felt that its large Chinese population would further reduce the Malay proportion of the Federation's population (*The SBS World Guide*, 1994: 505).

The power relationships of pre-independent Malaya can again be presented schematically (Wang, 1992: 230):

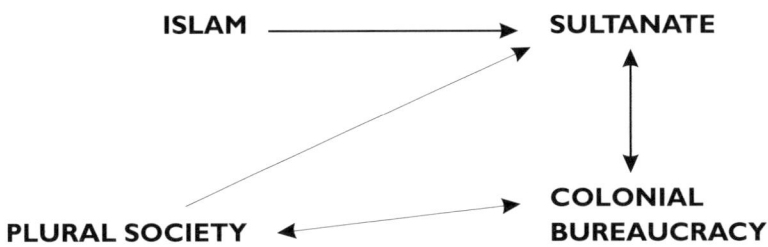

Figure 6: Power structure before Independence (1957)

The most obvious difference from the kerajaan model is the replacement of the Chiefs by the Colonial Bureaucracy, who maintained a strong if more mutually beneficial relationship with the Sultanate than the Chiefs did. The rulers were able to continue as the Islamic authority within their states, in return for which they supported the British – evidenced by their support for the Malayan Union proposal. Islam was more isolated than before and was undergoing a process of 'purification,' influenced by Islamic Modernism in the Arab world in the 19th and early 20th centuries and associated with an emphasis on unmediated and independent interpretation of *The Qur'an* (von der Mehden, 1993: 13). The Plural Society developed from the earlier 'Others' category, but was now massively boosted by the influx of Chinese and Indian workers. The Malayan nationalism that came into being in the late 1940's was predominantly a Malay nationalism. Consequently, in terms of the prioritization of identity criteria 'the Malay is first of all a Malay, then a Muslim and then a Malayan; the Chinese first of all a Chinese, then a Buddhist or a Christian if he is religious and then possibly a Malayan; and the Indian is first of all an Indian, then a Hindu or Muslim and then possibly a Malayan' (Joseph Strayer, quoted in Wang, 1992: 192). To identify oneself as a Malayan is therefore a third-level consideration. This weak nationalism, which in other contexts might well be considered a positive attribute, continued the ethnic separateness and absence of cultural interaction that had existed for over a century.

Parsee Theater and Bangsawan

However, there were countertendencies towards heterogeneity and hybridity, expressed through cultural practices and activities that arose from the interaction between local cultural traditions and various immigrant communities. The most important of these was the Bangsawan, the dominant pre-cinematic cultural form that became very popular in Malaya at the end of the 19th century. Bangsawan was itself modeled on the Indian Parsee (or Parsi) theater. So once again, the principal influence on Bangsawan was Indian, although in this case the British presence in Colonial India was also to be an important element. The Parsees were Zoroastrians of Persian origin, who became India's first commercial bourgeoisie and bought up theaters in Bombay in the middle of the 19th century (Rajadhyaksha and Willemen, 1999: 171). This stimulated the rise of modern Indian theater, which initially took root in the major 'British' commercial cities like Bombay and Calcutta, the cities that together with Madras would also become the dominant film production centers. This Parsee theater differed from the more traditional Indian performance modes in two significant ways (Karnad, 1989: 335):
1. payment for attendance, which radically altered the relationship of the audience members to the event and to the institution, and stands in contrast to the traditional patronage system, seen in its final 'glorious' moments in Satyajit Ray's elegiac 1958 film JALSAGHAR (The Music Room);

2. the introduction of the proscenium arch, which renegotiated the performer (and performance) relationship with the attendee, who in the traditional mode was more of a participant, but would now be more appropriately called a spectator, although the 'participant' element never really disappeared and is still evident in the very enthusiastic involvement of Indian film viewers in the film 'performance.' The proscenium arch was part of a broader westernization of Indian culture, such as Company School Painting (Indian artists attempting to incorporate European naturalism in their work) and Pat Painting (the mass production of folk painting; the word 'chitra-pat' means 'mural' and is the Hindi word for cinema). These elements all coalesced in the figure of Raja Ravi Varma, whose 'academic' paintings of Indian gods were to have lasting influence on their representation in film and television and whose impact on stage and film backdrops was enormous (Rajadhyaksha and Willemen, 1999: 45-46, 80, 174, 230).

The plays performed in the Parsee theater reflected the multiple influences of its creation. They ranged from Arabic-Persian romantic melodrama to stories from the Indian epics, from adaptions of Shakespeare to Victorian melodrama, with new material created from Persian and Urdu sources (Rajadhyaksha and Willemen, 1999: 172). Perhaps the most important Indian contribution to this theatrical form was the inclusion of music and dance into the performance (Karnad, 1989: 336). Music and dance had always been central to Indian cultural life and were to remain so irrespective of the actual medium of performance. So their presence in Indian film was only to be expected. All of the plays adapted to the Parsee theater tradition were in the melodramatic mode: the heightened emotion, stock characters, music and dance combine to form 'music drama' – the literal meaning of melodrama.

Parsee theater troupes traveled throughout India and to the Malay Archipelago, where the first performance was in the 1870's in Penang, by now an urban center with a substantial Indian and Indian-Malay population, which was already familiar with the sorts of Arabic-Persian and Indian stories presented in the Parsee theater and had some understanding of Hindustani. Locally, this theater form was called 'Wayang Parsee'– an attempt to contextualize it to the new environment. However, the popularity of Wayang Parsee eventually waned because of the absence of new material and the local company collapsed. A Penang businessman bought the theatrical materials and thus began the first Bangsawan group (Mohd Anis Md Nor, 1993: 36-37).

Tan Sooi Beng (1993), an ethnomusicologist from the Universiti Sains Malaysia in Penang, has written an important book on Bangsawan. The book examines this popular cultural form in great detail, with a particular emphasis on the musical forms. The following summary of the book's arguments concentrates more on Bangsawan as an urban entertainment phenomenon, dealing with its subject matter, its employment of a variety of cultural material and its narrative structuring, while noting some of the musical aspects. The importance of Bangsawan is its very direct influence on and interrelationship with Malaysian cinema, a link that will be pursued in greater detail in the next chapter.

Bangsawan literally means 'of noble birth' and referred to the fact that the plays dealt almost totally with royalty. These stories came from the same traditions as Parsee theater: the Arabic-Persian romances, the Indian epics, European plays, especially Shakespeare and Victorian melodrama, but now also Malay and Chinese stories (p. 35); in the 1930's the stories were also derived from popular films (p. 48). This multi-ethnic content was matched by the multi-ethnicity of the management and the performers of Bangsawan, and also of its audience (pp. 18, 26). Like Parsee theater, Bangsawan incorporated the proscenium arch and payment for attendance; unlike Parsee theater, the main language was Malay (p. 26). Bangsawan became popular in the 1890's, reaching its peak in the 1920's and 1930's. Its popularity was due to a number of factors (pp. 27-32): the use of the Malay language made it accessible to most people, unlike Parsee theater and imported films (even the Malay accents of Indonesian films proved to be a problem); Bangsawan songs and entire plays were available on record and played on the radio (this commodification of performances was to culminate in film versions of Bangsawan plays after World War II); the introduction of amusement parks in the large cities provided a consolidated and centralized, yet extremely broad range of entertainment, such as Bangsawan, Chinese opera, Parsee theater, European theater, gambling halls and dance parlors and eventually films (these parks were owned by entrepreneurs like Shaw Brothers, who would later dominate film production and exhibition in Malaya); and Bangsawan was an urban substitute for traditional festivities on feast days such as the Muslim Hari Raya Aidil Fitri, the Hindu Deepavali and Chinese New Year – interestingly, Hari Raya remains a sought after release date for new Malay movies (see the newspaper advertisement for IBU MERTUA-KU (My Mother-in-Law, 1962) in chapter 4).

Bangsawan's primary difference from Parsee theater was its links to traditional Malay theater, especially the Wayang. It was similarly an oral form and thus depended on fixed narrative structures and stereotypical characters (p. 103). Bangsawan's aristocratic stories were organized according to the Wayang's plot structure of starting and finishing with a court scene. While there was less digression and greater narrative linearity as a result of European influences, the active, even intrusive participation of the audience did retard the narrative flow (p. 109). Such audience behavior is reminiscent of audience involvement in Indian film presentations. Like Wayang, there were clearly defined heroes and villains; the importance of such traditional role-functions is made very apparent when Bangsawan adapted Shakespearian plays to its performance mode: a 1930's version of *Hamlet* started and ended in the palace (even though Shakespeare's play opens in a graveyard); fitted the characters to the stock roles, so that Hamlet was allowed to remain alive; introduced songs and dances; and inserted new scenes, e.g. a scene where multi-ethnic characters are buying tickets to attend Hamlet's dumb show (pp. 125-129).

As with Parsee theater and Wayang, Bangsawan always incorporated music, songs and dances into its performances, between acts and between short plays. These interludes separating story segments were called 'extra turns' and were often as popular as the advertised plays (p. 35). The subsequent influence of Bangsawan on film included the incorporation of such songs and dances into the films – as in Bangsawan, these songs often remained unrelated to the narrative itself. The songs and dances of Bangsawan came from the same variety of sources as the stories, representing a complex interaction of musical traditions as well as specific citings of a particular tradition (p. 83). Inevitably, Bangsawan changed over the decades by including new stories and new musical and dance idioms. The most interesting of these changes was the increasing emphasis, from the late 1920's onwards, on Malay historical stories, Malay songs and instrumentation. Tan attributes this to the rise of Malay nationalism during this period (p. 51), to which I referred earlier in this chapter. Not only were the stories reworking 'nationalist' narratives like the *Hikayat Hang Tuah* (Kassim Ahmad, 1966: 2), but the Bangsawan plays also started to shed the traditional gods, fairies and evil spirits from their performances (Tan, 1993: 47). This tendency towards realism also reduced the emphasis on songs and dances as the focus shifted to a more western theatrical tradition. As will be discussed in the next section, Tan Sooi Beng argues that the Bangsawan that developed and flourished in Colonial Malaya was drastically and consciously 'Malayized' after the events of 1969, but she does not suggest, as I would, that the first indication of the rejection of Bangsawan's multi-ethnicity occurred in the 1930's under the influence of Malay nationalism, which was, after all, stimulated by Malay perception of increasing non-Malay economic and political power. In the next chapter, I want to suggest that the Malaysian film industry also slowly, if in a slightly later time frame, became more Malay-oriented.

Bangsawan's attempts to respond to Malay nationalist calls for more relevant subject matter and staging were not sufficient for many of the Malay intelligentsia, who found a greater sense of realism in the new theatrical form called 'Sandiwara,' which was more directly influenced by European theater and was fully scripted; Malay historical and contemporary themes dominated the plays and this contributed to the nationalist agenda (Nanney, 1988: 166). This is evidenced in a Sandiwara play first performed during the Japanese occupation, called *Pahlawan Melayu* (A Malay Warrior), which presented the Hang Tuah/Hang Jebat conflict in the traditional manner, with Tuah remaining the hero, whose loyalty to the Sultan was beyond question (Nanney, 1988: 167). The decline of Bangsawan was to be expedited by the development of a local film industry in the 1950's. Bangsawan did not disappear – it was just appropriated by Malaysian cinema; in the 1970's, Bangsawan was to be revived by the government, which was set on reaffirming and creating Malay traditions. What did disappear was its 'musical and cultural syncretism' (Tan, 1993: 193), based on multi-ethnic creative interaction and the response of diverse ethnic communities in the new urban centers in the Peninsula.

My concentration on Bangsawan is to be seen in the context of the multiplicity of its social and cultural connections and, most importantly, because of its major role in the construction of a local film industry. Other cultural forms were equally active and equally affected by the enormous changes occurring in the Peninsula during the colonial period. It is not possible to bring all these into the argument, with the exception of a brief reference to the novel. A. Wahab Ali has detailed the influence of this European literary form on the Malay Hikayat tradition (1991), but I want to comment on a novel that is often regarded as the first fully-fledged, realistic Malay novel. While A. Samad Said wrote *Salina* in 1961, its relevance here is its setting in the early 1950's in a poor kampung on the outskirts of Singapore. The novel concentrates on a group of people in the shantytown scarred by their war experience and attempting to survive in a hostile environment. While the subject matter contributed to its characterization as a realist novel, it was criticized for its lack of psychological plausibility by A. Teeuw in the foreword of the novel (A. Samad Said, 1991: xi) and for its repetitiveness by the author himself (A. Samad Said, 1994: 11). The writing is indeed repetitive as characters constantly rework and reformulate their attitudes and feelings towards each other, but, then again, such an approach is characteristic of an oral culture – it is also apparent in some of the films of the 1950's, e.g. the comedies of P. Ramlee. The most idealized relationship in the novel is between two innocents, Hilmy and Nahidah. Eventually, when briefly alone in the communal bathroom, they tentatively declare their love for each other, but very quickly their personal emotions become transformed into a passionate plea for the recognition and importance of Malay literature (A. Samad Said, 1991: 353-366). The scene may be problematic as psychological realism, but this outpouring of Malay nationalist fervor erases the characters in order to plead for the survival of Malay literature and culture in the face of European colonialism (identified here as English literature). The characters' own survival and happiness is sacrificed for the greater good of Malay society and culture. This attitude to self and society places A. Samad Said within the 'Generation of '50' literary movement that developed in Singapore in the 1950's. Writers like Asraf denounced the overemphasis on individualism (almost invariably identified with the poem *Aku* by the Indonesian writer Chairil Anwar)[9] in favor of community-centered, even 'raja-centered', social and cultural behavior (Matheson, 1985: 10, 46).

Singapore in the 1950's became the pre-eminent Malay cultural center; despite the fact that it was primarily an ethnically Chinese city, it was also the socio-cultural capital of the Malay Peninsula (Lockard, 1991: 21). One of the 'Generation of '50' writers, Keris Mas, described Singapore as a cosmopolitan city, which became a center for broadcasting, publishing and film-making, and thus attracted young Malays from all over the Peninsula (quoted in Matheson, 1985: 3). The attraction of Singapore to young Malay intellectuals and nationalists is poignantly presented in Kassim Ahmad's 1950's short fiction, *A Common Story*, in which the protagonist recalls the excitement of Singapore's political and cultural pluralism (a 'Melaka of the 1950's'), while at the same time expressing great concern about the survival of traditional Malay kampung culture (Kassim Ahmad, 1968).[10] Kassim Ahmad was to play a major role in the reorientation of the Hang Tuah/ Hang Jebat debate in the 1960's – a reorientation that had begun with the rise of Malay nationalism in the 1920's.

The radical changes that occurred in the Peninsula as a result of European colonialism were to have profound effects on Malayan society and culture. The influx of millions of migrant-workers altered the demographics of the region and led to major changes in the new society. One of the unintended consequences of colonialism all over the world and certainly in the Malay Peninsula was the inevitable and often sudden interaction between communities of different social and cultural backgrounds. These connections, voluntary or forced, would affect all of the parties involved, including the local peoples and the colonizers. The colonial period in the Peninsula saw the writing down of the important stories and histories of the pre-colonial period and these began to function as 'narratives of nation.' It is, however, salutary to note that the concept of a Melakan Golden Age was ideologically beneficial to both the colonizer and the Malay court culture, since it reinforced a view of society as static and unchanging (Proudfoot, 1994). On the other hand, the example of Bangsawan highlights the productive consequences of cultural interaction in the construction of a localized hybrid cultural form, which was in turn reshaped by the influence of Malay nationalism with its emphasis on *Malay* historical narratives. Nevertheless, the new urban centers like Singapore acted as social and cultural magnets and laboratories and became the prime sites for the production and distribution of nationalist and popular culture.

Postcolonial Malaysia

While the terms 'pre-colonial' and 'colonial' are relatively unproblematic and often used to describe a historical period, the same cannot be said for the term 'postcolonial.' Certainly, it is possible to state that postcolonial Malaysia refers to the period from Independence in 1957 to the present time. However, postcolonialism also implies the termination of colonialism, its demise. As such, it appears to be camouflaging the continuity or re-emergence of a range of practices that could still be labeled as imperialist or colonialist, whether political, economic, social or cultural. This has led to the application of the term 'neo-colonialism' to this phenomenon, to highlight its 'repetition with difference' relationship to colonialism (Shohat and Stam, 1994: 40). The power structures after independence were initially not that different from those before independence, particularly in a country like Malaya that gained independence without a full-scale revolution (as in Indonesia). Nevertheless, the relationship of a new nation to its colonizer and other national and supranational entities are never simply based on political or ideological 'imperialism.' Malaysia, especially in recent years, has continued to rail against its colonizer (e.g. the 'Buy British Last' campaign) and against what Malaysia identifies as that colonizer's 'local branch,' Australia – a paradoxical situation in a terminological mine field, in which Australia is also frequently categorized as a postcolonial nation. This prelude to an examination of post-independence Malaysia recognizes the conditional nature of the postcolonial label. The following discussion argues that the crucial political, social and cultural concerns of Malaysia are intra-national *and* a consequence of colonialism.

Malaya became an independent nation on August 31, 1957, with Tunku Abdul Rahman as Prime Minister. As part of its Sultanate history, it instituted a unique system of elective constitutional monarchy, that still exists today, where the king ('Yang di-Pertuan Agong,' lit. He who is made Chief among Chiefs) is elected by the nine hereditary Malay rulers of Peninsular Malaya from among their number for a five-year term. In 1957, the Malays represented less than 50% of the new country's population. Singapore became substantially independent in 1958 and this occasioned a reversal of the migration by Malays to Singapore that occurred in the early 1950's. Malaya was concerned about the possible communist control of Singapore and proposed its incorporation into Malaya (Andaya and Andaya, 1982: 271). As Singapore was predominantly ethnically Chinese, this would further reduce the proportion of Malays in the overall population; negotiations eventually brought Sabah and Sarawak (territories on the island of Borneo/Kalimantan) into the union to boost the Malay population and restore the 'ethnic balance.' The new nation was formed in 1963 and called Malaysia. It was immediately in conflict with Indonesia and the Philippines over the breakup of Borneo. Then in 1965, Singapore seceded from Malaysia to become an independent nation, partly as a result of conflict between the Malay-dominated government and the Chinese-dominated Singaporean political party. Andaya and Andaya argue that it was ironic that while the Malaysian government 'had preserved the unity of the Malaysian Federation in the face of diplomatic and military pressures from Indonesia and the Philippines, it succumbed to the threat of violence among its own people' (1982: 276). Much of the above scenario was driven by ethnic community concerns about control and survival, so that the eventual construction of the nation was primarily based on ethnic population numbers. Despite these machinations, the period from 1957 to 1969 was perceived as a period of economic development, social integration and tolerance; even as late as April 1969, the Prime Minister confidently proclaimed 'the fusion of the cultures of all our people into a Malaysian cultural identity' (quoted in Solehah Ishak, 1987: 6).

The power relationships in the new nation had altered appreciably since the end of direct colonization (Wang, 1992: 229):

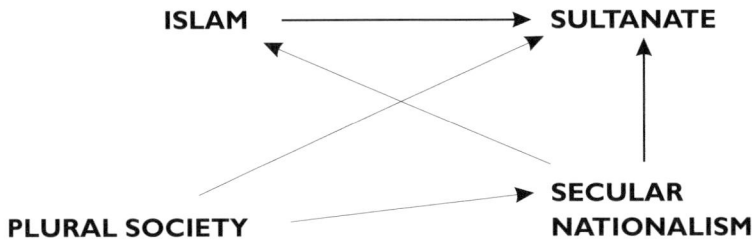

Figure 7: Power structure in the 1960's

Independence introduced a powerful new force: Secular Nationalism, replacing the Colonial Bureaucracy, which had in turn replaced the Chiefs. The Secular Nationalists were predominantly Malay (as previously discussed) and they sought to harness the Sultanate and Islam as contributing elements to the construction of nation. This model begins to identify the increasing gravitation of power to the bottom right-hand corner of the diagram. The Sultanate has retained some formal power within the constitutional-monarchy structure and as autonomous religious leaders in the individual states (Ackerman and Lee, 1988: 43). Islam is more isolated than before and would not resume its power base until the 1970's. The Plural Society is of minimal significance and represents the non-Malays, who had economic power but little political power.

The catastrophic events of May 1969 came as a shock to almost everyone. If Melaka represented the Golden Age, the dream of Malay power and culture for the new nation, then May 13, 1969, was its nightmare. It is the pivotal turning point in Malaysian history – nothing would ever be the same again. In that respect, it brings to mind the 'civil war' in Indonesia in September 1965. In both cases, it is easier to make these sort of generalized doomsday comments than to describe the events themselves, which, perhaps like the Melakan Sultanate narratives, have become contested versions premised on the perspectives adopted by a particular storyteller or dalang.

Perhaps provocatively, I want to start with the version that overtly announces its objectivity: the pre-credit sequence of the 1992 Australian film, TURTLE BEACH, which, to my knowledge has never been screened in Malaysia (although Malaysian objection to the film is not primarily based on the pre-credit sequence). Its putative objectivity is immediately signaled in the opening shot of a Teletype machine gradually typing out the following headline: 'State of Emergency.... Malay racial hatred explodes against Chinese and Indian minorities....' The camera tracks out to reveal a room full of such machines but void of people – the technology providing information seemingly un-manipulated by human agency. There is a dissolve to a Chinese cook chopping the head off a slaughtered pig followed by shots of Malays throwing bombs into cars and shops, leading to a shot of the Chinese cook calculatingly throwing the pig's head into the Malay (Muslim) crowd, which then proceeds to chase him and his fellow Chinese. A European female photographer, later identified as the Australian journalist Judith Wilkes, frantically photographs these events. Finally, the film audience is provided with a viewpoint – the objective, unbiased recording of these terrible events by an outsider. The typed statement at the beginning of the film is now literally visualized by the photographer and by the film itself. The Malays, armed with knives and poles, now corner a Sikh and chop his head off. This action mimics but also differs from, by virtue of its brutality, the earlier butchering by the Chinese cook. The Malays now turn their attention to Judith, but she is saved at the last moment by her male colleague, who drags her into a car now pursued by a large group of threatening Malays. Such a 'rescue mission' involving Europeans saving other Europeans trapped in third-world violence and chaos recurs constantly in films and television programs[11] and here sets the stage for a series of brutalities undertaken by Malays in the film. The film 'objectively' identifies the Malays as the perpetrators of the violence by its employment of a western journalistic discourse.

Karl von Vorys' 1975 book *Democracy without Consensus* provides a detailed study of Malaysia's political system, especially the relationship between the country's ethnic profile and the possibility of a workable political system. The book's perspective is academic and therefore 'disinterested.' It discusses the election of May 10, 1969, and its aftermath and argues that the Chinese and, to a much lesser extent, the Indian communities initiated the conflict, resulting in a Malay backlash in which 'they went *amok*' (von Vorys, 1975: 329), killing a number of Chinese. While this statement is not further developed, it implies that the actions of these Malays were understandable if not acceptable, *because* it represented a Malay cultural response. Similarly, the Malays are typically described in the book as reacting to, rather than initiating, political or physical conflict. Karl von Vorys blames the Opposition Parties for the outcome of the elections and for the armed confrontation that occurred, especially those parties that defined themselves as non-communal (von Vorys, 1975: 264). However, the argument's 'objectivity' is as suspect as that of TURTLE BEACH – in a footnote on page 332, it is suddenly revealed that the author was in Malaysia during the election and had been at the home of the Chief Minister of Selangor, Dato Harun: a leader of the militant communal wing of UMNO, the dominant – and Malay – party in the government before and after the election (Andaya and Andaya, 1982: 294). The Malay perspective, presented through reasoned academic argument, now begins to look like a more committed position.

In what almost appears like a counter-argument to von Vorys (which it is not), Solehah Ishak notes that '[b]lame has been heaped on the Chinese, and on the Malays, depending on which side the writer favours' (Solehah Ishak, 1987: 7). This self-conscious neutrality continues in her unwillingness to apportion blame; instead she details the cost in human life from the riots: 196 deaths and 439 injured (Solehah Ishak, 1987: 8). The employment of statistics is, nevertheless, a retreat into objectivity, even a form of fatalism that constructs the event as a natural disaster.

The final story of the conflict that I want to mention is the traditional, historical approach adopted by Barbara Watson Andaya and Leonard Y. Andaya in their *A History of Malaysia*. First, they lay the groundwork: the political coalition in power before the May 1969 election, the Alliance, had been the government since Independence (and has remained so since 1973 under a new name, the National Front). The Alliance was principally composed of three political organizations each identified as an ethnic party: UMNO (United Malay National Organisation), MCA (Malayan Chinese Association) and MIC (Malayan Indian Congress). Allegiance was primarily ethnic with links between the parties only occurring as a means of providing a certain level of consensus. UMNO, as the Malay party, was the dominant partner in this Alliance (Andaya and Andaya, 1982: 266-268). Having identified this complex coalition, the authors proceed to discuss the 1969 election, identifying the primary issues as language and education, with the Malay language (Bahasa Melayu) replacing English as the official language and the language of instruction in the National Schools (pp. 278-279). Many non-Malays perceived this as a Malay bias and felt that 'their' political parties, MCA and MIC, were not protecting their interests sufficiently. The 1969 election reflected this dissatisfaction with the increased support for parties outside the Alliance, especially parties that labeled themselves as non-communal. The result shocked the Alliance government, even though it retained the majority of seats. The day following the election, the supporters of the non-communal parties celebrated by marching through the streets. The subsequent clash with UMNO supporters set off the violence. The Malay leadership blamed the non-communal parties for the violent Malay response, because those parties had attacked Malay privileges. The authors conclude their examination of the conflict by raising the 'old question...: how was a united and enduring Malaysia to be forged?' (Andaya and Andaya, 1982: 280-281). While the overall argument is still based on ethnic differences and the tremendous difficulty of maintaining those differences in a productive and harmonious relationship, the discussion is centered on politics and political machinations. The perspective is almost Olympian and based on principles of human action that could not be more different from those operating in TURTLE BEACH.

The events of May 1969 are still so sensitive in Malaysian society that it is unlikely that there could be a Malaysian film made about the conflict in the foreseeable future.[12] For a writer and critic like Hamzah Hussin, this is a tragedy in itself. He considers it important for there to be a film set in a community where Malays and Chinese people lived closely together, dealing with their responses to the riots and the impact of the riots on their relationship with each other (Hamzah Hussin, 1994a). Such a quotidian perspective contrasts with the much longer historical view referred to earlier in this chapter, where Muhammad Yusoff Hashim, in writing about the submerged (ethnic) tensions within Melakan society in the 15th century, suggests that the society born in Melaka will continue to have 'differing ambitions' (Muhammad Yusoff Hashim, 1992: 253). Perhaps the link between this Melaka and the 'antiMelaka' of 1969 is a little too tenuous, although the intervening historical homogenization and separatism of the Peninsula's ethnic communities would certainly make it an arguable scenario.

These (hi)stories of the May 1969 crisis highlight not just the different perspectives of the various tellers, but also the conflicting positions of the major protagonists involved in those events. This might contrast with the relative unanimity of Melakan narratives like the *Sejarah Melayu* and the *Hikayat Hang Tuah*, although, as has been mentioned, these stories are also constantly being reinterpreted and contested. Perhaps the problem with the 1969 events is that there is little reinterpretation or analysis going on in Malaysia – the debate is virtually closed. However, there certainly were some quite swift responses by government to the riots. The majority of these were intended to strengthen Malay economic, educational and cultural power. Nevertheless, the government also set up an agency to improve the relationship between the ethnic communities, although in time it was amalgamated with the body concerned with neighborhood security (Akerman and Lee, 1988: 138-139), indicative of the contradictory agendas of cooperation and containment.

Before proceeding with the post-1969 developments, it is useful to bring some population statistics into the argument (Ibrahim Saad, 1983: 59-61). In 1975, the population was just over 10 million, with 53.6% categorized as Malays, 35.2% as Chinese and 10.4% as Indians. These categories are unevenly distributed throughout the country, with the Malays concentrated in the northern and eastern states, while the non-Malays live mainly on the west coast. Furthermore, the urban-rural balances are also skewed, with the Malays primarily rural (82%), the Chinese slightly more urban than rural (50.7%) and the Indians mainly rural (62.3%). Finally, the religious affiliation as determined in the 1980 census were Muslims 53%, Buddhists 17.3%, Confucians and Taoists 11.6%, Christians 8.6%, Hindus 7% and Others 2.5% (*The SBS World Guide*, 1994: 361). The Malays were now once again the dominant ethnic group (by population) in the country, but they overwhelmingly resided in the rural kampung and engaged in farming activities. On the other hand, the Chinese were predominantly urban dwellers and represented the economic power in the country. The religious denomination figures can be superimposed upon the ethnic categories to confirm the strong correlation between religion and ethnicity; the discrepancies result from category definitions ('Malay' includes Christian Kadazans from East Malaysia) and the presence of Indian Muslims and some Chinese Muslims (*The SBS World Guide*, 1994: 361).

The major government initiative after the 1969 riots was the New Economic Policy (NEP), which intended 'to "eradicate poverty" and to end ethnic identification with economic role' (Ong, 1990: 259). This represented a policy of positive discrimination in favor of the Malays, who were now identified as bumiputera ('sons of the soil') – a strong assertion of identity through the construction of autochthonous status, rather than a literal description, since the NEP encouraged Malay urbanization. Once again migration, this time intranational, was to be influential in changing the economic, social and cultural condition of Malaysia. The objective of the NEP was to increase bumiputera equity capital control from 2.4% in 1970 to 30% in 1990 (Ong, 1990: 259); the actual figure in 1990 of 23.5% (*New Straits Times*, 1994b) is still remarkable and the NEP has made a crucial contribution to Malaysia's economic growth (NEP's role in improving ethnic relationships is more debatable).

Other policy initiatives included a new state ideology, the 'Rukunegara' ('pillars of the nation'), which is based on five principles: belief in God, loyalty to King and Country, the supremacy of the Constitution, the rule of law, and mutual respect and good social behavior; the change in name of the language from Bahasa Melayu to Bahasa Malaysia to remove connotations of ethnic exclusivity and ownership – since 1988 there have been calls for a return to the original name, which did take place in the late 1990's; and a National Cultural Policy (NCP), of which there is more below.

In the 1970's, Islamic revivalism took hold in Malaysia. It was part of a worldwide Islamic renewal (Ackerman and Lee, 1988: 57), but its role in Malaysian society was also quite specific, being influenced by the post-1969 economic and social directions. The rapid industrialization and the resultant urbanization of many Malays fragmented their traditional kampung-based identities in the face of modernization, westernization and materialism, making the 'dakwah' ('call to religion') movement attractive as a means of consolidating a sense of common identity (Solehah Ishak, 1987: 20-22). The dakwah movement was particularly popular with the newly urbanized Malay youth, both those in educational institutions and those working in the factories in the Free Trade Zones. For many 'Islam was a "more comprehensive value system" than Malay custom... some insisted on being re-identified, saying, "I am Muslim rather than Malay"' (Ong, 1990: 271). Although, as Judith Nagata points out, the distinction is not necessarily a major departure, as Islam and Malayness had become synonymous (Nagata, 1980: 416). This doesn't mean that the emphasis on Islam is not significant. It led to the establishment of a number of organizations, the largest and most important of which was the Islamic Youth Movement of Malaysia (ABIM), led by Anwar Ibrahim, who warned that Islam opposed 'development which propagates inequality and which is void of moral and spiritual values' (quoted in Ong, 1990: 267). The statement's anti-development rhetoric counters the objectives of the NEP and represents the never-ending struggle in Malaysia between Islam and secularism. 'The task at hand for the Malay elite is to strike an acceptable balance between secularism and Islamic traditionalism without upsetting the economic applecart' (Lee, 1990: 75-76). The influence of organizations like ABIM was evidenced by blatant attempts to attract Anwar Ibrahim into politics, first by the Islamic Party (unsuccessfully) and then by UMNO, which quickly recruited him into the ministry and promoted him to Deputy Prime Minister (Solehah Ishak, 1987: 25).[13]

Wang Gungwu's power structure diagrams have demonstrated the tensions that have always existed between the various elites and have traced their changing relationships. The 1980's diagram highlights the post-1969 political and economic changes (Wang, 1992: 231):

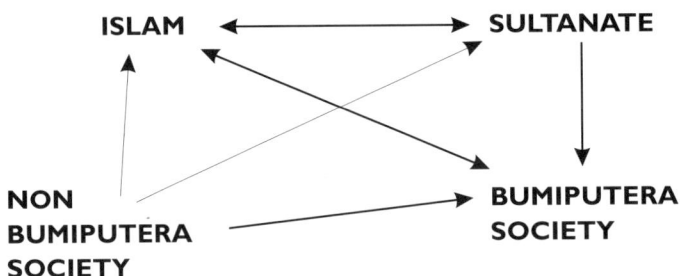

Figure 8: Power structure in the 1980's

As noted in the previous diagram, the power base in the society continues to shift to the bottom right-hand corner, now renamed the Bumiputera Society, which remains a separate entity from the non-Malays, the Non-Bumiputera Society, a distinction now legislated under the NEP. The power base of Islam has strengthened appreciably throughout the 1970's and is in constant debate and struggle with the nationalists (largely identified with the Bumiputera Society) about the proper governance of the country (Milner, 1993: 115). The Sultanate has suffered grievously in the 1980's (and 1990's), with their powers of veto and their excessive lifestyles much reduced by the 'presidential' Prime Minister, Dr. Mahathir Mohamad. The relationship between Islam and Malayness has been described as dialectical (Hussin Mutalib, 1990: 31). They represent almost contradictory world-views, best expressed as Islam's inclusiveness and universality versus Malayness' exclusiveness and communal identity. On the other hand, the two are inseparable: to be a Malay means to be a Muslim and for non-Malays to convert to Islam is to 'masuk Melayu' (i.e. 'to become a member of the Malays,' although that will not necessarily bring bumiputera status). Non-Malays, who are non-Muslims, perceive Islam as a Malay religion, another aspect of the aggregate that constitutes Malay identity (Hussin Mutalib, 1990: 163). Politically, the two are also closely linked, but in a more pragmatic manner. Islam is frequently used by the government to fight Islam and to legitimize Malay secularism and economic development – Dr. Mahathir Mohamad never tires of reminding Malaysians that 'Malaysia aspired to be a model Islamic nation and wanted to prove to the world that a nation governed by an Islamic administrator could also achieve progress' (Saiful Azhar Abdullah, 1994).

The dakwah movement also drew attention to the non-Islamic aspects of Malay custom (adat), such as the Hindu-influenced marriage ceremonies, the animistic folk cures used by the bomoh, the practice of 'silat' (Malay martial arts) and the Indian-Hindu elements in the Wayang (Nagata, 1980: 415). At the social level, the movement has sought to increase male control over public and domestic domains, thus countering the bi-laterality inherent in adat. 'ABIM members insisted that women's first duties were to their husbands and that wives should obey their husbands just as all Muslims should obey Allah' (Ong, 1990: 271). Publicly, women were encouraged and even intimidated into wearing a head-cloth and avoiding western clothing – Ong suggests that these measures strived to institute sexual and ethnic segregation, once again reinforcing the indissoluble link between Islamic and Malay identity (Ong, 1990: 270). The influence of these proposed gender 'realignments' on government was evidenced in the partial co-opting of its ideology. In 1984, it was announced that the population should increase from the present 14 million to 70 million in 100 years time to meet the labor demands of the fast growing economy. Implicit in this proposal is the presumption, strongly asserted by the dakwah movement, that women's primary role is that of being mothers; the population policy might also mean to drastically increase the Malay proportion of the population (Ong, 1990: 272). Despite these pressures on gender identity, Karim argues that Malay women still retain a considerable amount of autonomy, due to the continuing strong influence of adat, which acts 'as an "equalizer" actively attempt[ing] to formulate women's position vis-a-vis men in non-hierarchical ways despite Islamization and other allied processes' (Karim, 1992: 219).

The National Cultural Policy and its Consequences

The National Cultural Policy (NCP) was formulated at a congress held at the University of Malaya in August 1971, and the announced policy consisted of three main principles (quoted in Mohd. Taib Osman, 1984: 282):
(a) the national culture of Malaysia must be based on the cultures of the people indigenous to the region;
(b) elements from other cultures, which are suitable and reasonable may be incorporated into the national culture; and
(c) Islam will be an important element in the national culture.

Some have argued that this policy is part of the 'politics of ambiguity' typically employed in Malaysia as a form of conflict regulation (Ibrahim Saad, 1983: 66). However, it has primarily been interpreted as representing a core culture based on Malay culture and Islam, while accepting aspects of Chinese and Indian culture as long as they do not contradict the Malay culture. The role of the various aboriginal groups in this arrangement is not clear (Chopyak, 1987: 433; Solehah Ishak, 1987: 14). The NCP may well be more contentious than even the language policy and the NEP. The Prime Minister in 1978 introduced the slogan, 'Culture is the cornerstone of unity' (quoted in Ibrahim Saad, 1983: 63), but others insist that while '[non-Malays] are willing to become Malaysians politically; culturally however, they are determined to remain Chinese and Indians' (quoted in Solehah Ishak, 1987: 14). Government officials made it very clear how they interpreted the NCP. The Minister of Culture, Youth and Sports said in 1979, 'The characteristics of a national culture have emerged... At state functions, there are no dances except Malay dances' (Tan, 1989-90: 163-164).

The government actively intervened in the promotion of cultural activities considered to represent the three principles of the policy: universities encouraged research in Malay folk arts; festivals were organized to promote traditional Malay performing arts; and certain Malay popular arts were selected to exemplify traditional Malay culture – these included Zapin and Bangsawan (Tan, 1989-90: 139-142). Zapin was a dance form introduced by Arab settlers in the Peninsula before the 14th century, but it became a contemporary dance in Bangsawan and in Malaysian films, and it was this more popular form of the dance that was appropriated by the NCP. It was an ideal cultural form for the purposes of the NCP, as it met all of its criteria: 'a dance tradition indigenous to the peoples of the Malay Archipelago... created from the syncretic processes of Malay-Arab culture... [and it] manifests the arabesque form of Islamic visual art' (Mohd Anis Md Nor, 1993: 88-89). The situation with Bangsawan was rather different. Its discussion in a previous section of this chapter focused on its hybridity and multi-ethnicity, so that its 'elevation' to a Malay traditional art required some radical surgery, including the 'invention of tradition', the Hobsbawm phrase that Stuart Hall identified as central to the construction of national cultures.

Bangsawan had lost much of its popular support by the 1950's partly because of Malaysian cinema, but it became virtually extinct in the 1970's due to the increasing popularity of television (Tan, 1993: 176). It is rather ironic that its appropriation by the NCP was also to be its rescue from certain oblivion. A 1977 workshop to discuss the future and survival of Bangsawan concluded that it 'deserved to be revived and popularized because it "manifested the culture of the Malays and a type of Malay theatre"' (Tan, 1993: 178). This was actually more of a goal than an accurate description of the Bangsawan that had been popular in the early 20th century. Bangsawan was in fact reshaped to resemble the more traditional Malay theater forms like Wayang, although Wayang itself became problematic for the NCP because of its pre-Islamic characteristics. The new Bangsawan was well and truly 'Malayized' (and not 'Malaysianized'): the stories were now only Malay stories, the costumes, backdrops and props were Malay and featured Malay symbols like the Sultan's yellow umbrella, the throne and the kris (a traditional dagger). Furthermore, the musical instruments and the music were 'Malayized' and those Malay songs used in the pre-1930's Bangsawan were given a more overt Malay character (Tan, 1993: 179-183). Bangsawan's history was therefore reconstructed or invented to suggest a homogeneity that had not been there; it is a form of neo-traditionalism or, as Tan says, it is 'artificially traditional' (Tan, 1993: 187). This is one reason for its lack of popularity. Non-Malays as well as younger Malays were not and are not attracted to this ideologically manufactured entertainment form. There was similar disinterest by non-Malays and middle-class Malays in the other revived indigenous cultural forms; those who attended were, not surprisingly, the recently urbanized Malay workers (Mohd. Taib Osman, 1984: 284).

In contrast to these NCP changes to Bangsawan, the Tuah/Jebat debate developed through less orchestrated political, social and cultural forces. Whereas traditionally Hang Tuah had epitomized all the qualities of the Malay hero, there was now a move to elevate Hang Jebat as a figure to be emulated. It is generally recognized that the change in Jebat's status occurred in the earlier decades of the 20th century as a response to colonialism. This involved an equation of feudalism and colonialism, so that Jebat's rebellion against the Sultan could be transferred to the Malay rebellion against the British presence; Jebat was therefore redefined as a nationalist and a worthy leader (Muhammad Haji Salleh, 1991: 162). The person considered most responsible for re-evaluating the Jebat character was Kassim Ahmad, who compiled and annotated an edition of the *Hikayat Hang Tuah* in 1966 and a separate publication, *Characterisation in Hikayat Hang Tuah*, in the same year. Kassim Ahmad's socialist views (he was a politician at the time) constructs a Jebat who 'is a rebel of the nationalist turn of mind... a prophet and hero of Malay nationalism' (Kassim Ahmad, 1966: 33). Kassim Ahmad notes that the 1956 film HANG TUAH introduced the 'first note of scepticism as to Hang Tuah's rightful title to honour as a hero' (Kassim Ahmad, 1966: 3). These attitudes were also entering Sandiwara plays. Ali Aziz wrote a play in 1959 called *Hang Jebat Menderhaka* (Hang Jebat Commits Treason), which concentrated on Jebat rather than Tuah and portrayed Jebat quite sympathetically, although not a hero; Tuah's character is also somewhat different – he refuses to kill Jebat, allowing him to die in Tuah's home from the earlier inflicted wounds (Nanney, 1988: 167-168); this play became the basis for the 1961 film HANG JEBAT. Usman Awang's play *Matinya Seorang Pahlawan* (The Death of a Warrior) presents Jebat as an un-ambivalent hero figure who despises the blind loyalty of Tuah and the injustice perpetrated by the Sultan (Nanney, 1988: 168-169). In the 1970's plays like Johan Jaaffar's *Kotaku Oh Kotaku* (My City Oh My City), Jebat becomes a warrior for the urban poor: 'I fight for those who are weak. I oppose oppression. I oppose exploitation... ' (quoted in Solehah Ishak, 1992: 89).

These are not the only re-interpretations of the Tuah/Jebat story. In a book on the problems of leadership in Malaysian society, Shaharuddin b. Maaruf identifies Tuah and Jebat as ruthless warriors, who were as bad as each other. For him, neither can serve as a model for modern Malay society (Shaharuddin b. Maaruf, 1984: 20-38). Kamaruddin M. Said also rejects both Tuah and Jebat, only to confer the status of hero on the Bendahara (Prime Minister); he is today's hero because of his 'maturity in thinking and diplomacy' (Kamaruddin M. Said, 1992: 179) – my immediate reaction was to construe this interpretation in terms of the current occupant of that particular position. The political use of the Tuah/Jebat issue is ongoing and was employed in the debate in the early 1990's about the excessive power and 'conspicuous consumption' of the Sultans. Clive Kessler has also referenced the Tuah/Jebat relationship in his discussion of the centrality of 'followership' and the associated obligations involved in Malay political culture. In doing so, he makes a playful link between the words 'merdeka' (freedom, independence) and 'menderhaka' (to rebel, to commit treason) – perhaps Jebat's present popularity results from the conjunction of the two concepts (Kessler, 1992: 147-149). Salleh Ben Joned would disagree with such an argument, since he believes that the idea of treason is still 'unthinkable to the Malay mind' and that it was perhaps Jebat's treason that drove him to run amuk (Salleh Ben Joned, 1994a: 128). He also rejects Kassim Ahmad's analysis of Jebat and replaces it with his own perspective: Jebat was an anarchist, a hedonist and a sensualist; Salleh Ben Joned usefully emphasizes an aspect of the *Hikayat Hang Tuah* that is little referred to: its sensuality and eroticism. This is illustrated by a scene where Jebat reads and sings to the Sultan, who is so enchanted by Jebat's voice that he lays his head in Jebat's lap; similarly, the court women and concubines are entranced by Jebat: 'In the light of the blood bath about to come [Jebat's running amuk], there is an undercurrent of the sinister in the uncanny sensuality of this scene' (Salleh Ben Joned, 1994a: 153-154). That such an interpretation is problematic in an NCP environment is demonstrated by the government's refusal to include Ramli Ibrahim's dance-drama of the Tuah/Jebat story in an ASEAN television cultural exchange program, because 'some parts were "erotic" and that it did not reflect Malaysian culture' (Tan, 1989-90: 141). Ramli Ibrahim has also attempted to revive the traditional, bawdy Malay comic theater, Makyong, in his play *In the Name of Love*; Makyong is banned in its native state of Kelantan, because the fundamentalist Islamic government objects to women playing men's roles (Vatikiotis, 1994: 41).

The 1971 National Culture Congress categorized the literatures produced in Malaysia according to NCP principles: literature written in the Malay language in Malaysia was defined as the National Literature of Malaysia; literature written in other bumiputera languages was called Regional Literature;

and literature written in Mandarin, Tamil and English was labeled Sectional Literature. The Regional and Sectional Literatures were regarded as Malaysian literature, but their targeting of particular groups denied them the name of National Literature (quoted in Solehah Ishak, 1987: 16-17). In the theater, this led to the development of a Malaysian theater using the Malay language, replacing the English-language European theater that had held sway until this time (Solehah Ishak, 1987: 44-45). This was an important cultural change, but, as is apparent from the literature categorizations above, it meant that English and other language plays by Malaysians were not encouraged. Tan argues that the independence of such playwrights from the state (and this was to include Malay writers as well) was actually to their benefit and led to greater innovation, esthetically and also multiculturally, e.g. *The Cord* by K. S. Maniam, *1984 Here and Now* by Kee Thuan Chye and Ramli Ibrahim's *Kalau Kau Mau* (Tan, 1992: 293). In contrast, the post-1969 Malay playwrights are 'prisoners of development... captives of State Structures' (Solehah Ishak, 1987: 162); 'the State, as creator and destroyer of the arts, is finally the real *dalang* which controls... [the] playwrights' (Solehah Ishak, 1987: ix).

The national literature written in Bahasa Melayu, as defined by the NCP, was also influenced by the dakwah movement of the 1970's and led to the development of an identifiable Islamic literature ('Sastera Islam'), which was supported and encouraged by the government through literary competitions (Ungku Maimunah Mohd. Tahir, 1989: 289). The important Malay writer, Shannon Ahmad joined the dakwah movement in the early 1970's and described Islamic literature as 'literature produced in the name of Allah and for the good of all mankind' (quoted in Ungku Mainunah Mohd. Tahir, 1989: 290). Shannon Ahmad's definition of Islamic literature is emphatically Islamic, but is also inclusive in its relevance to all peoples, even though that may imply a proselytizing function. Yet the role of Islam *in* his novels appears not to have changed radically from his pre-dakwah novels (Aveling, 1996: 220-223; Banks, 1987: 129-131). His best known novel, *Ranjau Sepanjang Jalan* (*No Harvest but a Thorn* in the English translation) was written in 1966 and tells the story of a large farming family trapped in poverty and misfortune, yet having an unshaken belief in God. The more general point is that Shannon Ahmad's Islamic literature is holistic rather than sectional, unlike the views of certain other Malay writers and critics. Salleh Ben Joned despairs of the views of people like Mohd Affandi Hassan that Islam radically and totally transformed the Malay world-view and eradicated all pre-Islamic concepts and values. The present threat to Malay literature is deemed to be the corrupting transformation of this world-view by westernization. Western literary influence is considered to be 'totally secularistic,' i.e. hostile to things spiritual and metaphysical, and the West is philosophically and morally materialistic. Mohd Affandi Hassan thus defines the word secular to mean 'un-Islamic' and so 'un-Malay.' Furthermore, he suggests that non-Malays engaged in Bahasa Melayu writing, have motives that are 'highly dubious and the consequence of their involvement, together with that of the '"total secularisation" of literature, is a "new barbarism"' (Salleh Ben Joned, 1994a: 75-76).

The conflation of anti-Islam and anti-Malay is not new, but here they begin to acquire a sense of paranoia and isolationism. The blame is firmly placed on the non-bumiputeras for not accepting all aspects of the NCP, especially their lack of commitment to Bahasa Melayu. This is not primarily an attack on the languages of the Indian and the Chinese communities, but on the language of the former colonizer: English. Paradoxically, others argue that English might be the most appropriate language for the country, 'a better medium of integration... not identified with any particular ethnic group' (Salleh Ben Joned, 1994a: 58). While this has a certain validity (and has been accepted in a number of other postcolonial countries), it is very unlikely to occur in Malaysia, where the tools of national identity construction are so firmly in the hands of the Malays. Salleh Ben Joned, one of Malaysia's most interesting and provocative writers, worries about the presence of the root-word 'bangsa' ('race') in the Bahasa Melayu word for national, nationalism and nationality, 'kebangsaan', and hopes that, in contrast to the principles of the NCP, Malaysian society can adopt the term 'kebudayaan rojak', meaning a salad culture (similar to its use in Australian multiculturalism discourse), a term despised by the bumiputera elite (Salleh Ben Joned, 1994a: 50, 57).

Malaysian cinema was not directly affected by the NCP. To begin with, it was at a very low point in the early 1970's, both economically and esthetically. Secondly, it was already generally in line with the NCP principles, with its concentration on the Malay experience, presented through localized cultural practices that were shaped by the cultural and filmic traditions of its immigrant peoples. The presence of Islam in the films before the 1970's was quotidian and relatively underemphasized, unless it was a major narrative issue (as in SEMERAH PADI, 1956). As a generalization, the films of the 1980's and 1990's tend to highlight Islam somewhat more overtly, but without the strong conviction of dakwah literature.

There has been little direct interaction between Malaysian literature and cinema. Most of the obvious links have already been mentioned in the course of this chapter: Sheppard's book on Hang Tuah and the 1956 film; the 1959 Hang Jebat play and the 1961 film; Shannon Ahmad's *Ranjau Sepanjang Jalan* and the 1983 film of the same name.[14] To my knowledge, there is only one film director who works in both cinema and theater: Rahim Razali, who directed and starred in an English-language version of Usman Awang's play, *Matinya Seorang Pahlawan* (The Death of a Warrior) (Mazlan Nordin, 1993). More recently, he wrote and directed a play called *Hulu Melaka* (lit. up-country Melaka), which concentrated on Hang Tuah's exile from the Sultanate (Fatimah Abu Bakar, 1995: 3). Rahim Razali's interest in the Tuah/Jebat relationship is very apparent in his films, e.g. MATINYA SEORANG PATRIOT (Death of a Patriot, 1984), discussed in chapter 4.

Conclusion

In the 1980's, Malaysia's Prime Minister, Dr. Mahathir Mohamad proposed a bold set of objectives for the country called *Vision 2020*, which strives for full industrialization by the year 2020. It is further accompanied by the desire to create by that time 'a united Malaysian nation which is ethnically integrated and harmonious [and] a liberal and tolerant society in which Malaysians respect each other's creeds and customs' (Salleh Ben Joned, 1994a: 55, 56). During my stays in Malaysia in the early 1990's, there were frequent television campaigns reminding Malaysians of these targets. The advertisements and the general discourse about *Vision 2020* invoked, sometimes overtly, the Melakan Sultanate, projecting 2020 as the commencement of a second Golden Age. This is the recurrent rhetoric of nationalism, where to go forward necessarily requires one to go back, to employ the past to construct the future. The reference to Melaka seems only partially relevant to the actual process of achieving the *Vision 2020* goals. First, the emphasis at present is almost totally on industrialization and development, whereas cultural issues and the humanities are undervalued and underfunded.[15] This contrasts with the economic and cultural power of Melaka. Second, Melaka's existence as a *Malay* reference point presents its own problems. On major (ethnic/religious) feast days in Malaysia, there is always strong government encouragement given to the idea of 'open house.' At Hari Raya Aidil Fitri (the end of the fasting month of Ramadan), the Prime Minister and other Malay/Muslim dignitaries invite people, particularly from the Indian and Chinese communities, to visit their homes;[16] the same applies to the Hindu feast of Deepavali, to Chinese New Year and to the Christian feast of Christmas. The newspapers and the television news programs cover these events at some length. It is an admirable show of inter-ethnic and inter-cultural communication, but it is precisely a show. Malaysian society is still fundamentally driven by intra-ethnic relationships and not the 'lines of connectedness' presented on these feast days. The most obvious example of this emphasis on the 'vertical' is the membership of political parties – direct membership to the National Front is discouraged and affiliation occurs through the ethnically defined political parties, UMNO, MCA and MIC. The

National Front (called the Alliance until 1971) has governed Malaysia since independence, but its days appear to be numbered. There is increasing disunity within UMNO and this was greatly exacerbated by the dismissal of Deputy Prime Minister, Anwar Ibrahim, in 1998 and his incarceration in 1999. Clive Kessler has suggested that the Mahathir era is fast coming to an end and that Malay political unity may well be fraying (Kessler, 2001: 22). Furthermore, bumiputera privileges and quotas (instituted under the NEP) are under attack, especially the availability of university places for non-Malays; there are also Malay criticisms of non-Malay lack of involvement in the civil service, the army and the police, with some references to the non-bumiputeras as 'bangsa asing' ('foreign race') (Shamsul Akmar, 2001: 4; A. Kadir Jasin, 2001: 11). The hierarchical identification of self in terms of ethnicity and religion ahead of 'Malaysianness' has clearly not changed greatly since the 1940's. The 'lines of connectedness' are constructed within communities, both spatially (urban Malays to their home kampung,[17] Indians and Chinese to their home countries) and temporally (Malays to Melaka, the Chinese and Indians to their own cultural traditions).

There is no more graphic an example of this isolationism than the statistics that correlate cinema attendance by ethnic group with the national or language origin of the film being viewed (Grenfell, 1979: 167):

		Ethnic Group		
		Malay	Chinese	Indian/Other
Language	Bahasa Melayu	23%	0	1%
or	Chinese	7%	81%	0
Origin of	Indian	34%	1%	83%
Film	English	35%	18%	16%

Figure 9: Language distribution of cinema attendance by ethnic group[18]

The Chinese overwhelmingly watch Hong Kong, Taiwanese and Mainland Chinese films; if not, they watch English-language films, but almost never films made in Bahasa Melayu. The same scenario occurs with Indian audiences. The situation with Malay audiences is more complex. Their first preference is for English-language films, followed by Indian films and only then films in Bahasa Melayu. The separation along ethnic lines is starkly drawn, with only English-language films cutting across all the communities. Another perspective on the figures is that 90% of the audience at Bahasa Melayu films is Malay. These statistics suggest that Bahasa Melayu cinema is a weak cultural force, despite the Malays being the most powerful political force in the country. Bahasa Melayu cinema therefore occupies only a marginal position in Malaysian film culture – a paradox that will be discussed in the following chapters.

This brief and necessarily selective examination of Malaysian society and culture is, of course, another version of the 'narrative of a nation', if one that attempts to highlight its constructedness. Unlike the narrative structures of the traditional oral and written stories, this version has employed a rather strong linear narrative and cause/effect motivation (an approach typical of western historiography), although it has attempted to identify and emphasize particular events and suggest synchronic connections. These voluntary and forced 'lines of connectedness' (migration, trade, cultural interaction, colonialism) are central to the formation of the multiple and complex cultural identities of the peoples of Malaysia, yet they tend to be severed, erased or lost in the construction of a national culture, based on origins and tradition, on nostalgia and continuity. The hybrid culture of the Malay Archipelago was characterized as a Melakan Golden Age, which became the political and cultural touchstone for the Malays, especially after European colonial powers gained control of the Peninsula. The tendencies towards both homogeneity and heterogeneity, towards the center *and* the margin, shaped community identities under colonialism. With the political formation of nation – Malaya, then Malaysia – a particular version of nation was constructed, one that eventually became untenable, as demonstrated by the tragic events of May 1969. This led the government, as the 'guardian' of national identity, to legislate a new Malaysian identity, one enshrined in the NCP, which suppressed difference by re-affirming and even inventing origins and traditions that ensured a particular interpretation of Malaysianness. However, cultural activity is ultimately more complex and serendipitous than formal principles and policies. The Malaysian film culture, discussed in the next chapter, exemplifies the never ending oscillation between uniformity and hybridity in the construction of a local culture, which, paradoxically, persists only because of the enduring presence of the 'non-local' and the heterogeneous, factors themselves shaped by broader local and global historical and social forces.

3 Film in Malaysia

> 'The Malaysian film industry was founded on
> Chinese money, Indian imagination and Malay labour'
> (Hamzah Hussin, 1994a).

> 'The Pandava Brothers meet the Shaw Brothers in the Land below the Wind.'[1]

Introduction

Malaysia does not figure very prominently in the rankings of world cinema; in fact it is hardly mentioned in the general discussion of film in academic books and journals or in more popular film books and magazines. I am aware of only two substantial entries on Malaysia in Euro-American film publications, which, whether we like it or not, still constitute the dominant discourse on cinema in the world. There is a chapter on Malaysia (and Singapore) in John A. Lent's interview-based book on Asian film industries (Lent, 1990: 185-200) and regular entries (since at least 1972) by the Malaysian film critic Baharudin Latif in the annual *International Film Guide*. Roy Armes' 1987 book *Third World Film Making and the West*, which, despite its title, is a broad survey of filmmaking in Asia, the Middle East, Africa and Latin America, devotes two short paragraphs to Malaysia, including the statement: 'With production directed at the needs of the domestic market, no directors of international standing have emerged...' (Armes, 1987: 150) – a contention both tautological and highly questionable (even taking the words 'domestic market' very literally, counter-examples to such an argument include Ritwik Ghatak, Lino Brocka, Youssef Chahine, Mizoguchi Kenji and Ozu Yasujiro). The Geoffrey Nowell-Smith edited *The Oxford History of World Cinema*[2] does not mention Malaysia, nor the rest of Southeast Asia, except for Indonesia, while Katz' *The Macmillan International Film Encyclopedia* disregards even that country; both of these 'world surveys' do cover India, China, Hong Kong, Taiwan, Japan, Australia and New Zealand (Nowell-Smith, 1996; Katz, 1994). A book written in English about Malaysian media devotes one chapter to its cinema (Grenfell, 1979). It was published in 1979 and is concerned with mass-media audience research, an approach not of direct relevance to this book. As might be expected, there is more recognition of Malaysia in Asian film publications, but even here it is one of the least acknowledged and least regarded of Asian cinemas.

The situation is not much more encouraging if the distribution and exhibition of Malaysian films outside of the country is examined. Malaysian films have had only limited access to the Indonesian market over the years, while receiving some exposure at Asia-Pacific Film Festivals and other Asian film festivals. The 39th Asia-Pacific Film Festival held in Australia in 1994 included two Malaysian films, ABANG 92 (Brother 92, 1993) and WIFE, WOMAN & WHORE (PEREMPUAN, ISTERI &..., 1993) (Pattison, 1994). To my knowledge, no Malaysian film has ever been commercially screened in Australia and SBS (Special Broadcasting Service, Australia's multicultural television channel) has shown just two films, A HANDFUL OF RICE (RANJAU SEPANJANG JALAN) and DEATH OF A PATRIOT (MATINYA SEORANG PATRIOT), both more than ten years ago. A few years ago, SBS screened a Malaysian film made for television, THE ARSONIST (KAKI BAKAR, 1995), a program still banned in Malaysia. Incidentally, KAKI BAKAR was selected for the Directors' Fortnight at the 1995 Cannes Film Festival; the first time a film from Malaysia had been invited to such a prestigious event (Vasudev, 1995: 76).[3]

This chapter provides an overview of this unknown (outside Malaysia) and unsung film industry, which has produced just under 600 feature films between 1933 and 1993 (Jamil Sulong, Hamzah Hussein and Abdul Malik Mokhtar, 1993), by no means an insignificant number. In a roughly equivalent period (1930-1989), Australia produced 700 feature films (quoted in Jacka, 1993: 74). The following discussion of the film industry in Malaysia is incorporated into a historical analysis of film culture in Malaysia, which concentrates on the films made in Malaysia *and* the films and film cultures from countries such as India, China, Indonesia and others, to the extent that they contributed to the overall film culture of Malaysia and, inevitably, to Malaysian cinema itself. Malaysian cinema is therefore characterized as a cinema that exists in interrelationship with other cinemas and cultures, as all national cinemas do. The term 'national cinema' is used with some reluctance because of its tendency to imply a certain uniqueness and distinctiveness, where difference is posited in contrast to other national cinemas, rather than within and between all cinemas. Nevertheless, the book's focus on a specific film culture like Malaysia makes a discussion of national cinema essential.

National Cinema

The previous chapter argued that national identity and national cultures were discursive constructs, which create a set of cohesive and coherent attributes of a nation. National cinema is a particular version of this selfsame phenomenon.

Discussions of national cinema are typically agenda-driven, proposing a specific set of images ('imaginings') of both cinema and nation, so that one 'naturally' belongs to the other and is absorbed by it. The cinema is then a means of 'speaking the nation' in all its (constructed) uniqueness. The connection between 'speaking the nation' and 'selling the nation' becomes all the more inevitable when the rhetoric of both nationalism and marketing emphasize qualities of uniqueness, distinctiveness and patriotism. The term 'representing the nation' therefore acquires an economic as well as an analytical and cultural objective – it is not just 'how' a cinema represents the nation, but also 'how successfully' it does so. The recognition of the interconnectedness of such discourses is important and is unfortunately an aspect of national cinema missing in Andrew Higson's otherwise useful discussion of the subject. He identifies four ways in which the concept of national cinema has been mobilized (Higson, 1989: 36-37):

1. in economic terms, with an emphasis on the film industry and its production, distribution and exhibition sectors;
2. its textual characteristics, which involve the 'identification' of a common style and common themes;
3. a consumption-based approach, which examines the films that domestic audiences are watching, including non-domestic films; and
4. its cultural value, stressing the quality and worthiness of that cinema for the nation and its image.

A substantial part of the article is then devoted to defining the 'imaginary coherence, the specificity, of a national cinema' (Higson, 1989: 38), by contrasting national cinemas in order to establish difference (and thus identity) and by examining national cinema in relation to the discourses of nation already operating within the country. Both methodologies reinforce the rigidity and imperviousness of the border of the nation, one by accepting the presumed, discrete entities of nation states, the other by linking the national cinema to other internal manifestations of national identity. While Higson does continually insist on the overwhelming influence of American cinema on the formation of national cinema, his perspective underemphasizes the transformative power of cultural interaction, wherever that might occur. National cinema is still a circumscribed, coherent concept that invites comparison with the ways that auteurism has been theorized.

It is therefore intriguing that Philip Rosen's review of two studies of national cinemas suggests that nationality may be characterized as an intertextual symptom, an element of coherence in the films of a nation (Rosen, 1984: 70); such an approach is strikingly similar to psychoanalytical conceptions of auteurism (Caughie, 1981: 200). Unfortunately, the symptom of coherence can easily and seductively become the desire for coherence, potentially reaffirming the traditional concept of national cinema – a situation that once more resembles critiques of auteurism, where the auteurs were still important analytical constructs, if now in quotation marks – 'John Ford' rather than John Ford (Caughie, 1981: 200). More promising is Rosen's proposal that nationhood is a component of a film's textual address (a strategy also adopted in critiques of 'classical' auteurism), 'an unstable, shifting variant, effective to different degrees at different points in time' (Rosen, 1984: 82). This is useful because coherence is thus constantly qualified and even in 'danger' of fragmenting. At the end of the article, Rosen makes the interesting comment that it is 'at least theoretically possible for a historian to argue that the cinematic output of a given nation during a given period does not embody that particular kind of intertextual address one would call a national cinema' and while this 'is a limit case which may be unlikely,... film industries in colonized countries could provide objects of interesting studies in this regard' (Rosen, 1984: 83). It might be tempting to propose the application of this proposal to a 'colonized' country like Malaysia, but that would just confirm that the dissolution of national cinema could only occur at the margins, in the 'third world.' A bolder proposal would be to push the concept of national cinema from center stage altogether.

Paul Willemen attempts such a strategy through refocusing interest away from national identity towards cultural specificity, whereby 'the specificity of a cultural formation may be marked by the presence but also by the absence of preoccupations with national identity' (Willemen, 1994: 210). National identity and its cohort, national cinema, are therefore no longer at the center of the argument, representing only a possible component of a film's cultural heterogeneity in a particular domain (such as a country, a region or any other defined category). As already discussed in chapter 1, the cross-cultural analyst must match this emphasis on cultural specificity with a methodology 'of double-outsideness, hybridity and in-between-ness [that] is the precondition for any useful engagement with "the national" in film culture' (Willemen, 1994: 218). The Bakhtinian character of Willemen's cultural studies approach also highlights the relevance of some of Bakhtin's relational notions of culture, e.g. heteroglossia and polyphony. If heteroglossia stresses the 'manylanguagedness' of a cultural community, in which different interests are always competing with each other, polyphony suggests harmony and a plurality of voices; crucially, the two concepts are not defined as opposites but as oppositional, being in constant and creative interaction (Stam, 1989: 229). Furthermore, in contrast to Rosen's proposition that national cinema may be a less important characteristic of the cinemas of 'colonized' countries, Bakhtin's approach concentrates on the margin (e.g. the carnivalesque), but only to '[interrogate]... the center from the margins,' resulting in a 'more open, reciprocal, de-centered negotiation of specificity and difference' (Stam, 1989: 234). These notions of reciprocity, de-centering and cultural specificity are particularly relevant in examining film cultures and publications on national cinemas; they will be applied to film in Malaysia later in this chapter, but more immediately to some examples of national cinema discourse.

National Cinema Texts

Susan Hayward's *French National Cinema* is the first in a National Cinemas series of books to be published by Routledge under the general editorship of Susan Hayward. While most books on national cinemas have substituted the particular nationality for the word 'national,' Hayward's series of books pointedly retains 'national' as part of the title, thereby insisting upon its importance as a defining characteristic of cinema. In the preface to her book, Hayward introduces the concept of difference, but applies it solely to the relationship between the popular, mainstream cinema and the avant-garde, oppositional cinema in France (Hayward, 1993: xi). The book then examines this difference in the three ages of French cinema: classical, modernist and postmodernist. The historical approach and conceptual framework adopted by Hayward is 'a synchronic and diachronic filling in of the gaps between the auteurs and movements' (p. xi). Auteurs, movements, themes and styles have been the staple of national cinema discourse and Hayward employs them to identify seven typologies relevant to the 'enunciation of the "national" of a cinema': 'narratives, genres, codes and conventions, gesturality and morphology, the star as sign, cinema of the center and cinema of the periphery, [and lastly] cinema as mobilizer of the nation's myths and of the myth of the nation' (pp. 8-9). Through these typologies, the book argues the difference of French national cinema as one of esthetic alternatives that constantly feed off each other as the mainstream changes the avant-garde and vice versa. Even the typology of center/periphery refers to the antagonisms between Hollywood and the French cinema and between the central indigenous cinema and artisanal/auteur cinema (p. 13). All the other heteroglossia of this film culture is suppressed or at least submerged. Discussion of the French colonial film is unfortunately limited to its general contribution to the construction of nation, rather than representing a crucial component of nation formation. Only when briefly discussing colonial films made by women, e.g. Claire Denis' CHOCOLAT (1989), does Hayward address the 'marginal' of colonialism, but she locates this in the female European characters of these films (pp. 252-253). Med Hondo's SOLEIL O (1970), a major film by a Mauritanian director living in France, is not included as a liminal text of French national cinema, but casually mentioned as one of a number of films dealing with everyday racism in France (pp. 272-273). Nor does the book refer to the French Ministry of Coopération's unique system of funding African filmmakers, which provides substantial production finance while at the same time exercising editorial control, esthetically and ideologically, over their films (Diawara, 1992: 21-34) – this would have represented a challenging 'test-case' for notions of coherence and difference in national cinema. Closer to 'home' is the book's treatment of Jean Renoir's 1934 film TONI. There are some cursory references to its setting in the south of France (p. 30) and to its story, the problems of immigrant workers (p. 120), but there is no recognition of the film as a 'border-text,' one where difference is celebrated as being at the heart of esthetics, culture, society and identity. This is the approach adopted by Jonathan Buchsbaum, who describes the world of the immigrant workers in TONI as 'heteroclite, syncretic, polyvalent, in constant flux' and the film expresses that flux 'thematically, visually, aurally, and linguistically' (Buchsbaum, 1996: 32). Hayward's book represents an example of the hermetic study of national cinema, looking within the nation for its identity, untroubled by the increasingly fluid borders between societies and cultures; the book's title is indeed a most accurate, if regressive, description of its contents.

The *Encyclopaedia of European Cinema* seems to herald a quite different perspective by circumventing the category of national cinema altogether, instead focusing on a more heterogeneous domain. But this is only superficially the case. First, the book insistently identifies its entries by nationality (and in bold type), whether they be individuals, specific cinemas or film movements. Secondly, the category of European cinema itself takes on the attributes of a national cinema and the book has a certain fortress mentality about it, perhaps most graphically illustrated by Jean-Luc Godard's quote at the head of the Introduction about American cinema being the ruin of the cinemas of Europe (Vincendeau, 1995: xiii). There are entries on individuals who were born outside Europe, but they are few and in a sense this just accepts the inevitability of their presence in terms of status and influence, e.g. Raul Ruiz and Stanley Kubrick (interestingly, Med Hondo, referred to above, is not included despite him being domiciled in Paris since 1958). On the other hand, figures like Ingrid Bergman, Greta Garbo, Alfred Hitchcock, Fritz Lang and Ernst Lubitsch are categorized as Europeans, as part of a European diaspora. Their inclusion is matched by the exclusion of 'third world' filmmakers working in Europe, e.g. Sohrab Shahid Saless and Tevfik Baser in Germany and the inevitable (given the Godard quote) absence of entries on American filmmakers, who have worked in Europe over the decades, e.g. those who made films at Cinecitta in the 1950's and 1960's (Robert Aldrich, Clint Eastwood, Lee Van Cleef). The border, if now surrounding a whole continent, remains intact and acknowledges only those of European birth. Despite the Introduction's stated interest in 'the Europeans who are not included in the notion of Europeanness' (Caughie quoted in Vincendeau, 1995: xvi), the book pays no more than lip service to that aspiration. As Ien Ang stated at a conference on European cinema: 'The problem for Europe, then, is to learn how to marginalise itself,... so that Europeans can start relating to cultural "others" in new, more modest and dialogic ways' (Ang, 1992: 28).

Surprisingly, there are few books on American cinema as national cinema. Perhaps this suggests that American cinema is generally perceived as an international cinema (Higson, 1989: 38). Nevertheless, writings on American cinema tend to be more inclusive than the two texts discussed above. Andrew Sarris' *The American Cinema* is regarded as a landmark in auteur 'theory' literature, but, despite the national cinema connotation of its title, it includes filmmakers like Fritz Lang, Ernst Lubitsch, F. W. Murnau, Max Ophuls and Jean Renoir in its list of 'Pantheon Directors' (Sarris, 1968: 9). This might simply be a strategy for boosting the status of American cinema, which, some would argue, needs all the help it can get. However, the 'retention' of Alfred Hitchcock and Ingrid Bergman (among others) in a book on European cinema could be seen to function in the same way. The two strategies provide a contrast in terms of their attitudes to identity and place. The book on European cinema primarily considers place as 'home' and as origin; the perspective is thus diasporic and the links are attachments to the anterior culture. Sarris' book has an immigrant culture perspective, where the 'lines of connectedness' are more interactive and more directed to their roles in the posterior culture. This is a view of Hollywood as a polyglot or heteroglossic culture, where filmmakers from many parts of the world bring their styles and attitudes, which are in turn inevitably reshaped by the new social and cultural environment in which they find themselves. A study of Hollywood as a place where 'newness enters the world' has still to be undertaken and would counter the prevailing view of Hollywood as the decimator of cultural difference.

The book by David Bordwell, Janet Staiger and Kristin Thompson on the Hollywood classical cinema is, in many respects, the other side of the coin to Sarris' book. It proposes a rather monolithic even static view of cinema, one that categorizes Hollywood (and most other cinematic 'modes of production') as a stable set of formal characteristics. Here difference is absorbed or, as the authors argue, is 'bounded'; the book takes the limit case of film noir, in which 'issues of transgression and subversion, stylization and realism, foreign influence and domestic genre intersect' only to conclude that film noir 'no more subverts the classical film than crime fiction undercuts the orthodox novel' (Bordwell, Staiger and Thompson, 1985: 74-77). Difference by and large exists only outside the Hollywood system, as demonstrated in the book's final chapter, 'Alternative modes of film practice' (pp. 378-385), which was to become the starting point for Bordwell's subsequent book on narration in film (Bordwell,

1985). Nevertheless, Bordwell, Staiger and Thompson do not reject the influences of immigrant (or sojourner) filmmakers on the classical style, a style that in its detail is immensely flexible if totally resilient as a system (pp. 367-377). More importantly, they characterize the classical style, if not as international, then certainly as more than national, with Hollywood signifying a mode of production that exceeds the boundaries of the American cinema as national cinema. Tom O'Regan's perceptive article on Hollywood identifies some of the contradictions implicit in any discussion of Hollywood: the distinction between Hollywood and American cinema, Hollywood as a national and international film industry, its cultural specificity and archetypal character and its proclivity towards both homogenization and difference – culturally, esthetically, economically. O'Regan argues that these characteristics make it 'the only national cinema which is not a national cinema... [b]ut Hollywood movies do not disavow their "Americanness"; rather their Americanness just does not typically appear to be what they are principally about' (O'Regan, 1992: 328).[4] As will be discussed later in this chapter, there are other 'supra-national' cinemas that function in somewhat similar ways, if in more circumscribed film markets, e.g. Indian cinema, Hong Kong cinema, Egyptian cinema.

Japanese society has often been categorized as mono-cultural and unique, contributing to a particular construction of national identity that insists on distinctiveness and homogeneity. This view is strongly held and argued within Japan, but is equally contested both within and outside of Japan (McCormack, 1996). Noel Burch's enormously influential and controversial book, *To the Distant Observer: Form and Meaning in the Japanese Cinema* (Burch, 1979), adopts the former view. While Burch writes of 'a system of contradictions' and 'a boundless text,' he contains these centrifugal tendencies within an overarching concept of Japanese 'otherness,' derived principally from Roland Barthes' book on Japan (Barthes, 1982). The difference of Japanese cinema is not primarily internal (differences in the film styles of Ozu and Mizoguchi are deemed less important than their common 'otherness'), but lies in its contrast to the western representational system. Burch in effect uses Japanese cinema's supposed indifference to 'illusionism' to attack the 'codes of illusionism' of western cinema and western culture in general (Burch, 1979: 66). This agenda-driven objective has led to Burch (and Barthes) being charged with 'Orientalism' (Malcomson, 1985). In order to maintain the 'otherness' of Japanese cinema, Burch constructs a pre-war Golden Age, when the influence of the West was not just minimal, but consciously rejected. Films made after the defeat of Japan were admired by Burch to the extent that they continued their previous strategies or they were slighted because of their incorporation of western representational characteristics. Burch's obsession with non-western modes of representation contributes to the book's emphasis on homogeneity and mono-culturalism and leads him to disregard the popular commercial genre cinema of Godzilla science-fiction films, Tora-san comedies and ZATOICHI samurai films, none of which are even mentioned in his book. Finally, Burch's assertion that much of Japanese cinema was homogeneous and consciously non-illusionist has itself been questioned by an increasing number of film researchers.[5]

Ella Shohat's writings on Israeli cinema offer a stark contrast to those of Burch, by focusing on the relationship between the complex and conflicting political context of Israel/Palestine (with the name itself a contested aspect of nationhood) and its cinema. Shohat problematizes categories of identity such as East/West, First World/Third World, diaspora/homeland (as both origin *and* destination), colonizer/colonized, Ashkenazi Jews/Sephardic Jews, Jewish Israelis/Palestinian Israelis, and traces their representations throughout the history of the local cinema. She concludes her study by comparing the representations of Palestinians and Israelis in the 'Palestinian Wave' of Israeli cinema and in the Palestinian cinema itself. An Israeli film like THE SMILE OF THE LAMB (1985) makes tentative gestures towards incorporating Palestinian characters, which speak Arabic and are given some spectatorial identification, even though the film continues to privilege the 'reluctant occupier' – the liberal Jewish Israeli who is ultimately the real victim (Shohat, 1989a: 262-263). The Palestinian film, WEDDING IN GALILEE (1987), constructs identities for the Palestinian Israelis, identities that emphasize history and subjugation, but also diversity and cultural hybridity, e.g. the wedding's mingling of Muslim and Christian customs, the 'seduction' of the Israeli female soldier by the Palestinian women and the multiplicity of perspectives and voices granted by the film (Shohat, 1989b). The cinema(s) of Israel/Palestine thus become part of the larger process of negotiating cultural identity and cultural interaction, however difficult that might be; labeling this as just another national cinema runs counter to both the realities and the aspirations of the local inhabitants.

Studies of Australian cinema have tended to be more concerned with essentialist notions of identity than have those of American cinema, less obsessed with homogeneity than Burch on Japanese cinema and less focused on social and cultural difference than Shohat's work. Australian cinema, like Australian culture in general, is rather self-conscious about its status as Australian, irrespective of whether this is expressed positively or negatively. It is also extremely conscious of being an English-language cinema and the consequent direct competition with American and British films, both at home and abroad. Sylvia Lawson's 1979 article 'Towards Decolonization: Film History in Australia' describes Australia as a postcolonial, but not a post-revolutionary society. For Lawson, this 'lack' has limited the scope of Australian cinema, which is unable to match the vitality and politicization of film practices of the cinemas of

China, Cuba, and the 'third world' (Lawson, 1979: 70). There was only one moment in its history when Australian cinema was able to address its audience in the same confident way that the films of Glauber Rocha address his audience – these were the silent 'neo-realist' comedies like THE SENTIMENTAL BLOKE (1919) and ON OUR SELECTION (1920). The neo-realist label is not accidental, with Lawson invoking Renoir and de Sica when discussing these films – in fact, she suggests that the Australian films anticipated the European films in style and themes (p. 70). Lawson's 'bad objects' are the early sound films and the mainstream cinema of the 1970's, both shaped too insistently by and for the Hollywood system. The article is strongly polemical, proposing a turning away from the direction taken by Australian films in the seventies and towards a modest European art cinema (since the third world model is, by definition, unavailable). Rather less obviously and unstated, Lawson's valorization of the silent comedies implies a view of 'Australianness' that is rather nostalgic, homogenous and focused on the 'Aussie Battler' coping with women and harsh environments (both significant 'others' in Australian culture).

Brian McFarlane and Geoff Mayer's *New Australian Cinema: Sources and Parallels in American and British Film*, like Lawson's article, defines Australian cinema in terms of other national cinemas and cinema movements/genres. It is an equally polemical work, proposing that Australian cinema 'embrace' the melodramatic mode of address so long favored by Hollywood, rather than the more reticent approach of contemporary Australian and British cinema (McFarlane and Mayer, 1992: 241).[6] The purpose of this shift seems to originate in the need and desire to increase the popularity of Australian films, both at home and abroad. While this proposal is admirable in challenging the continuing emphasis on the 'Australianness' of Australian cinema, its conservatism is apparent in its insistence on sharply defined categories: the classical cinema (Hollywood melodrama) *or* art cinema (the European tendency proposed by Lawson) (McFarlane and Mayer, 1992: 239). In fact, the book eschews any discussion of heterogeneity, whether on the level of mode of address or cultural identity. Films like JEDDA (1954), MAD MAX: BEYOND THUNDERDOME (1985) and NIGHT CRIES (1989) (not discussed, although all made well before the book was published) can be labeled as melodramas, but their melodramatic and cultural hybridity are not in keeping with the book's rigid categories.

Susan Dermody and Elizabeth Jacka's second volume of *The Screening of Australia* examines films made in Australia from the early 1970's to the mid-1980's through the 'constraints' of national cinema (Dermody and Jacka, 1988). In many respects, their approach is rather reductionist, since it limits the discussion to the 'Australianness' of Australian cinema. Frequently, the authors ask whether a particular film is especially Australian or indicate that a film asserts its Australianness. This emphasis on national identity runs somewhat counter to the more questioning remarks they provide on the subject of national cinema itself. While setting the Australian cinema against the homogenizing tendency of Hollywood – at war with Hollywood but at the same time imitating Hollywood's stylistic paradigm – the authors worry about the overpowering hegemony of the concept of national identity, when 'it is, at any given time, only one of several terms like class, race, gender and region, from which an essentially historical identity can be constructed' (Dermody and Jacka, 1988: 19). In a follow-up book to *The Screening of Australia*, Elizabeth Jacka is ready to jettison the centrality of the national in favor of the 'local' or what I referred to earlier in this chapter as cultural specificity: 'the local does not entail any particular exclusion of what is not Australian; the local in a postmodern society is a huge accretion of influences from many sources' (Jacka, 1988: 126), with 'Australianness' being just one of these influences. No longer would analyses of films like MAD MAX: BEYOND THUNDERDOME and NIGHT CRIES need to be confined to issues of national identity, Hollywood imitations or Aboriginal cinema. Similarly, it would allow the inclusion of films made in Australia in the 1960's and 1970's by immigrant filmmakers like Giorgio Mangiamele and Ayten Kyululu, whose work has been omitted from or perhaps suppressed in histories of Australian film (Conomos, 1992: 12). Annette Hamilton's article 'Fear and Desire: Aborigines, Asians and the National Imaginary,' takes the debate about identity further 'within' and further 'without,' by confronting the 'fear and desire' of cultural interaction as evidenced by the representations of Aboriginal people and Asian people in films made in Australia (Hamilton, 1990). The increasing interest in issues of cultural interaction, hybridity and difference helps problematize the still powerful investment in national identity and national cinema formations.

There are, of course, other ways of categorizing cinema based on political, social and cultural criteria, e.g. 'third world' cinema, 'third cinema,' African cinema, Latin American cinema, Asian cinema, Black cinema and so on. Each of these projects provides new perspectives on the subject of cinema and society (as does the national cinema project itself), but each also has the tendency to construct an essentialist domain, a monolithic system immune to local cultural specificity. The following two examples should make the point. Teshome Gabriel's writings on 'third world' cinema and 'third cinema'[7] have brought long-neglected attention to the filmmaking activities of individuals and groups from the 'third world.' This is, however, accompanied by a reductionist approach to that cinema. First, he excludes films regarded as products of commercial film industries from places such as India, Hong Kong and Egypt, and secondly, he constructs particular and essentialist notions of space/time manipulations for his chosen 'third world' films, e.g. the emphasis on the long take (a 'sense of time and rhythm of life') and the wide-angled shot (a 'sense of community') in 'third world' films, in contrast to the fast cutting and preponderance of close-ups in western films (Gabriel, 1989: 44-45). The second example relates to Asian cinema, a category that has tempted some to tentatively propose a similar overarching homogeneity to that of Gabriel's, e.g. Donald Richie's 'Narrative Traditions: East and West' (Richie, 1991). The title of Richie's article reflects much of the discourse on Asian cinema: its difference from the West and thus, often only by implication, its internal similarities (such an approach resembles much of the writing on national cinema). Like Gabriel, Richie concentrates on certain formal characteristics, e.g. the close-up and the movement towards characters in western cinema connotes empathy, whereas the move away from the character has the same function in Asian cinema (examples are given from films by Kurosawa Akira and Satyajit Ray) (Richie, 1991: 14-15). Richie is less essentialist than Gabriel, acknowledging cultural and esthetic difference within Asian cinema, but the emphasis on the East/West dichotomy serves to obscure the long-standing cultural interactions within Asia and the relationships between its various and often quite different cinematic traditions. The following discussion of film in Malaysia strives to remain conscious of these interactions and relationships, whatever their source – the focus, after all, is on the destination.

The Film Industry and Film Culture in Malaysia

The history of the Malaysian film industry is the history of local production, distribution and exhibition. On one level, this history is quite distinct from a study of Malaysian film culture, which would concentrate on the circulation and reception of film in Malaysia. This second approach does not limit itself to locally made films, although it might well concentrate on them. In the case of Malaysia, it would also pay attention to Chinese (mainly Hong Kong), Indian (Tamil and Hindustani), American, Indonesian and other films shown in cinemas, viewed on video, watched on television and discussed in the media. On another level, this film culture is inextricably linked to the local film industry, where, over the decades, 'immigrant' filmmakers have shaped the local industry, while imported films have influenced the cultural and esthetic character of local films. The following discussion of film in Malaysia tracks this industry/culture relationship from the 1900's onwards, identifying and explicating the major influences and the extent to which they were adopted locally.

Up until 1981, a film company in Malaysia could operate in all three sectors of the industry (production, distribution and exhibition) and this was the situation during the studio era when Shaw Brothers and Cathay-Keris virtually controlled the whole industry. However, as in America (as a result of the 1948 Paramount case), this vertical integration eventually became illegal (Baharudin Latif, 1981). In Malaysia, the dismantling of these vertical links was largely due to film producers complaining to the government about their difficulties in gaining access to film exhibition outlets (Baharudin Latif, 1977). However, the distribution/exhibition sector in Malaysia largely remained monopolistic because the same companies distributed local and imported films and also owned the cinema chains throughout the country. Indicative of the complex ethnically oriented profile of the Malaysian film industry is the fact that Chinese Malaysians have dominated the distribution/exhibition sector as well as the thriving video distribution system. In recent years, there has been a steady increase of Malay Malaysians in this sector largely as a result of the government's bumiputera policy applying to all business enterprises – the requirement that Malays own at least 30% of the corporate wealth of the country. Consequently, Malay companies have bought into the two major distribution/exhibition organizations (Shaw Brothers and Cathay) and Malay business people now sit on the boards of all film companies.

The production sector is traditionally divided into two historical periods: the studio era from 1947 to 1977 and the independent (bumiputera) phase from 1974 onwards (Baharudin Latif, 1989a: 45). This is a common distinction and one that occurred in many other film industries, such as those in America, Australia, India and Hong Kong, although the causes and timing of these structural changes were always quite country-specific. Production actually started in Malaya in the 1930's, but it was fragmentary and on the whole rather unsuccessful – it also came to a sudden halt when the Japanese invaded the Peninsula.

The studio era was dominated by two organizations, Malay Film Productions (Shaw Brothers) and Cathay-Keris, both owned by Chinese businessmen and located in Singapore. The films were almost totally made by Indian directors, although in the 1960's the number of Malay directors steadily increased. In the early 1960's a third studio, Merdeka Studio, was set up in Kuala Lumpur. Despite the almost total exclusion of non-Malay actors/characters, many of the studio films attracted a broad, ethnically diverse audience.

The independent phase of the industry has centered on Kuala Lumpur, with the production companies largely headed by Malay Malaysians. The films are made by Malay directors and writers and there are very few Chinese Malaysian and Indian Malaysian filmmakers. To confuse the picture, Hong Kong filmmakers come to Malaysia and make films that are then dubbed into Cantonese or Mandarin for eventual release in Malaysia and other 'Chinatown' destinations. The bumiputera films are largely Malay in content and character, despite the stated desire of everyone in the industry to make Malaysian rather than Malay films. If there are external influences, they increasingly come from Hong Kong and America rather than India. The audiences for these films are predominantly Malay, there being little 'cross-over' except for films that introduce Hong Kong-style action and special effects, e.g. XX RAY (1992), films that attract a non-mainstream 'art-house' audience, e.g. PEREMPUAN, ISTERI &..., or films (very few) that manage to appear more ethnically inclusive, e.g. MEKANIK (Mechanic, 1983).

Early Film-going in Malaya

The arrival of cinema in Malaya occurred at much the same time as it did elsewhere in the world. Many histories of national cinemas breathlessly announce the date on which a film screening first took place in that country. When comparing a number of these histories, it becomes clear that the dates do not differ much. After all, the communication and supply networks in the European colonies were already well developed by the end of the 19th century. So to discover that film screenings were common in Malaya before the beginning of the 20th century is not at all surprising (Lent, 1990: 186). In the early 1900's, film companies from countries as diverse as Britain (the colonizer), France and Japan toured the Peninsula – a Japanese company's screening in 1906 included items on the Russo-Japanese war (Tan, 1993: 9).[8] One source refers to film production beginning in Singapore in 1907; although no further information is provided (Fuziah Kartini Hassan Basri and Raja Ahmad Alauddin, 1995: 59), it would most likely be material shot by the British. In the 1920's and early 1930's, films from China, India, Indonesia, and western countries were shown throughout the Peninsula (Tan, 1993: 10). Mohd Anis Md Nor mentions that Hindustani films were particularly popular because their themes, songs and dances resembled the Wayang Parsee and Bangsawan already familiar to local audiences; Arab films from Egypt and Lebanon were equally popular because of their religious and nationalist themes and their songs (Mohd Anis Md Nor, 1993: 45). Western film distribution companies were so attracted to Malaya that in 1930 there were five production and distribution agents in Singapore (Fuziah Kartini Hassan Basri and Raja Ahmad Alauddin, 1995: 59).

The multiplicity of sources of films was not matched by the diversity of ownership of the local cinemas. By the 1920's, most of these were in the hands of the Chinese. One of the first was Ho Ah Loke who started buying cinemas in the Malayan town of Ipoh in 1926; in the early 1930's, he sold all his interests to Runme Shaw (De Cruz, 1981). The Kuala Lumpur-born Loke Wan Tho had also acquired cinemas in Kuala Lumpur and Singapore in the 1930's under the name of the Cathay Organisation (Lent, 1990: 188). Both he and Ho Ah Loke were eventually to set up the Cathay-Keris studio in the 1950's. The Shaw brothers had been actively involved in the local entertainment industry since the late 1920's, when two of the brothers, Runme and Run Run, came to Singapore from China and bought into cinema chains (Jarvie, 1977: 41-42) and into the burgeoning entertainment parks that were all the rage in Singapore, Penang and Melaka. These parks were multi-purpose centers that contained food stalls, magic shows, gambling stalls, cabarets, dance stages, Bangsawan stages, Chinese opera stages and cinemas (Mohd Anis Md Nor, 1993: 42-44). The entertainment park business led the Shaw brothers to actively promote Bangsawan. They helped to start up Bangsawan troupes in the 1930's and then contracted these troupes to perform in their parks throughout the region (Tan, 1993: 31). When the Shaw Brothers film studio, Malay Film Productions, was at its most successful in the 1950's, the company owned more than 160 theaters throughout Malaya and Singapore (Law, 1992b: 119).

Cinema-going had become a very popular entertainment choice and was beginning to rival that of Bangsawan. Stevenson (1974: 219) suggests that, apart from the racecourse, the cinema was the only place in colonial Malaya where 'all races and classes freely congregated.' This appears to be somewhat of an exaggeration and it is not surprising that a similar case was made for Bangsawan. The descriptions of patrons at 'A Night at the Movies,' quoted by Stevenson (p. 219), are strikingly similar to the Bangsawan 'audience profile' sketched out by Tan Sooi Beng (Tan, 1993: 26-28).

The British in Malaya

The British influence on Malaysian film culture is largely restricted to the period prior to the commencement of local film production. Hamzah Hussin believes that audiences were never attracted to British films because the films were very verbal and emotionally cold, just as the British themselves were unpopular because they isolated themselves from the local people (Hamzah Hussin, 1994a). The legacy that Britain has left is not to be found in the filmic practices themselves but in the constraints within which these practices are able to operate: the censorship system. There was nothing specifically Malayan about the system they instituted – it was just another aspect of generalized colonial control.

On September 18, 1926, *The Times* (London) published a report from 'a correspondent' entitled 'The Cinema in the East (Factor in spread of Communism)' (*Review of Indonesian and Malaysian Affairs*, 1981). The story expressed concern about the 'rapid growth of Communist propaganda among the natives of those regions [i.e. Malaya and the Dutch East Indies]' and the increasing contempt shown by these 'natives' towards Europeans, where there had once been 'genuine respect' (p. 151). The correspondent then suggested that the cause of these alarming trends was the cinema, particularly the American cinema, with its 'scenes of crime and depravity' and 'pictures of amorous passages' (p. 152). Such scenes, the correspondent went on to argue, contributed to the loss of respect for the European, especially the European woman, and led to crimes that mimicked those shown in the films. This in turn 'prepared the minds of the people [the "natives"] for the disintegrating influences of Communist propaganda' (p. 154). The report clearly made the still popular connection between social behavior and filmic (and other) representations, and proposed that this link was particularly present 'in the minds of unsophisticated natives' (p. 153).

It is a most interesting cultural text and speaks volumes about imperialism, colonialism and racism. The 'correspondent' was in fact Sir Hesketh Bell, GCMG, a former Governor of Uganda, Northern Nigeria, Leeward Islands and Mauritius, who wrote this report after his tour of the Malay Archipelago and Indochina in 1926 (Stevenson, 1974: 211). While his views were regarded as somewhat extreme, there was certainly a general belief at the time that films had lowered the regard by local people for Europeans (p. 210) and for European civilization: 'Hollywood has scattered broadcast over the brown and black and yellow worlds a grotesquely garbled account of our civilization' (Aldous Huxley, quoted in Stevenson, p. 211). It is more than coincidental that whenever cinema is mentioned here, the reference is to American cinema, a point that will be discussed a little later.

Bell's report demanded that the British government do more about tightening censorship in the colonies. However, places like British Malaya already had strict film censorship criteria and enforcement procedures; this was in stark contrast to the absence of censorship in Bangsawan theater, which was not seen as a threat by the British (Tan, 1993: 100). In 1925, 12% of films entering Malaya were totally banned, while 90% of the remainder were censored to some extent (Stevenson, 1974: 215). The Official Censor of Malaya stated that certain scenes and situations were unacceptable for 'Eastern audiences' and these were (in addition to those already deemed 'objectionable even to a European audience'): dress immodesty ('every Western woman is immodest from an Eastern point of view'), methods used by criminals ('Chinese in Singapore had successfully used methods adopted from the screen'), gambling scenes and intimate inter-racial marriages and attachments ('of course, all that has to be stopped') (pp. 215-216). The British Board of Film Censors, in their report for 1929, specifically listed stories that were unacceptable in films shown in the colonies. Once again, they included stories about inter-racial intercourse (whether 'moral or immoral') and ones that showed 'white men' and 'British officers' in a bad light: topics that reinforced that loss of respect that Bell talked about in his report. Perhaps surprisingly, the Board of Film Censors also objected to stories 'calculated to wound the susceptibilities of foreign peoples' (p. 223). This was an issue already of concern to the local people in Malaya. Starting in 1927, Cinema Vigilance Committees were established in a number of the Peninsular states. These committees included 'Asians' and in some cases the majority of members were 'Asian.' The Committees expressed concerns not just about the representations of Europeans but also about the representations of the local peoples and their religions in the films (p. 218). While their objections were made known to the Official Censor, it is not clear what effect that had. However, their response, like that of the colonial administration itself, was always a matter of prohibition and censorship rather than a proposal for counter-representations or self-representation, especially by the colonized themselves.

Whereas film censorship was clearly presented as a solution to the deterioration of the image of the European and therefore of stopping the slide towards Communism, another aspect of Bell's report was more coyly addressed. His criticism was not really of cinema in general, but of American cinema. While this was presented as a moral argument, it really had more to do with nationalism, trade and economics. American films dominated not only Malayan screens, but also British screens and those of most other countries. In 1930, the percentage of American films in the British Malayan market was 71%, while in Britain it was 75% (Thompson, 1985: 5). On the other hand, the proportion of British or Empire-produced films shown in the colonies was less than 10% – no specific figures are given for Malaya (Stevenson, 1974: 213); presumably, the other 20% were Chinese and Indian films. Much was made in the late 1920's of the importance of increasing the proportion of 'Empire productions' (p. 213), but the rationale used was not just economic. One British writer on Malaya regarded the 'Yankee monopoly... a scandal from every point of view – educational, financial, patriotic, imperial, moral' (p. 211). This paralleled the prevailing view in Britain itself that Hollywood films 'tended to glorify criminals and encourage gangsterism' (p. 211). A government official argued that the 'gradual substitution of British films for foreign [i.e. American] films' would result in films that were 'clean and wholesome' (p. 216), and the Attorney-General of Malaya wanted the British film industry to be given special support in the colonies, since the cinema 'is today the most universal means through which national ideas and national atmosphere can be spread' (p. 217). These arguments about the social, moral, national and educational advantages of British films contradict the fact that British film producers in the 1920's and 1930's were desperately trying to break into the American market for primarily economic reasons. They were also more than willing to 'follow to a large extent American ideas and customs... [even though] the results were usually pale imitations' (Thompson, 1985: 127). The 'Empire films' made by both British and American producers in the 1930's were remarkably similar in content, style and cultural stereotyping, e.g. SANDERS OF THE RIVER (Britain, 1935) and LIVES OF A BENGAL LANCER (USA, 1935) (Richards, 1983: 251). Economic gain was of equal importance to the American film industry, which realized that it needed to comply with the British censorship regulations (both in Britain and in its colonies) because the British Empire constituted about 50% of Hollywood's foreign income (Vasey, 1992: 627).

While it might be an overstatement to suggest that the push for a greater number of British films in the colonies was solely an economic objective, it is difficult to deny that it was the primary one (economic gain was one of the driving forces behind colonialism as a whole). What is also not explicit in the statements of the time is the importance of employing cultural products like films to assert the ideology of Empire and colonialism (although it would obviously not have been expressed in those terms). The frustration of not being able to present a predominantly British image of the world (and therefore a more 'appropriate' image) to the peoples of the colonies is apparent in these statements. This is not to argue that the American perspective was any less shaped by the prevailing ideologies of racial superiority and colonialism. The British, no less than the Americans, were well aware of the propaganda value of film. While this was usually pursued through documentaries, the propaganda potential of feature films was not ignored: '[they]... strike subconscious cords and reinforce or modify prejudices or opinions already held' (Report of the British Government Committee set up in 1938 to coordinate propaganda quoted in Richards, 1983: 248).

It is clear that the motivations for such a regulatory system were quite complex, involving more than the morality issues routinely associated with censorship. The arrangement, whereby the censorship structure and guidelines were quite different within Britain as compared to the colonies, is one that was typical of the colonial system in general. Interestingly, postcolonial governments were often happy to maintain the systems inherited from the colonizers. In Malaya, this is evident in the censorship system that will be discussed later in this chapter, but it also applied to the broadcasting structure. The new Malayan government enthusiastically retained the British 'colonial service model' of broadcasting designed to safeguard the authority of government. This contrasts with the 'metropolitan model' (i.e. the BBC), which stressed a public service function (Karthigesu, 1988: 309).

Origins

Apart from the rush to nominate the first film screening date in a country, national cinema histories, like national cultures more generally, seek to identify a moment of origin and therefore the commencement of a distinctive tradition. This origin represents the beginning of local production and is often a reference point of esthetic and cultural importance, whether it be a filmmaker or a specific film. Traditional histories of American cinema have nominated D. W. Griffith and the 1915 film THE BIRTH OF A NATION (for these purposes, a most appropriate title; forging the bond between cinema and nation) as the foundational figure/text. More recently, the mantle has fallen on E. S. Porter and THE GREAT TRAIN ROBBERY (1903) and even pre-cinematic figures like Eadweard Muybridge (Christie, 1994: 70). The Australian cinema echoes the American situation by traditionally citing Raymond Longford and THE SENTIMENTAL BLOKE as the esthetic reference point. The much earlier THE STORY OF THE KELLY GANG (1906) has now become the focus of attention and has been called 'the world's first narrative film of substantial length' (Murray, 1994: x); both this film and the Longford film support the larrikin and bush tradition that has defined the dominant strain of Australia's national identity formation. In France, on the other hand, there has been little controversy about the 'founding fathers': Louis Lumière and Georges Méliès, perhaps partly because they neatly characterize the twin (and warring) destinies of film: documentary and fantasy.

The origin of Indian cinema is generally associated with D. G. Phalke, who was inspired to filmmaking after seeing THE LIFE OF CHRIST in 1910 and applied its Méliès-like magical images to a story from the *Mahabharata*, to make RAJA HARISHCHANDRA (King Harishchandra) in 1913 (Rajadhyaksha and Willemen, 1999: 177). Intriguingly, the foundational text in China is not so much a person or a film as a place: Shanghai. It has been called 'the womb of the whole country's film culture' (Tan, 1994: 74) and from the 1920's onwards became a crucial anterior text for filmmaking in Hong Kong, Taiwan, Indonesia and Malaya. Indonesia represents a more complex example, as might well be the case in a colonized, multi-ethnic society. The debate about origin is linked to ethnicity and language: the first Indonesian film was made in 1926 by a Dutchman and a German, the first locally-made Chinese film was made in 1928 by recent arrivals from Shanghai and the first Indonesian film in the Malay language was scripted by an Indonesian and directed by a Dutchman in 1938 (Salim Said, 1992: 99-102). The status of each of the films is thus dependent on one's definition of 'Indonesianness.'

While complex ethnicities are equally applicable to Malaysia, there is no ambiguity or conflict about origin here – it is a 1933 film called LAILA MAJNUN. As was the case with Indonesia, and unlike the other cinemas discussed, this film was not principally 'authored' by indigenous filmmakers. Perhaps this is not surprising given the colonial context in which a western technology such as film was introduced. This doesn't mean that Westerners were 'better' at using this technology, but that those who brought the technology were more likely to control the means of production, whether they were European, Chinese or Indian. However, in terms of the origins of the 'original' Malayan film, there is a greater level of displacement than in most other cases; this film epitomizes and heralds the complex cultural interactions that would constitute filmmaking in Malaysia.

LAILA MAJNUN, India and Indonesia

LAILA MAJNUN was made in Singapore and produced for the Motilal Chemical Company of Bombay by its owner, Indian businessman K. R. S. Chisty (sometimes also spelled Christy and Chistry), and directed by B. S. Rajhans, a Punjabi who had recently arrived from India where he had gained some filmmaking experience. The story was Persian-Arabic in origin and had been staple Bangsawan (and probably Parsee theater) entertainment in the early 20th century. Its formal strategies were also based on Parsee theater and Bangsawan, as well as on the early Indian sound film. The film employed Bangsawan actors, musicians and set designers and, like Bangsawan, was in the Malay language. A newspaper advertisement for the film refers to 'enchanting Egyptian and Arabic Dances!', 'lilting songs in Classical Malay!', 'Natural Scenes of Malaya never before filmed!' and its stars Fatima Benti Jasman 'of H.M.V. Records Fame' and Syed Ali Bin Mansoor 'the Renowned Artiste of the Bangsawan stage' (Tan, 1993: 11). Labeling it as 'The Most Spectacular Malay Talkie Ever Brought to the Screen!' suggests that it wasn't the first Malay sound film. In fact, Indonesian sound films had been shown in the Peninsula the previous year; it was their popularity that had stimulated the production of LAILA MAJNUN (Raja Ahmad Alauddin, 1992: 83). The film's complex cultural history is reminiscent of the Malaysian cultural hybridity discussed in the previous chapter. In that respect, its Malayan identity was never in any real doubt. Its cultural credentials could also not have been more impeccably in line with the 1971 National Cultural Policy (NCP). Its Persian-Arabic (or Persian-Islamic) story and its Middle Eastern musical and dance tradition, which included the already sanctioned Zapin dance form, made the film an ideal NCP cultural product. Added to that were the presence of Malay Bangsawan performers and traditional Indian components (Parsee theater, music and dance) that had been acknowledged as acceptable cultural influences for post-1969 Malaysia.

LAILA MAJNUN was, according to those who saw it, a rather stilted film that looked like a recorded stage play (Baharudin Latif, 2000: 123). While there are no known copies of the film in existence, it is nevertheless important to further discuss this 'poor quality,' lost film, perhaps exactly because there could be no more fitting an example of cultural origin – one literally lost in the past. However, it is not a product of indigenous cultural purity; on the contrary, its multiple traditions counter any tendency towards essentialism. I want to now explore some of the 'lines of connectedness' in more detail by tracing the transportation of the Laila and Majnun legend from the Persian-Arabic world to India and on to Southeast Asia, as well as its transformation from legend to poem to Parsee play to Indian film, and from Bangsawan play and Indian film to Malayan film.

The Indian Parsee theater's introduction of the proscenium arch was, in a technological sense, reified by the development of cinema, even though the construction of space and time was to be quite different. Cinema's threat to Parsee theater was its ability to increase the spectacle of song and dance routines, but this was not to eventuate until the advent of the sound film. Nevertheless, Indian silent film had quickly identified Parsee theater as a source of story material. RAJA HARISHCHANDRA, claimed as the first Indian feature film, was a popular Parsee theater adaption of a *Mahabharata* legend (Rajadhyaksha and Willemen, 1994: 225). The arrival of the sound film technology in India was to transform the industry. Finally song and dance, so central to Parsee theater and traditional Indian culture, could be exploited to the fullest in the new medium and this led to the demise of Parsee theater as a popular entertainment form (Das Gupta, 1991: 16). The first sound film, ALAM ARA (1931), also adapted from a Parsee play, immediately laid down what were to become the parameters of Indian cinema. 'All the sound films produced in India in those early years had a profusion of songs. Most also had dances. The Indian sound film, unlike the sound films of any other land, had from its first moment seized *exclusively* on music-drama forms' (Barnouw and Krishnaswamy, 1980: 69). Paul Willemen, advocating a hybrid and 'impure' conception of Indian cinema, notes that the director of ALAM ARA went on to make a Persian film *in Bombay* in 1933 that is commonly accepted as Iran's first sound film (Rajadhyaksha and Willemen, 1999: 9). The Indian film historian B. D. Garga claims that it was the Calcutta-made film LAILA MAJNU (1931), more than ALAM ARA, that 'established the unshakeable hold of songs on our films which continues till today' (Garga, 1995: 24). The Malayan LAILA MAJNUN has been described as having the characteristics of a typical Indian film of that time:

melodrama, spectacle, songs and dances (Baharudin Latif, 1992: 2), elements that in turn were derived from the Parsee and Bangsawan theaters.

Laila and Majnun, 'the quintessential lovers of the Perso-Islamic world' (Kakar and Ross, 1992: 43) have been called the 'Arabic Romeo and Juliet,' a problematic assignation, since it implies that the European story is the anterior text (a similar form of Orientalism is apparent when it is suggested that the *Mahabharata* is India's *The Iliad*). This situation is not improved when references to Laila and Majnun in Indian films are replaced in the English subtitles by the names Juliet and Romeo – as occurs in Raj Kapoor's AWARA (The Vagabond, 1951). While there are similarities between the two stories, Majnun, in particular, is a very different character. He pines away in loneliness for his absent lover, Laila, wanders through the bazaars singing her praises, eventually becoming a madman, which is what Majnun literally means (Kakar and Ross, 1992: 45). The story is recognized in the Persian-Islamic world as a parable of the Sufi religious experience, where Majnun 'exemplifies the Sufi mystic, who contemplates the full perfection of the Beloved only in Image' (Kakar and Ross, 1992: 52). In popular culture, Majnun came to represent a passive, unhappy hero figure, unrequited in the loss of the beloved. Sudhir Kakar calls this typical character of 1950's Indian cinema the 'Majnun-lover' (Kakar, 1990: 35); the character was also to crop up frequently in Malaysian film, starting of course, with the 1933 LAILA MAJNUN. The popularity of the Laila Majnun legend in the Islamic world (although its currency extends well beyond that world) is so great that in India alone fifteen film versions of the story have been made. The Indian filmmaker, B. N. Rao, who directed films in Singapore in the 1950's and 1960's, produced a Malayan version of the story in 1962. The respected Indonesian director, Sjumandjaja, made a version of the Laila Majnun story in the 1970's; Salim Said's comment on the film is scathing and perhaps ignorant of the story's origin (it is ironic that the story has here become just another piece of western popular culture 'sadly' taken up by Indonesian filmmakers): 'Sjumandjaja churned out such lightweight fare as LAILA MAJENEUN, a film which transported WEST SIDE STORY from New York to Jakarta' (Salim Said, 1991: 93).[9]

The origin of the story helps to explain the presence of Arabic dances referred to in the advertisement for the 1933 film, although the dances would most likely have been part of the Indian tradition too. But what about the specific reference to Egyptian dances? It was mentioned earlier that Egyptian films had been popular in Malaya because of their nationalist and religious themes, but the main attraction for local audiences lay in their Arabic songs and dances. As with Indian cinema, the earliest Egyptian films were stage adaptions and included songs and dances by the country's best-known performers (Malkmus and Armes, 1991: 29).[10] The Malaysian film director Jamil

Sulong mentions that singers/actors like Mohamed Abdel Wahab were well known to the Malayan film-going public in the 1930's (Jamil Sulong, 1989: 60), as Oud Kalsoum and Farid El Atrache were to become over the next decades, the latter's life and film career bearing an uncanny resemblance to that of the Malaysian director/star P. Ramlee. Egyptian cinema became the dominant Arab cinema during the 1930's and maintained a continuing, if limited, connection with the Malaysian film culture.

The advertisement for LAILA MAJNUN also refers to the songs being in 'classical Malay.' This may well have been a way of stressing the Malayan origin of the film. The Indonesian film TERPAKSA MENIKAH (Forced Marriage, 1932), the 'first Malay talkie,' when shown in Malaya in 1932 was criticized for using 'bazaar' Malay with a Javanese accent, rather than the high Malay heard in Bangsawan; the film was also criticized for its social and sexual daring and its vulgarity (Tan, 1993: 29). Nevertheless, TERPAKSA MENIKAH and other early Indonesian sound films were very successful in Malaya, because they embraced a theatrical tradition that was quite similar to Bangsawan. The popularity of these films may well have been the stimulus for the production of LAILA MAJNUN (Mohd Anis Md Nor, 1993: 45). In the 1920's and 1930's, both countries had urban, commercially popular theater forms that influenced their respective film cultures: the Malayan Bangsawan and the Indonesian 'Tonil,' from the Dutch word for stage plays, 'toneel,' and 'Komedi Stambul,' so named because most of the plots came from Stambul, the Malay name for Istanbul (Tan, 1993: 18). However, at least in the early 1930's, the ways that these theaters interacted with their nascent film cultures were quite different. As described above, Bangsawan provided the Malaysian film industry with actors, performance styles and stories; in return, the films became the sources of new dances for Bangsawan (Tan, 1993: 44). There was much less interaction between popular theater and film in Indonesia, at least until later in the 1930's (Salim Said, 1991: 21). This had a lot to do with the ethnic composition of the audiences and the filmmakers.

The first feature film in Indonesia was made in 1926 by a Dutchman, Heuveldorp, and a German named Kruger. It was called LOETOENG KASAROENG (The Enchanted Monkey) and the story was based on a West-Javanese folktale. This European involvement in filmmaking, which continued for the rest of the decade and included at least one Englishman, is quite unlike the Malayan situation. The result was a series of films (including the afore-mentioned TERPAKSA MENIKAH) aimed primarily at the Eurasian audience in Indonesia. However, this audience found these films distasteful for their representation of Eurasians as 'primitives' and preferred imported films, the most popular of which were Hollywood and especially Shanghai films (Salim Said, 1991: 22-23). As in Malaya, Chinese involvement in Indonesian films had initially been confined to film distribution and exhibition, with Shanghai films as their principal product. It soon became clear that certainty of supply of films was essential to the survival of their distribution and exhibition business; this motivated Shanghai filmmakers to come to Indonesia and set up production companies in partnership with Indonesian-born Chinese. The first locally-made Chinese film, LILY VAN JAVA (The Lily of Java, 1928) was shot and directed by the Wong brothers and starred Lily Oey, all of whom had recently arrived from Shanghai, and the film portrayed the life of Jakarta's upper-class Chinese (Salim Said, 1992: 100). It set the pattern for later films in its use of Chinese stories, Chinese actors, and Chinese and Malay subtitles (Salim Said, 1991: 16-18) – the audiences for these films were clearly people of Chinese descent.

With the arrival of sound the situation changed, partly because a 'significant percentage of the Chinese community in Indonesia did not speak the language of their forefathers' (Salim Said, 1991: 22). While the stories tended to remain Chinese or Malay-Chinese, the actors and settings were becoming more Indonesian. The production of the film TERANG BOELAN (Full Moon) in 1937 represented a consolidation of this tendency towards 'Indonesianization,' and also heralded a new direction for Indonesian film. Often described as the first full length Indonesian film in Malay, it was scripted by an Indonesian journalist Saeroen, photographed by David Wong (a native-born Chinese and not related to the Wong brothers) and directed by a Dutchman, Albert Balink. The film's production profile is thus a confluence of the various interests in the Indonesian film industry over the previous ten years. The new tendency represented by this film was that its story was an adaption of the 1936 American film JUNGLE PRINCESS, which was set in Hawaii and starred Dorothy Lamour. TERANG BOELAN used exotic local settings, added keroncong music (a popular, Portuguese-influenced musical form), spectacle, songs and actors who were carefully chosen for their looks and singing ability (Salim Said, 1991: 26). This reworking and 'indigenizing' of successful foreign stories was to become the dominant strain of the Indonesian cinema for decades to come. Of course, the idea of remaking successful foreign films was not new even then and the Shanghai films of the 1920's and 1930's had themselves given 'Chinese backgrounds and costumes to imitations of foreign, usually American, films' (Leyda, 1972: 50). Of particular interest was TERANG BOELAN's success in attracting audiences from well beyond the Chinese film-going community. Indonesians who had in the past dismissed locally made films and those who had found the Malay popular theater (i.e. Tonil and Komedi Stambul) a more relevant form of entertainment were most enthusiastic about this film. This was at least partly due to the recruitment of actors for the film from this popular theater and the fact that the scriptwriter, Saeroen, had himself worked in Komedi Stambul (Heider, 1991: 15-16).

The similarity between the two early film industries are striking: Chinese dominance of distribution and exhibition, an influential theatrical tradition based on melodrama, song and dance that provided stories and talent, and non-indigenous control of production. However, the Malayan film LAILA MAJNUN was an amalgam of Arabic, Indian and Malay cultures, while the early Indonesian films were more directly shaped by the Shanghai tradition. These differences help to define the specificity of these film cultures, even when the two societies – Malaysia and Indonesia – have so much in common in terms of ethnicity, language, religion, history and colonialism.

The Indonesian influence on LAILA MAJNUN was the recognition that Malay language films were attractive to Malayan audiences, however different the spoken dialect might have been. There are contradictory reports about the success of the film, some calling it a box office failure (Jamil Sulong, 1990: 8), while others suggest that its popularity encouraged Shaw Brothers to enter film production (Baharudin Latif, 1989a: 46), but it could as well have been the interest generated in Malaya by Indonesian films that stimulated Shaw Brothers to make films for the Malayan market. Following the box office success of the Indonesian film TERANG BOELAN in Malaya, a Chinese production company that had been active in the Indonesian film industry decided to also set up a production facility in Singapore in 1938 (Baharudin Latif, 1992: 4). This was the Tan and Wong Film Company, of which one partner Tan Koen Yauw had been the largest producer of silent films in Indonesia (Salim Said, 1991: 21), while the other partners were the Wong brothers referred to earlier as the creators of the first Chinese film in Indonesia. This new company's first (and only) film was called MENANTU DURHAKA (Rebellious-in-Law), made before the war and directed by B. S. Rajhans, the Indian director who had made LAILA MAJNUN in 1933. Their decision to use an Indian, instead of a Chinese or Chinese-Indonesian director, may well have been based on Rajhans' previous experience in working with Bangsawan actors and technical staff; in a rather qualified way, he was more 'local' than any other film director. The film's popularity stands in stark contrast to a series of unsuccessful films made by Shaw Brothers in Singapore at about the same time.

Shaw Brothers

The Shaw brothers were part of the enormously influential Shanghai film diaspora. By the early 20th century, Shanghai was the premier, westernized Chinese city and the source of the May Fourth Movement, which advocated the social and intellectual reform of China through the inclusion of western ideas

(Clark, 1987: 5). It also became the center of film production in the country in the 1920's and 1930's and excelled in a wide range of genres from social films, martial arts films and melodramas to song and dance films (Tan, 1994: 81). During the 1930's, as the political conflicts and the economic crisis worsened, left-wing film studios were established in Shanghai and produced films that were extremely critical of the status quo, e.g. THE GODDESS (1934), CROSSROADS (1937) and STREET ANGEL (1937). This last film, quite typical in this regard, applied Hollywood melodrama conventions, particularly those of Frank Borzage, to the social realities of life in Shanghai. The film also includes a number of songs, which are subtitled and use a 'bouncing ball' technique to encourage audience participation. Some of the social melodramas made in Singapore in the 1950's similarly combined musical numbers, social criticism, melodramatic characterization and stylistic excess. However, it would be a mistake to attribute these 'left' tendencies to the Shaw brothers.

The Shao brothers (as they were then called) had set up the Tianyi Film Company in Shanghai in 1925 and the following year established a distribution company in Hong Kong. Tianyi was a very conservative production company and the move south was a business decision that recognized Hong Kong as a major distribution center for Chinese films (Tan, 1994: 75). In the same year, two of the brothers, Run Run and Runme, came to Singapore to build cinemas and buy entertainment parks that would supplement their distribution business (Law, 1992b: 119). In the 1930's, Tianyi opened a branch production company in Hong Kong to produce Cantonese films for the Southeast Asia market (Law, 1994: 37). The dispersal of the Shanghai film industry was largely determined by outside political forces, such as the Sino-Japanese war in 1937, the civil war from 1946 and the subsequent defeat of the Nationalists by the Communists in 1949; each of these set off a wave of migration to Hong Kong (and to a lesser extent to Taiwan and other parts of Mainland China). While some of the Shanghai filmmakers continued to make 'didactic films' in Hong Kong, Tianyi Film Company made the same sort of entertainment films that it had produced in Shanghai (Tan, 1994: 81). The influence of the Shanghai film culture on Hong Kong was profound and is only now being researched in any detail;[11] it is outside the scope of this book, although some further comments are relevant in the next sections of this chapter.

After investing heavily in film exhibition, the two Singapore-based Shaw brothers realized the need to ensure continuous product for their film theaters, at the same time working towards a monopoly system by making it difficult for competitors to enter the market. The success of Malayan and Indonesian Malay-language films led them to import used film equipment from Shanghai to start their own film production activities in Malaya (Baharudin Latif, 1992: 3). The production company was called Shaw Brothers; the reference to

Warner Bros. was not accidental and extended to an almost identically shaped logo. Prior involvement with Bangsawan was to benefit their filmmaking enterprise greatly, and the films they produced before World War II starred the country's best-known Bangsawan players. These early films, which included IBU TIRI (Stepmother), MUTIARA (Pearl), TOPENG SHAITAN (Satan's Mask) and TERANG BULAN DI MALAYA (Full Moon in Malaya – a local remake of the 1937 Indonesian hit; the song 'Terang Bulan' provided the tune of the Malaysian national anthem, *Negara Ku*, lit. My Country),[12] were all made by Chinese directors brought in from Shanghai, but the films were not popular with local audiences. This may have been due to their directors' unfamiliarity with Malay culture or because the films were based on Sandiwara and not Bangsawan plays (Jamil Sulong, 1989: 56), suggesting that the more realistic Sandiwara drama was less attractive to film audiences. Jamil Sulong also describes the films as being very stagy, consisting mainly of long shots of the performers. Hamzah Hussin believes that the failure of these films is indicative of the broader lack of cultural involvement by the Chinese in Malaysia ('they convey a mentality of being temporary residents'), unlike in Indonesia, where the Chinese were already a part of Indonesian culture (Hamzah Hussin, 1994a).[13]

The Japanese invasion of Malaya in 1941 shut down film production for six years, although it had already been struggling for some time due to the scarcity of film stock and audience reluctance to spending money on non-essentials (Baharudin Latif, 1992: 4). Only Japanese films and Indian feature films were allowed to be shown during the Occupation – the Japanese decided that Indian (particularly Hindustani) films were harmless entertainment, whereas they totally banned all Chinese films because of the conflict between Japan and China (Krishnan, 1994a). This would also help explain why local production ceased – it was controlled by Chinese businessmen. A film studio belonging to a producer called Miu Hang-nee, who came to Singapore from Shanghai before the war to make Malay-language films, was seized by the Japanese. In 1946, Miu reclaimed his studio and made a film called BLOOD & TEARS OF THE OVERSEAS CHINESE, to expose 'the cruel treatment meted out to overseas Chinese by the occupiers' (Teo, 2000b: 162). Some propaganda films were produced by the Japanese in Singapore (Jamil Sulong, 1990: 9), but they mostly screened Japan-made films as part of a campaign of 'Nipponization.' The films included propaganda films, newsreels, informational films and also feature films to demonstrate the qualities of Japanese social and cultural life (White, 1995). Timothy White claims that these films contributed to the stylistic and generic development of the 1950's Malayan films, e.g. that the BUJANG LAPOK series of comedies that P. Ramlee made show the influence of Japanese nonsense films.[14] P. Ramlee's film style was also indebted to post-war Japanese films by Ozu Yasujiro, Mizoguchi Kenji and especially Kurosawa Akira – this matter will be addressed when discussing specific P. Ramlee films in the next chapter.

The wartime film production situation was quite different in Indonesia. Here the Japanese produced propaganda shorts, but also feature films (which were strongly propagandist) that starred Indonesian actors. The Japanese had a major influence on the future of the Indonesian cinema by creating 'an attitude towards film and filmmaking that was radically different from that of the past' (Salim Said, 1991: 36). This included a perception of film 'as a means of social communication... an awakening of the [Indonesian] language... a greater sense of national consciousness' (Salim Said, 1991: 34).

The emphasis on LAILA MAJNUN in this section has been greater than it, as a specific (and lost) film, perhaps warrants, but the film underscores many of the cultural influences and interactions that were to define the local films in the 1950's. The pre-war production activities of Shaw Brothers introduced the only other major contributor to the post-war film industry: the Chinese entrepreneur. The Indian directors and the Chinese producers should also be seen as a continuation of the massive migratory and diasporic (sojourner) forces of the 19th and early 20th century referred to in the previous chapter (just as the Hollywood 'czars' came from Eastern Europe as part of the mass migration into the USA). These Indian and Chinese nationals combined with the local cultural community to create that strange film culture identified by Hamzah Hussin at the head of this chapter.

The Golden Age

The re-emergence of local film production in Singapore after the war signaled the beginning of the studio system in Malayan filmmaking, which was to last for over twenty years. The first post-war film actually preceded the studio era and its failure was indicative of the changing conditions of the industry. K. R. S. Chisty and B. S. Rajhans, the producer and the director of the 1933 LAILA MAJNUN, teamed up again to make SERUAN MERDEKA (Call for Independence) in 1946. This time the film failed at the box office, largely because Chisty could not gain access to exhibition outlets, which were owned by Shaw Brothers (Mohd Anis Md Nor, 1993: 52). SERUAN MERDEKA is now considered an important film, because it featured Malay and Chinese protagonists fighting together for freedom (Hamzah Hussin, 1994b), a significant theme, given the antagonism that had developed between the Malays and the Chinese during and after the Japanese Occupation.

The Indian Connection

Shaw Brothers also returned to film production, but rather more successfully than Chisty. They established a studio in Singapore in 1947 under the name of Malay Film Productions (MFP) and engaged the same B. S. Rajhans as their director; in fact until 1950, Rajhans was their only director, completing eight films for the studio in this time. The success of these films was undoubtedly the result of Shaw Brothers' stranglehold on the exhibition sector that they had bought up before the war. However, the appointment of an Indian director also suggests a lesson learned from their pre-war production experience – the value of Indian directors rather than Chinese ones in a market so strongly shaped by Indian culture. The films that Rajhans made were based on Indian folklore, myths and legends as well as on contemporary social issues, e.g. SINGAPURA DI WAKTU MALAM (Singapore at Night, 1947) dealt with the problems of Malay youths leaving the kampung for the city (Tan, 1993: 32). MFP was so taken by its working relationship with Rajhans that it sent agents to India to recruit other Indian directors. Besides the Indian-Malayan cultural connection already referred to, Indian directors were favored because India had a well-developed film industry, Indians were familiar with English (the legacy of a shared colonial power) and Indian directors were cheaper than Hollywood ones (Matsuaka Kanda, 1995: 50). The first two recruits, L. Krishnan and S. Ramanathan were of Tamil origin and both had lived in Malaya in their youth before returning to India – their 'local knowledge' was instrumental in their selection.

L. Krishnan is one of the few who has remained in Malaysia after his directing career, and he is now a distinguished Malaysian citizen, with the honorific title of 'Datuk.' I met him in 1994 and want to briefly sketch his early career as an example of the involvement of these young, inexperienced filmmakers in the Malayan film industry. He was born in Madras and migrated with his family to Penang in 1928 when he was six years old. L. Krishnan became an interpreter for the Japanese during the war and in 1943 joined the Indian National Army, whose goal, under Subbad Chandra Bose, was to expel the British from India; not surprisingly, the army was supported by the Japanese. Inevitably, when the British returned to Malaya, L. Krishnan was repatriated to Madras. Here he entered the Tamil film industry and became an assistant director. In 1948 he directed a Sinhala film called AMMA; this might seem puzzling, but many of the early Sri Lankan films were shot in South India with local crews and technicians (Abeyesekera, 1997: 4).[15] The following year, L. Krishnan took an appointment as a film director at Shaw Brothers' MFP, partly because of his familiarity with Malaya. His first film was BAKTI (Devotion, 1950), which was based on *both Wuthering Heights* and *Les Miserables*! It was also the first film to star P. Ramlee, who was to become the Malaysian cinema's one superstar during the 1950's. L. Krishnan made nine films for MFP, before moving to help launch the competitor studio, Cathay-Keris. In 1960, he left Singapore and contributed to the establishment of Merdeka Studio in Kuala Lumpur, but left it over disagreements in 1963 to move into private business, where he eventually founded a film production company, a color film laboratory and a sound studio. He remains highly regarded in the Malaysian film industry, has strong views about the current state of the industry and is a Governor of the Malaysian Film Academy. His feature film career covered the rise and fall of the studio system, during which time he directed 34 films (Krishnan, 1994a).

Other Indian directors followed, but these were less familiar with the local conditions than L. Krishnan and S. Ramanathan. The last of them, Dhiresh Ghosh, was initially recruited by Indonesian producers (of Chinese origin), but his one film there was not successful. This was also the case with a number of other Indian directors and it made people like L. Krishnan refuse offers of employment in the Indonesian film industry (Krishnan, 1994b). The effectiveness of Indian directors in Malaya, as opposed to the earlier failure of Chinese directors there, contrasts starkly with the reverse situation in Indonesia and perhaps indicates that the 'cultural competence' of the two immigrant communities is quite specific. Shaw Brothers also enticed a number of already well-known Indian directors to work in Singapore, notably B. N. Rao and Phani Majumdar. Both eventually returned to India to continue their careers there; each made a number of distinguished films for MFP and in the case of Rao also for Cathay-Keris. Rao's HUJAN PANAS (Hot Rain, 1953) and Majumdar's HANG TUAH will be analyzed in some detail in the next chapter and represent examples of the work of the Indian filmmakers in Malaya; it is remarkable that during the 1950's (the height of the studio system), Indians directed 107 of the 149 films made.[16] All of these directors were first employed by MFP; some, like L. Krishnan, transferred to Cathay-Keris, while only L. Krishnan and Dhiresh Ghosh eventually worked at Merdeka Studio.

The Studio System

Shaw Brothers under its own banner (1937-41) and as MFP (1947-69) produced 170 Malay-language films, with its output peaking in 1951. During these early years, its only competition came from a number of independent companies, which were also owned by Chinese businessmen; the films were made by Indian, Indonesian, Chinese and the first Malay director, A. R. Tompel, although it is instructive that he used an Indonesian pseudonym, Armaya. Once again cinema availability was the problem, but this time a solution was found through the amalgamation of these companies (one of which was owned by

Ho Ah Loke) with Cathay Company, an exhibition and production organization owned by Loke Wan Tho, to form Cathay-Keris, which was also located in Singapore and became MFP's only rival in the 1950's (Baharudin Latif, 1992: 4-5). Cathay-Keris survived from 1953 to 1972 and made 123 films. Production activities peaked in the early sixties, when MFP was no longer a serious competitor, but their combined output, together with the first films from the newly established Merdeka Studio in Kuala Lumpur led to the release of a total of 23 films in 1963, a level of production not since exceeded.[17]

The studio system, like that of the studios in Hong Kong with which the Shaw brothers and the Cathay-Keris owners were familiar, was based on Hollywood in its emphasis on expediency, efficiency and cost-consciousness. MFP set up two production units, enabling two films to be shot at once, one in the studio while the other was on location (Jamil Sulong, 1990: 35). The typical schedule was three weeks with budgets of about RM 60,000 (equivalent to AUD 30,000 in today's terms) and each studio aimed to release one film a month (Baharudin Latif, 1989b: 46). The studio era is generally considered to be the most successful period of the Malaysian film industry, due to the political and economic stability of the country and the Hollywood-inspired star system (Fuziah Kartini Hassan Basri and Raja Ahmad Alauddin, 1995: 60), but Philip Cheah claims that the films were not very successful, with only three of Cathay-Keris' films between 1952-58 making a profit (Cheah, 1997: 55). While this seems a poor economic result, since Cathay-Keris made 29 films during that period, it represented the first six years of their activities. More generally, it needs to be remembered that film production by both studios was a means of providing product for their own cinemas, which also showed other films produced or distributed by the same or affiliated companies. Local production also enticed audiences to frequent other films, by making cinema-going a regular event and by promoting upcoming attractions.

Despite the above-mentioned suitability of Indian directors, scripting and communication problems did occur. The scripts were written in English, Hindi or Tamil and then translated into Malay, often lacking the local language nuances. Many of the actors were also illiterate, whereas the producers and directors, with a few exceptions, were limited in their ability to speak Malay (Ainon Haji Kuntom, 1973: 9). The presence of Chinese cinematographers compounded the problem and often required hand signals to facilitate communication (Jamil Sulong, 1990: 35). The scripts were usually adapted from successful Indian, Chinese or American films, but also from Bangsawan plays. The limited knowledge of Malay culture meant that few films drew upon traditional or contemporary Malay literature, a situation that has changed little over the years. Some of these cultural problems were overcome when Malay directors and scriptwriters were given the opportunity to make films. Both studios instituted an apprenticeship system, whereby Malays were made assistant directors for about eight years before they were allowed to direct in their own right, with the same opportunity being given to their leading stars after they appeared in a number of films; this arrangement led P. Ramlee to direct his first film in 1955, Roomai Noor in 1956 and Jamil Sulong in 1959. Filipino directors were also introduced in 1955; they were considered to be as appropriate as Indian directors with the extra advantage of speaking a language, Tagalog that is related to Bahasa Melayu. Whereas Indian directors had introduced the performance styles, filming methods and cinematic traditions of Indian cinema, the Filipino directors brought shooting and lighting techniques that reduced the overall shooting time – the Filipinos had learned these approaches from American filmmakers. The most prolific director was Ramon Estella, who made 12 films in Singapore. He was a truly itinerant filmmaker, having worked in America, Vietnam, Italy as well as in the Philippines (Co, 1990). Eddie Infante, who was the first Filipino director to work in Singapore, wrote of the cultural similarities between Malay kampung life and the world of the Muslims in the southern Philippines. He also contrasted, perhaps rather nostalgically, the fast-paced Filipino cinema with the slower and gentler rhythms of the acting style of P. Ramlee and of the films themselves (Infante, 1991: 152-153). While Jamil Sulong does not mourn the passing of the studio system with its associated economic and artistic control of directors (Jamil Sulong, 1994), most commentators, including L. Krishnan and Hamzah Hussin, who both worked within that system, still extol its virtues: effective planning, quality scripts, regular work, competitiveness, the ability to absorb a failure at the box office and a creative studio culture (Krishnan, 1994a; *New Straits Times*, 1986; Baharudin Latif, 1994b).

Not surprisingly, most of the studio films of the 1950's retained the formal strategies of the Indian film: melodramatic, episodic and digressive narratives that focused on family and genealogy, always integrated with songs and dances. These were also part of the Bangsawan tradition, which while itself succumbing to the popularity of Malay films continued its influence through the presence of actors, technicians, musicians, performers and stories in the films of the 1950's. Jamil Sulong acknowledged that most of the films he directed had been Bangsawan plays (Jamil Sulong, 1989: 59). The songs and dances were, as in Bangsawan, from a wide range of traditions, but their staging was often determined or altered by the Indian directors. Thus the frequency of garden, forest, mountain and moonlit love scenes – the romantic trope of the pathetic fallacy, where nature becomes the metaphor for human emotion, is common in Indian literature and cinema (Rajadhyaksha and Willemen, 1999: 348). The Arab-introduced Zapin dance form was also re-choreographed into a lead-chorus arrangement typical of Indian films; it furthermore enabled the lead dancer to sing to the chorus' accompaniment (Mohd Anis Md Nor, 1993: 55). At the same time, the song and dance styles were in a constant process of transformation through more general American, Latin American, Indonesian, Middle Eastern and Indian influences. Unlike the length of the typical Hindi film, Malay films had to be limited to 90-105 minutes for cinema scheduling reasons (Jamil Sulong, 1990: 70). This constraint reduced the number of songs/dances to five or six (from an average of about ten in 1950's Indian films). The song and dance routines were also less narratively motivated than in Indian films – this may well be due to the Bangsawan tradition, where songs and dances were performed during breaks in the performance (the so-called 'extra turns'). Besides, the songs and dances were to be appreciated as performances in their own right and had social and economic consequences beyond the film itself, e.g. in night clubs and record sales.

As mentioned in the previous chapter, Singapore in the 1950's was a cosmopolitan city and a Malay cultural center, even though it was a predominantly Chinese city in terms of population. Nevertheless, it is striking how few Chinese stories and Chinese characters turn up in the films made there, despite the Chinese ownership of the studios (it might be compared to the absence of overtly-identified Jewish characters in Hollywood films).[18] There were equally few Indian characters, but at least the stories and esthetic aspects of the films were strongly shaped by Indian traditions. Some films did draw on Hong Kong genres like ghost films and vampire films, e.g. PUTERA BERTOPENG (A Masked Prince, 1957) and ORANG MINYAK (The Oily Man, 1958); the latter was directed by L. Krishnan, who also took a Chinese story for ANTARA SENYUM DAN TANGIS (Between Laughter and Tears, 1952), which had a 'multi-ethnic cast and a multicultural theme' (Krishnan, 1994a). More intriguingly, L. Krishnan made a local version of the 1936 Tamil film DEVDAS (based on a popular Bengali novel of the same name frequently filmed in India) called SELAMAT TINGGAL KEKASIHKU (Farewell, my Beloved, 1955), in which he changed the story into a relationship between a Malay man and a Chinese woman; this made the film controversial, especially in the strongly Muslim state of Kelantan (Krishnan, 1994b). This film has also been cited as exemplifying the sort of cultural 'mistakes' that occur when an 'outsider' attempts to create a local story: in the film, a man picks up his dead friend's body – an act quite appropriate for a Hindu, but offensive to Muslim custom (Hamzah Hussin, 1994a).

P. Ramlee

Such cultural 'problems' were expected to disappear with the advent of Malay creative control. Nevertheless, the Malay-directed films retained the Indian film style and narrative predilections. This is particularly evident in the work of the most highly regarded Malay director, P. Ramlee, who had acted in many of the films made by the Indian directors. It has been suggested that he changed his name from Teuku Zakaria bin Teuku Nyak Puteh to P. Ramlee because such a contraction was in the South Indian tradition (Kee Hua Chee, 1992: 18), a tradition he was strongly influenced by while growing up in Penang.[19] B. S. Rajhans (the director of LAILA MAJNUN and once again playing a pivotal role in the industry) found him performing in a Bangsawan play in Penang and employed him as a playback singer (Mahirin Binti Hassan, 1978: 75). The playback singer, who sang the songs that the actor on the screen mimed, was a crucial figure in the Indian film industry, often better known and more lauded than the screen actor – a response indicative of the status of song in Indian cinema. The Malaysian playback singer performed a similarly important function, although, when P. Ramlee became an actor, he sang all his own songs. P. Ramlee went on to become the foremost composer, singer, actor and film director of the late 1950's and for many, the best of all time. His long-term influence on Malaysian popular music was immense and is extensively discussed in Craig Lockard's article (1991). Musically, he amalgamated indigenous traditions with styles from other cultures, including 'Latin American dance music, Hawaiian music, Indian film music and Western popular music' (Lockard, 1991: 19).

This interest in hybridity is equally evident in his films and will be explored in the next chapter. Song and dance were to remain important in his films and he often played the character of a singer/composer, providing narrative motivation for his musical performances. The characters he played are very much in the vein of the 'Majnun-lover' previously mentioned (Kakar, 1990: 35): a romantic, passive protagonist, who accepts personal and family setbacks without question; he differs from Kakar's model in often responding to his fate in a surprisingly aggressive manner towards the end of a film. This character type was embedded within the melodramatic form, with an emphasis on heightened emotion and starkly delineated conflicts, exemplified by constructing the relationship between hero and heroine across class, ethnic or religious borders, a melodramatic formula common in Indonesian and Malaysian popular fiction (Quinn, 1987: 51).

This approach to character interaction – the Laila/Majnun phenomenon – was also at the heart of the Indian cinema and Indian popular literature (e.g. *Devdas*), and its most successful and impressive proponent in the 1950's had been Raj Kapoor (one of India's megastars). P. Ramlee has been compared to Raj Kapoor, but, as L. Krishnan pointed out, P. Ramlee also composed and sang his own songs (Krishnan, 1994b). He was labeled 'the Charlie Chaplin of Asia' by two Japanese film industry figures (Mahirin Binti Hassan, 1978: 78); obviously an honor, but the comparison is very misleading and is more appropriately applied to Raj Kapoor, who consciously modeled himself on Chaplin (Sahai, 1987). An equally powerful figure to P. Ramlee was the Tamil actor and sometime director, M. G. Ramachandran, fondly known as MGR, who dominated Tamil cinema and Tamil politics from the 1950's to the 1970's (Pandian, 1992). P. Ramlee was often encouraged to enter politics, but refused because he felt committed to his art (Mahirin Binti Hassan, 1978: 76). As a popular singer, who became a major star in melodramatic films, P. Ramlee is reminiscent of Zhou Xuan, the star of the Shanghaiese film STREET ANGEL and many subsequent films in Hong Kong. I mentioned earlier that he resembled the Egyptian songwriter/singer, Farid El Atrache, but P. Ramlee also directed many of the films in which he starred. Perhaps 'multi-skilling' was inevitable in a small-scale film industry, but the quality of his many contributions to each film makes him such an exceptional figure in cinema. P. Ramlee appeared in 63 films and directed 34 films, in only one of which he did not also star. He died in 1973 at the age of 44, probably already past his prime creative period in both the film and music industries.

The high regard in which he is still held today is demonstrated by the frequency with which his films are shown on Malaysian television and the inevitable reference to him when I mentioned my interest in Malaysian film to people in Malaysia. (Hamzah Hussin believes that P. Ramlee only became really popular after his death, *due to* the repeated screenings of his films on television (Hamzah Hussin, 2001). P. Ramlee's films are loved for their music and for their acute social analysis of the condition of the Malays, who were suddenly caught up in rapid social, political and cultural changes in the 1950's and 1960's. One can reasonably speak of a P. Ramlee industry that has 'exploded' in the last decade, including television specials (Zieman, 1997), hagiographies like Ahmad Sarji's book (1999), as well as the National Archives-run 'shrines': the P. Ramlee House in Penang (where he was born) and the P. Ramlee Memorial in Kuala Lumpur (where he lived for the last ten years of his life) – there are also streets named after P. Ramlee in both Penang and Kuala Lumpur.[20] For current filmmakers, P. Ramlee is rather a problematic figure, because general audiences and film producers alike want films with the popularity and universality of P. Ramlee's films, while also expecting contemporaneity and modernity (Raja Ahmad Alauddin, 1993).

Figure 10: The P. Ramlee House, Penang

However, P. Ramlee is not adulated by all; people like Hamzah Hussin downplay his esthetic and social contribution to Malaysian film, while acknowledging the impact of his songs (Hamzah Hussin, 1994b). Others, like the playwright Johan Jaaffar damn him with faint praise – admiring his versatility, while questioning his innovative ability (Johan Jaaffar, 1984). This has led to the valorization of Hussain Haniff, the director of HANG JEBAT, at the expense of P. Ramlee, with one critic labeling Hussain Haniff as 'Singapore's most revered director' (Cheah, 1997: 55).[21]

Hamzah Hussin, himself a major figure of the Singaporean Golden Age in both Malay literature and Malay film, insists on distinguishing between the importance of these two cultural forms. The literary community was overwhelmingly concerned with merdeka (independence) and with social issues, often expressed in quite 'leftist' terms. Film and popular culture in general were much less so; even P. Ramlee's films were not primarily or consciously about social issues (Hamzah Hussin, 1994b). There might be something of a high culture bias to his proposition and I will argue that P. Ramlee's films continued the same contradictory attitudes to social concerns as did the Indian films of the 1950's. Nevertheless, P. Ramlee, as well as many Malay writers, decided to return to Malaya after Independence in 1957. L. Krishnan, although not for the same reason, also left Singapore and together with Ho Ah Loke (an owner of Cathay-Keris) literally built Merdeka Studio on the outskirts of

Kuala Lumpur (Lent, 1990: 189). Merdeka Studio was active for twenty years and produced 89 films between 1960 and 1981, peaking in the early 1970's, but the output of the studio has always been rated well below that of the two Singaporean organizations. P. Ramlee himself did not move to Kuala Lumpur until 1964, but despite this bringing him 'closer' to his culture, his films there never achieved the popularity and cinematic glory of the Singapore days. In the 1950's, his films and those of other directors attracted multi-ethnic audiences and created an incorporative sense of 'Malaysianness' (the term is deliberately used ahead of its time) that has disappeared since; despite the repeated call by contemporary filmmakers for a *Malaysian* cinema, it is in reality a *Malay* cinema.

Indian Cinema

Indian films remained very popular with Malayan audiences in the 1950's, extending to the non-Indian Malaysian audiences, who enjoyed the songs and dances and recognized the obvious similarities to the locally made films, even though these films were neither subtitled nor dubbed into the Malay language. In general, audiences preferred Hindi films to Tamil films, because they were shorter, had less dialogue and more movement and spectacle, more melodious songs and more beautiful stars – their lighter skin-tones were considered more attractive (Krishnan, 1994a; 1994b). The preference for Hindi films was not confined to the Peninsula; it was also the case in India itself, the Indian diaspora and in other parts of Asia and Africa. Ravi Vasudevan discusses reasons other than those cited by L. Krishnan, including the Hindi films' construction of 'an overarching north Indian, majoritarian Hindu identity,' which simultaneously defined all else as 'other' (Vasudevan, 1995: 306). The Malaysian novelist, A. Samad Said, obviously very familiar with this cinema, discusses Hindi film stars like a true fan, pointing out the qualities of actors like Dilip Kumar, Raj Kapoor, Dev Anand, Nargis, Madhubala and Nimmi, noting the preponderance of suffering lovers and not averse to commenting on Nimmi's beauty (A. Samad Said, 1994: 203-205).[22] A more detailed discussion of the cultural and esthetic relationship between Hindi films and Malayan films will be undertaken in the next chapter.

Hong Kong Cinema

In order to remain conscious of the interconnections between the various film cultures, it is important to recognize that the Chinese businessmen who owned the two Singapore studios were also actively involved in the Hong Kong production scene. The Shaw brothers' Tianyi Film Company had been operative in Hong Kong since before the war and in the 1950's two Shaw studios were making Mandarin and Cantonese films there (Jarvie, 1977: 45). Run Run Shaw left Singapore in 1959 to form the Shaw Brothers Studio in Hong Kong. This was in response to Loke Wan Tho, one of the owners of Cathay-Keris, buying a studio in Hong Kong some years earlier; its films, mainly in Cantonese, were a major source of supply for the Southeast Asian market (Law, 1992b: 120). Shaw and Loke were thus competing in Hong Kong as well as in Malaya. It is even claimed that their rivalry saved the Mandarin cinema in Hong Kong from extinction (Teo, 1997a: 22). The Southeast Asian market, especially Singapore and Malaya was crucial to the Hong Kong film industry. Since its own domestic market was dominated by American films, it depended on overseas markets for its own survival. The Southeast Asian demand for Hong Kong films was so great that it contributed to the assembly-line production system developed there and referred to in chapter 1. Furthermore, this market also determined the sorts of genres that were being produced, e.g. the preference for romantic melodramas in Malaysia and Singapore, and martial arts films in Indonesia affected production decisions. (Leung and Chan, 1997: 144-145). Even the casting decisions for the extremely popular HUANG FEIHONG films were influenced by the opinions of the Chinese distributors in Singapore and Malaya (Rodriguez, 1997: 2). There were also films made specifically for the 'Nanyang' (lit. the Southern Ocean), the Chinese term for the Southeast Asian region (Andaya and Andaya, 1982: 17). These Nanyang films, with titles like SONG OF MALAYA (1954), LOVE IN PENANG (1954) and BLOOD STAINS THE VALLEY OF LOVE (1959), were family melodramas, dealing with the self-sacrificing woman, the weak man and, in the case of the last film, a love affair between a Chinese man and a Malay woman (Law, 1992a: 95, 96, 100, 101) – all themes that crop up in Malaysian films in the 1950's and 1960's. The Hong Kong based Shaw Brothers Studio also made at least one film in Singapore and Malaya: LOVE ON A LONELY BRIDGE (1959). The characters speak Cantonese, although with a local flavor, and the film is again a family melodrama, where an interfering mother destroys her daughter's love affair (Teo, 1997b). This level of attention to an overseas, although predominantly Chinese, market is quite remarkable for actually affecting the genres and the contents of films. Indian films never, to my knowledge, felt the economic or cultural need to do the same; nor in time did Hong Kong, which is now almost totally preoccupied with Greater China (Mainland China, Taiwan and Hong Kong), even though Southeast Asia remains a major market for these films (Law, 1992a: 95). The interaction between Hong Kong films and the Peninsular audiences is a powerful reminder of the complexity of a film culture, where a 'foreign' film industry is enmeshed in and dependent upon local exhibition networks (of course owned by Malayan and/or Hong Kong Chinese entrepreneurs) and local audiences (extending well beyond Chinese audiences).

While it has been argued that Hong Kong film had little direct influence on Malayan films in the 1950's and 1960's, unlike the Malayan influence on Hong Kong cinema discussed above, there is a marked similarity in the methods of interpolating songs in films, which is rather different from the Indian approach. The Mandarin melodramas made in Shanghai in the 1930's typically included songs and this tradition continued in the Mandarin musicals produced in Hong Kong in the post-war period. Most of the songs exist for their own sake and have rarely any links with the film's narrative (STREET ANGEL is a notable exception). Stephen Teo describes the songs as embodying the 'karaoke principle,' with the lyrics presented as subtitles to encourage audience participation (Teo, 1993: 32) – such subtitles are also present in Malay films of this period. In STREET ANGEL this is further accompanied by a 'bouncing ball' to encourage synchronization of response. The singer from that film, Zhou Xuan, was to become the leading exponent of the Mandarin melodrama musical, including the renowned SONG OF A SONGSTRESS (1948), which Teo labels an 'exploitation musical' for its inclusion of details of her own life (something that was also to occur in some of P. Ramlee's films).

The Cantonese opera film was one of the major genres of 1950's Hong Kong cinema and it replaced Cantonese opera for many of the same reasons that led to Bangsawan's disappearance in Malaya – by moving personnel (actors, directors, musicians, technicians), plots and stylistic elements from the theatrical form to film. Cantonese opera also influenced the martial arts films through gesture, movement and acrobatic spectacle (Li Cheuk-to, 1987). The Cantonese melodrama, which was very popular in Malaya and Singapore, similarly used Cantonese opera as a source of creative personnel, stories and conventions, once again reminiscent of the Bangsawan situation. Post-May Fourth Chinese literature and Hollywood melodrama also shaped the Cantonese melodrama: stereotypes include visual tropes such as thunder and lightning to signify danger and threat; ineffectual men, often artists and teachers; and the mother/son/wife triangle, in which the two women become rivals over the man (Law, 1986: 15-33) – many of these themes frequently cropped up in Malayan films as well. The songs in these films were as arbitrarily positioned in the narrative as those in the Mandarin melodrama musicals. In the Cantonese melodrama, WHEN BEAUTY FADES FROM THE TWELVE LADIES' BOWER (1954), the songs are minimally related to the story, rather abruptly inserted into the film, and performed in a declamatory way; there are altogether six songs lasting a quarter of the film's total running time. This is also the normal song quota of Malayan films, where the delivery is often directly to the audience (sometimes through an audience within the film). Despite the preference for melodramas, there were also other Hong Kong genres shown in the Peninsula. The horror films and vampire films were popular and did stimulate local production of similar films, although a film like P. Ramlee's SUMPAH ORANG MINYAK (Curse of the Oily Man, 1958) grafts horror elements onto a local fable and a typical melodrama of lost love. Martial arts films were equally loved, especially the HUANG FEIHONG series which started in 1948 and was revived in the early 1990's as the ONCE UPON A TIME IN CHINA series.

Indonesian Cinema

P. Ramlee's popularity as a film star in the 1950's extended beyond the Peninsula to Indonesia. It was an all too brief glimpse of a potentially huge market for Malayan films, but the Indonesians soon instituted a quota system, so that for every film from Malaya, three Indonesian films had to be shown in the Peninsula – this was at a time when Indonesian films had lost the popularity they once had in Malaysia during the 1930's. This protectionist policy has been the norm between the two countries and has severely limited the access of Malayan films to Indonesia (Baharudin Latif, 1989d). The studios tried other ways of ensuring distribution in Indonesia: bringing popular Indonesian actors and highly regarded directors like Usmar Ismail to Singapore (Raja Ahmad Alauddin, 1992: 84-85).

Salim Said is critical of Indonesian cinema of the 1950's for the opportunism of local producers, who were ready to make films in the 'Chinese style' (i.e. martial arts) and the 'Indian style' (i.e. melodrama and songs) if that was to increase their profits (Salim Said, 1991: 41-42, 101). The four Indonesian films of the 1950's that I have seen do have some elements of the 'Indian style,' but they are quite minimal compared to Malayan films of the same period. David Hanan has argued their cultural specificity (Hanan, 1992; 1997), but the films can also interestingly be related to other traditions. TIGA BURONAN (Three Fugitives, 1957, produced by Usmar Ismail) has a classical Hollywood style and something of the plot of westerns like HIGH NOON.[23] There is little that reminds of Malayan films, although the film does contain two songs, one that brings out the moral of the film ('stay within the law') and a rather unmotivated song about rice. The film does have a quite risqué scene between the protagonist and a local woman that would not have been possible in Malaya at that time. TAMU AGUNG (Exalted Guest, 1955, directed by Usmar Ismail) is imbued with the ideology of development, but is, at the same time, very critical of conflictual party politics, bribery and status; the 'exalted guest' is apparently a little-disguised caricature of President Sukarno (Sen, 1994: 40). These issues would never have been discussed so forthrightly in Malayan films and not even in contemporary Malaysian films, with the qualified exceptions of HATI

BUKAN KRISTAL (The Heart is not a Crystal, 1990) and RINGGIT KASORRGA (Playground, 1994). Usmar Ismail is often labeled 'the father of Indonesian cinema' and therefore might be seen as occupying a similar position as P. Ramlee. However, the comparison is not particularly useful: the singer/performer and sometime social critic P. Ramlee is far removed from the western-trained, strongly anti-leftist artist/producer and sometime entertainer Usmar Ismail (Sen, 1994: 38-39). Their differences are further accentuated by the political, social, cultural and film industry specificity of each country. HARIMAU TJAMPA (The Tiger from Tjampa, 1953) is a kampung-based revenge story, with a commentary provided by an off-screen group of unaccompanied male singers constantly repeating the refrain: 'What suffering life is!' The repressive authoritarianism of the village chief was recognized as a criticism of Indonesia's leadership (Hanan, 1997: 59). The Malayan film that most resembles it, SEMERAH PADI, presents the authoritarianism of its village chief much more positively. TJAMBUK API (Whipfire, 1958, produced by Usmar Ismail) details and perhaps exploits the whip culture of East Java to tell a revenge story (again a little like an American Western with whips replacing guns). There are a number of songs in the film and they do resemble the Indian and Malayan style of song construction. Of most interest is the portrayal of the brutal village chief's daughter as a very headstrong and independent woman; not until PEREMPUAN, ISTERI &... (1993) would a Malaysian film create such a figure. These examples highlight, once again, the distinctiveness of these two Malay cultures, despite the quite similar focus on kampung life in many of the films and despite the temporary interchange of film product in the 1950's.

The Decline

While the end of the studio era was previously given as 1977, the demise of MFP and Cathay-Keris occurred much earlier. MFP stopped making films in Singapore in 1967, while Cathay-Keris lingered on until 1972 (Baharudin Latif, 1989a: 46-47). The seeds for the decline had been sown years before. They include broad political/cultural reasons like Malayan independence in 1957, which gradually made Malayan filmmakers decide to leave Singapore, a fall in audience attendance due to the introduction of television to Malaya in 1963, and the failure of local films to remain relevant; the latter cause was accompanied by an increasing interest in Indonesian, Indian and Hong Kong films. The industry itself was attempting to cope with rising production costs and with major union disputes between the studios and the creative and technical staff (Baharudin Latif, 1989a: 46). As has often happened when a film industry is at a moment of crisis, MFP tried to spend its way out of trouble by making an expensive color and widescreen epic that would turn the tide. RAJA BERSIONG (The King with Fangs, 1968) cost RM 750,000, which was more than ten times the cost of the average film. The film was directed by Jamil Sulong and employed a Japanese crew, causing major production and communication problems (Hamzah Hussin, 1994a). Even though the story was written by Malaysia's first Prime Minister, Tunku Abdul Rahman, and was a nationalist epic set in northern Malaysia, the film failed at the box office (Jamil Sulong, 1994). A similar fate befell three other 'swan song' films made by MFP in the Malay language, but shot in Hong Kong. They were all made by Low Wai (Low Wei/Luo Wei), a Shaw Brothers director at the time, who was to direct Bruce Lee in THE BIG BOSS and FIST OF FURY, films that changed the face of Hong Kong and Southeast Asian film (and beyond). One of these Malay films was NORA ZAIN AGEN WANITA 001 (Nora Zain, Woman Agent 001, 1967), an example of the James Bond spy 'genre' that was sweeping the world and being re-invented everywhere, including Hollywood, Rome, Bombay and Hong Kong. Cathay-Keris continued to produce cheaply made, poor quality black-and-white films right to the end. AKU MAHU HIDUP (I Want to Live, 1970), a tawdry comedy/melodrama about prostitution and alcoholic excess, is an embarrassment to Hamzah Hussin, who was the film's script adviser (Hamzah Hussin, 1994a) – even its noirish lighting and shadow scenes (having Wayang overtones) cannot save it. Cathay-Keris films could no longer compete with the Indonesian films coming into Malaysia and eventually capitulated by importing and distributing them (Raja Ahmad Alauddin, 1992: 85).

P. Ramlee had left Singapore by 1964 to join Merdeka Studio, but his films there were not the successes, financially or esthetically, they once were. This seems ironic, given his and other Malay filmmakers' now closer proximity to Malay culture. However, times had changed and even P. Ramlee was no longer in tune with the region's socio-cultural priorities. Perhaps he also lost the creative edge that came from the close interaction within the filmmaking community in Singapore (Lockard, 1991: 22). His death in 1973 contributed to the end of Merdeka Studio in the following year (Fuziah Kartini Hassan Basri and Raja Ahmad Alauddin, 1995: 61). In 1966, the Shaw brothers took over Merdeka Studio, in effect moving their production base in the Peninsula from Singapore to Kuala Lumpur, but by the early 1970's their local films could no longer compete with their Hong Kong films or with the Indonesian films. Once again, Shaw tried to save the studio with an expensive color film, RAHSIA HATIKU (My Heart's Secret, 1974), based on *Little Women*, but the film was never released (Baharudin Latif, 1992: 9). Shaw held out for another three years, bringing Hong Kong production units to Kuala Lumpur to make most of the films, which were nominally directed by Jamil Sulong. Not surprisingly, a number of these films were copies of Hong Kong films of the late 1970's (Jamil Sulong, 1990: 267). The studio was bought by the Malaysian government to house the National Film Development Corporation Malaysia (FINAS) in 1985 (*Cintai Filem Malaysia*, 1989). The above changes graphically illustrate the increasing influence of Hong Kong cinema over the local film culture, at this stage most obviously in industry and audience preference terms, but when a new local industry took shape in the 1980's, also in generic and stylistic terms.

By the early 1970's, the demand for Malay language films was being met by Indonesia – their color and widescreen spectacles were attracting audiences away from the local product. The output of the Indonesian film industry exploded in the 1970's and genres such as Dangdut musicals (Indonesian popular music), mystic films, comedies and action films were as popular in Malaysia and Singapore as they were at home (Mohd. Kamsah Sirat, 1992: 89-90). The amazing success of the 1973 Raj Kapoor melodrama, BOBBY, only confirmed the continuing attraction of Hindi films for non-Indian Malaysian audiences (these films were not subtitled or dubbed) (Baharudin Latif, 1975: 266; 1992: 7). A Hong Kong film to more than match the popularity of BOBBY was THE BIG BOSS, the first of the Bruce Lee kung fu films; Hong Kong films were now becoming popular with non-Chinese Malaysians as well (Baharudin Latif, 1992: 7). English-language films continued to draw enthusiastic patrons from across the ethnic communities, ranging from James Bond films and Spaghetti Westerns (dubbed) in the early years to the beginning of the Lucas/Spielberg spectacles in the late 1970's; apart from an interest in western dramas by the middle classes, the preference was always for action films. The popularity of these very different films with Malaysian audiences was in stark contrast to the lack of enthusiasm for local films at this time. The years from the mid-1960's to the mid-1980's represent an intermediate stage, with one type of filmmaking disappearing (the studio system) and another replacing it (the bumiputera independents).

It is useful, however, to make some brief comments about Indian cinema and Hong Kong cinema during this period, when both film cultures transformed their cinematic traditions of the 1950's and early 1960's. In the Indian cinema, the tragic, passive Majnun hero-figure was being replaced by what Sudhir Kakar called the 'Krishna-lover,' who is anything but passive: 'an "eve-teasing" hero, whose initial contact with women verges on that of sexual harassment' (Kakar, 1990: 36). The reference is to Krishna as a mischievous lover constantly accosting the 'gopis' (cow-herdesses). The representative stars were Dev Anand and Shammi Kapoor (Raj Kapoor's younger brother) and the mood of the films was optimistic and saturated with the western popular culture iconography of the time. In an interesting article on some of Shammi Kapoor's films of the 1960's, Amit Rai speaks of the 'moment of the hybrid mimic,' where Elvis Presley is grafted to the Krishna trickster-figure and both are appropriated by the Shammi Kapoor persona (Rai, 1994: 65). BOBBY, made some ten years later, retains many of these characteristics: teenage love story with a happy ending and sixties 'pop' iconography, but returns to the 1950's tradition with its Majnun/Laila relationship characteristically located across a class divide. The obviously tacked-on happy ending was forced on Raj Kapoor by the distributors (Rajadhyaksha and Willemen, 1999: 416). Also released in 1973 was a film called ZANJEER, which starred Amitabh Bachchan as an avenging vigilante and introduced a new hero to the Indian cinema. Kakar labels Bachchan as a 'good-bad hero,' who lives outside the norms of society, but with a powerful private moral code; Kakar finds the origin of this hero-figure in the *Mahabharata*'s Karna, the illegitimate son of Kunti, the mother of the Pandava brothers (Kakar, 1990: 37-38). Bachchan epitomized this good-bad hero in his role as a criminal in DEEWAR (The Wall, 1975), in conflict with his policeman brother, and pining for a mother whom he cannot visit because of his life outside the law. His love relationship in the film is with a nightclub dancer, from whom he seeks admiration rather than love – the Bachchan lover is a withdrawn and unemotional lover (Kakar, 1990: 40). His love relationship with the landlord's widowed daughter in SHOLAY (discussed in chapter 1), is similarly distant and tragic. While some of the character elements of the Bachchan hero are evident in a few of the 1980's Malaysian films, they are minimal compared to the continuity of the Majnun figure.

Bachchan's fight scenes in DEEWAR are modeled on the Hong Kong action film (Rajadhyaksha and Willemen, 1999: 423) – perhaps one of the earliest such influences. It would certainly not be the last, as evidenced by the increasing use of kung fu-style scenes in 1980's and 1990's Indian action films. Hong Kong cinema in the 1960's was also to change, with the martial arts knight-errant hero taking on the more avenging aspects of the Italian Western (see chapter 1). The James Bond films were very popular in Hong Kong (and elsewhere), where FROM RUSSIA WITH LOVE (1963) broke all box office records in 1964. Characteristically, it immediately triggered a spate of Cantonese and Mandarin films about espionage (Ng Ho, 1983: 143). The most intriguing 'localized' manifestation of this was the *Jane* Bond films. As mentioned previously, the Cantonese melodrama and Mandarin melodrama musical were dominated by female characters, with the male being a weak, ineffectual and often sick person. Gradually in the 1960's, the Mandarin cinema 'rejuvenated the male hero,' particularly in the martial arts genre, whereas the Cantonese martial arts films continued to be the domain of the female hero (Sek Kei, 1996: 31-32). The Cantonese Jane Bond films were a contemporary example of this phenomenon. Typical of the saturation-and-replacement principle of filmmaking employed in Hong Kong, the cycle of films started in 1965, peaked in 1967, when it represented a third of the Cantonese output, and disappeared by 1971 (Sam Ho, 1996: 41). The emphasis was on action, but the Jane Bond character often had a relationship with a man, who always remained inferior to the heroine – thus maintaining the tradition of the weak male character in Cantonese cinema during this period. The Malaysian film referred to above as a James Bond type film, NORA ZAIN AGEN WANITA 001, is clearly an example of the Jane Bond cycle – not surprising, as it was made in Hong Kong in 1967 (but, of course, in Malay).

The decline of the Jane Bond films paralleled the decline of Cantonese cinema in general, as it was overwhelmed by the increasing domination of the Mandarin cinema, especially as epitomized by the Shaw Brothers Studio, which had improved technology (Shawscope), increased film budgets, pursued a star system (as they had in Singapore) and displayed the 'masculine heroism' of the martial arts films of Zhang Che/Chang Cheh, Shaw Brothers' premier director (Poshek Fu, 1997: 43-44). When Raymond Chow left Shaw Brothers in 1970 to form his own company, Golden Harvest, he developed a quite different organizational structure, but continued the improvements undertaken by Shaw Brothers. His first major hit was the kung fu film, THE BIG BOSS, directed by Low Wai and starring Bruce Lee. This was the first Hong Kong-made film to top the box office there, repeated the following year (1973) with first and second place (THE WAY OF THE DRAGON and FIST OF FURY) (Jarvie, 1977: 135-136); this started a trend that continued into the 1990's, although it is now in decline (Elley, 1998: 161). The impact of these films was enormous and initiated a kung fu cycle that is still evident today in the films of Jackie Chan (who combines martial arts with comedy). The Bruce Lee hero has something of the Bachchan rebel about him: an outsider, who deals with problems through his own resources and moral codes; a taciturn and withdrawn figure, for whom women are of negligible interest. Bruce Lee is the supreme example of the dominance of the male hero in Mandarin cinema, a tendency that permeated the Cantonese cinema in the 1980's and 1990's. The Malaysian actor/director, Jins Shamsuddin, performed in a number of Hong Kong Bond films in the 1960's, but the increasing masculinization of Hong Kong cinema is not particularly evident in the Malaysian films of the 1980's and beyond – the 'weak male' is still much more prevalent.

The Revival

Not surprisingly, the resurgence of the local industry originated in the post-1969 government policies, especially the National Economic Policy (NEP) of

1971 that intended to increase bumiputera equity control in all companies to 30%. In the film industry, the bumiputera companies began to appear in 1972 and were often set up by the filmmakers themselves. P. Ramlee, Jins Shamsuddin and others formed Perfima, which initially imported the still popular Indonesian films (Lent, 1990: 191), while the actor Samirah, her husband and Hamzah Hussin formed Sari Artis, later called Samirah Film Productions, which produced RANJAU SEPANJANG JALAN. Perfima survived P. Ramlee's death to become quite successful in the late 1970's by producing two of Jins Shamsuddin films. The breakthrough came in 1975, when a Sabah businessman, Deddy M. Borhan, produced, under the banner of Sabah Filem, KELUARGA SI CHOMAT (Comat's Family), a lightweight comedy in color and widescreen. It resulted in the return of local audiences to local films (Baharudin Latif, 1989b: 49) and demonstrated the possibility of film as a *Malay* business enterprise (Hamzah Hussin, 1994b). Others criticized these films as a tired blend of slapstick comedy and the Indian song and dance style (Mansor bin Puteh, 1990: 4). Nevertheless, finance became more readily available, stimulating the proliferation of bumiputera production companies, new directors and a level of production by 1982 not seen since the mid-1960's. However, the bumiputera 'assault' on the film industry did not extend to the exhibition sector, which remained under the control of Cathay and Shaw Brothers, making the release of local films in good quality cinemas very difficult. This changed to some extent, when first Cathay and later Shaw sold part of their equity to bumiputera companies (Lee, 1979).

Government Assistance and Controls

In 1976, the government decreed that all non-Malay films have Bahasa Melayu subtitles as a 'contribution to national unity and nation-building efforts' (quoted in Lent, 1990: 193). Furthermore, a few years earlier, a task force was set up to consider ways of protecting the industry; after years of investigation, indecision and industry pressure, a National Film Development Corporation (FINAS) was established in 1981 to encourage the development of the local industry and 'ensure that a sizeable portion of the total volume of business done in the production, distribution and exhibition sectors would be handled by Malays' (Baharudin Latif, 1981: 199). FINAS has always been regarded as a mixed blessing by industry people, providing support and training, but also hopelessly inadequate to the task of efficiently aiding a fragile and very commercial film industry (Ruhani Abdul Rahman, 1994 and 2001). Criticism also extended to the limited competition inherent in the new environment, leading to a lack of creativity and a sloppiness in scripting and pre-production (*New Straits Times*, 1986; Raja Ahmad Alauddin, 1994a). Some indeed wish to see the return of a vertically integrated industry to motivate exhibitors (still predominantly Chinese Malaysians) to screen locally made films (Krishnan, 1994b), while others hope for a government or privately funded scheme to stimulate an alternative cinema movement (Hamzah Hussin, 1994a).[24] Many of these debates have continued throughout the 1990's without being formally addressed by the industry. Even the National Film Policy, launched in 1997, but not activated due to the Malaysian financial downturn at the time, has had little impact.

The 1980's and 1990's saw the introduction of new directors into the industry, many having been trained overseas in the USA, England and India and very critical of the 'old' Malaysian cinema (Mansor bin Puteh, 1989-90: 33). Othman Hafsham, one of these young directors, loudly rejected the Hindi tradition with its 'wide angles, static shots, overacting, verbose scripts and song-and-dance numbers' (quoted in Lent, 1990: 199), advocating realism rather than melodrama – the latter remaining the preferred approach of the 'old guard' still making films (Baharudin Latif, 1989b: 51). I will argue in the next chapter that melodrama has continued as the dominant mode of expression, irrespective of any polemical old guard/new wave distinctions. During the 1980's, women became more active in film directing; Rosnani Jamil, an actor in films since the early 1950's, directed the first film by a woman in 1986 – her film MAWAR MERAH (Red Rose) is highly regarded and she continued to make films in the 1990's. Things were more difficult in previous decades – when in 1962 the actor Siput Sarawak wanted to direct a film from her own script, the studio, Cathay-Keris, agreed, but the film-workers union objected. Hussain Haniff eventually directed the film, having said that 'women are not qualified to direct'; Siput Sarawak was credited as adviser and scriptwriter, but she disowned the film, MATA SHAITAN (Eye of Satan), for its debasement of women (Rohani Mat Saman, 1989: 103). The best-known contemporary woman director is Shuhaimi Baba, one of whose films will be discussed in the next chapter.

FINAS is the central government organization for the film industry. At its Hulu Kelang site, it manages the Merdeka Studio Complex, consisting of post-production facilities, an equipment rental service and the Malaysian Film Academy. More generally, it runs incentive schemes that provide financial assistance to film companies and individuals: the Entertainment Tax Rebate Scheme and the Compulsory Screening Condition arrangement. FINAS also provides policy advice to the government. The Malaysian Film Academy conducts short training courses for industry and formal courses for individuals wanting to become filmmakers, with the best graduates then sent overseas for further study (Abdul Rahman, 1993). By far the most important (and controversial) functions of FINAS relate to the Entertainment Tax and the Compulsory Screening regulation. The Entertainment Tax Scheme requires 30% of box

Figure 11: FINAS, Hulu Kelang

office receipts of all films screened in Malaysia to be collected by state governments for FINAS, which returns 25% to a film's producer. This is an important system of industry support, often enabling films to make a profit as long as they are reasonably popular. The Compulsory Screening Condition is meant to give all local films a chance of some success by regulating that the films must be shown for at least seven consecutive days in the major cities and three in the smaller centers. If the film's takings exceed the 'hold-over' figure (i.e. a threshold amount per day), it must continue to be shown until it drops below that amount. Larger and more successful producers complain about FINAS' incompetence in monitoring and collecting the tax (state governments want to retain the money themselves) and criticize the Screening Condition, while others insist on their importance for the survival of the Malaysian cinema (Ruhani Abdul Rahman, 1994). It is clear that the industry is dependent on these support mechanisms, which fuel the commercialism of film production and can provide companies minimally interested in film with reasonable financial returns. A further criticism of FINAS is its control over the release dates of Malaysian films, which can occur months after their completion date. The demand by producers for attractive opening dates like school holidays and feast days cannot be met, given the limited exhibition outlets (Ruhani Abdul Rahman, 1994).

The control over the film industry further extends to censorship, which has continued to operate under the guidelines initially developed by the British, and based on the 'colonial service model' discussed earlier in this chapter, which presumes and enforces the role of cinema (and of the media in general) as arms of government. Hence, films are censored or banned if they oppose government policy or encourage anti-government feeling; glorify communism and socialism; glorify any particular race while denigrating others; glorify crime and immorality; deal with sadism, cruelty and excessive violence; insult 'public dignity'; and show behavior not acceptable to Malaysian society (Mohd Hamdan bin Haji Adnan, 1991: 65). The harshness of the regulations and of their enforcement encourages directors and producers to engage in self-censorship. It is certainly noticeable that films rarely approach any of the prohibitions listed above; if they do, as in RINGGIT KASORRGA with its themes of political corruption and sexual power play, the attack is suitably muted. Perhaps the most notorious censorship case of recent years was that of the film FANTASI, made in 1992, but not released until 1994, after certain changes were forced upon the filmmakers. The film deviated from Islamic teaching in its theme of reincarnation – a theme perfectly acceptable to the non-Muslim Malaysian community. Raja Ahmad Alauddin considers the ban as another instance of the insularity of the authorities and their failure to recognize the multiple identities of the Malaysian people (Raja Ahmad Alauddin, 1994a). Three years later, a film called AMOK (1995), was banned for being 'un-Islamic and not in keeping with the Malay culture,' because of its spiritualism, sex and violence; the ban was subsequently lifted by Dr Mahathir Mohamad himself, but the compulsory removal of ten minutes of footage made the film incomprehensible, resulting in a financial disaster (Ruhani Abdul Rahman, 2001). The effect of such scenarios is to drive filmmakers back to the safe middle ground of teen comedies and romances.

The censorship controversy surrounding Steven Spielberg's film SCHINDLER'S LIST (1993) is even more intriguing; the film was originally banned because of its 'over-zealous sympathy towards the victimised Jews' (Baharudin Latif, 1994c: 256). The anti-Zionist policies and rhetoric of the Malaysian government make this actually an unremarkable decision (television news in Malaysia refers to Israel as the 'Tel Aviv Regime'). However, the international outcry over the reason for the ban led Cabinet to overturn the Censorship Board's decision. Perversely, the film is still banned because Spielberg refused to remove scenes depicting sex and nudity as subsequently demanded by the censor. Equally paradoxical is the fact that the films of Steven Spielberg (himself a Jew) are probably the most popular western films shown in Malaysia (Baharudin Latif, 1994c: 256). Despite this example, it has been suggested that the Censorship Board is not primarily concerned with Hollywood films, which are after all western and therefore 'other,' but with Hong Kong films, especially those dealing with ethnic tensions. The target group is the young, Malaysian-born Chinese, and the fear is that they may develop a longing for their 'homeland' (Baharudin Latif, 1993b). This implicit lack of loyalty by the Chinese Malaysians to Malaysia was voiced by a number of people to whom I spoke (Samsuddin Rahim, 1994; Hamzah Hussin, 1994a).

The question of the cultural identity of Malaysian film is a constant issue, even for the least culturally minded film producer, since it is related to the need to attract a broad-spectrum audience. It is still the case that more than 90% of the audience for Malaysian films is Malay and that 'cinema is probably the most racially segregated activity in the country today' (Mansor bin Puteh, 1990: 6). The one exception universally mentioned was MEKANIK, directed by Othman Hafsham, which was a popular and critical success. Kee Thuan Chye, while acknowledging a certain triteness to the film, claimed it as 'a film for all Malaysians,' not 'completely in Bahasa Malaysia or peopled mainly by Malays' (Kee Thuan Chye, 1992: 133). The film did not start a trend – everyone may want a Malaysian cinema, but then acknowledges that what exists is a Malay cinema, one which Chinese and Indian Malaysians rarely sample. This is contrary to the experience of the music industry, which has developed a non-Malay audience and provided opportunities for non-Malays as performers, songwriters and producers (Lockard, 1995: 17-18). There are a few Indian-Malaysian mainstream producers and directors, e.g. Pansha, who produced PEREMPUAN, ISTERI &... and directed SUAMI, ISTERI DAN...? (Husband, Wife and...? in 1996), but most Chinese and Indian-Malaysian directors work on the margins of the industry or in television. FINAS itself continues to implore Malaysians to watch local films, in order to ensure industry economic viability and as 'one of the vital instruments for national unity' (*Suara FINAS*, 1992).

The events of the late 1990's have not been kind to the Malaysian cinema. The Asian financial crisis virtually crippled the film industry in 1997 and 1998. Since then there has been some improvement in box office takings, but film production is the lowest since 1979. In fact, the problems are more systemic than the above comments suggest. Most films fail at the box office; since 1995, only two directors have been able to entice Malay audiences to the cinema: Aziz Osman and Yusof Haslam, whose teen comedies and teen melodramas, starring pop singers and models, have become more and more formulaic. The serialization of their films is evident from their titles and stem from their commercial successes in the early 1990's: Aziz Osman's XX RAY, led to XX RAY II

(1995), PUTERI IMPIAN (Dream Princess, 1997), PUTERI IMPIAN II (1998), SENARIO THE MOVIE (1999) and SENARIO LAGI (Senario Again, 2000), while Yusof Haslam's SEMBILU was quickly followed by SEMBILU II (1995), MARIA MARIANA (1996) and MARIA MARIANA II (1998). The influence of SEMBILU can be seen in Yusof Haslam's own films, in Aziz Osman's PUTERI IMPIAN series, but also in IMPI MOON (Moon's Dream, 2000), made by Shuhaimi Baba, considered a director of serious (called 'heavy drama') films (IMPI MOON was a box office disaster). In this climate, Barahudin Latif's call for the return of Chinese and Indian entrepreneurs to the film industry to provide 'level headed business acumen' and attract audiences 'back into the cinemas to watch Malay [sic] films' is driven by more than a nostalgia for the studio era (Baharudin Latif, 2000: 143).

Ever since the foundation of ASEAN in 1967, there have been attempts at co-productions between some or all of the film industries, but nothing came of them (Raja Ahmad Alauddin, 1992: 86). Finally in 1989, a number of films were completed, one of the most popular of which was IRISAN-IRISAN HATI (Shreds of the Heart), directed by an Indonesian with Malaysian and Indonesian actors. The film is set during the 'Konfrontasi' (confrontation) between the two countries in 1964, but re-affirms the connections between the two cultures through a love story of an Indonesian soldier and a Malaysian woman (Lim, 1989: 212). While the co-productions were enthusiastically welcomed by the Malaysian film industry, hoping for another opportunity to 'crack' the Indonesian market, the Indonesian perspective was more pragmatic about the gains for its own industry: 'Joint productions with Malaysia caused no problems since the major roles in the films were generally assigned to Indonesians' (Salim Said, 1991: 127).

Popular Indonesian cinema continued to produce musicals, comedies, horror films and teenage films, many of which were exported to Malaysia and available in video stores, although the audiences for the films are now mainly limited to Indonesians working in Malaysia (Baharudin Latif, 1994a). Indonesian 'art' films have difficulty finding an audience in Malaysia, but they are highly regarded by a number of local filmmakers like Raja Ahmad Alauddin and U-Wei Haji Shaari;[25] directors like Teguy Karya and Slamet Rahardjo Djarot are envied and admired for making films that could never attract business or audience interest in Malaysia (Raja Ahmad Alauddin, 1994a). Some of these films also confirm that, unlike in Malaysia, the Wayang tradition is still relevant to cinematic exploration: TJOET NJA' DHIEN (Eros Djarot, 1989) structurally resembles the Wayang narratives discussed in the previous chapter and frequently employs back lighting to create shadow effects (as does Ami Priyoni's 1983 'Laila Majnun' film RORO MENDUT). Ironically, the Indonesian film industry has almost totally collapsed in recent years, due to the lifting of import restrictions on foreign films. This policy has favored American films, but not, as far as I am aware, Malaysian films, despite them finally gaining unimpeded access. The relationship between the two cultures remains an 'uncomfortable one, like that of older to younger brother' (Raja Ahmad Alauddin, 1994a). I encountered two views of Indonesia in my discussions with Malaysians, views that say more about Malaysia than about Indonesia: a Malay-Malaysian envy of Indonesian racial integration and its single language; an Indian-Malaysian perspective that Indonesia, because of the longer and stronger influence of Hinduism, was less strictly Islamic than Malaysia. Both represent a nostalgia and, of course, an idealization, although sadly they are quite diametrically opposed to each other.[26]

Hong Kong Cinema

The Hong Kong influence is increasingly eclipsing the Indian moon, which for so long graced the love scenes in Malaysian films. Malay martial arts, such as silat, have been present in Malaysian films since the 1950's, but, stimulated by the popularity of the Bruce Lee films of the 1970's, they have become more like kung fu, even in Malay historical programs, such as the television series TUAH AND JEBAT (1994). Aziz Osman believes that Malaysian actors learn their acting style from Hong Kong films (Aziz Osman, 1994) as, in the 1950's, they had imitated Raj Kapoor, Dilip Kumar and other Indian actors (Jamil Sulong, 1990: 21). Films like FANTASI and XX RAY contain special effects reminiscent of Hong Kong martial arts films (the special effects were actually produced in Hong Kong). Often, the Hong Kong influence operates at the superficial level of stylistic 'tics' – special effects, slow motion violence and the staging of action scenes.[27] There has also been an increased use by Hong Kong producers of Malaysia as a location for Cantonese language films and television series (Chin, 1989; Lim, 1993: 27). This trend extends to Southeast Asia in general, but treats the region, the Nanyang, in a quite different way from its representation in the 1950's films discussed previously. Probably starting with THE BIG BOSS, Southeast Asia becomes Hong Kong cinema's 'Dark Continent – a world of barbaric, ominous happenings,' epitomized by a series of jungle witchcraft films of the early 1980's (Li Cheuk-to, 1989: 94), but also evident in 'Vietnam war' films like Ann Hui's BOAT PEOPLE (1982)[28] and Tsui Hark's A BETTER TOMORROW III: LOVE AND DEATH IN SAIGON (1989).

Hong Kong has increasingly dominated the box office takings of Malaysian cinemas – in 1992 the ten top grossing films in Malaysia were all from Hong Kong, indicating the strong similarity between Malaysian and Hong Kong audience tastes (Baharudin Latif, 1993a: 242). This can be partly explained by the large Chinese Malaysian proportion of the population, but Chinese Malaysians are also more inveterate filmgoers than any other group in Malaysia (and wealthier as a group), making up an even larger proportion of the total film audience – an early 1980's survey put the figure at 70% (Mohd. Hamdan Hj. Adnan, 1988: 158). However, the non-Chinese, especially the young, are equally attracted to this action-oriented cinema, where subtitle reading needs be no more than an intermittent chore. A similar attitude draws these Malaysians to the Hong Kong-like American films like RAMBO III (1988), TERMINATOR 2 (1991), SPEED (1994) and TITANIC (1997), with their mix of action, spectacle and special effects. It is also worth noting that the top grossing film in Malaysia in 1994 was SEMBILU – a teen melodrama that has little to do with the Hong Kong style, although its fight scenes are certainly Hong Kong-influenced (Baharudin Latif, 1995: 240). Despite the generalization made, this film is still the faithful descendant of 1950's Hindi and Malayan films.

Hong Kong cinema's recent obsession with its own destiny, its relationship with the other Chinas and a related nostalgic tendency has led to an 'inwardlookingness' that seems to counter its popularity outside of Greater China: 'it has finally found a worthy subject – it has found Hong Kong itself as a subject' (Abbas, 1997: 23).[29] Yet the films retain an abstractness and a stylistic verve that allows them to remain 'readable' beyond their local context, much as the American cinema has always been. This is not always the case though; when I saw 92 LEGENDARY LA ROSE NOIRE (1992) for the first time, it was extremely difficult to make sense of an obviously intricate reference system. Only later did it become clear that the film was a nostalgic parody of Cantonese films of the 1960's, with title and content alluding to the first of the Jane Bond films, THE BLACK ROSE (1965) (Sam Ho, 1996: 46). Tsui Hark's THE LOVERS (1994) invokes the Mandarin musicals of the 1960's in a similar fashion. Even the action films that are popular beyond Hong Kong entertain such a nostalgic perspective, e.g. the 1982 Jackie Chan film, PROJECT A's mythical recreation of early British Hong Kong and Tsui Hark's ONCE UPON A TIME IN CHINA series, which revived the HUANG FEIHONG series of films of the 1950's and 1960's. In light of the earlier discussion of Hong Kong cinema, perhaps the most interesting instance of the nostalgic mode is the reconnection to Shanghai and to the Shanghai cinema of the 1920's and 1930's that was broken after the demise of the Shanghai-born Hong Kong filmmakers. Tsui Hark's SHANGHAI BLUES (1984) resurrects the musical melodramas exemplified by STREET ANGEL, while Stanley Kwan's CENTER STAGE (1991) is an innovative biography of the life of Shanghai's most famous film star, Ruan Lingyu, with Maggie Cheung recreating the role and also commenting on it from a contemporary perspective. A more popular film, AU REVOIR, MON AMOUR (1991), starring Anita Mui as a 'sing-song girl,' is 'an hommage to Shanghai, exploiting as it does, all the generic signs and conventions associated with Shanghai films'

(Teo, 1994: 24).³⁰ This nostalgic 'turn' shows no sign of abating, despite the return of Hong Kong to China in 1997 and the difficulties experienced by the film industry over the last five years. Wong Kar-wai's recent critical and commercial success, IN THE MOOD FOR LOVE (2000), 'reverberates with muted nostalgia for Hong Kong's elegant Golden Age [the 1960's], while [affirming] Hong Kong's propensity for overcoming adversity and withstanding loss' (Teo, 2000a: 13).

Indian Cinema

Indian cinema has not (yet?) received the international attention of Hong Kong films, although it is largely the male-dominated Hong Kong films of Jackie Chan, John Woo and Ringo Lam that have become popular in the West. However, it is exactly this sort of film that has become the staple of Indian cinema, triggered by the direction in which Amitabh Bachchan's protagonists took Indian film. Already in DEEWAR, the emotional commitment and loyalty of the Bachchan character were not to a woman, but to family and friend: 'Shashi Kapoor, who played the hero's brother or best friend in many movies, came to be popularly known as Amitabh Bachchan's favorite heroine!' (Kakar, 1990: 40). Gradually, Bachchan became a self-conscious 'text,' repeating and refining his persona until it became a parody of itself and a metatext.³¹ His 1990 film AGNEEPATH (Path of Fire), a typical revenge action film, contains scenes where the shooting of the protagonist causes riots in the streets of Bombay, until his recovery is announced. This replicates the events surrounding Bachchan's accident during the shooting of COOLIE (1983), when he almost died (Sharma, 1993: 178) – the country came to a halt, Indira Gandhi visited him in the hospital and many people offered to give their lives for his. Bachchan's 'offspring,' such as Anil Kapoor and Sunny Deol have maintained and even accentuated the 'spectatorial fascination with the male body in action' (Vasudevan, 1992: 5).

Indian films continue to be shown in Malaysia and remain attractive because of their emphasis on success through action and commitment – Hamzah Hussin cites this as a reason for the popularity of COOLIE in the 1980's and also for the revival of interest in Tamil films (Hamzah Hussin, 1994a). The latter phenomenon is most likely due to the films made by Mani Ratnam in the 1990's, which, unusually for Tamil films, were shown widely in India typically being dubbed into Hindi. Their popularity derives to a large extent from their stylishness and fast-paced editing. ROJA (The Fast, 1992) became controversial because of its intimations of Hindu nationalism, especially in the wake of the destruction of the Babri Mosque at Ayodhya by Hindu fundamentalists. The Tamil hero is sent to Kashmir, where he is captured and tortured by a band of pro-Islamic terrorists (Rajadhyaksha, 1996: 688-689). The film's success in Malaysia suggests on one level a lack of interest in the anti-Muslim message of the film in favor of its spectacle and music, and on another level a nostalgic nationalism within the Indian diaspora. In an interesting echo of the significance of the overseas market for the survival of Hong Kong films, Hindi and Tamil films are becoming more and more dependent on overseas returns. This is likely to result in the production of films that are attractive to overseas Indian audiences (much as Southeast Asian audiences shaped the star and genre characteristics of Hong Kong films) – it appears that romance and family genre films, like KUCH KUCH HOTA HAI (A Certain Feeling, 1998), are particularly favored outside of India (Vasudevan, 2000b: 124). Certainly KUCH KUCH HOTA HAI was very successful in Malaysia at a time when Malay films were failing at the box office (Baharudin Latif, 2000: 143).

Conclusion

This discussion of film in Malaysia has been undertaken in the context of the debates on national cinema presented at the beginning of this chapter. The adoption of headings like 'Origins,' 'The Golden Age,' 'The Decline' and 'The Revival' to chart the history of this film culture is an ironic reference to the archetypal national cinema discourse mentioned in chapter 1. By employing these labels, I have inevitably forced the discussion into the 'straight jacket' of national cinema periodization, but only to further emphasize the inevitably multiple and continuing connections and interactions between film (or any other) cultures that always defeat any attempted reductionism.

Malaysian film has always been incorporative, based on the interaction of Malayan, Indian, Chinese and other film cultures, which themselves are shaped and reshaped by various influences. Malaysian film is heterogeneous and hybrid because of all these influences and because of the presence of other filmic and cultural traditions within the country. The chapter's repeated discussion of Indian, Chinese and Indonesian cinema alongside Malaysian film strives to demonstrate an interdependence that is rarely recognized in national cinema discourse. The cultural borders are not rigidly national and not focused on uniqueness or distinctiveness; instead, the borders allow the negotiation between the cross-cultural and the intra-national, engaging issues like ethnicity, religion and gender to construct notions of cultural identities. Like the previous chapter, this chapter has highlighted the complex 'lines of connectedness' that have existed throughout Malaysian cultural history, despite formal and informal attempts to constrain its heterogeneity. Indian and

Chinese/Hong Kong films have continued to attract audiences within the country, even if the emphasis has shifted more to the latter since the 1970's. However, Malaysian films themselves have remained remarkably 'faithful' to Indian cinematic traditions, despite the country's more general re-orientation from the West to the East, exemplified by the government's 1982 'Look East Policy,' which proposed that Malaysia's economic development be modeled on countries like Japan. These Malaysian films, a selection of which will be examined in detail in the next chapter, exhibit extensive cultural and stylistic 'lines of connectedness', but, paradoxically, apply these inclusive characteristics to a largely exclusive perspective – that of the Malays, as actors/characters on the screen and spectators in the cinemas. This tension between 'Malayness' and 'Malaysianness' – a recurrent theme in the preceding chapters – remains the core 'problematic' of cultural identity, and may well be the most productive definition of that cultural identity.

4 Malaysian Cinema

> 'Are Malay films for the Malays only?'
> (Film Forum topic, quoted in Zainal Alam Kadir, 1996).

> 'Is [a Malay film] a film with *jiwa Melayu*
> (Malay in spirit) or merely a film in *Bahasa Melayu*?'
> (Mahadi J. Murat, film director and invited forum panelist, quoted in Zainal Alam Kadir, 1996).

Introduction

It may have been noticeable that there was only minimal discussion of specific Malaysian films in the previous chapter, except for the peculiar case of LAILA MAJNUN. This chapter remedies that situation by presenting detailed analyses of a number of films made in Malaysia, not in order to fill a void seemingly made invisible by the presence of imported films, nor to now focus upon the 'center' – the Malaysian national cinema. It is precisely the notion of a center that is being rejected, since it presumes a nationally circumscribed cinematic identity, defined through unique thematic and formal characteristics. On the contrary, a specified cinema, like Malaysian cinema, is constructed from the interaction of cultural forces in that particular location and expressed in the films through issues such as ethnicity, religion, gender, tradition/modernity, intra- and international migration and esthetic options such as narrative voice, stylistic exposition and generic characteristics – cultural and film analysis perspectives that will be applied to the group of films that follow these introductory comments.

This chapter emphasizes the cultural specificity of films in their interplay with local and other cultural forces. In other words, the intention is to consider how the films 'speak of, around and beside the nation' rather than how the nation 'speaks the films' or even how the films 'speak the nation.' The films are discussed chronologically – this approach has the danger of constructing a teleological argument about national cinema's triumph in the face of adversity and the inevitable progression towards cinematic excellence. However, a diachronic perspective does allow the tracking of influences and their persistence or abandonment – this will be graphically illustrated in the intertextual relationship that exists between the first film discussed in this chapter, HUJAN

PANAS (1953) and the last, SEMBILU (1994). 'Lines of connectedness' run through the films and link them to the cultural and filmic traditions that were discussed in previous chapters.

Thirty feature films were selected as a sample of the output of the Malaysian film industry.[1] The choice of films was actually quite limited, being dependent upon the video holdings of a number of government and commercial sources – the Film Archive, located within the National Archives of Malaysia, does not hold copies of feature films.[2] Nevertheless, an early decision was made to cover a fairly broad historical range, while also attempting to include films considered significant or representative by film critics and industry figures. This was not achieved as easily as it might appear, due to the scarcity of documentation about Malaysian films in English. However, the selected films include nine of the ten films Baharudin Latif nominated as his Centenary (1895-1995) 'Ten Best Malaysian Films' (Baharudin Latif, 1995: 238).[3] This might seem like an investment in the 'canon' and, to an extent, it is recognition of the currency of these films within Malaysian film culture (implicit in the fact that the above organizations held or sold these particular titles). More importantly, the films come from the 'Golden Age' and the 'Revival' periods constructed in the last chapter. The exception, GERIMIS (Drizzles, 1968), was made at the height of the 'Decline' period, but is really a very late, if unrepresentative, example of the 'Golden Age.' Once again, my focus on the conventionally recognized high points of local filmmaking was not planned, but it was inevitable given the status of those periods, just as it was not surprising that films from the 'Decline' period were difficult to find. The generic categorization is particularly interesting. Despite the temporal difference between the two eras, most films from both the 1950's/60's and the 1980's/90's are urban or rural melodramas. Of the selected films, only eleven will be examined in any detail – these represent influential and culturally significant works of Malaysian cinema and also confront the arguments of this book most directly. A number of the other films will be included in the discussion to the extent that they confirm or qualify the arguments.

The Indian Cinema of the 1950's

As is apparent from the list of selected films, the predominant genre in Malaysian cinema is melodrama. Though perhaps its pervasiveness signals the inappropriateness of identifying melodrama as a genre; it might be more productive to suggest that melodrama is a supra-generic mode of address within which particular genres operate. This overarching view of melodrama has also been applied to the popular Indian cinema (Thomas, 1987: 303-305). This cinema in many respects literalizes the original meaning of the term 'melodrama' – music drama – to a greater extent than other cinematic traditions do. The combination of Indian traditional performance modes employing music and dance (village theater forms like Kathakali, Ramlila and puppet theater)[4] with European theatrical (narrative) forms (Shakespeare, Victorian melodrama) became the basis of Parsee theater and later Indian film, especially the 'All-Indian' Hindi film. This heritage has influenced the form of this melodramatic mode of address: loosely structured, digressive narratives, where cause/effect, realism and psychological motivation are of minimal concern, while music and dance as spectacle and the emotional involvement of the audience are of paramount importance.[5]

The melodrama is organized around a clearly defined good/evil dichotomy, which requires a conclusion of 'moral ordering' rather than narrative resolution (Thomas, 1995: 163); the narrational strategies of suspense and surprise have little relevance in such a structure. Good is typically associated with tradition and resides in family obligations, epitomized by the archetype of the Mother, with the mother-son relationship overshadowing all other family links. The Mother figure draws on the character of Sita in the *Ramayana* and includes references to her sons, her absent husband (Rama), the ordeals (including fire) she has to undergo and her acceptance of her fate. The personification of evil is, of course, her polar opposite, the Villain, who disregards family and fate, while indulging in lechery, brutality, smoking and drinking (signifiers of the West) – the mythical reference is to Ravana, the 'foreigner' who abducted Sita. Thomas suggests that the hero is positioned between these two poles and must resolve his attraction to both by finally upholding the moral order (Thomas, 1995: 168-173).

This broad melodramatic form is employed in a range of genres, such as mythologicals, historical films, stunt films, fantasy films and, of immediate interest, 'socials.' Socials are films that deal with contemporary life, often identifying the conflict of negotiating family and modernity as a crisis for the protagonist, who may or may not succeed in that enterprise. The social films of the 1950's are probably the high point of this genre as represented by the films of Mehboob Khan, Bimal Roy, Raj Kapoor and Guru Dutt – an article on their films is not surprisingly called 'The Great Four of the Golden Fifties' (Masud, 1995). Music is ever present in Indian melodrama, even in the socials and these same directors are also considered to have raised the art of 'song picturization' to a level not seen again in Indian cinema; the compulsory songs were visualized to illuminate the themes and emotions of the films and not necessarily to function as a component of narrative drive – more the case with Hollywood musicals (Chatterjee, 1995: 197-198).

The male protagonist of Hindi films in the 1950's was characterized by Sudhir Kakar as a 'Majnun-lover' (see chapter 3), but in the 1950's social melodramas, this renouncer-hero[6] is more specifically embodied in the figure of Devdas. Devdas was the protagonist of a popular Bengali novel of the same name, written in the 1910's, and the character came to signify romantic obsession and failure, having an almost morbid fascination with loss, the beloved, the mother, childhood and home (Vasudevan, 1994: 103).[7] The figure of Devdas was popularized in a celebrated 1935 film, which was remade in 1955 when it was directed by Bimal Roy and starred Dilip Kumar, who had already played a number of Devdas-like roles in earlier films, such as ANDAZ (A Matter of Style, 1949). The Devdas renouncer-hero recurs throughout 1950's Hindi films like DEEDAR (Sight, 1951) also with Dilip Kumar, but the figure is reformulated in Guru Dutt's PYAASA (The Thirsty One, 1957). Whereas Devdas was a weak, narcissistic hero, Vijay in PYAASA renounces the world because of his disgust for it (his final song talks of a society that is the enemy of man), and his desire for a new world with his beloved, the prostitute Gulab. Dutt's next film, KAAGAZ KE PHOOL (Pale Flowers, 1959), incorporates the Devdas theme overtly into the film by having a film director, Suresh, working on a new version of *Devdas*; it soon becomes clear that Suresh is himself a Devdas figure, crippled by an inability to act, destined, as he says in the film, to carrying 'the burden of countless worries.'

The complementary protagonist to the Devdas figure in 1950's Hindi cinema is the hero who negotiates a place in society (Vasudevan, 1994: 97) through a resolution of his doubtful genealogy, a crucial issue in a cinema and a culture that is obsessed by kinship ties. The archetypal example is Raj Kapoor's AWARA, in which the hero, Raj, lives with his mother in a slum area, while the heroine, Rita, and her father (although he is in fact only her guardian, since he is actually Raj's father) reside in a sumptuous two-story house – such single parent (often of the opposite gender to the offspring) pairings are extremely common in Indian and Malaysian cinema, as is the implied class contrast. In AWARA, both women (the mother and the heroine) eventually sacrifice themselves to enable the reunion between father and son to occur – the film's Majnun/Laila story is thus transformed into a moral tale of patriarchal power. The film sets up a pseudo-class division between hero and heroine (pseudo, because Raj is actually the son of a judge), with Raj involved in crime to support his mother, who was ejected from the judge's house at the beginning of the film for a presumed liaison with a criminal, echoing the *Ramayana*'s Rama/Sita/Ravana relationship. The film's message about the social basis of poverty and crime is set in counterpoint to an equally insistent biological determinism in the figure of the criminal, who becomes the incarnation of evil in the film.

The formal strategies of these films were derived from the Hollywood continuity system, so elaborately analyzed by David Bordwell in *The Classical Hollywood Cinema* (Bordwell, Staiger and Thompson, 1985: 1-84). This continuity system is accompanied by the more spectacle-based esthetics of 'the iconic' and 'the tableau,' derived from the frontality of the Parsee theater (and Victorian melodrama). Both the iconic and the tableau represent moments of stasis in the ongoing spatio-temporal momentum of the film, where particular meanings and emotional states are presented to the viewer and/or to a character (Vasudevan, 2000a: 105-106). AWARA makes constant reference to a photo of Rita and frequently frames Raj's mother as image and icon.

The concept of the image and of the look are central to Hindu culture, where seeing (darsan) the divine image is the most 'significant element of Hindu worship' – the look is reciprocal, with the deity presenting itself to be seen and the devotees receiving their darsan (Eck, 1985: 1, 6). It may seem surprising that the Indian Muslim emperors appropriated this concept from Hinduism, despite the more limited divinity of their kingship ('the shadow of God on earth,' whereas the Hindu king was considered the actual incarnation of Vishnu),[8] but in fact the daily ritual of the Mughal court revolved around the emperor giving darsan to his subjects from a viewing window (he is thus framed as an image) and the people taking their darsan of him (Brand, 1995: 7, 132). The adoption of such an image-based concept by Muslims (a religion of the book) is intriguing in light of the application of darsan in Hindi cinema *and* Malaysian cinema.

Ravi Vasudevan (1994: 106-107) applies the darsan perspective on looking to Hindi cinema and contrasts it to the theorization of the look in American cinema by writers like Laura Mulvey (1975), where power, especially male power, is articulated through looking at women. Vasudevan suggests that in Hindi cinema, looking revolves around the exercising of authority through taking or rejecting the look (the deity position), with the woman's look being equivalent to that of the devotee. Both DEVDAS (1955) and PYAASA contain sequences where the woman's look at the man is presented as engaging in darsan, with the employment of continuity editing, iconicity and the tableau, together with devotional music and lamps, constructing the hero as a divine image (Vasudevan, 1995). There is also a beach scene in AWARA, where the woman's desiring look at the man is coded in a similar fashion. The 'darsan effect' is no less patriarchal than the 'Mulvey look,'[9] but it employs a different cultural paradigm, which can in turn become transgressive by using that same strategy to problematize the authority of the male and the desire of the woman (Vasudevan, 1994: 121) – the best example is actually the Malaysian film, PEREMPUAN, ISTERI &..., discussed later in this chapter.

The above discussion of Indian cinema has focused almost exclusively on Hindi commercial cinema, because this is the pervasive Indian film culture in India and in Malaysia (as well as in other parts of the Indian diaspora); this is also the film culture that the Indian directors working in Singapore employed, even if they had worked in other cinematic traditions in India – after all, the Malayan cinema was a strictly commercial cinema. The Indian 'art cinema' of Satyajit Ray was certainly known in the Peninsula in the 1950's, but its realist tendencies were not adopted in the local films, despite some claims to the contrary – these claims will be examined in relation to specific films. The films of Ray's Bengali contemporary, Ritwik Ghatak were also of negligible influence, even though he worked in the melodramatic mode; a melodrama like MEGHE DHAKA TARA (The Cloud-Capped Star, 1960) combines myth, melodrama and realism to construct an epic cinema of critical and historical analysis (Rajadhyaksha and Willemen, 1999: 364-365), a cinema that stands outside the more mainstream melodramatic tradition. The Hindi social melodrama was to have a marked effect on the films made in Malaysia by the Indian directors, by Malaysian directors like P. Ramlee and even by the bumiputera directors like Yusof Haslam. More specific cross-references to Indian and other film traditions will be made in the discussions of the Malaysian films in the following sections.

HUJAN PANAS (Hot Rain, B. N. Rao, 1953)

The title refers to the phenomenon of a sun shower, which is considered a bad omen in Malay culture; it suggests the co-existence of light and darkness, hope and despair, good and evil – the Manichean universe beloved of melodrama and the structuring principles of this film. It has a typical melodrama plot, with its sudden changes of fortune, unrequited love, hatred, loss and a hopeful resolution; a film in which the protagonist desires the modern, aggressive, independent woman only to be betrayed by her, finally realizing that the traditional, patient and more passive woman represents his true salvation. While there are similar plot elements in American melodramas like THERE'S ALWAYS TOMORROW (1955) and SOME CAME RUNNING (1958), the specific configurations described here have more in common with Indian films like DEVDAS, Raj Kapoor's SHREE 420 (Mr 420, 1955) and PYAASA. P. Ramlee's own IBU MERTUA-KU and the 1994 Malaysian film, SEMBILU, rework the same basic premise. The presence of an Indian director highlights the interaction between the Hindi melodramatic tradition and local cultural/thematic concerns, such as the passive/active male protagonist, gender relations and Malay exclusivity.

Figure 12: HUJAN PANAS advertisement

The relationship between Amir and the two women is very effectively and economically defined in the film's opening sequences. Amir (P. Ramlee) is sitting at the piano absorbed in composing a love song; there is a cut to a medium close-up of Hasnah standing silently in the doorway. Her desiring look at the as yet unaware Amir conveys her feelings through its coding as darsan, the viewing of the deity by the devotee (like the scene from PYAASA referred to in the previous section, although here the effect is more curtailed and more prosaic). In the ensuing conversation, Hasnah accepts that her love for Amir is unreciprocated and acknowledges Amir's desire for Aminah (Siput Sarawak), for whom he is writing the song – its reference to the beloved as a 'heavenly peacock' ('Merak Kayangan') already suggests Aminah's unattainability.[10] In the following sequence, Hasnah again enters a room, this time Aminah's dressing room. Aminah also has her back to the door, but, whereas Amir was composing musical images of and for his beloved, Aminah is solely concerned with her own mirror image; this self-absorption is reinforced when Aminah goes on to rhapsodize about her own beauty. Throughout the film, Aminah is constantly positioned in front of mirrors, signifying an obsessive desire for the self, a narcissism that will be her undoing. When Amir eventually enters

Aminah's dressing room in the same scene, her lack of interest in him is underlined by her return to the mirror and so to herself.

The character traits defined in these two sequences remain fixed throughout the film, as is typical of melodrama, with the narrative functioning to demonstrate the inevitable consequences of the characters' interaction. Hasnah acts as a sort of intermediary between Amir and Aminah suppressing her own desire, while continuing to motivate, protect and eventually save Amir. She may resemble the suffering woman of melodrama, but she is also an active agent. In a number of scenes, Hasnah is in the background of shots, actively looking at and listening to Aminah talking to the nightclub owner – the information gathered goes to help Amir's career. Hasnah's drive is in stark contrast to Amir's passivity and resignation, traits characteristic of the Devdas figure of Indian cinema and quite unlike the active/passive gender division in western melodrama (Nowell-Smith, 1987: 72). When he is eventually rejected by Aminah, Amir's response to his plight is to renounce the (music) world and wallow in his loss. Only Hasnah's forceful arguments about his responsibility to his son, to her and to his music make Amir reconsider his attitude and his obligations. In nearly killing Aminah after the death of their son, Amir exhibits a most un-Devdas-like trait, although the melodramatic mode does require the punishment of evil (i.e. Aminah) and the return of the world to order, a world that had not reacted to the destruction of innocence and goodness, epitomized in the film by the son. This outburst of violence following long periods of resignation to the condition of the world is a recurrent motif in Malaysian cinema (it is not at all characteristic of Indian cinema) and suggests a response reminiscent of amuk – that sudden and almost uncontrollable release of aggressive behavior, previously referred to in chapter 2.

The conclusion of the film is an accommodation between Amir and Hasnah premised on her assertions about the virtue of patience and the acceptance of the co-existence of good and evil. It is a happy ending, but not an emotional one; the real (tragic) love story of the film is that between father and son, a theme that would be explored more overtly in ANAK-KU SAZALI (My Son Sazali, 1956). The film thus pursues the movement of desire from Hasnah to Amir to Aminah to Hassan (her lover), who eventually rejects her, resulting in Aminah turning back to Amir, who having lost his only true love, his son, completed the circle by finding solace in Hasnah – a more complex and more optimistic circular pattern than that of WRITTEN ON THE WIND (Douglas Sirk, 1956), in which 'Dorothy Malone wants Rock Hudson who wants Lauren Bacall who wants Robert Stack who just wants to die' (Elsaesser, 1987: 64).[11]

The mise-en-scene of HUJAN PANAS is certainly not as baroque as that of the Sirk film or of the films of Raj Kapoor and Guru Dutt; while the plot and the stock characters are typical of melodrama, the film's style is very plain, exhibiting none of the excess or overt emotion often associated with melodrama. Most of the scenes are constructed around medium close-ups of two characters conversing and/or a series of two-shots, filmed in shallow focus and shot almost frontally, reflecting the Parsee theater and Bangsawan origins of Indian and Malayan cinema. The influence of Bangsawan is also noticeable in the song and dance routines in the film, which tend to interrupt the narrative and yet remain quite unrelated to it; they are, however, strongly motivated by the film's story of singers performing in a nightclub. This is an important distinction, which contrasts with the weakly motivated, but strongly narrativized songs in Indian socials, e.g. PYAASA. The songs are often presented frontally to the camera/film audience with few cutaways to the nightclub audience – this, as well as the weak narrativization of the songs, is reminiscent of the Cantonese opera films and melodramas of the same period. P. Ramlee films are very often set in a musical world, thus naturalizing the fact that characters sing; this is quite unlike Hindi films, where characters, whatever their occupation, sing through an 'unnatural' shift in the performative register. The P. Ramlee singer-songwriter also continually replays his own life story: that of an aspiring musician, who is eventually given a 'break' (as he was by B. S. Rajhans in a Penang Bangsawan theater) and who becomes successful. In this way, the P. Ramlee film 'genre' is biographical, recalling the Chinese 'exploitation musical' melodramas of Zhou Xuan (Teo, 1993: 32).

HUJAN PANAS was B. N. Rao's first Malayan film after a successful career as a director in the Tamil film industry, where he had made films like GUMASTAVIN PENN (Clerk's Daughter, 1941), a melodrama of class conflict, sexual desire and death, and considered an 'early attempt at realism in Tamil cinema' (Rajadhyaksha and Willemen, 1994: 180, 271).[12] The reference to realism is interesting given the almost total artificiality of HUJAN PANAS, except for the pre-credit sequence, which is a 'mini-documentary' of people in Singapore walking along the streets and catching buses home from work. These scenes have nothing to do with the film's diegesis at all, but they do recognize the existence of a multi-ethnic community, which is totally absent from the ensuing fictional story.

Despite all of the Indian influences on the film (direction, story, mode of address, formal strategies), the film presents a homogenous Malay world, where difference is reduced to the distinction between a traditional, reserved and passive Malay woman (Hasnah) and her nemesis, the modern, westernized (signified by Aminah smoking cigarettes) Malay woman, who is punished for her independence. The identity of the male is therefore constructed through this conflict between tradition and modernity – a scenario common to Indian and perhaps all melodrama. It is somewhat complicated in HUJAN PANAS due to the fact that Amir is even more passive than Hasnah, who persists in steering Amir towards an outcome he recognizes as necessary, but seems unable to achieve and perhaps does not even desire. Amir's immobility, in which he is 'frozen' by fate, is reminiscent of Majnun and Devdas and creates a 'still center' in the film, where the conflicts occur around Amir through the tensions between the two women. The final outcome for the protagonist is therefore dependent on which of the women wins the battle. This passive masculinity is not necessarily a criticism of masculinity and the male protagonist's hero status is not diminished by his inaction. Nor is the traditional woman valorized solely for her subservience – she actively intervenes in the narrative to achieve the desired outcome for the protagonist, but also for herself, since the protagonist is not likely to act on her behalf. Such behavior reflects aspects (traces?) of women's equality and autonomy (bi-laterality) in traditional Malay society (Karim, 1992: 2-5). These complexities of gender relations counter some of the sweeping generalizations made about the representation of women and issues of power and control that have circulated about Malaysian films (Banks, quoted in Lent, 1990: 199, footnote 3). Subsequent Malaysian films continue to explore such gender ambivalences as well as employing the recurrent theme of a woman asserting herself in the presence of a reluctant/disinterested man, who is the object of her desire.

PENARIK BECA (The Rickshaw Driver, P. Ramlee, 1955)

It is an interesting paradox that PENARIK BECA,[13] the first film by a major Malay filmmaker, has more Indian attributes than HUJAN PANAS, which was made by an Indian director. This runs counter to the prevailing wisdom about the influence of the cultural credentials of filmmakers on films; it is also contrary to the arguments voiced at the time and in retrospect that increased Malay creative involvement would lead to greater Malay cultural presence in the films. This attitude is implicit in the following statement: 'Almost single-handedly P. Ramlee transformed the Malay film industry by putting Malay social drama in the modern context' (Aishah Ali, 1981: 39), suggesting a monoculturalist agenda not evident in a close examination of this and subsequent films by P. Ramlee and other Malay directors. In his first film, P. Ramlee maintained the Indian cinematic tradition of his Indian mentors, at the same time introducing aspects of Japanese cinema, while ultimately locating the (melo)drama in a clearly identified Malay (rather than Malayan or Malaysian) context. L. Krishnan confirmed P. Ramlee's adaptive and incorporative esthetic tendencies when commenting on his tendency to absorb Indian film culture into his own filmmaking approach (Krishnan, 1994a). Perhaps the Malay-focused implication of Aishah

Figure 13: PENARIK BECA poster

Ali's comment is more validly applied to P. Ramlee becoming a model for future Malay directors by demonstrating the capacity of Malays to take creative control (Raja Ahmad Alauddin, 1994a) – the popular success of PENARIK BECA (Baharudin Latif, 1989c: 64) further contributes to this interpretation. It is also significant that P. Ramlee's first directorial effort touched on social and economic divisions within the Malay community, a theme constantly returned to in his work. He is also quoted as saying: 'My art is not for money. My art is for society... As artistes [sic] we should never forget the ordinary man, the trishaw-pedaller, the laborer, or the slum-dweller...' (quoted in Lockard, 1991: 23). These sentiments about his themes and his audience align him with Indian directors like Raj Kapoor and Bimal Roy rather than with Satyajit Ray.

Structurally, the plot resembles Raj Kapoor's AWARA in its pairing of a poverty-stricken sole mother and her son (Amran, a rickshaw driver, played by P. Ramlee) against a financially well-off, aggressive father (Marzuki) and his daughter (Azizah). However, it is not a 'man of the world' scenario like AWARA, in that the male protagonist of PENARIK BECA is totally defined within the Majnun/Devdas mould. The poor son and mother/rich daughter and father dichotomy, so beloved of Indian popular cinema, was thus swiftly adopted by P. Ramlee and was to be employed in a number of his other films (e.g. SEMERAH PADI and IBU MERTUA-KU). This plot structure – the generational and class-impeded romance – is ideally suited to the melodramatic mode because of these stark contrasts, which are dependent on stock characterizations, coincidence and a reduced emphasis on the cause/effect chain. These characteristics are clearly derived from the Indian socials, but also from the Wayang and Bangsawan narratives. Marzuki is the only character that 'develops' during the course of the film through being 're-awakened' to his social responsibility to the poor. For the most part, the characters interact conflictually in a series of schematic permutations, the most complex of which occurs in the scene where Amran drives Azizah home after sewing class, to be confronted at the door by Marzuki and his new friend, Ghazali. The camera tracks laterally so as to position the two pairs of characters on either side of a round pillar. Marzuki hits Azizah, who falls to the ground – her mother rushes out of the house to protect her, while Amran strains forward but ultimately does nothing. There follows a new pairing of the two women on one side of the pillar and Ghazali and Marzuki on the other side, leaving Amran by himself. The shots represent the sort of tableau found in Indian cinema and referred to earlier in this chapter – a set of images that enunciate a fixed set of social and gender relationships.

The film is constructed as a series of narrative events that are butted onto each other, lacking the chaining component of the cause/effect sequencing and the transitional scenes often used to convey character departure and arrival. Coincidence, that most depreciated of narrative agents in western film, is here used without 'camouflage' or self-consciousness; as in the Wayang and in films like AWARA, coincidence is the true motor of the narrative. In PENARIK BECA, this revolves primarily around the villain, Ghazali. It is he who harasses Azizah and attacks Amran; his running down Mazruki brings him back into the plot and also brings immediate recognition from Azizah and Amran,[14] although neither speak of their previous encounter with Ghazali. Finally Ghazali's friend, who had accompanied Ghazali at the beginning of the film when they accosted Azizah, happens to be riding by Amran's shack just as Azizah visits him; the friend's recognition of Azizah is as inevitable as is the instantaneous presence of Marzuki, Ghazali and his friend at Amran's door, where Marzuki again hits Azizah, this time for sullying the family name.

Stylistically, the film combines quite different approaches – this indicates a willingness to experiment with stylistic options, but it gives the film a fragmented quality. Much of the film employs the proscenium arch compositions reminiscent of Bangsawan and Indian cinema, but they intermittently extend to carefully designed two-dimensional frames-within-frames that recall the films of Ozu Yasujiro. At times the editing is also Ozu-like, as when Ghazali joins Marzuki and his wife for a meal and the two-dimensionality of the images are maintained by cutting at 90° rather than the more typical continuity cut of around 30°. The Japanese influence may seem surprising, but it is not accidental. The previous chapter referred to the Japanese cinematic presence in Singapore during World War II; furthermore P. Ramlee himself learned Japanese during the Occupation (Kee Hua Chee, 1992: 18) and later often mentioned his interest in Japanese films (White, 1995). However, these stylistic elements are not consistently employed – at other times, long takes and tracking shots are the dominant approach. When Amran returns home after 'saving' Azizah from Ghazali, he dismounts from his rickshaw. The camera pans with him as he enters the shack and frames him and his mother in long shot as he tells her about his good luck (having been asked by Azizah to take her to her classes everyday). The scene fades out when Amran closes the shutters outside of which the camera has remained throughout the scene. This simple, yet effective single take bears comparison with one of Mizoguchi Kenji's famous sequence shots. Mostly though, the editing is quite rudimentary and the Indian-style tableaux shots are transformed into the standard diagonally composed continuity shots when the characters engage in discussions or confrontations. On the other hand, given the emphasis on frontality, there are very few point-of-view shots in the film.

The musical component of this melodrama is in the Indian tradition to a much greater extent than HUJAN PANAS was. Surprisingly for a P. Ramlee film, this is not a performance-based musical. Consequently, the songs arise out of the narrative, but are unmotivated by the action. There are only three songs in the film and they are all solitary reveries by Amran/P. Ramlee, with the partial exception of the first one. This song is initiated by Azizah and her girlfriends at a seaside picnic, to which they were brought by five rickshaws, with Azizah driven by Amran. Amran walks away from the other drivers almost immediately and disappears from the scene. Halfway through the song, Azizah hears a male voice singing in the distance; she leaves her friends to follow the voice, which sounds alluring, yet so melancholy. This is a remarkable conjunction of the diegetic and the non-diegetic, introducing an element of performance otherwise absent from the film. Azizah recognizes the voice as Amran's while the Malayan audience would instantly recognize it as the voice of the country's most popular singer, P. Ramlee. It is thus quite significant that the first song he sings in his first directorial effort emphasizes his voice. Azizah, along with the audience, follows the voice until its body is found – an audio-visual conjunction takes place, one that also signifies the more ambitious 'coming-into-being' of P. Ramlee as singer-songwriter-actor-scriptwriter-director.[15] Appropriately, the song he sings mourns the chasm between the poor and the rich, visualized by the increasing distance between him and Azizah as the scene progresses. At the conclusion of the song, Amran talks to her about how distasteful being a carrier of people is to him, likening himself to a 'wild beast.' This invocation of one of P. Ramlee's favorite poems (Ché-Ross, 1996), Chairil Anwar's *Aku* (referred to in chapter 2) is interesting for the very different meaning P. Ramlee gives it. The poem includes the lines 'I am a wild beast/Driven from the herd' (Salleh Ben Joned, 1994a: 117). The defiance and resentment implicit in these lines become a lament in the film about being a social outcast (once again linked to the Devdas sentiment) – Amran's acceptance of his situation is the antithesis of Chairil Anwar's anarchistic denunciation of the system. The location also softens the social comment, for it resembles the idyllic landscape found in romantic musical numbers in Indian films.

The third and last song, called 'Azizah,' is also both 'inside' and 'outside' the film. It is a song about a desired but unattainable woman (similar in sentiment to the song the protagonist of Hujan Panas was composing), picturized in a very stylized, stark landscape, through which Amran/P. Ramlee moves in an equally stylized and even stilted fashion. The song is narratively appropriate within the film and is still regarded as one of the 'national treasures' of Malay popular music (Lockard, 1991: 20). However, it was composed back in the 1940's and won P. Ramlee a song competition in 1947 – the song remained popular partly because of the ongoing speculation as to the identity of 'Azizah,' presumed to have been P. Ramlee's unrequited love, but never revealed by P. Ramlee or anyone else (Kee Hua Chee, 1992: 20). While not a performance-based musical, the film thus continues the 'exploitation musical' aspect already evident in Hujan Panas. This self-consciousness extends beyond the P. Ramlee character. Early in the film, Azizah and some of her friends decide to go to the cinema to see a 'good movie' – it is Iman (Faith, 1954), an MFP film starring the actor playing Azizah, Saadiah.

The film's gender roles can be placed into three categories, represented by Marzuki and Ghazali, Azizah and her mother, and finally Amran. Marzuki and Ghazali characterize the aggressive male, brutal and condescending to women – in Marzuki's case this is particularly evident in his treatment of his daughter, whom he physically assaults twice in the film. Ghazali is the villain of the film, much in the mould of the villain of Indian cinema: nasty, greedy, a threat to order and yet ultimately supine. Azizah's mother is almost irrelevant to the film, except to further demonstrate Marzuki's disdain and brutality towards women. Her attempt to protect Azizah from her husband is futile – the violence of fathers against daughters and the attempts of mothers to protect daughters recur in P. Ramlee's films, most complexly in Antara Dua Darjat (Between Two Classes, 1960). Azizah does exhibit a certain amount of defiance towards the 'patriarchal order,' certainly more so than her counterparts in Indian films like Andaz and Awara. Amran stands out in contrast to the other males in the film as the passive male protagonist, who needs to be encouraged into a relationship by the woman and then bemoans the fact that he is suffering because of his love. This Majnun/Devdas characteristic is not condemned by the film, but it is once again overturned at the end of the film, when Amran, having meekly accepted his own fate and that of the women in the film (including his mother), now engages Ghazali in a lengthy and vicious fight. The gender/power overtones implicit in this fight are crystallized in the moment when Ghazali stands over the exhausted Amran and thrusts the kris (the traditional Malay dagger that was hanging on Marzuki's bedroom wall) slowly towards Amran from between his legs. Amran quickly reverses the situation, takes the kris from Ghazali and throws it at the ceiling – such phallic assertiveness is incompatible with the Majnun/Devdas stereotype.

In a sense, the gender roles are complicated by their links to class positions. Amran's passivity is also a realization of his economic impotence. On the other hand, Ghazali is accepted by Marzuki because he *appears* to be of his own class. Ghazali's greed is insatiable and unqualified in contrast to Marzuki's similar behavior, which is presented as a dangerous tendency that may take over his better self. Marzuki's disdain of the poor is epitomized in his attack on his daughter for being unable to distinguish brass from gold (i.e. Amran from Ghazali) – the judge/father in AWARA exhibits a strikingly similar attitude to the poor. Interestingly, Amran's mother accepts the socio-economic divide as unquestioningly as Marzuki, when she tells Amran that they are quails, who should not aspire to be eagles. After Amran finally overwhelms Ghazali and Marzuki regains the money Ghazali had stolen, Marzuki and his family arrive at Amran's shack. Just prior to this, Marzuki is privileged with the only voice-over in the film, in which he regrets his attitude to the poor. Marzuki as patriarch dominates the final meeting in Amran's shack and the fantasy accommodation across class boundaries is as unconvincing as similar resolutions in Raj Kapoor's films.[16] The film ultimately sentimentalizes poverty and actually positions itself with Marzuki in the final scene. On the other hand, Amran returns to his passive role, accepting Marzuki's pronouncements without comment and the film ends with him and Azizah departing from the shack in silhouette and thus renouncing the 'real world' – earlier in the film, both were visualized as being trapped by their environment and their family. The relationship between Amran and Azizah is also affected by class differences – only by crossing the chasm can the woman initiate a relationship, with her class power now able to cancel out her lack of gender power.

The rich/poor dichotomy is also grafted onto a westernization/traditional differentiation. At the beginning of the film, Ghazali and his friends leave a Joget Hall (a singing/dancing entertainment center), complaining that the dances and songs are not western – we hear a singer stressing the importance of Malay culture. Later on, Marzuki's family is conspicuously shown eating the western way (bread and butter on plates eaten with knives and forks; tea poured from a teapot). These indicators of westernization combined with Marzuki's greed and ruthlessness signify the dangerous consequences of increasing industrialization and wealth acquisition in urban Malayan centers like Singapore in the 1950's. It is therefore significant that the film's resolution (of conflicts) occurs in the shantytown – the closest that the film approaches the traditional kampung world – where there exists a sense of community noticeably absent from Marzuki's urban environment. However, the shantytown where Amran and his mother live is purely a cipher of poverty, having none of the life force of a similar setting in A. Samad Said's novel *Salina*. Amran's work as a rickshaw driver is likewise condensed into a signifier of poverty; this is in stark contrast to the protagonist of Two Acres of Land (1953), where there is a great emphasis on the difficult and exhausting work that rickshaw driving really is. The Indian film is regarded as an early realist film (despite the presence of a number of popular songs[17]); Penarik Beca fits more easily into the Bangsawan performance tradition and frequently betrays its predominantly studio setting, despite its documentary introduction to Singapore in the pre-credit sequence (similar to, but much briefer than, the beginning of Hujan Panas).

The long brutal fight between Amran and Ghazali that takes place in Marzuki's house, involving the use of the traditional kris, has Hang Tuah/Hang Jebat overtones. The parallels are limited, but they might be expressed as follows: Marzuki, like the Sultan, treats Amran/Tuah badly and outlaws/exiles him, preferring Ghazali/Jebat, whose betrayal of the Sultan and invasion of his house/palace is subsequently punished by the returning hero. As in the traditional interpretation of the Tuah/Jebat tale, the distinction between hero and villain is totally unambiguous – the heroic status of Hang Tuah is more ambivalent when P. Ramlee actually plays that character in the historical melodrama Hang Tuah, made the year after Penarik Beca.

Hang Tuah (Phani Majumdar, 1956)

Phani Majumdar was already a well-known film director in India,[18] before he was invited to Singapore by Shaw Brothers to make a film about that quintessential Malay subject, Hang Tuah (Matsuoka Kanda, 1995: 48). Majumdar's screenplay for the film was adapted from *The Adventures of Hang Tuah*, written by another outsider, an 'orang puteh' (white man), M. C. ff Sheppard, a Malayan civil servant, who was to become an influential figure in Malay histori-

Figure 14: Hang Tuah poster

cal/cultural affairs. The ensuing film functions as a respectful interpretation of this key Malay foundational narrative, while at the same time offering a critique of centralized power and its relationship to ethnicity and gender.

Sheppard's book was loosely based on the *Hikayat Hang Tuah* and the *Sejarah Melayu* (both of which were discussed in chapter 2), but he acknowledged that 'many details [were] imaginary' (Sheppard, 1962: 132). Sheppard confined his narrative to some of Hang Tuah's major adventures, using the story's characters from the Bangsawan version if there were discrepancies between the two traditional sources (Sheppard, 1962: 132).[19] In keeping with Hikayat and Bangsawan conventions, Sheppard's version emphasized event and action and displayed minimal interest in Tuah's psychological motivations. On the other hand, the almost exclusive focus on Hang Tuah, the employment of causality and the absence of repetition are characteristic of the European (written) narrative tradition and are in stark contrast to the digressive, repetitive quality of the *Hikayat Hang Tuah*, which was written down, but written down to be read aloud in public (Errington, 1979: 36). Sheppard's story starts with the first adventures of Tuah and his four friends as boys, whereas the *Hikayat Hang Tuah*, after the initial invocation to Allah, clearly identifies its subject matter: 'This is the story of Hang Tuah, who was very faithful to his lord...,' only to then launch into a lengthy discussion of the genealogy of the Melakan Rajas (Errington, 1975: 52). This is an affirmation of origin and legitimacy – a strategy common to most national epics – but it also stresses that Tuah's actions are totally circumscribed by the position and power of the Raja. Sheppard's book was first published in 1949 (it is still the only English version of the story) – it is therefore surprising that its judgment of Hang Jebat remains so similar to that of the *Hikayat Hang Tuah* (i.e. Jebat as villain, Tuah as untroubled hero), given the reinterpretation of Jebat's status that was already in train prior to World War II (see chapter 2).

The film deviated from Sheppard's story in some significant ways. It introduces a new female character, Melur, while omitting Tuah's later adventures except for the Tun Tijah episode, which the film inserts before the tragic fight between Tuah and Jebat. In the film, Tun Tijah falls in love with Tuah 'naturally,' whereas in the book he gives her a love potion – in both versions, Tun Tijah is given a potion to forget Tuah. The film omits any reference to Jebat living with one of the Sultan's wives in the now vacated palace, where Jebat ruthlessly kills the woman before confronting Tuah, in order to 'polish my kris' (Sheppard, 1962: 73). More importantly, in the book Tuah guarantees fair play in his fight with Jebat, but then blatantly deceives Jebat by stealing the magical kris from him. Tuah suffers no remorse for his duplicitous actions – his only response is one of delight in being made Laksamana (Admiral). These changes increase the romantic aspects of Tuah's character in the film, bringing him more into the Devdas/Majnun domain; love and doubt soften the absolutism of blind loyalty as a principle, and deviousness as a method of operation, setting the scene for a more ambivalent ending. The film's omission of Jebat's sexual exploits and violent behavior also reduces his villainous attributes, thus making Tuah's subsequent behavior less acceptable. Interestingly, both versions omit the *Hikayat Hang Tuah* episode of Jebat running amuk after the fight with Tuah and before his death, when he kills thousands of Melakans with the implicit approval of Tuah (Errington, 1975: 111-112) – the motivation for such behavior is difficult to defend in naturalistic texts like Sheppard's book and the film, and would certainly have made emotional identification impossible.[20]

Like a Wayang performance, the film is constructed from a small number of settings that are constantly revisited: palace, natural environment, palace (Becker, 1979: 225). Much of the film is set in Melaka, identified by an emblematic shot of the Sultan's palace located at the top of the Melakan hill; the shot, which recurs a number of times, has some formal resemblance to the Wayang's 'pokok beringin,' a leather mountain-shaped 'puppet' that has mythical and symbolic significance, but also acts as a recurrent marker of events within the performance (Matusky, 1993: 18). These shots function as much more than mere establishing shots for events taking place in Melaka – they underline the role of the palace as the center of power and control, exercised by the Sultan through 'instruments' such as Hang Tuah and his companions. Interestingly, once that power is abused (Tuah's 'death') or challenged (by Jebat), the palace image disappears from the film. The Melakan scenes are marked by court ritual and formal court language that constrain the characters within the hierarchical structure of power and unswerving loyalty. This is echoed in the film by the presence of flat framed, two-dimensional compositions and lateral tracking shots within the palace. When chaos does occur – the amuk attack on the Bendahara and Jebat's revolt – it is expeditiously neutralized.

Melaka is constructed as a male domain, where women disappear from sight – Radin Mas Ayu and Tun Tijah don't exist visually or narratively once they enter Melaka, while Melur arrives in the center only to be made a dayang, after which she is soon murdered. The only woman to survive in Melaka is Tuah's mother, whose role as nurturing figure provides legitimacy – the character and the actor's performance are very reminiscent of the stereotypical Indian film mother. Melaka, like Malaysian film generally, is ethnically homogenous; Sheppard makes some reference to Indian merchants and to the Chinese quarter (Sheppard, 1962: 36), but the film's characters are all Malay, with the exception of Tun Ali. While unstressed in the film (and the book), the historical Tun Ali was of Tamil-Muslim origin (Muhammad Yusoff Hashim, 1992: 239). The two most prominent court conspirators are therefore both outsiders: Tun Ali and the Javanese Pateh Kerma Wijaya – the former survives his connivance, but the latter is killed by Melur. In summary, Melaka is represented as a male monocultural society that absorbs, contains or destroys difference, quite at odds with the cosmopolitan community described in various historical accounts (Thomaz, 1993; Muhammad Yusoff Hashim, 1992).

The margin, on the other hand, exhibits (limited) social and gender flexibility. There are three journeys away from Melaka and each of them revolves around a woman, who then travels to or is taken to Melaka. Early in the film, Tuah (P. Ramlee) and his four friends go to the sacred mountain, Gunong Ledang, where a guru trains them in martial arts that will help maintain Melaka's power and glory, but it is also the place where Tuah meets Melur. He first speaks to her after watching her dance with a group of other women, identified as Jakun (Ché-Ross, 1996), an orang asli tribe. The dancing is very vigorous and is characterized as 'primitive' (the same way that tribal dancing is often represented in Hollywood films) in contrast to the Tuah's refined dancing in Pahang later in the film. The love affair between Tuah and Melur is therefore generically coded as tragic (based on a cultural difference impossible for lovers to surmount – this is somewhat qualified when it is later revealed that Melur was actually a Melakan kidnapped by the orang asli tribe!). The doomed nature of their relationship is echoed in the sad, haunting song that Melur and Tuah sing as they first meet at the pond and that Melur continues to sing when looking for Tuah in Melaka and also at the moment of her death. Their meeting at the pond is mediated by the reflection of the moon in the water. The moon is associated with love and provides a link between absent lovers in Malaysian and Indian cinema, but it is also specifically linked with Hang Tuah, whose fate as a great warrior was foretold as a child by his father, who dreamt of the moon being above or falling on the boy's head (Errington, 1975: 98; Sheppard, 1962: 12). Despite pledging his eternal loyalty to Melur, Tuah leaves the next day without saying farewell to her, being totally concerned with his greater loyalty to the Sultan. When later in the film, Tuah meets Melur in the palace, he does show some emotion about their (permanent) parting. Nevertheless, Melur's death has no particular consequences within the film – the Tuah/Jebat fight that follows her death is concerned with more abstract principles of (male) loyalty and friendship.

The second journey away from Melaka takes Tuah, his companions and the Sultan to the Kingdom of Majapahit in Java, where the Sultan is to marry the King's daughter. The departure and arrival is presented in a stylized way, occasioning the only voice-over in the film (which tells of the journey and the Sultan's marriage to Radin Mas Ayu) accompanied by a set of static images of the Sultan and the Bendahara seated on an elephant, preceded and followed by Melakan nobles and soldiers, including Tuah and friends, 'traveling' from Melaka to Majapahit. While obviously a cheap production solution, it is also reminiscent of the Wayang's method of presenting journeys, especially as it is accompanied by gamelan music. In keeping with the structure of Wayang plots, a palace scene is typically followed by a journey scene, which culminates in a battle scene (Becker, 1979: 220), a sequence of events precisely followed in the film. In the Wayang, journey scenes, like action scenes in general, are initiated by the dalang's description of the nature of the events and are accompanied by tunes that evoke the form of the activities (Sweeney, 1972: 57). Similarly, in the film, the voice-over describes the action, while the elephant-walking shots are supported by appropriate gait-like rhythms from the gamelan orchestra. The end of the journey dissolves into a long scene of the King and his nobles together with the Sultan, his new wife and his entourage watching a performance of 'Wayang Wong' – a form of Wayang that substitutes human dancers for the leather puppets. A demon – signified by the performer's large size, uncouth dancing gestures and grotesque mask – drags a young woman away, only to be confronted by a slim, refined young man, who slays the demon, using a kris and silat (Malay martial arts). This battle scene tells the core story of the *Ramayana*, in which Ravana abducts Sita and takes her to his palace in Lanka; eventually Rama arrives, kills the ogre and rescues his wife, Sita.

This episode has interesting parallels throughout the film, ranging from Tuah abducting Tun Tijah and taking her to Melaka (from which she is not 'rescued') to the Tuah/Jebat fight (raising the question of whether Tuah is unequivocally the Rama figure and Jebat the Ravana figure), and finally in Melur's dance before Pateh Kerma Wijaya and her subsequent killing of him (Sita killing Ravana herself – an action forced on her by the absence/disinterest of Rama/Tuah). A more traditional interpretation of the *Ramayana* story immediately follows the dance, when the Javanese warrior, Tameng Sari, enters the royal hall and fights with Hang Tuah, with the former clearly presented as Ravana and the latter as Rama.[21] While Tameng Sari is more abstracted in the film than in Sheppard and the *Hikayat Hang Tuah*, the fight acts as a prelude to the later Tuah/Jebat conflict, even though the crafty, deceitful way that Tuah manages to take Tameng Sari's magical kris is not replicated in the film's denouement.[22] This performance scene also includes the only tender moment between the Sultan and Radin Mas Ayu, when he looks at her and smiles (the fact that it occurs when Rama enters to save Sita from Ravana adds an interesting dimension). It is also the last time she is seen in the film and probably the only time the Sultan exhibits any human qualities.

The film's third and final 'boundary event' is Tuah's kidnapping of Tun Tijah, undertaken by Tuah on his own accord, because the Sultan's marriage proposal to the daughter of the Bendahara of Pahang (Tun Tijah) was turned down. While Tuah's behavior is calculated and manipulative, Tun Tijah genuinely falls in love with him. After arriving in Pahang, Tuah is invited by the Bendahara's son, Tun Zainal, to join him and his friends that evening for singing and dancing. They dance/sing the 'Joget Pahang' (a joget is a lively Malay dance), with Tuah (predictably) the outstanding performer. Tun Tijah watches him unseen from another room and is instantly besmitten by him. Her response is reminiscent of Hasnah's towards Amir in Hujan Panas (and Melur's in this film), theorized as darsan in Indian cinema and based on the intense visual engagement of the worshipper with the God-image in Hindu culture. The ensuing love scenes between Tuah and Tun Tijah are very similar to the Tuah/Melur ones (garden, moon, love poems, song). The link is made overt when Tuah, back in his room remembers Melur and sings 'their' song; Tun Tijah hears it from her window and proceeds to hum the same tune. Tuah then recalls the song he sang to Tun Tijah earlier that evening about forsaking riches for love ('Berkorban Apa Saja') and reminds himself that his love for his Sultan and country is and must be greater than any other love. Tuah persuades her to elope with him, but once they have fled Pahang, Tuah admits to her that he is taking her to Melaka to be the Sultan's bride. When Tuah eventually gives her a magic betelnut that will make her forget him, she sings this song back to him, more in sorrow than in defiance – the shot frames her behind vertical wooden slats in the cabin of the boat taking them to Melaka, signifying that her entombment is already well advanced. Her grief dominates the scene and contrasts with Tuah's emotionless response. The last we see of Tun Tijah is in the film's second 'journey scene,' in which she and Pateh Kerma Wijaya ride elephants (in separate shots) in procession through Melaka. It is quite significant that all the film's songs take place within these three sequences located outside Melaka, graphically contrasting spheres that allow for the possibilities of human interaction to the hierarchical, martial society that is traditionally presented as the epitome of Malay culture. Both Melur and Tun Tijah are sacrificed by Tuah for these 'higher purposes.' Despite the class differences of the two women, the similarities of the expression of their love for Tuah and their eventual demise (disappearance/death) confirm the fate of all women in such a patriarchal society.

Despite the film's basis in traditional Malay culture, it conforms to the musical-melodrama mode discussed earlier in this chapter. While the Malay dance and song ('Joget Pahang') is performed by Hang Tuah and a group of men as a distinct event, the two other songs are integrated into the narrative in the best Indian film tradition. These songs are located in love scenes that take place in verdant gardens and under moonlight, where the lovers' discourse is through formalized love poetry – elements characteristic of Indian musical numbers, even though here the poetry is the Malay 'pantun,' a concentrated and highly intricate quatrain format used to seek 'confirmation or denial of romantic feelings in the other party' (Karim, 1990: 30); its verse form is 'closest to song and music' and frequently became lyrics for traditional and contemporary songs (Muhammad Haji Salleh, 1991: 37). When Hang Tuah 'courts' Tun Tijah, her pantun asks him to speak of love, but he replies that he cannot express his feelings in mere words and so begins to hum a tune – here the pantun elegantly dissolves into a song, which is thus narratively justified *and* motivated by the action. This particular song, addressed to a princess, suggests that the only true measure of love is the willingness to sacrifice all one has – a sentiment to which Hang Tuah himself does not actually subscribe, but which he expects the princess to adopt for his sake. The song has intertextual reverberations, as it was originally composed for Norizan, then the consort of the Sultan of Perak, who was to become P. Ramlee's second wife in 1955 (Mahirin Binti Hassan, 1978: 78). The song in the film may well function as an indictment of the deceitful Tuah character in stark contrast to P. Ramlee's employment of the song when wooing Norizan; once again the strategy recalls the 'exploitation musical' element so prevalent in P. Ramlee films.

The film seems very reverential towards the Tuah legend, manifested in the slow-paced and somewhat ponderous approach to the staging of the action. The conflict between two different kinds of (blind) loyalty – to one's lord or to one's friend – are not examined in any depth. On the other hand, the gradual questioning by Hang Tuah of his absolutist commitment to the Sultan and his consequent rejection of emotional attachments (to Jebat, Melur and Tun Tijah) do make this a revisionist interpretation of the *Hikayat Hang Tuah* and Sheppard's book – apparently the first note of skepticism about Tuah's hero status in any version of the story (Kassim Ahmad, 1966: 3), but it needs to be pointed out that Tuah's doubts only surface after he has (very willingly) killed Jebat. However, despite the views of the commentators, who compared HANG TUAH unfavorably with the 1962 HANG JEBAT,[23] the film does cast doubts on the model this Golden Age foundational narrative represents for the soon to be independent Malaya/Malaysia. By concentrating on the narrative events set outside Melaka (which occupy more than half of the film's running time), it is possible to interpret the film as questioning the validity of centralized power and its attendant ideologies of gender and ethnicity.[24]

SEMERAH PADI (P. Ramlee, 1956)

The first images of the film are of clouds swirling across a turning and gradually approaching earth that eventually reveals a map of the Malay Archipelago and closes in on an area in present day northern Sumatra. The music accompanying these images is somber and the voice-over is incantatory:

> 'In the name of Allah, the most Gracious, the most Merciful
> Turning page after page of history
> Volume after volume
> Many many years ago
> In the Malay Archipelago
> When Islam first became the religion
> New laws were made
> As written in the Koran full of wisdom
> The Chieftain and people are the devotees
> A village by the name of SEMERAH PADI.'[25]

At this stage the map dissolves into a mountain range, followed by a slow tracking shot into the village, as the credits unfold and the title song is played.

This remarkable opening resembles the beginning of traditional (oral) texts like the *Hikayat Hang Tuah* and the *Sejarah Melayu*, with the customary invoca-

Figure 15: SEMERAH PADI advertisement

tion to Allah and the reference to the origin of community. While the 'hikayat/sejarah' tradition unproblematically combines the mythical and the historical, the film's opening visuals and commentary locate its story in a specific geographic space and historical time.[26] However, this 'precision' is then eroded by the village's symbolic name (lit. 'as red as a rice padi [at sunset]') and by the names of some of the main characters – Teruna (lit. young, unmarried man) and Dara (lit. maiden, virgin) are the names of the archetypal Malay couple (Ché-Ross, 1996). The initial images and voice-over are also reminiscent of the dalang's opening words in a Wayang performance, which follow 'the strategy of moving from widest physical context to narrowest, from the place of the kingdom among all kingdoms, the mountains around it, the sea, the town, the houses...' (Becker, 1979: 237). All these elements combine to provide the film with a powerful ancestry that more than compensates for its contemporary fictional origin, and construct it as a foundational narrative as significant as the Hang Tuah story.

The credits and long shot of the village/kampung dissolve to a padi field, where men and women are tending the rice plants. It is an idyllic scene portraying community work, laughter and music making. After a considerable number of shots of various individuals at work, the camera concentrates on a woman, who is looking across to a man taking a water buffalo through the padi field; it is already clear that she is attracted to him and, as they talk, it is equally obvious that he enjoys her company – her name is Dara and his is Aduka (P. Ramlee). The workers leave the padi field for their meal. Aduka washes his feet and follows them, only to be met by Dara, who has brought food for him to eat. Aduka is quite playful and teasing, but Dara is more intense in her feelings for him. It is a beautiful sequence of peace and harmony (in mood, it resembles the end of SEVEN SAMURAI), photographed to emphasize the physicality of people and things – Semerah Padi seems a Garden of Eden untouched by pain and sorrow. However, intimations of 'The Fall' are actually already present. After all, his name is not Teruna and he is therefore not the person destined for Dara. Furthermore, Dara is constructed as the desiring one. She is granted the only close-up in the scene; this could suggest a retrospective point-of-view shot of her by Aduka, but this is not the case – the close-up defines her look as darsan, as her desire for him and his presence as a godlike object of desire. The signs of disaster are there to be read; even so, this is the only scene in the film that is at all dominated by happiness and laughter.

SEMERAH PADI is a variation on the Laila/Majnun story. Dara is the daughter of the kampung headman and her parents want her to marry Teruna (of course!), the headman's deputy. Teruna's parents seek this match as much as Teruna himself does, but it is clear that Dara has no time for him. Even so, she obeys her father and is betrothed to Teruna. The villagers dance in celebration, but are interrupted when a wounded villager, Kecewa (lit. forsaken), is brought to the headman. Kecewa found his wife in bed with a stranger, both of whom then attacked the husband. Kecewa dies and Aduka and Teruna are sent to arrest the culprits. The lovers, Jejaka (lit. youth) and Galak (lit. shameless, fierce), refuse to submit and fight the warriors until exhausted. They remain defiant; the headman finds them guilty of adultery and murder and sentences them to death by impalement ('sula'), the traditional *Malay* punishment for adultery.[27] Jejaka's brother, Borek, takes vengeance upon the kampung by brutally killing men and women and burning down houses. The kampung is barely able to defend itself – a situation exacerbated when an envoy of the Sultan asks the headman to supply 'volunteers' to fight pirates. Teruna is chosen to lead the volunteers, leaving Aduka in charge of the defense of the kampung. Borek kidnaps Dara and is only saved from being sexually assaulted by the opportune arrival of Aduka, who kills the villain and takes the unconscious Dara to a hut, where her desire for him eventually results in them having sexual intercourse. Upon his return, Teruna finds a weeping Dara and a repentant Aduka, who asks Teruna to kill him. Teruna forgives him and tells him to leave the kampung. The kampung headman is not so forgiving and gives Aduka and Dara 100 strokes each with the rotan as punishment for committing adultery. Aduka and Dara are finally married, although no one seems particularly happy, least of all the married couple.

Historically, the film is set in the era prior to the Hang Tuah story. This pre-Golden Age period is a critical moment in the self-definition of the Malay people. The film concentrates on the important role of Islam in the creation of community, but this is continually linked to the concept of 'bangsa' (lit. race, family, nation), to construct a 'narrative of a nation' that combines the secular and the religious, or perhaps more accurately, defines the national through the religious. The kampung becomes the site of this 'identity formation,' shaped by the resolution of a series of crises that are internal and external, moral and secular. The 'newness' of Islam is implied in the conversation Teruna has with the headman after his return from a nearby kampung – Teruna mentions that they were starting to build a mosque. However, the film is primarily concerned with Islamic law as an instrument of moral and social order. While the kampung has an imam, seen presiding over the betrothal ceremony, the dispenser of this law is the headman, the undisputed and sole arbiter of justice (the kampung's socio-political-religious system resembles the kerajaan model discussed in chapter 2).

The issue that triggers the film's deliberations on crime and punishment is adultery. In fact, SEMERAH PADI's publicity stills all carry the statement 'Hukum Zina Dalam Islam!' (lit. the law of adultery in Islam!) above the title of the film (Jamil Sulong, 1990: 141-143). The betrothal of Teruna and (the reluctant, but obedient) Dara is carried out by the imam, but announced to the villagers by the headman. The celebratory traditional dance, a spectacle of order and harmony (the song's tribute to Semerah Padi matches the Edenic world visualized in the post-credit sequence) is disrupted by the cries of the fatally wounded Kecewa, who tells the headman of his wife's adultery. The betrothal and the transgression are thus directly linked, acting as both a warning to Dara (and Aduka) and (like the dance in HANG TUAH) a premonition of subsequent events. Jejaka and Galak exhibit a reckless abandon in their desire for each other that is not evident in Aduka and Dara's relationship, but the adulterous couple's 'lovemaking' in the hut before their capture does visualize what is elided when Aduka and Dara sleep together in another hut. The headman, in sentencing the lovers to death, suggests that the adultery they committed led them to murder and warrants the full force of the law of Islam – at the same time he warns the villagers (who include Dara and Aduka) that they will be similarly punished if they follow in the footsteps of Jejaka and Galak. Such behavior, more importantly, is categorized as blatant treachery to God, nation (bangsa) and religion. The death by impalement is performed in front of all the villagers, with Aduka singing the Muslim call to prayer over the dying lovers.

Somewhat later in the film, Teruna and Dara are once again together, this time by themselves. Dara responds to his questions about their future home with minimal enthusiasm and a polite deferral to his decisions. For a second time, their legally sanctioned association is disrupted by intimations of discord. In this case, the headman has to adjudicate Solomon-like on the conflict between two villagers; once again, they are judged by the laws of Islam and their punishment requires them to help each other complete their work. The scene is more didactic than the earlier ruling, but essentially serves the same purpose: to affirm the value of Islam to uphold moral and (now) social order. The film goes on to present Islam as an even more powerful force, when the headman, unable to convince a group of captives to reveal the name of their leader, acknowledges their loyalty, but at the same time, warns them that Semerah Padi's villagers are *more* loyal, because their loyalty is to the teachings of Islam. The implication is that these captives are not Muslims and thus inferior to Semerah Padi's villagers; nevertheless, they are to be punished according to Islamic law: death after the morning prayers.

The culmination of these thematic concerns is the adultery and punishment of Dara and Aduka. Technically, their sin is not adultery, but the Malay/Arabic word 'zina' covers both adultery and fornication. The earlier 'warning' about adultery was heeded by Aduka, who made all possible efforts to keep away from Dara. She, however, is much less reticent and the absence of Teruna, away fighting the pirates, makes their meeting (melodramatically) inevitable – it is signaled by a cymbal clash (as was her pre-betrothal meeting with Teruna). She seeks him out, but Aduka ignores her, leaving her sitting beside a moon-reflecting pond wiping away her tears (a scene reminiscent of Melur's sadness after Tuah left Gunong Ledang in HANG TUAH). As 'punishment' for her frankness, she is abducted by Borek, the leader of the marauding band and about to be raped by him, when Aduka comes to her rescue. He carries her unconscious body to a hut for shelter against a violent thunderstorm (always a sign of foreboding). Her regaining consciousness is presented in medium close-up, which emphasizes her breasts as well as her face. At first it seems coded as Aduka's point-of-view, but, as in the film's first sequence, this is not the case. The image connotes *her* desire for him, an interpretation confirmed by the film cutting to a wider shot, showing Aduka self-absorbed in removing his wet shirt, while Dara now looks at him passionately. Aduka stands in the teeming rain to avoid her insistent declaration of love. He is facing the camera, while in the background, Dara slowly walks out into the rain, never ceasing to look at him. The desired body, presented in all the sexual physicality available to Malay cinema at this time, is that of Aduka; Dara's look engages the darsan discourse once again and Muslim propriety is nowhere to be seen. Aduka takes her back into the hut and throws her to the ground, but she grabs hold of his leg and pleads with him. The lighting has become more melodramatic (predominantly from below) and the camera slowly tracks back to present, in a tableau shot again typical of Indian cinema, the bare-chested Aduka with Dara crying at his feet. However, Dara is the sexual aggressor here and her willingness to sacrifice everything for Aduka (recalling the absolute commitment of Galak to Jejaka), makes him succumb to her pleas. The camera modestly pans to a burning torch, which is blown out by a gust of wind. Passion and desire won't surface in the film again.

The punishment for their transgression is dispensed by the headman in accordance with Islamic law, but this time it is accompanied by pleas for clemency from Teruna and some of the villagers (but not the mothers of the two victims). Even the headman himself seems reluctant to continue with the canings, but he argues that he cannot and must not break the law of Islam. Earlier, Teruna had forgiven Aduka, but not Dara, to whom he referred to as 'rotten meat.' Dara does ask forgiveness from her father, but again he is restrained by his role as law dispenser; she then prostrates herself before him, signifying her submission to the law, while at the same time saying that her love knows no law. The headman doles out equal punishment to both Dara and Aduka, but the film punishes only Dara. Teruna asks Aduka why his commitment to Islam has faltered, but no such inquiry is made of Dara, who comes to represent the unreconstructed pre-Islamic symbol of sexual desire. The compassion of Islam enables the film's resolution to take place, since the marriage of Aduka and Dara is permitted by law. The actual wedding ceremony is not shown and even the film's final shot of the bersanding, the Indian-derived custom of viewing the seated married couple, offers little joy for anyone.

Aduka's character is weak and passive, a victim of a woman's passion that he is unable to resist – Aduka's Devdas-like behavior signals his lack of direction and ultimate dissolution. Unlike previous P. Ramlee characters, Aduka is not presented as the film's hero, for he betrays his religion and his community. Teruna tells him to leave Semerah Padi to avoid punishment (by the headman). However, Aduka is resigned to his fate, actively seeking death at the hands of both Teruna and the headman, who rejects revenge and instead invokes the new Islamic sanctions. Teruna emerges as the film's most positive figure, forgiving his friend and accepting the impossibility of marrying Dara (whom he, in any case, claims to love less than he loves Aduka). His commitment to community transcends his personal interests: when Aduka is sent to capture the adulterous couple, Teruna offers to accompany him, despite it being his betrothal ceremony – he says that country and religion are more important, a sentiment with which the headman agrees. Teruna, the loyal deputy headman, is Hang Tuah to Aduka's Hang Jebat, who committed treason by committing adultery, because that moral offense threatened the coherence of the community of Semerah Padi.

The adultery of Jejaka and Galak also sets in motion the film's commentary on social order and disorder, by introducing the threat of the 'other.' Jejaka is the first of the film's outsiders, whose death leads his brother Borek to vow vengeance on Semerah Padi's headman. However, it is the internal conflicts that really lead to the invasion of the village by Borek's band: Galak's adultery and the dispute between the two villagers. Borek and his men have observed the latter scene, which acts as a trigger for his decision to kill the headman. The attack on Semerah Padi (to attack the village is to attack the headman) is presented as the actions of brutal savages; the maniacal laughter accompanying their slaughter is contrasted with the melodramatic screams and agonizing deaths of the kampung men and women, clearly defining them as 'other'; also our 'other,' as they threaten us by swinging their machetes at the camera. The threat of chaos and anarchy lies over the kampung and soon extends beyond Semerah Padi to include the whole of the Sultan's domain. However, the enemy is not just external, he has found sanctuary within the kampung. While Teruna and others help rid the Sultan of pirates, Aduka manages, almost by chance and at great personal cost, to find and kill the internal foe, Borek. The elimination of the threatening 'others' (Borek and his men, the pirates *and* the desiring women, Galak and Dara) forms and consolidates the identity of the bangsa and the central role of Islam within it. While the film doesn't end in personal happiness, it has demonstrated the powerful role of religious conviction and community commitment in establishing order. It is, however, a hierarchical order centered on the absolute power of the headman and based on Islamic law: the 'newness' that has entered this world. Interestingly, the headman remains in his house throughout the film, leaving it only to judge or lecture his people. He doesn't lead them in battle; like the Sultan in HANG TUAH, he employs others (e.g. Teruna and Aduka) as the 'instruments' of his power. The film constructs the origin of a new religious and social system, but it also, not surprisingly, speaks to its own era. Completed the year before independence, it can be seen as a discourse on governance and the role of Islam in the new nation.[28] Its concern with external and internal threats, while identified as marauders and raiders in the film, might also suggest the dangers of communist insurgents/guerillas and non-Malay communities to the survival and identity of Malay/Muslim society, occasioning the call to sacrifice by the headman in the film and by Malay leaders in the early 1950's.

Given the forest setting and its themes of loyalty and faithfulness in the face of disorder, it is not surprising that SEMERAH PADI evokes the films of Kurosawa. In fact, the influence was quite conscious; Jamil Sulong recalls that he, P. Ramlee and Omar Rojik talked about Kurosawa's camera placements and camera movements and that Aduka's walk through the forest was based on that of the woodcutter in Kurosawa's 1950 film, RASHOMON (Jamil Sulong, 1990: 147, 152). The camera certainly follows Aduka through the forest accompanied by drumbeats, but the outcome, where he jumps into the clearing to confront Borek like the bogey man in a bad melodrama, destroys the mood and the carefully constructed rhythms that precede it. Nevertheless, the film adeptly employs tracking shots and mise-en-scene stagings in total contrast to P. Ramlee's previous film, PENARIK BECA. The first meeting of Dara and Teruna, after she returns from visiting Aduka and his mother, is elegantly shot in a mobile single take, utilizing deep space and diagonal composition to highlight Teruna's interest in her, while she simultaneously manages to hide her feelings about him yet still recollect her recent meeting with Aduka. The attack on the kampung by Borek's men resembles the frightening invasion of the potter's village in UGETSU MONOGATARI (Tales of Ugetsu, 1953), but lacks the dispassionate tone of the Mizoguchi film – the villains and the victims are too quickly caricatured as grotesque ogres and terrified innocents.

Malaysian film critics praised the film for its adoption of Kurosawa-like techniques (Baharudin Latif, 1989c: 63), but the film is actually much closer to the Indian melodrama tradition. Kurosawa's changing perspectives and Mizoguchi's distanced emotional stance are both too 'cold' for an esthetic based on intensity and heightened drama (for Indian audiences, even Hollywood's melodramatic style is considered too dispassionate). SEMERAH PADI continues the gestural acting style, expressive lighting, signals of foreboding (plot 'forecasts,' musical stings) and coincidence (when the headman and his wife discuss Teruna as a possible son-in-law, he appears at their door). There is also a 'telepathic' moment, when Teruna, still away from the kampung, suddenly awakens and calls Dara's name, immediately after Dara and Aduka make love. Such 'telepathic' sequences are recognized for their 'essential "Indianness," in conveying fate's dominion over individual destiny' and part of the Indian melodramatic tradition from DEVDAS (1935) onwards (Rajadhyaksha and Willemen, 1999: 262). The film's only song is narratively significant in being the only instance of Aduka overtly indicating the great sadness that has befallen him because of Dara's betrothal to Teruna. Sitting by a running stream under a crescent moon, Aduka's demeanor and mournful singing signify his dejection, even though he is singing the community-oriented title song that was earlier heard under the credits (also sung by P. Ramlee, but with a female chorus). The two dances, one in celebration of Dara and Teruna's betrothal, the other farewelling the men chosen to fight the pirates, are based on the traditional Zapin village dances, which were typically performed in front of the headman's house (as they are here), but originally only by male dancers (here there are separate rows of male and female dancers and the song is sung by a woman) (Mohd Anis Md Nor, 1993: 54, 10). The influence of contemporary dance styles and Bangsawan are apparent in the presentation of these dances in the film: performance by both sexes, choreography for a proscenium stage presentation and a lack of interaction between dancers and community (Mohd Anis Md Nor, 1993: 12, 52). The 'authenticity' of these dances are therefore culturally, if not ethnographically, accurate, a contention equally applicable to the status of Indian film music in relation to its traditional musical form.

It is interesting to compare SEMERAH PADI to the Indonesian film, HARIMAU TJAMPA (already referred to in the previous chapter). Both films are concerned with kampung headmen, who wield power over their subjects. The Indonesian film unequivocally criticizes the headman's abuse of his position and his essential corruptness (in that respect, he stands in for the narratively invisible Dutch colonial power); Semerah Padi's headman is equally absolute in his control over his people, but his power is presented as being in the community's best interest. The melodramatic mode is evident in both films, but in HARIMAU TJAMPA, this is muted by the naturalistic lighting that results from its location shooting. P. Ramlee employs a more Indian-oriented style of lighting and studio-dependent staging. The Indonesian film's critique of authoritarianism (and, by implication, of Sukarno's leadership) could not be further from the Malayan film's concurrence and support, even propaganda, for that country's eagerly awaited independence (Indonesia's post-independent political realities represented a very different context).

SEMERAH PADI's sober and ultimately tragic conclusion (the marriage of Aduka and Dara) may seem puzzling given the film's ideological commitment to heralding in a new nation. However, the eradication of individualized, traditional (pre-Islamic), and aberrant social and moral behavior is a crucial precondition for the creation of a new and homogenous ethno-social structure. The film's historical-mythical narrative, which is presented *as if* it was a foundational text, is thus constructed as a proposal for the governance of the soon to be independent nation of Malaya.

HANG JEBAT (Hussain Haniff, 1961)

The film's title succinctly signals a shift in emphasis in the treatment of the traditional story as compared to the 1956 film, HANG TUAH. In the earlier film, Hang Jebat only became a significant character once the court officials began plotting the demise of Hang Tuah – even then, Jebat remained secondary to Tuah, acting as a foil for his actions and a trigger for his eventual moral doubt.

Figure 16: HANG JEBAT advertisement

HANG JEBAT reverses this situation. Jebat totally dominates the film and his conflict is as much with the Sultan as with Tuah, who is little more than a stock character constantly affirming his loyalty to the Sultan and his condemnation of Jebat's betrayal. Even in the final scene, as he comforts the dying Jebat, Tuah's conviction of the righteousness of his actions overwhelms any emotional response to the impending loss of a close friend. Yet, the film's revisionist interpretation of the Hang Tuah story is tempered by its predominantly traditional stylistic and cultural characteristics.

HANG JEBAT is based on Ali Aziz' 1959 play, *Hang Jebat Menderhaka* (Hang Jebat Commits Treason), which itself was part of a broader re-interpretation of the Tuah/Jebat relationship that took place in Malay society in the 20th century. The play stresses Jebat's individuality and his personal and social convictions, thereby undercutting the role of fate so central to the Hang Tuah story and to the Malay world-view, while adopting elements of western dramaturgy and philosophy (Nanney, 1988: 167). The film, scripted by its director and the playwright, similarly presents Jebat as a tragic figure doomed by his own inflexibility and inner turmoil. The narrative trajectory is much more in the classical Hollywood mold than HANG TUAH (and most other Malayan films of this period), replacing the hieratic form of the earlier film with an emphasis on psychological realism, individual characterization, the continuity system and narrational strategies like suspense and surprise.

HANG JEBAT assumes much greater pre-knowledge than the earlier film, because it only deals with a very small portion of the Hang Tuah saga. In story terms, the film is closer to the *Hikayat Hang Tuah* than to Sheppard's book or Majumdar's film. There is much greater emphasis on Jebat's occupation of the palace and his involvement with the dayang, on the expediency/deceit with which Tuah grabs the magical kris that enables him to fatally wound Jebat and on the inclusion of Jebat's amuk episode, during which he kills a large number of Melakans before staggering into Tuah's house to die in his arms. On the other hand, the film introduces the character of Dang Baru, a dayang belonging to the Bendahara, who becomes Jebat's lover and wife (a retrospective status announced by Jebat on his deathbed – his transgressions did not include immorality!). A more interesting inclusion is a scene in which Jebat offers the people food and gives them jewels from the palace treasury – this will be discussed at some length below. The film diverges most from the *Hikayat Hang Tuah*, Sheppard's book and the 1956 film in its delineation of the main characters. Jebat may not be designated as a hero-figure, but he is the protagonist with whom we are asked to sympathize, although this does fluctuate throughout the film. Initially, Jebat is an anguished soul, set to avenge the terrible wrong inflicted upon his beloved friend, Hang Tuah. Frequent close-ups, tracking shots into his face and voice-overs provide perspectival and emotional identification with Jebat.

Jebat seems to delight in the Melakan people's awareness of his interdiction and he repeatedly parodies the court behavior of the Sultan. It leads to a remarkable scene, where Jebat occupies the palace and invites the people to eat palace food and to take home the Sultan's jewels, which, he argues, belong to the people anyway. Jebat rejects their attempts to pay homage to him, saying that, unlike the Sultan, he does not crave power. In effect, Jebat here implies the creation of a new polity, based on a revolution by the people against the absolutist hierarchical system represented by the Sultan (and Tuah) – this proposition well exceeds the crimes that are traditionally considered to constitute Jebat's treason: personal revolt against the Sultan and defilement of the palace. It is a truly radical agenda, since it rejects the identification of the state as kerajaan – the condition of having a raja (Kessler, 1992: 136) – and thus the central principle underpinning the Melakan Sultanate; it is therefore not surprising that the film quickly drops this theme. After this first 'democratic' gesture, Jebat sends the people home, telling them he will invite them again so that he can 'return' more of the Sultan's riches – the film does not make any subsequent reference to such an event. Furthermore, Jebat is now increasingly defined as hedonistic in his enjoyment of the 'pleasures' of the palace (food, music, the dayang), as power-hungry, when he considers himself as 'a king to all in sight and a Sultan in his heart' (appropriating the roles he had earlier denounced) and as insane, a condition that will inevitably lead to the amuk episode; only on his deathbed does Jebat return to the personal anguish he initially harbored. These changes in Jebat's character complicate his persona, but do not actually produce a complex figure. In that respect, the psychological realism mentioned above is less than convincing, with Jebat occupying a series of roles that recall the stock characters of Wayang, Bangsawan and previous Malay cinema.

It might well be more productive to contrast Jebat's changing emotional states with those of the Sultan, who, according to tradition, ought to remain the film's center of intolerance and intransigence. At the start of the film, the Sultan is angry and abusive, demanding a public affirmation of allegiance from all his court officials now that Tuah has betrayed him. In that context, Jebat's vengeance is perfectly reasonable. Once he has named Jebat as the new Laksamana, the Sultan remains narratively insignificant until Jebat's behavior becomes intolerable for him to bear. As Jebat taunts the now quite helpless ruler and becomes more imperious himself, the Sultan begins to assume the mantle of sanity and reason. This recuperation of the Sultan (and thus of the system he represents) contrasts with the increasing insanity of the democrat (even Marxist?), Jebat. When the Sultan apologizes to the ever-loyal Hang Tuah for his hasty judgment, the film's sympathies definitely lie with these men and no longer with Jebat. This is further confirmed by the mood of the people outside the palace when Tuah and Jebat are fighting each other. Their earlier praise for Jebat has now turned to hatred, as they seek to kill him for his betrayal – of the Sultan and, therefore, of the Sultanate. Order is restored, Wayang-like, and the rebellious Jebat is reduced to a tragic figure, unable to overcome, Hamlet-like, the conflicts within himself – the film's daring agenda is defused, withdrawn and erased.

Only the women remain loyal to Jebat. Hang Tuah's wife, a character that usually doesn't enter the story until well after the events covered in this film, is more affectionately treated by Jebat than by Tuah, who, upon his return from exile, even accuses her of unfaithfulness with Jebat (once again, the Rama/Sita/Ravana 'syndrome'). Similarly, Dang Baru never wavers in her love for Jebat. Like Jebat, she is not concerned about the Bendahara's response to her relationship with Jebat (despite being the Bendahara's 'property'). Both Dang Baru and Jebat rejoice in her pregnancy and Jebat later calls her the Datin Laksamana (the Lady Laksamana). On Jebat's deathbed, she affirms her faith in him and after he dies pronounces Jebat's behavior as a lesson for future generations.[29] It is indeed fitting that she speaks the film's final words, which suggest a contemporary relevance to Jebat's motivation, even though the film does construe his actions as tragic and doomed to failure. The group of dayang that Jebat invites into the throne room become 'his' women, although no sexual relationships are directly suggested by the film. Their support for him is repaid near the end of the film, when Jebat halts his fight with Tuah to allow Dang Baru and the dayang to leave the palace before the inevitable outcome. This contrasts with the fate of these women in the *Hikayat Hang Tuah*, where Jebat 'kills the seven hundred palace women – not one remains. Their blood flows under the palace like a heavy rainfall' (Errington, 1975: 109).[30] The earlier scenes where Jebat lies on the throne surrounded by the dayang come as close as the film does (and probably can) to conveying the eroticism and sensuality that Jebat induces in others in the *Hikayat Hang Tuah*, when he recites a story and 'his clear sweet mellifluous voice soothes the raja to sleep and makes the palace women lustful' (Errington, 1975: 117) – this episode led Salleh Ben Joned to label Jebat as a hedonist-anarchist, rather than the political rebel proposed by Kassim Ahmad (Salleh Ben Joned, 1994a: 127). Jebat's continuing affiliation with the women in the film does imply (and no more than imply) something of this hedonism.

Jebat's rescue of Dang Baru, as she is being sexually assaulted by one of Pateh Kerma Wijaya's henchmen, initiates a love affair that, despite the brutal context of their meeting, resembles the relationship between Hang Tuah and Melur in the earlier film. Dang Baru and Melur are both additions to the traditional story and both function as the main protagonist's love interest. In both films, the first romantically characterized meetings are set in idyllic garden-like settings and occur at night in the presence of a full moon. In HANG JEBAT, the scene begins with Dang Baru singing a traditional Malay love song, while walking through the moonlit woods close to the beach. Jebat then arrives and their conversation, while a little more frank, is much like that in HANG TUAH. It is the film's only love scene and employs all the characteristics of the Indian love-song format. The song is integrated into the plot as an expression of her joy and love for Jebat, but paradoxically, the scene's excessive length actually 'freezes' the narrative; this is further exacerbated by Dang Baru's disappearance from the film until the climactic palace fight – her intermittent presence in the film is also reminiscent of Melur's role in HANG TUAH. The film otherwise exhibits only limited Indian influence: the performance style and musical 'warnings' at moments of crises being the most obvious examples of that melodramatic tradition.

While there is only the one song in the film, there are two dance numbers. The second of these is performed by the dayang for Jebat and the people he invited into the palace; its purpose is thus similar to the distribution of food and jewels: to give the Melakan people access to the pleasures of this previously taboo world. The first dance is much more significant. It purportedly celebrates the Sultan's appointment of Jebat as the new Laksamana. When being presented with Tuah's magical kris, Jebat kisses it and stares at it obsessively. The dayang then dance and sing in praise of the new Laksamana – one of the dancers is holding a kris, thus mimicking the ceremony that has just taken place. The dancers are frequently filmed from ground level and from overhead, creating formal patterns set against the abstract designs painted on both the ceiling and the floor. This scene has been labeled as a bold experiment with mise-en-scene and cinematography: 'For HANG JEBAT, [Hussain Haniff] featured a Busby Berkeley-type dance sequence, hanging an overhead camera to capture elaborate body patterns of a Malay folk dance' (Cheah, 1997: 55). This Busby Berkeley 'effect' was quite commonly incorporated in many film musicals and also in Indian and Malay melodramas – HUJAN PANAS contains a performance number that constantly cuts to overhead shots of the dancers as abstract designs. In Malay films, these Zapin-inspired dances were often filmed from above to create circular and arabesque floor patterns (Mohd Anis Md Nor, 1993: 56);[31] these stylistic flourishes also conformed to the non-figurative nature of Islamic art.

The mood of the dance becomes more somber as the camera executes a lengthy overhead tracking shot from the dancers to the seated Sultan. To repeated close-ups of an upset-looking Sultan and a frowning but nodding Jebat, who seems to recognize its significance, the dancers enact the tragic story of Tuah and Jebat – the dancer with the kris is now stabbed by a fellow dancer, who then holds her in her arms as she dies. The dance then reverts to the more cheerful opening style, with the women singing about the newly appointed warrior loyally and willingly giving his life for his Sultan – quite a misreading of the future, after the perspicacious forecast of the slower middle dance. Everyone is now happier except Jebat, who seems to understand the relevance of the performance. In that respect, the film does characterize his enterprise as fate-driven, contrary to the earlier comment that this Jebat had a greater sense of individual control over his destiny than the Jebats of previous versions of the story. However, it might be more useful to regard this dance as a sign of foreboding, an omen that Jebat consciously disregards; on the narrational level, the scene suggests some self-knowledge on the part of the narrative – both of these perspectives align this fascinating, condensed version of the Tuah/Jebat legend with the similarly functioning, if more opaque, Ravana/Sita/Rama dance at the court of Majapahit in HANG TUAH.[32]

As with other versions of the story, the actual conflict between Tuah and Jebat is considered the core event (the spectacle whose outcome, like the fratricidal war in the *Mahabharata*, is inevitable), and this film extends the fight into a lengthy physical and verbal battle that begins to approach its presentation in the *Hikayat Hang Tuah*, where the two warriors alternate fighting with discussions and eating over a period of some seven days – all undertaken with a lack of personal animosity and an absence of passion (Ché-Ross, 1996), difficult to 'motivate' in contemporary psychologically driven narratives. This film emphasizes the anguish and the sad loss of friendship, especially as voiced by Jebat. One of his pleas to Tuah is actually made to the audience, with Jebat moving into close-up and speaking to the camera, thereby obliterating Tuah totally from view. It is almost as if he seeks the viewer's intervention, without Tuah's presence complicating the issue. There are a number of interruptions that lengthen the scene and function to delay the inevitable conclusion: the shots of Hang Kesturi killing some of the crowd that seek to enter the palace to kill Jebat, the departure of the women from the palace, and the scene where some of the crowd run under the palace and jab their spears through the floor, almost wounding Hang Tuah. This causes Jebat to propose, not surprisingly given the earlier comments about his 'sexual' exploits, that they adjourn to the Sultan's bedroom, where, just as inevitably, he is quickly ensnared in the curtains by Tuah and fatally wounded by the magical kris that Tuah had deceitfully retrieved from Jebat. Tuah then calmly walks out of the palace leaving Jebat to bind his wound so that he can undertake his amuk, an episode central to the *Hikayat Hang Tuah*, but only staged here in a brief scene – even so, its 'unmotivated' brutality sits uneasily in a text with pretensions to realism.

Just as Jebat has tended to eclipse Tuah in recent decades as the preferred character, the film HANG JEBAT has also increasingly been considered a masterpiece of Malay cinema at the expense of HANG TUAH (Hamzah Hussin, 1994b; Cheah, 1997: 55). The film has even been compared to Kurosawa's THRONE OF BLOOD, Eisenstein's BATTLESHIP POTEMKIN (1925) *and* Welles' CITIZEN KANE (1941) (*Wings of Gold*, 1994: 44), a puzzling combination if ever there was one. The Kurosawa reference is of some relevance, but more for the similarly shot and edited forest scenes and accompanying ominous drumbeats of RASHOMON than the stark, stylized and ritualized THRONE OF BLOOD. The film's fluid camera work and expressive compositions do however reflect something of Kurosawa's work in general, for which Hussain Haniff had expressed some admiration (*Wings of Gold*, 1994: 43). Other commentators have responded more negatively to HANG JEBAT, either because of its denigration of Hang Tuah's hero status (Jamil Sulong, 1994) or because the films rising critical standing is indicative of the 'creeping Islamization and ethnocentrism of contemporary Malaysian society' – HANG JEBAT's Indian Muslim director being favored over the non-Muslim Phani Majumdar (Krishnan, 1994b).[33]

I have attempted to argue that HANG JEBAT is not as innovative as its supporters would claim and that HANG TUAH is not as traditional as its detractors might suggest. The arguments about the qualities of the two films are obviously set to continue in parallel with the ongoing reinterpretation of the Tuah and Jebat figures themselves. The most interesting Tuah/Jebat references in recent Malaysian cinema occur in the films of Rahim Razali, especially MATINYA SEORANG PATRIOT, in U-Wei Haji Shaari's PEREMPUAN, ISTERI &... and Aziz Osman's XX RAY II: films that incorporate elements of the legend into contemporary stories about Malaysians, demonstrating the continued relevance of the story to Malaysian cultural life.³⁴ The first two of these films will be discussed in detail later in this chapter.

IBU MERTUA-KU (My Mother-in-Law, P. Ramlee, 1962)

Figure 17: IBU MERTUA-KU advertisement

IBU MERTUA-KU may well be the swan song of the studio era; it wasn't the last Malay film made in Singapore (1967) nor P. Ramlee's final film there (1964), but its thematic density and stylistic bravura were a summation of the 'genius' of the studio system (to adapt one of André Bazin's best-known phrases). It is also P. Ramlee's most complex work, largely because of its adeptness at integrating a web of transtextual references. This process of doubling (the relationship of the anterior to the posterior text) is accompanied by a multitude of 'mirrorings' within the film itself. Much of this material is derived from his own earlier films, but Hindi cinema and Cantonese melodrama provide reference points that contribute to what became a highly personal text: 'A heavy melodrama told in a parable of his own experience' (Kee Hua Chee, 1992: 22).

Only one of these references appears to have been overt. The notorious scene in which the protagonist, Kassim Selamat (P. Ramlee), gouges out his own eyes is 'borrowed' from the 1951 Indian film, DEEDAR (A. Samad Said, 1994: 204). However, a closer examination of this 1951 Indian melodrama reveals further intertextual affinities. DEEDAR's lead actor was Dilip Kumar, the quintessential Devdas figure of Indian cinema even before he actually played that role four years later – P. Ramlee's characters are similarly shaped by that powerful cultural stereotype. Like DEEDAR, IBU MERTUA-KU is a lost-and-found narrative, in which the characters, through deceit, loss of memory or physical afflictions such as blindness, (mis)recognize each other with fateful consequences. Both protagonists and their first loves are separated by class differences and through fate, resulting (for different reasons and at different ages) in their blindness, after which they are given permanent shelter by a parent and daughter of a lower social class. A strong relationship develops between the protagonist and the daughter, one which is tested when an eye specialist, who has in the meantime married the protagonist's first love, restores his eyesight, enabling him to see his (now unavailable) beloved. His response to this situation is the self-blinding referred to above and leads to his departure from his first love's world with his second love.

While some specific events in the two films are identical – the self-blinding is immediately followed by the second beloved's sudden awakening and calling of his name, a 'telepathic' moment endemic to Indian cinema – there are also major differences: Kassim Selamat actually marries his first love, Sabariah, who returns to her mother – the mother-in-law from the title, who had totally disapproved of the relationship in the first place, largely because Kassim Selamat was an entertainer.[35] These 'differences' actually align the Malayan film with Cantonese Nanyang melodramas like LOVE IN PENANG, although, not surprisingly (given the discussion about gender dominance in Hong Kong cinema in the previous chapter), its protagonist is a female singer; this Cantonese film is said to '[reprise] most of the clichés of the genre: opposition from a feudal-conscious family to an unsanctioned match, the self-sacrifice of woman, the weakness of man' (Law, 1992a: 96) – comments equally applicable to IBU MERTUA-KU (in fact, 'Love in Penang' would be a more appropriate title for the Malayan film than its actual one).

Structurally, the film employs the doubling and mirroring paradigm characteristic of Indian films like AWARA (mother/son, father/daughter) and PYAASA (hero/helper, first beloved/second beloved), as 'localized' by P. Ramlee in his earlier films, especially ANTARA DUA DARJAT, where the dichotomies of past/present, kampung/Singapore, poor hero/rich heroine, upper class/lower class, hero/helper, heroine/servant are accompanied by the obsessive repetition of narrative events and are even alluded to in the title of the film itself. IBU MERTUA-KU's most schematic parallelisms occur in the film's first half hour, which is generically coded as a comedy, partly because of these doubling strategies – Kassim Selamat and Sabariah arrange to meet each other for the first time, but independently send their helper/servant instead to determine the other's physical attractiveness. There are other strong similarities between ANTARA DUA DARJAT and IBU MERTUA-KU, ranging from narrative events like the concocted death of the lover/wife and the return from Europe of the lover's betrothed (who is evil/deceitful, perhaps befitting such 'contamination'), through to both films' emphasis on the intolerance of the upper classes. Ismadi, the eye specialist who returns to Singapore early in the film, and his sister, Hayati, who seems most anxious to finalize the marriage arrangements between her brother and Sabariah, are, as already suggested, reminiscent of similar characters in ANTARA DUA DARJAT; in the earlier film, these characters are intent on acquiring the bride's inheritance, whereas here, perhaps because of the intertextual cross-reference, their over-solicitous concern for Sabariah's mother suggests, but never confirms, a similar intention. In ANTARA DUA DARJAT, as in a number of P. Ramlee's other films (especially SUMPAH ORANG MINYAK), the focus on intolerance and greed leads to overt and often awkwardly inserted social commentary, with the didacticism often 'crippling' the narrative and the characterization. IBU MERTUA-KU, while pursuing similar themes, contains them more effectively within its melodramatic mode of address.

Once Ismadi presents Sabariah, now uncharacteristically coy, with a necklace, the film abruptly switches from comedy to melodrama. This shift in tone is achieved through two 'empty' shots that function a little like Ozu's transition shots – the first is of a large wall-painting of a sailboat, the second is a high-angle shot of a living room with that same painting on its back wall; meanwhile the music has turned ominous and urgent. The next shot identifies this as a room in Ismadi's house, as Hayati and her husband enter his consultation room to announce the wedding date. The dramatic turn of events is particularly signaled by the high-angle shot, with its implication of an impersonal agency (fate) now controlling the course of events. The film intermittently returns to such a perspective, but from now on it will always contain the major protagonists, ritualistically performing their predetermined roles, 'trapped' within fate-orientated narrative conventions like doubling and repetition – the very essence of melodrama.

The relationship of the two women to Kassim Selamat is the most obvious of these 'repetitions with difference' and identifies the film as a more complex remake of HUJAN PANAS. At the beginning of the film, Sabariah, the daughter of a rich widow, is called to her room by her servant because Kassim Selamat is singing on the radio. The song is 'Jangan Tinggal Daku' (Don't leave me), which recurs a number of times in the film; it is clear that Kassim Selamat is a celebrated singer/saxophone player (like so many P. Ramlee characters), but Sabariah's response is quite remarkable. Exhibiting both ecstasy and desire, she strokes the radio and swoons on her bed. Her behavior is totally shaped by his voice, since she has never seen him; she decides to call him at the radio station and ask him for a date, to which he readily agrees. The desire expressed by Sabariah for Kassim's voice is significant within the film, but it also suggests the desire of the viewer/listener for P. Ramlee's voice – an intertextual reference (and marketing strategy) previously encountered in PENARIK BECA. Sabariah breaks off her engagement to Ismadi, incurring the wrath of her mother, who forces Kassim to marry her daughter, whom she then summarily expels from her house and excludes from her will. Later events in the film suggest that Sabariah's desire for Kassim was in fact a superficial infatuation, which itself stimulated his interest in her. Kassim's passivity is evident in his acceptance of the desires and dictates of others – once again invoking the Devdas figure, but it is also reminiscent of Majnun, the forlorn lover driven crazy by a world that cannot understand his loss.

The 'honeymoon' in Penang and its aftermath signal the end of their relationship and Sabariah's pregnancy provides her mother with the opportunity to take her back to Singapore. In time, Kassim, who remained in Penang, is advised that Sabariah died during childbirth. Kassim's grief overwhelms him to the extent that he spends the next two years isolated in a dark room, gradually going blind. Unable to afford even that small room, he wanders aimlessly around Penang until he falls asleep in front of a house gate where he is found and given accommodation by an older woman, whose daughter, Chombi, is herself grief-stricken due to the death of her husband three months earlier. When asked his name, Kassim says it is Osman. On one level, this is an attempt to remain incognito, but it also signifies the birth of a new person, shaped by the suffering he has endured – in keeping with the melodramatic tradition, the blindness has brought insight and understanding. The long sequence that follows his admission into this sorrow-filled household has certain features in common with the opening sequence already discussed, but the repetition/difference dynamic is such that the resultant relationship and emotional intensity are totally different. This sequence is probably the most complex and moving in all of P. Ramlee's films and possibly in all Malaysian cinema – its melodramatic excess, narratively and stylistically, is not so much reminiscent of Douglas Sirk as of Frank Borzage (one of his films has the following intertitle: 'Souls made great by love and adversity,' a fitting subtitle for this Malayan film) or the Kurosawa of THE IDIOT.

The sequence starts with Chombi alone in her room, weeping uncontrollably in front of her dead husband's photo. Kassim asks to be taken to Chombi's room, where he gently warns her that such grief can have disastrous consequences, as it did for him – his story moves the mother so much ('your narrative is so tragic') that she invites him to remain with them. Kassim is returned to his room, while the mother tries to console Chombi. They hear Kassim singing in his room and, as if in slow motion, they turn their heads towards the sound. The song is called 'Di Mana Kan Ku Chari Ganti' (Where can I find a replacement) and its lyrics sum up Kassim's despair *and* hope. The words also restage the film's repetition/difference paradigm referred to earlier: 'If my fate is so written/What can I do/*Where can I find a replacement/Who is like you...*/ How bitter my heart feels/I'm left alone without a companion/The world which was bright has become dark' (my italics).[36] After the first two lines quoted above, the film cuts to a high-angle shot of Chombi, who as if in a dream, slowly stands up and leaves the room. In the next shot, she walks down the corridor towards the camera while Kassim sings the italicized lines – linking their similar situations *and* the inevitable 'replacement' that each will become for the other. As Chombi walks along the corridor, she initially seems uncertain of where the singing is coming from, but eventually arrives at Kassim's door where, still crying, she falls to her knees, all the time listening to and looking at him. The song causes her to remember her husband, visualized as a double exposure of her still looking at Kassim, while in the background she is holding her husband's hand (he is dressed in army uniform, implying that his death was probably due to the communist insurgency that was still active in the early 1960's in northern Malaya); Kassim has a similar recollection, where he and Sabariah are framed at a window, while in the foreground, he finishes his song. While Chombi remains transfixed by Kassim's performance, there is no indication that he is aware of her presence at the door.

The film's 'compulsion to repeat' returns us to Chombi's room where she is now asleep in bed, watched over by her dozing mother. They are awakened by a loud metallic-sounding noise. Once again, the high-angle shot of the room shows Chombi rising from her bed (the dream reference is even stronger here) and it is followed by the shot of her walking along the corridor towards Kassim's room. Chombi and her mother arrive at his door to see him searching for the cup they had heard him drop. Chombi rushes to help him; as she does so, her image is reflected in a number of mirrors in the room. When she eventually stands up, the camera tracks slowly around her face – the mise-en-scene and camera movement combine to signify her 'resurrection from the dead.' Her mother wipes away her tears and Kassim, presuming they have left the room, prays to God for their protection; Chombi is now kneeling next to Kassim's bed and gazes at him with great intensity.

Chombi's response to Kassim's voice recalls Sabariah's erotic display earlier in the film – the two events illustrate the power of Kassim's music/voice to generate an intense attraction, almost involuntarily drawing the woman towards him. Both situations are darsan-driven, but the mood of the second sequence is closer to the religious/mystical rapport between a devotee and the deity – the alternation between the high-angled 'predestined' shots and the more tentative corridor shots further mimic the combination of fate and desire that drives that engagement. The initial lure is aural, but this is soon replaced by an emphasis on the gaze that is all the more intense because it cannot be returned (Kassim's blindness) – Sabariah's and Kassim's concerns about their self-image is replaced by Chombi's evacuation of self and absorption in the beloved. Such self-abnegation may also be characterized as an assertion of 'patriarchal authority.'[37] The patriarchal 'deification' of Kassim/Osman (and of the performer P. Ramlee) is certainly evident in this scene and perhaps in the film as a whole, but the ending of the film does suggest a more complex gender relationship.

The aural-visual conjunction of the two women's relationship with Kassim stands in stark contrast to the aural/visual dichotomy of Kassim and Ismadi. Kassim is the musician, listened to and looked at as the site of attention, while Ismadi is the eye-specialist, who actively intervenes to restore Kassim's sight. However, Ismadi is also associated with the male gaze (cf. Mulvey, 1975), illustrated by the large photos of Sabariah on the walls of his house that he longingly admires even after her marriage to Kassim. She is the object of his desire, whereas Kassim was the object of hers. Ismadi seeks to cure Kassim's blindness to appease his own guilt in deceitfully taking Sabariah from Kassim, but he cannot 'see' that Kassim's subsequent recognition of Sabariah and their son will inevitably lead to Kassim's self-mutilation (befitting a film about blindness and vision, misrecognition and recognition are crucial narrative devices). As the now blind Kassim leaves Ismadi's house, accompanied by thunder and lighting (generic signs of chaos and disorder), he is met by Chombi and her mother. In the last (high-angle) shot of the film, they walk away into the darkness.[38]

This darkness, which duplicates Kassim's second blindness, is not a sign of moral disintegration or tragedy. In fact, the ending can be construed as an optimistic resolution, for Kassim's blindness allows him to return, literally and emotionally, to Chombi's world. This is also her desire: 'And now I take you back, you are again blind, but I am happy. Come, let us go home, Kassim.' His dependence on her and her devotion to him neatly complement each other – to characterize this as the reaffirmation of patriarchy is misreading the complexity of the relationship. Certainly, Chombi is the more traditional of the two women in her demeanor and life-style (as Hasnah was in HUJAN PANAS), although Sabariah's assertiveness towards Kassim is swiftly replaced by a shyness, even coyness, when in the presence of Ismadi (somewhat like Azizah in PENARIK BECA, where I discussed the differences in gender behavior within and across class boundaries). Kassim's acceptance of his fate and lack of resistance to the dictates of Sabariah's mother and Ismadi make him P. Ramlee's most passive protagonist, although, in keeping with the Malay cinema's version of this Indian stereotype, there is a final moment of aggression – here, of course, self-directed.

Singapore, the metropolis, comes to represent intolerance and class-consciousness in contrast to Penang, the island of love and self-realization, a haven from the 'world' where social distinctions do not exist and where blind tramps are readily given shelter. In that respect, Penang is the kampung component of the archetypal kampung/city dichotomy, one of the most significant and recurrent themes of Malaysian cinema, especially in the films of recent decades. Like the kampung, the Penang of the film is ethnically homogenous (as is the Singapore of the film – this is quite ironic, considering that these two cities were and are the most Chinese of Malay(si)an cities). Penang's multi-ethnic population is only apparent in some brief scenes of the harbor and the city of Georgetown; as in the opening shots of Singapore in HUJAN PANAS, such diversity seems accidentally 'caught' by the documentary camera before it is quickly suppressed in the ensuing fiction. However, on a cultural level, Singapore was already losing its Malay identity by the early 1960's, following its exclusion from the then independent nation of Malaya. P. Ramlee was to physically return to Malaya in 1964, but perhaps the ending of this film already signals his desire to leave this 'foreign' place for a Malay destination. In this context, Chombi's (and the film's) final words are highly charged: 'Come, let us go home, Kassim' – that Penang was also P. Ramlee's birthplace would have given these words extra resonance. This final intertextual 'moment' is indicative of IBU MERTUA-KU's density and heterogeneity, qualities apparent in a number of the previous films discussed, but here developed to the point where the film's 'Malayness' is, paradoxically, its adventurous interweaving of very diverse cultural and social materials.[39]

MATINYA SEORANG PATRIOT (Death of a Patriot, Rahim Razali, 1984)

Figure 18: MATINYA SEORANG PATRIOT poster

During the kampung funeral of Haji Shahban, the 'patriot' from the title, his Melati Holdings company co-directors, having remained in Kuala Lumpur and clearly unmoved by his death, consider the qualifications of his son, Safuan, to be his replacement on the board. Accompanied by a low-angle shot of Safuan being embraced by mourners at the funeral, one of the directors describes him as 30 years old, two years married, no children, educated at Malay and English schools, not a university graduate, preferring his father's business, a silat expert like his father, chairman of the local youth club, not interested in politics, honest, clean, brave, direct and having a strong nationalist streak like his father. It is not a portrayal that the co-directors approve of – the film goes on to find them corrupt and responsible for Haji Shahban's death – but the 'like father, like son' reference is endorsed by the film as a rather good definition of the ideal Malay. Even the brutal revenge that Safuan and his brothers exact upon Haji Shaban's co-directors does not substantially tarnish this image. MATINYA SEORANG PATRIOT examines the viability of Malay values in a world where corruption in business (and perhaps in politics) is considered acceptable and even necessary. This kampung/city contrast is part of the broader traditional-modernity paradigm that underpins the whole film, thematically, culturally and cinematically.

The film's long credit/opening sequence covers the burial and the company directors' deliberations mentioned above in a quite complex narrational arrangement of shifting perspectives, flashbacks and image/sound displacements, conveying the impact of the past on the present and the interconnection of apparently distinct events. This sort of stylistic bravura is new in Malaysian cinema and reflects the different influences upon this new generation of filmmakers. Rahim Razali worked in advertising before making this film and has acknowledged being inspired by the films of Francis Ford Coppola (Somboon, 1984: 11).[40] However, the 'modernism' of the beginning of MATINYA SEORANG PATRIOT is not maintained throughout the rest of the film, which returns to the more traditional character-motivated flashbacks and telepathy-triggered cross-cutting of earlier Malaysian cinema. This ambivalence, or perhaps lack of conviction, permeates the whole film, characterizing it as a text 'in-between,' uncertainly looking forward, while constantly looking over its shoulder.

Most of the kampung scenes involve the family's response to Haji Shahban's death (mourning, revenge arrangements, silat practice) and flashbacks of him training his sons to be Malay warriors. The first of these flashbacks occurs during the funeral, while the sons carry his body to the grave. The father admonishes his sons for their lack of fitness as the five of them struggle to hold up a tree trunk (visually resembling the wrapped body at the funeral), but the point of the scene is to emphasize the power of combined, resolute effort. Only two of the five sons, whose names, rather schematically, all start with an S, play significant roles in the film, but their number and destined tasks construct them as contemporary versions of the five Pandava brothers in the *Mahabharata* and, more consciously, as Hang Tuah, Hang Jebat and the three lesser 'Hangs' from the *Hikayat Hang Tuah*. Reference to these two cultural texts recurs in a later flashback, where the father reminds his now young sons that they are the descendants of warriors and that he is teaching them silat to make them proper human beings. Steeped in the Malay animistic tradition, silat is a martial arts form that combines physical prowess with spiritual and emotional development.[41] Blessing his children with incense, he advises them to be fair and correct in their judgments, which will then shape their actions – the situation is strongly reminiscent of Krishna's advice to Arjuna before the cataclysmic battle in the *Mahabharata*. Haji Shahban then tells them to understand Tuah's loyalty *and* Jebat's rejection of injustice and tyranny. Razha Rashid suggests that the silat guru typically summons warrior spirits as models for his students, becoming 'the director of this seance of "dead" heroes'

(Razha Rashid, 1990: 77) – an apt description of the atmosphere of this scene. The Tuah/Jebat ethical stances are central to the film's (ambivalent) moral outcome, while the Tuah/Jebat fight is evoked in the silat confrontation between the two older brothers at the end of the film.

The familial harmony evident in these flashbacks starts to falter after Haji Shahban's death. The brothers are practicing their silat in the same enclosure as in the flashback, but suddenly the tension between the second son, Saiful, and one of the other sons breaks out in aggressive fighting, which ceases just as quickly, with them all embracing each other. Typical of the film's strategy of withholding plot information, it is not until just before the final fight between Saiful and Safuan (the oldest brother) that the first part of that scene is introduced as a flashback. One of the brothers calls Saiful a coward and a 'mommy's boy' and holds their mother responsible for the death of their father. Saiful says they are crazy. Safuan then hits him and points out that seeking revenge is not madness, but amuk, which was the mark of great heroes and is the proper description of their united efforts to avenge their father, who had himself threatened retribution against those who sought to destroy him. The film presents Haji Shahban and his sons as model Malays, but based on a conception of 'Malayness' that looks to the past, to legendary heroes like Hang Tuah and Hang Jebat (and further back to the elemental battle in the *Mahabharata*). In that respect, its themes of family loyalty and revenge exist outside society, whose only representatives in the film are, by default, the businessmen that are the targets of that revenge. Nevertheless, the conflict within the family – sons against sons and sons against mother – does suggest a criticism of that very Malay warrior culture that Haji Shahban has instilled in his children, but the film, while open about the familial tensions, is mute about their consequences and about that moral code's value and relevance in late 20th century Malaysian society.

The film's antagonists are clearly identified: organizations that thrive on corrupt practices and individuals that adopt unacceptable moral behavior – both are associated with the rejection of Malay kampung values in favor of westernized, metropolitan-centered expediencies. Men like Yusuf Mahmud, the Chairman of Melati Holdings, have compromised themselves in this new, materialist environment, while others, epitomized by Jamali, are contaminated by the evils of modernity: sexual profligacy, alcohol, blackmail and corruption. Jamali was the company director, who recited Safuan's resume in the opening sequence with an unconcealed antipathy towards the (kampung) values Safuan embodied. Not surprisingly, he is also the first of the board members to be killed by the unidentified assailants. Jamali, earlier identified as a married man is celebrating Safuan's failure (engineered by Jamali) to win a seat on the company board in his city apartment with his girlfriend. Alcoholic drinks, rock music, Playboy posters and showering with his girlfriend mark Jamali's decadence. These 'hedonistic' activities are intercut with point-of-view shots of an unknown person ascending the stairs to Jamali's apartment. The black-clothed intruder slashes at Jamali's body with a long knife and proceeds to slowly and sadistically kill him; this brutal attack is itself intercut with quite revealing shots of his girlfriend, who remained in the shower, unaware of Jamali's fate. The rock music-driven editing creates exciting rhythms and the repeated 'sexy' shots of the woman's naked body are strongly voyeuristic – 'pleasurable' spectator responses encouraged by the film, which has just 'killed' Jamali for his engagement in such activities, thus seriously compromising the film's condemnation of these 'depravities.' [42]

With two other directors dead and Yusuf the next likely victim, it is revealed that Haji Shahban had accused his co-directors of corruption and intended to discuss the matter with the Prime Minister. The film does not make any direct link between business and political corruption, but suggestions of collusion or at least, lack of political resolve in this matter remain. At an early kampung meeting, where Safuan's candidacy for the board is being discussed, a poster on the wall proclaims: Clean. Efficient. Trustworthy. This was Dr. Mahathir Mohamad's slogan on coming to office in 1981 (Ché-Ross, 1996) and Hamzah Hussin considered this scene to be a subtle criticism of the government of the day (Hamzah Hussin, 1994a).[43] Yusuf eventually decides to visit Haji Shahban's family to confess to his wife and sons that he and his board members had blackmailed Haji Shahban. Jamali's 'research' had uncovered that Haji's wife had, before her marriage, agreed to pose in the nude for her boss, a top English colonial administrator. When Haji Shahban was confronted with these photos at his house, he collapsed and died in Saiful's arms, holding a crumpled photo in his hand. The sons therefore knew about these photos for some time, but their mother, when presented with this revelation by Yusuf, is totally shaken and immediately seeks her sons' forgiveness. The sons show little sympathy for their mother, who now realizes that they are planning revenge for her husband's death and wonders who they are 'at war with.' These references to nakedness, shame and a brutal 'war' with Haji Shahban's business partners once again suggest the *Mahabharata*: the Pandavas' battle with their relatives, the Kauravas, being triggered by the sexual humiliation of Draupadi, the Pandavas' wife. The deception and depravity at the heart of this urban culture is now fully exposed by the film.

When Jamali's girlfriend walks into the living room, earlier in the film, and sees his blood-splattered body, she screams. This is immediately followed by a shot of Haji Shahban's wife waking up screaming and asking God's forgiveness. On the surface, this is a clever device joining two scenes, while the call to God by Haji Shahban's wife represents her subliminal telepathic awareness that one of her sons has committed the murder. In retrospect, it can be argued that it is a premonition of her own responsibility for her husband's death. However, the connection between the two women is perhaps less innocent – in both cases sexual display is linked to death; a third, more subtle example involves Yohanis' 'forwardness' with Saiful in his room – when she sits on his lap and they embrace, the film cuts to a flash of lightning, which then provides the realistic context for the murder of the third director, killed during a thunderstorm by another black-clothed 'avenging angel.' The correlation between sexuality and death is not made by the film, but it is crucial in shifting the conflict, which was earlier identified solely as a kampung/city one, into the family itself. The film is not particularly sensitive to these gender/sexuality issues, or to the broader representation of women; apart from the implicit and explicit guilt of the mother, the character of Yohanis is transformed from a confident, independent businesswoman to a helpless, whimpering bystander at the climactic fight.

The final Tuah/Jebat fight is triggered by Saiful's protection of Yohanis in the face of threats by Safuan and the other brothers. Saiful argues that Yohanis, although Yusuf's daughter, is not responsible for her father's actions, to which Safuan retorts that while their mother sinned, their father died. Safuan's commitment to the father is thus unambiguously pitted against Saiful's 'feminine' plea for justice, tolerance and forgiveness. The two brothers dress in the traditional warrior garb and, to the sounds of gamelan music, engage in a vicious silat conflict, which ends when Saiful is knocked unconscious after hitting his head against a picture of Haji Shahban on the wall. The blood stain on the picture seems to implicate Haji Shahban in Saiful's (and their mother's) treatment, perhaps representing a critique of the values he had espoused – however, it is rather difficult to find sufficient evidence for such an interpretation, indicative of the film's general sense of ambivalence. The film concludes with Yohanis cradling the still unconscious Saiful in her arms, while Safuan and the other three brothers give themselves up to the police, thus accepting their responsibility for the murders and recuperating their status as upright Malays. As Saiful awakes, the blue police car lights flicker across his body; he attempts to stand up (to follow his brothers?), but Yohanis holds him back in the final freeze-frame. The film's resolution is personal and familial and seems to have bypassed the social and political context of Haji Shahban's death, just as the more recent film, RINGGIT KASORRGA is unwilling to pursue its theme of political corruption. Saiful's Jebat is granted resurrection and his rejection of the tyranny of revenge (and loyalty) locates the film firmly within the camp of Tuah/Jebat revisionists.

Saiful therefore becomes the ideal Malay (a status originally bestowed upon Safuan and Haji Shahban), who acknowledges the modern complexity of Malaysian culture, yet reaffirms the centrality of Malay traditions (much like the tenets of the 1971 National Cultural Policy discussed in chapter 2). The issue of Malay cultural identity is first raised lightheartedly when Yusuf comes home for lunch and is welcomed by his daughter, Yohanis, as 'pater.' Her mother objects to this non-Malay term for father and later defends her attitude by serving 'Thai soup' on the grounds that it is a Malay, not a Thai, dish – earlier, however, she had been watching a video of THE WORLD OF SUZIE WONG (1960)! The more serious discussion of Malay identity revolves around Yohanis' argument with her boss, Hasnul, about the cultural focus of a publicity show they are arranging for clients. Hasnul considers her approach as too 'ethnic' and 'national' and demands a more 'universal' presentation. At this moment, Saiful enters the room and literally performs a response to Hasnul's 'universalism.' Saiful's 'lecture' on cultural identity initially accepts the beneficial influence of other cultures on Malay culture (Portuguese steps in Malay dance, Chinese and Latin American rhythms in Malay songs), but then calls a halt on further intermingling ('our culture... doesn't need to be more universal'). He then sarcastically confronts Hasnul: 'But you are right. The clothes are too Malay. So perhaps the dancers should wear cowboy hats, Malay shirts, Japanese slippers and loincloths like Tarzan. Universal enough? Sometimes we all seem to be illiterate. We don't know our own culture.'[44] Hasnul, feeling insulted, leaves the room, but Yohanis is overjoyed by this man and, in the tradition of Malay and Indian melodrama, already in love. Saiful's outburst, endorsed by the film, is not only an attack on the urban, westernized Malay executive, Hasnul, but also on the incorporative implications of Raj Kapoor's famous opening song in SHREE 420, which starts with the following words: 'My shoes are Japanese, my trousers are English, the red hat on my head is Russian but my heart remains Indian.'

Saiful subsequently inducts the 'culturally ignorant' (i.e. urban, westernized) Yohanis into traditional Malay culture, including a Wayang performance, where he even plays in the dalang's orchestra. Her wondrous response to the shadow puppets is matched by her look at him playing the flute behind the screen – Saiful *is* Malay culture. He is also, at this moment, the beloved intently gazed upon by the devotee. This (probably) unconscious reference to darsan is itself matched by the unacknowledged Indian influence on the Wayang. The film's cross-cultural references are employed and acknowledged, only to be denied and rejected; the hybridity of Indian culture and Malaysian culture are ultimately discredited in favor of a Malay homogeneity.

Paradoxically, the Indian 'connection' exists in the film's form as well, although its reference point is the Indian cinema of the 1950's.[45] The mother/son(s) scenario is reminiscent of the Indian cinema's fascination (obsession?) with this particular dyadic relationship, which remains secure at the end of the film, despite the strain that her 'unfaithfulness' has placed on that relationship. The Indian influence is also evident in the film's employment of strategies like telepathy, an attribute particularly associated with the mother. The cross-cutting techniques also function to create a sense of foreboding and predestination – while cleverly edited together, such scenes are linked by a fate-oriented omniscience and purpose typical of 1950's Indian and Malay cinema. There are also references to the Malay cinema's Golden Age in the casting of Saadiah as the mother (Saadiah was a major actor of the 1950's, starring in films like PENARIK BECA, HANG TUAH, SEMERAH PADI and ANTARA DUA DARJAT) and the inclusion of a P. Ramlee song, sung by the village children in the presence of Haji Shahban (the only song in the film).

MATINYA SEORANG PATRIOT is the earliest of the 'bumiputera' films discussed in this chapter and represents the transition from the Golden Age films to those of the 1990's. The 'death of the patriot' is a cause for mourning (and retribution), but it also has (tentative) overtones of the end of an era and a rethinking of traditional values and heroes – in this respect, the film's title glosses the Usman Awang's Hang Jebat-oriented play, *Matinya Seorang Pahlawan* (The Death of a Warrior, 1961). Furthermore, Islam is more overtly present in this film than in films from previous decades. Obviously, a film involving the death of a Malay is likely to contain a Muslim funeral ceremony, but there are a number of scenes set at Haji Shahban's grave that stress the religious aspects of Malay identity to a greater extent than the films of the previous decades did. The most remarkable is where the Haji's wife and Safuan's wife are pouring holy water and strewing flowers over his grave, while reciting from *The Qur'an*. The opening image of the scene is composed as a long shot of the two women at the grave, with a superimposed photographic mask that contours the image in the shape of the top of a mosque, suggesting the holiness of the site and perhaps the sanctification of Haji Shahban (the Haji means that he had made the pilgrimage to Mecca). There is also a reference to 'khalwat' (lit. close proximity), when Saiful, alone with Yohanis in his room, asks whether she is frightened of 'getting caught'; she replies that then they would get married. Khalwat crops up in many contemporary Malaysian films as a relatively minor plot element, as it never did in earlier films. It doesn't imply that the couple have had or are about to have sexual intercourse, because the khalwat usually functions as a form of control over characters or even blackmail (because the couple can be charged by the religious police). Whatever the films' attitude towards the practice, it does reflect the greater emphasis on Islam in Malaysian society.[46]

FENOMENA (Phenomenon, Aziz M. Osman, 1989)

Figure 19: FENOMENA poster

FENOMENA's plot and themes are strikingly similar to those of the Rahim Razali film, TSU FEH SOFIAH (The Convert, 1985): the protagonist, an outsider (non-Malaysian/non-Muslim) from another culture (western, urban) returns to the place of her youth, where something momentous happened to her as a child (a miraculous cure, a mother's death). This place is culturally significant and imbued with traditional Malay magic, but also 'infected' by Muslim 'fundamentalists.' She becomes attracted to an older, rather lonely, widowed man, who has a child with a serious illness, which requires expensive western medical treatment (in TSU FEH SOFIAH the child is not related). The woman heals/renews herself by saving another (the man, the child), but dies/disappears at the end of the film. While some of these plot elements might well resemble the American woman's film of the 1940's, e.g. REBECCA (1940) and NOW, VOYAGER (1942) (Doane, 1987), it would be a mistake to pursue that relationship too far. The films' concerns are much too local and their melodramatic reference point remains the 1950's/1960's Malaysian cinema (e.g. IBU MERTUA-KU) and its antecedents, the Indian and Chinese cinema (with the latter 'providing' the female protagonist that is so rare in the former). I am concentrating on FENOMENA rather than TSU FEH SOFIAH, because the cultural implications of westernization, Islam and the kampung tradition on Malay identity are more clearly articulated in the former film.

The 'childhood scene,' loved by Indian and Malaysian cinema,[47] opens the film and casts its shadow over the rest of the film. A subtitle mentions the place and the time: Bukit Besi, Terengganu, 1966. The most important of these descriptors is the general location, Terengganu, one of Malaysia's East Coast states, which have always been considered more 'Malay' than the more culturally hybrid West Coast. The film's kampung, Bukit Besi, is therefore especially Malay, a place where Islam has accommodated itself to animism. A doctor arrives to treat a distressed young girl (Isabella), daughter of an English mine manager and a Malay mother, but he cannot find anything wrong with her. As he leaves, a local bomoh (Malay magician/medicine man), Wak Labib, asks if he might look at Isabella and the parents reluctantly agree. He whispers some prayers over her and strokes her crying face, while a traditional Malay healing song, 'Ulek Mayang,' is heard on the soundtrack. The child seems comforted and even cured, to the joy of her parents and the bomoh. The mystical healing power of tradition and place is set against the failure of western medicine, just as Malay culture will come to be favored over western culture later in the film (and kampung culture over city culture).

Isabella, now a young woman, arrives at Kuala Lumpur's Subang Airport, where she is found to be carrying syringes in her baggage. The popularized Malaysian image of Westerners is instantly evoked and repeated throughout the film, despite the fact that it is quickly obvious that Isabella needs injections to combat her dizzy spells. Kuala Lumpur itself becomes something of a living hell as she desperately tries to find a hotel, in which to recover from her affliction. Nobody seems willing to help her, until, as she loses consciousness in the crowded street, we see a few longhaired youths looking at her. Malaysian audiences would recognize them as members of the 'heavy-metal-tinged' band, Search (the description is Lockard's, 1995: 24). The band had been seen earlier rehearsing in a recording studio, a scene that was then narratively unconnected to Isabella's plight, but the all-male band, especially its lead singer, Amy (short for Suhaimi), becomes the crucial link between Isabella and the East Coast. Isabella is given shelter in the band's house, treated as a sanctuary within Kuala Lumpur, which is otherwise never revisited in the film – the scenes in Search's recording studio represent a performance space rather than an actual location. The coincidence, inherent in melodrama, enables Isabella to find a photo in the house of Wak Labib standing next to Amy's brother, Azlan. It is now revealed that Amy also came from Bukit Besi and he becomes the guide to her return to 'source.'

Isabella, half Malay, but an English citizen, seems to be beset by a restlessness that is attributed to westernized, urbanized young people, seeking an alternative to the rationalist and materialist world. Doctors have given her six months to live (the injections only provide temporary relief) and she has decided to find a cure in the place of her birth, quoting a Malay proverb: 'If I lose my way at the end of my journey, I must return to the beginning of the road.' Her illness, never explained or identified in the film, is more of a metaphoric sickness, a cultural disease that requires a more mystical and natural remedy. Isabella rediscovers her origins in her Malay identity and she becomes the instrument through which Azlan and his daughter, Seri, are rescued from their respective emotional and physical afflictions.

The first shot of contemporary Terengganu shows a young girl, Seri, standing on the beach looking at the ocean. She looks to be the same age as the Isabella of the opening 'childhood scene.' The link between them is reinforced during Seri's leisurely stroll through the kampung (Bukit Besi), talking to her grandfather, Wak Labib, and watching men arm-wrestling in a thatched hut. Her wanderings through this familiar world are reminiscent of, yet in stark contrast to, Isabella's frantic flight through Kuala Lumpur. Apart from making further connections between the kampung girl and the western woman, the scene also sets in motion the film's idealization of the kampung. Even, or especially, for an urban Malay audience the significance of the kampung cannot be underestimated. Many Malays return to their family's kampung on feast days, not just to visit relatives, but also to revisit the 'heart' of their culture: 'All Malays will agree on the tremendous evocative power of the word "kampung," including those city born and city bred' (Sweeney, 1989: 110). Isabella's journey with Amy to the kampung, though not physically shown, is a most significant Malay cultural activity. The film continues to emphasize the idyllic nature of the kampung in two further sequences, in which Isabella and Seri walk along the beach – these sequences also trace Isabella's growing affinity with this environment. In one of her regular diary entries (into a micro-cassette recorder – operating as a 'realistic' voice-over), she notes her unexplainable improving health and contrasts it to Seri's earlier blackout, which Wak Labib treated in much the same way he helped the young Isabella 24 years earlier.

It turns out that Seri has a hole in her heart, a condition requiring an expensive overseas operation. Her father, Azlan, whose wife died in the kampung while he was studying in England (the danger of leaving home?), has withdrawn from the world, wallowing in melancholy and self-pity, emotional states that cripple his ability to help his daughter. Isabella tries to make contact with him by mentioning that she heard he was a good musician, like his brother, Amy – she presumes it to be a Malay cultural trait. Azlan sarcastically responds by saying he understood that she was a drug addict, perhaps a western cultural trait. Whatever the seriousness of these comments, they reinforce the film's broader agenda of glorifying Malay culture at the expense of western culture, which, together with Kuala Lumpur, becomes the film's 'other.' Despite his gruffness, Azlan does appear to be 're-awakened' by Isabella's presence – a change beautifully captured by his tentative plucking of the strings of his old guitar, at once sensuous and mystical, with the guitar representing his desire for Isabella as much as the return of his musical interest. Isabella convinces Amy to give a concert in the kampung, with proceeds helping with Seri's travel and medical expenses. As she voices her impatience for Amy's arrival, he walks into shot, a coincidence presented as unselfconsciously as such events were in earlier Malay and Indian films. The two then rudely shatter Azlan's reverie, but when Amy and Azlan embrace each other, Azlan's re-entry into life seems assured. Azlan's Devdas-like characteristics, his transformation through love and the rekindling of his spirit are strongly reminiscent of the sequence in IBU MERTUA-KU, where Kassim and Chombi help each other out of their despair and depression (if one substitutes Isabella for Kassim, there are some strong similarities between the two films). The relationship between Isabella and Seri has also been transformed into one of (surrogate) mother and daughter, thus constructing a putative family that seems destined to epitomize the kampung ideals.

Isabella's gradual 'Malayization' has been evident in the modest Malay clothing she has been wearing since arriving in Terengganu, but its critical realization occurs during a ritual prescribed by Wak Labib to treat her illness, finally making the connection between her ailment and her cultural transformation overt. The custom of bathing in flowers, 'Mandi Bunga,' is believed to bring fortune and good health, but here the metaphoric cleansing is also a rebirth into Malay identity. The song accompanying Isabella ladling flower petals over her (clothed) body is the same one heard when Wak Labib prayed over her as a child: 'Ulek Mayang,' in which seven sea princesses are called upon to cure the subject. The camera's 'looks' at various parts of her body being covered by water and flowers is quite fetishistic and represents a frankness atypical of Malaysian cinema. As a moment of exuberant self-absorption and self-realization, it looks forward to Azlan's 'erotic' caressing of his guitar. Whereas the spell of that experience was broken by the sudden entry of Isabella and Amy, the 'look' here becomes voyeuristic by cutting to a shot of Azlan watching her leaving the (outside) shower recess – the male protagonist thus occupying the 'look' previously directly addressed to the spectator. However, the nature of the visual exchange then changes once again, as

Isabella returns the gaze, smiling as she places a towel over her shoulders, eventually 'forcing' Azlan to look away. Only then does she turn and walk away. If these final shots of the sequence have a darsan aspect to them, they also signify a boldness on the part of the woman not seen before in Malaysian cinema (in previously discussed darsan scenes, the male has been unaware of the woman's gaze); this boldness is most fully elaborated in the Kali-like gaze of Zaleha in PEREMPUAN, ISTERI &..., which will be discussed later in this chapter.

On the predicted day of her death, Isabella is seen to be calmly finalizing her affairs apparently ready to embrace her fate. Her audio-diary entry confirms the resolution of the film's narrative threads and her role in that outcome: Azlan's revival, Seri's trip to London and the returned harmony within the kampung after the rock concert (see below). Isabella has achieved her personal salvation through her re-awakened Malay identity and her predestined fatal attack is presented as an epiphany that she awaits with anticipation: she sits on her bed in silence with light streaming on her from above (the film's poster is dominated by this image); the slow dissolves from medium shot to long shot present the room as a holy place and the final return to a close-up signals the beginning of the attack and the end of her life, with her falling out of frame in slow motion. Seri (of course) tells the others, but this time neither western drugs nor Wak Labib's incantations suffice. With the 'Ulek Mayang' once again on the soundtrack, the camera tracks in to a close-up of Isabella's face, which now resembles those ecstatic moments of her 'Mandi Bunga' ritual cleansing. Azlan's response to her 'death' is to run out of the room to his wife's grave beside the ocean. He seems unable to cope, but then he hears Isabella's voice telling him not to grieve and to have a happy life; he turns around to the source of the sound and finds Seri standing there with Isabella's cassette recorder in her hand.[48] Isabella and Seri have now become one, with Isabella speaking through the young girl; their mysterious closeness throughout the film has finally been consummated in Isabella's reincarnation in/as Seri. This is a dangerous direction for a Malaysian film to take, so it is not surprising that the film only hints at such a conclusion.[49]

Apart from the repeated use of the traditional 'Ulek Mayang' song and the background score by M. Nasir (who also plays the role of Azlan), the music in the film is by Search. As mentioned earlier, Search's Amy plays a significant role in the film and the band performs in the kampung to enable Seri to receive medical treatment. Like many songs in P. Ramlee films, the Search music in the film is strongly performance-based, overpowering or 'freezing' the narrative at that point. The first song, called 'Fenomena' takes place in a Kuala Lumpur disco early in the film. Isabella is an admiring spectator, but suddenly she has another attack and rushes to the toilet for an injection. This is narratively significant, but the film is quite disinterested in her plight, preferring to return to the Search performance. Their second song is even more interesting: the band is recording 'Gadis Misteri' in a studio and their performance is intercut with slow motion shots of Isabella and Seri walking through the kampung. The intercutting can be taken as the concurrence of two distinct narrative events, but the slow motion shots also function as the 'picturization' of the song in the Indian film tradition, with the lyrics about a mystery girl, whose beauty the singer desires to glimpse – obviously referring to Isabella. These lyrics then add a further layer of reference. It is almost as if Amy (himself never romantically interested in her) is voicing the emotions Azlan felt when he looked at Isabella's 'Mandi Bunga' in the immediately preceding sequence. The concert at Bukit Besi is a straightforward performance piece, clearly intercutting footage from an actual concert (such a large audience is unlikely in a kampung!); the concert's second song, 'Isabella,' about lovers from two different worlds, includes shots of Isabella and Seri on stage with the band. Interestingly, all the main characters attend and enjoy this concert, as they had the earlier traditional Malay court dance in the kampung. Unlike in MATINYA SEORANG PATRIOT, rock music does not signify a westernized, urban negativity – the traditional and the modern can co-exist as long as they work for the welfare of the people.

The Muslim 'fundamentalists' in the kampung, whose censorious behavior is always signaled by discordant ominous music, object to the rock concert by tearing down advertising posters and actually protest at the performance with their own placards. Amy is clearly aware of such a response; he initially refuses to perform in the kampung, because 'we are a rock band, not a Mosband.' Islamic opposition to western-style rock music was a topical issue in the 1980's in Malaysia, due to the power of the 'dakwah' movement: 'stage shows by pop singers... have occasionally been disrupted or protested as "morally degrading"'; Kelantan, the state north of Terengganu, governed by an Islamic political party (PAS), banned popular music as immoral (Lockard, 1995: 21).[50] In keeping with the film's theme of kampung harmony, the 'fundamentalists' are forced to apologize for their behavior, including their negative response to Isabella's presence (she is considered a non-Muslim). In fact, their apology is accompanied by the listing of the amenities her father's mining company built for the local community: a school, a mosque and a tar-sealed road (such western 'generosity,' if that is what it is, would not necessarily be appreciated by PAS members).

I have so far been silent about what was considered the film's own fatal compromise with rock music. Apparently, FENOMENA was 'revamped to cash in on the popularity of the song "Isabella"' and the inclusion of Amy as 'the second male lead' (Baharudin Latif, 1990: 3). The name of the album from which that song came was 'Fenomena' and Search's producer was M. Nasir (Lockard, 1995: 24), the composer and male star of this film. Aziz Osman claims that Search's inclusion in the film does not suggest the powerful influence of rock music on contemporary popular film (Aziz Osman, 1994), but their presence in the film, musically and diegetically, is extremely significant, including the name of the film itself – the influence of popular music on Malaysian cinema was to peak with the release of the 1994 film, SEMBILU, in which rock stars virtually play themselves and perform their already popular songs. Azlan and Amy's embrace in that quite sublime moment of Azlan's 'resurrection' can also be read as an extra-diegetic embrace between rock star and producer. The intertextuality of this scene and Search's involvement in (and interruption of) the film does not represent a new trend in Malaysian cinema. My previous analyses of P. Ramlee films have also identified and commented upon the textual and commercial implications of such strategies.

FENOMENA was Aziz Osman's first feature film and it was highly acclaimed by critics like Baharudin Latif, who hailed Aziz Osman as the P. Ramlee of the 1990's for his ability to make intelligent yet popular films (Baharudin Latif, 1994a). FENOMENA remains his most interesting film for its sensitive portrayal of a woman's search for fulfillment through her rediscovery of self and cultural identity.[51] This 'return to source' narrative signals a strong desire to re-map Malay identity (it is Malay rather than Malaysian) in the face of growing industrialization and westernization, but it ultimately represents a regressive tendency, which here finds in place (the East Coast) what earlier films like HANG TUAH found in the past (Melaka's Golden Age).

SELUBUNG (Overcast/Veil of Life, Shuhaimi Baba, 1992)

SELUBUNG continues to draw on the East Coast myth just as strongly as FENOMENA, but its role as a source of Malay tradition, identity and spiritual power is here more directly integrated with the activities of urban Malaysian society, even extending to broader international issues. However, these inclusive tendencies are contained by the film's governing focus on Malay/Muslim communal concerns in the face of external threats posed by malevolent, international forces.

Barahudin Latif, praising this debut film by a London-trained woman director, describes it as 'a complex and off-beat story of a young woman maturing into responsible adulthood through three loves – that of a close friend, the displaced children of Palestine and the cumbersome advances of her persistent male employer, which almost amounts to sexual harassment' (Baharudin

Figure 20: SELUBUNG poster

Latif, 1993a: 240). The rather negative judgment of the third 'love' doesn't deny the fact that it comes to dominate the film at the expense of the humanitarian theme and to the almost total exclusion of the childhood friendship. There are actually two endings to the film, both signified by that now overused device, the freeze-frame. What is significant is that the first of these closes the international story with a long shot that emphasizes the group involved in sending provisions to the Middle East (which includes the heroine, Mas), with a superimposed dedication to the workers of MSRI, a charity organization, on which the film's Rescaid Organisation is based, while the second ending returns to a previously seen two-shot of the lovers, Mas and Kamal, as the credits roll up the screen, leaving no doubt as to the film's primary concern.

The three stories also define the three spaces of the film. First, Mas' friendship with E.J. originates in their Terengganu childhood, secondly, her commitment to the plight of the Palestinians is located in a Lebanese refugee camp and the Kuala Lumpur Rescaid office, although the person through whom this commitment is realized is Halim, also a Terengganu childhood friend and thirdly her romantic attachment to Kamal is a Kuala Lumpur experience, if once again continually connected to the Terengganu East Coast world. It is therefore not surprising that the opening sequence is the now familiar 'childhood' scene, which comes to 'haunt' the film, as did the similarly positioned scene in FENOMENA.

Soft focus shots of an old man caressing butterflies settling on his arms dissolve to a scene on the beach, where a young girl looks intently at a drum being struck, while an older man chants a song appeasing the sea spirits to the accompaniment of a gamelan orchestra; the young girl walks back to join another girl and a boy, all of whom are enthralled by the experience. The superimposed title, 'Terengganu, 1969,' will come as no surprise to Malaysian audiences. In retrospect, it can be deduced that the young girl is Mas and the older man her godfather, while reasonable speculation suggests that the other children are E.J. and Halim. E.J. and Mas frequently return to this location during the film, but Halim is only identified with the Rescaid work in Lebanon. The mystical power of the East Coast eventually also reaches Kuala Lumpur, when towards the end of the film, it occasions the 'resurrection' of Mas.

The swift dissolve from this mystical landscape to the Perth (Western Australia) skyline, accompanied by a local radio announcer publicizing that evening's rock concerts, is totally unexpected and represents a sudden cultural rupture, perhaps mimicking the social and cultural disorientation that overseas students (especially Muslim students) are said to experience. Such alienation is more directly expressed in the next scene, where a group of Malaysian students, including Mas, E.J. and Halim, leave a student common room, disgusted with the images of Palestinians under siege showing on the room's television set. Inviting a European student to join them for a meal, they leave behind two other European males, who, without emotion and beer in hand, watch a woman being tortured in a jail (whether this is now a fictional program is not clear). In the following scene, unrelated to the preceding narrative, and thus directly addressing the Malay viewer, Islam itself is under attack. An unidentified man sprays 'Arabs go home' on a wall, throws gas on a framed quotation from *The Qur'an* and on a number of books, including one called 'Truth,' and sets the room on fire. A title identifies this as a mosque in a Sydney suburb, burned down following unrest in the Middle East. Culturally, socially and politically, Australia is a dangerous and intolerant place for Muslims, who respond in two ways: a turn towards Islamic community and 'fundamentalism' or a humanitarian solidarity with the Palestinian people. E.J. is attracted to the former alternative, through the figure of Brother Musa, a member of Tabligh, a worldwide Islamic 'fundamentalist' missionary group. Brother Musa preaches Muslim separateness in the face of abhorrent western sexual and moral values. Mas represents the less extreme position by joining Rescaid, striving to sensitize Muslim and other students to the plight of the Palestinians and to seek donations for material support. On the other hand, Halim makes a more direct commitment by volunteering to work as a doctor in the Lebanese refugee camps.

This tension *within* the student Muslim community (while most of the students are Malays, the arguments are about different interpretations of Islam) is illustrated by the changing relationship between E. J. and Mas. E.J. becomes Brother Musa's second wife and is forbidden from mixing with Mas and her friends, particularly by Musa's increasingly deranged first wife, Hani, who also bitterly attacks a Malaysian student counselor, calling her a child of Satan, presumably because of her westernized behavior and appearance. The subsequent tragic episode of Hani's (accidental?) killing of E.J.'s baby (told in numerous flashbacks in the first half of the film) highlights the psychological disorientation caused by the cultural environment in which they are 'forced' to live. Apart from a lover's quarrel between Mas and Kamal, all of the film's conflicts are externally activated, whether it be the intra-communal strife discussed above, the killings in Lebanon or the destruction of the Kuala Lumpur Rescaid office (by the Sydney arsonist). In that respect, Shuhaimi Baba's international canvas is something of a ruse, since its primary function is to reaffirm the desire for home and community (whether Muslim, Palestinian or Malay). Consequently, the cut from Hani, looking tormented and psychotic, standing in a Perth street to the skyline of Kuala Lumpur induces a collective sigh of relief. This return 'home' is directly contrasted with the earlier 'departure' from Terengganu to Perth. The shots of Kuala Lumpur are similarly supported by radio announcements, but rising above this sound montage is P. Ramlee's voice, singing 'Menceceh Bujang Lapok' – the archetypal Malaysian, popular-culture figure welcomes Mas (and the spectator) back home.

Mas' first port of call on returning to Kuala Lumpur is the office of Rescaid, where she meets the manager, Dr. Sardar, a Palestinian woman, a strong and committed leader, who initially appears to function as a role model for Mas. While Mas becomes actively involved in Rescaid, her relationship with Kamal replaces all others and Dr. Sardar remains an important but secondary figure. This also applies to E.J., when she returns to Malaysia after the death of her child and Musa's decision to join Halim in Lebanon (representing Musa's conversion to the humanitarian solidarity cause). However, neither Mas nor the film forget the importance of Terengganu and Mas visits her father there immediately after first meeting Dr. Sardar in Kuala Lumpur. From now on, the film alternates between Kuala Lumpur and the East Coast, often without strong narrative motivation, but significant for the cultural osmosis that results from these linkages. During one of the Terengganu scenes, Mas renews her acquaintance with her godfather and with the drum ceremony she had attended as a girl. The impact of this Malay cultural tradition is so powerful that she is suddenly surrounded by a multitude of butterflies, which her godfather suggests will bring her luck. Mas' connection to and 'investment' in her culture will eventually grant her a miraculous cure, one that neither western medicine nor Kamal's love is able to achieve. The bombing of the Rescaid office seriously injures Mas, who seems unlikely to survive until her godfather and his fellow villagers chant the Muslim Testament of Faith in their Terengganu kampung. Butterflies begin to invade her mental world (superimposed over shots of Dr. Sardar, the Palestinian children and her godfather) and soon literally fill her hospital room, accompanied by a canopy of light that shines down upon her (as it did on Isabella at the end of FENOMENA). Inexplicably and suddenly, she comes out of the coma. Perhaps just as mysteriously, with overtones of premonition, Kamal's mobile phone rang just before these prayers began, while he stood in tears next to his car overlooking Kuala Lumpur at dawn. The potent combination of East Coast mysticism and Muslim faith, representing the essence of Malay cultural identity, has made this 'resurrection' possible.

This emphasis on Malay communal identity – as in all other Malaysian films, Malay concerns predominate here – is somewhat counterbalanced by the humanitarian solidarity theme, based on the universalist character of Islam. Mas' Rescaid work, which quickly engulfs her actual job and the company she works for (headed by Kamal), signifies a community that transcends ethnic boundaries – the 'ummah,' although still based on exclusivity, encompasses all of Islam. The Rescaid activities are focused on helping Muslims in the Middle East; that this is also characterized as supporting Palestinians suggests a constructed contiguity of Palestinian and Muslim identity, reminiscent of the intrinsic relationship posited between Malay and Muslim identity – the Palestinian film, WEDDING IN GALILEE proposes a much more complex cultural and religious hybridity for the Palestinian people.[52] Nevertheless, the film's concern with the plight of the Palestinians is heartfelt and Halim's and later Musa's medical treatment of wounded children are altruistic acts, which eventuate, in Halim's case, in the ultimate sacrifice. These scenes, set in Lebanon, are powerful in their own right, although they are quite brief and are primarily concerned with a vague commitment to survival in dangerous circumstances, rather than a confrontation with the political and humanitarian issues implicit in the conflict. The never-distant Malaysian connection is quickly introduced by converting the initially objective Lebanese scenes into images accompanying the reading of letters back home. The second of these is a letter from Musa informing E.J. of Halim's death. Its effect on Mas is most surprising, given the little we have seen of her and Halim together in Perth. Mas is devastated and her emotional reaction erases the impact of the Lebanon scenes, which now come to represent a plot device in Mas' relationship with Kamal.

No one, not even Kamal, seems able to console Mas, although it becomes clear in the next scene that her grief is only a prelude to a greater crisis, since Halim's death is never mentioned in the film again. The revelation that Kamal is a married man causes a rift between them that occupies the total attention of the film for some time, until it is mended in a scene that would be more at home in a comedy than a romantic melodrama: Mas, back in Terengganu with E.J., is confronted by Kamal on the back of a rental truck, proposing to her (through a loudspeaker), now that he has divorced his wife. The love story dominates the film, not just at the expense of the other stories, but actually through those other stories. Even the limited attention paid to Mas' professional career as an engineer is eroded, first by the Rescaid work and then by Kamal, who as head of the engineering company, redefines her as a lover rather than an employee or colleague. Kamal resembles the Azlan character from FENOMENA to some extent – the older, desirable, divorced/widowed attractive male, both played by M. Nasir – but the similarities stop there. Baharudin Latif's description of his treatment of Mas as sexual harassment may be a little extreme, but it does catch Kamal's forwardness and his perseverance in the face of Mas' rejection of him. Mas is an impressionable young woman, who falls under the spell of a worldly, rich man and exhibits none of the assertiveness and self-assurance of Isabella in FENOMENA – perhaps surprising in a film made by a female writer/director.

These references to FENOMENA are not fortuitous, because SELUBUNG is also the story of a woman returning to Malaysia to rediscover herself in her culture through an attachment to a man and a reconnection to her childhood. Music has a significant role in both films. While FENOMENA had Amy and the band Search, SELUBUNG has Pinto, played by the singer Hattan, a quite unimportant character narratively, who performs regularly in the second half of the film, even recording a song for Rescaid with Mas and Kamal (the singer M. Nasir, who also composed the film's musical score). All of these songs are narratively motivated and performance-oriented (as in P. Ramlee films), culminating in a Kuala Lumpur charity concert for the Palestinian children, sponsored by McDonald's (the acceptable face of the West?). Unlike the quite similar Search concert in FENOMENA, this sequence attempts to draw together all of the film's narrative threads, creating a montage that also becomes a 'picturization' of Pintu's concert song about the refugees, with Palestinian children escorted from the plane and taken by bus to the concert, where they are paraded on stage behind the singer. Their safety in Kuala Lumpur is contrasted with monochrome footage of Halim caring for these children in war-ravaged Lebanon and shots of Kamal's anguished vigil beside a seriously injured Mas in a hospital bed. E.J. is present in some of these scenes, but the story of this childhood friendship has long disappeared from the film.

Some Malaysian critics suggest that Shuhaimi Baba's films treat 'Malay society in a dichotomous way by interspersing urban city life with rural kampung life' (Fuziah Kartini Hassan Basri and Raja Ahmad Alauddin, 1995: 65). This certainly applies to her second film, RINGGIT KASORRGA (which admittedly these critics then go on to discuss), but SELUBUNG intermeshes the two Malay worlds to a much greater extent than other contemporary films do (where the city is often negatively characterized), although the East Coast kampung does remain the dominant life force (quite literally) that enables the urbanized, industrialized society to become culturally relevant. The enemy is not within (except to the extent that western terrorists, like the Sydney arsonist, can freely enter Malaysia); it is an external malevolent force that actively targets, culturally and physically, Malay and non-Malay Muslims, whether in Perth, Sydney or Lebanon.

Paradoxically, given this attitude about the West, the film's style is 'international' and its use of English, even among the Malays themselves, suggests a cosmopolitan overseas-educated outlook. While still a melodrama (with some social claims), it lacks much of the Malay film form still evident in films like FENOMENA. Barahudin Latif would 'blame' Shuhaimi Baba's western training; he was very relieved when Aziz Osman withdrew from a Dutch university, since such exposure to European cinema would have 'ruined his cultural perspective' (Baharudin Latif, 1994a),[53] but SELUBUNG's style signals a trend evident in much of contemporary Malaysian cinema, which often has an 'undervisualized' television look that makes the films stylistically indistinguishable (perhaps not surprising given the television origins of most of these young directors). SELUBUNG is, in fact, quite typical of current filmmaking practice in its focus on beautiful, young people, especially young women, to an extent not apparent in most other cinemas.[54] Many of these actors come from advertising and are often Pan-Asian – this predilection for beautiful, pale-skinned young women is derived from Hindi cinema, which is, for that reason, favored over Tamil cinema in Malaysia (Krishnan, 1994b).[55] Deanna Yusof, who stars as Mas, is a 'model-turned-actress of Malay and Swiss parentage' (Fuziah Kartini Hassan Basri and Raja Ahmad Alauddin, 1995: 67). While a Malay-European lineage is narratively appropriate for Isabella in FENOMENA, it is somewhat problematic for the character of Mas, whose kampung origin is so directly invoked. This caveat applies even more strongly to the Pan-Asian actor, Sofia Jane Hisham, who stars in the realist kampung drama, PEREMPUAN, ISTERI &..., and who is meant to represent the archetypal Malay woman.

PEREMPUAN, ISTERI &... (Woman, Wife &..., U-Wei Haji Shaari, 1993)

Figure 21: PEREMPUAN, ISTERI &... poster

This film is widely considered to be the most controversial film in contemporary Malaysian cinema; its notoriety preceded its release, because Malaysian women's groups sought a change to the film's working title: PEREMPUAN, ISTERI & JALANG (Woman, Wife & Whore) (Fuziah Kartini Hassan Basri and Raja Ahmad Alauddin, 1995: 63). The censor forced the removal of the final word, leaving the title as PEREMPUAN, ISTERI &..., and eventually also trimmed three scenes,[56] which were considered too sexually explicit for local audiences (interview with Pansha, RENTAK KARYA, 1994).[57] Despite its Malay subject matter, the film attracted middle-class audiences from across the ethnic spectrum, who otherwise would never watch a Malay film, but who considered this an example of the more international 'art cinema' (Raja Ahmad Alauddin, 1994a), although the nature of the subject matter – characterized by one critic as 'a nympho's journey into degradation and self-destruction' (Baharudin Latif, 1994c: 255) – would have provided its own momentum. Perhaps not surprisingly, the film's reception was quite contradictory: some considered it anti-Malay (a negative picture of Malaysian rural society) and misogynist (Cheah, 1993: 28), while others called it a 'truly Malay film' and an attack on female oppression (Amir Muhammad, 1993). As I will go on to argue, the issues are more complex, making such 'black and white' judgments difficult to support. The analysis concentrates on the means by which the film constructs sexuality, desire and masculinity and their link to money and exchange in order to critique that most traditional Malay cultural icon, the kampung and, by implication, Malaysian society in general.

The writer, Hamzah Hussin (1994a; 1994b) was one of the few people I interviewed, who had serious reservations about the film, principally because of its lack of a 'Malay voice'; he felt that it had a 'foreign' perspective, partly due to it being a remake of BITTER MOON (1992). The connection with Polanski's film is not all that obvious to me, but Hamzah Hussin's comments do reinforce PEREMPUAN, ISTERI &...'s categorization as an 'art film' (frank sexual behavior being one of its generic markers). Making more of an analytical, rather than critical observation, Raja Ahmad Alauddin (1994b) considered the film to represent an outsider's point-of-view of Malay culture. From an auteurist perspective, none of these remarks are surprising. U-Wei lived in New York for about eleven years, attending film school and making experimental films, before returning to Malaysia in 1987: 'You can never go home... therefore you must go home!' (Cheah and Vasudev, 1995: 15) – U-Wei Haji Shaari's ambivalent statement succinctly capturing the outsider-insider status noted above. PEREMPUAN, ISTERI &... is his first Malaysian feature film, after working in television drama since 1987. Its affinities with American cinema lie in the 1950's small-town melodramas of directors like Douglas Sirk and Vincente Minnelli.[58] A contemporary reference point is the Chinese film, JU DOU (1990), whose heroine is similarly sacrificed in the name of patriarchy. Such broad-based international intertextuality is very unusual for a Malaysian film – the local perception of its 'otherness' is therefore not all that surprising.

Whereas SELUBUNG ranged widely geographically, while remaining rather insular culturally, PEREMPUAN, ISTERI &... applies its international cultural credentials to the quintessential concerns of Malay cinema: the kampung as the signifier of Malay culture, family conflict and gender power, melodramatic mode of address, the darsan look and the Hang Tuah/Hang Jebat relationship. U-Wei Haji Shaari's perspective on these issues does not mean to reaffirm Malay solidarity, but instead seeks to analyze and critique these concerns. The Malay kampung is defined by activities that underline its Malay exclusivity: 'nasi kangkang' (see below), circumcision, 'korban' (sacrificial offering), 'mandi sungai' (river bathing) and 'tangkap basah' (being caught 'red-handed') (Amir Muhammad, 1993: 26). This insular world is shaken to its foundation by the arrival of the woman, Zaleha.[59] The only Malay film that invites comparison with PEREMPUAN, ISTERI &... is SEMERAH PADI, also an emphatically Malay story where female sexual desire throws a kampung into physical and moral disarray – this world is only returned to order by the erasure or the social legitimization of that desire. The earlier film's resolution was the forced marriage of the protagonists; in PEREMPUAN, ISTERI &... the forced marriage of Zaleha and Amir actually launches the kampung narrative – in that respect the latter film is the contemporary elaboration of the consequences of the P. Ramlee film.

The film's early scenes economically define the relationship between the two protagonists. Zaleha elopes from a kampung marriage to Amir and weds her lover in a Thai mosque. Amir tracks them down, kills the husband, rapes Zaleha and sells her into prostitution. Zaleha is an 'absent presence' in these scenes, invisible or silent in the face of Amir's aggression. Only when he reclaims her from the pimp six months later does she appear more confident and assertive. The characters in these preliminary scenes have no history apart from the inferences that might be drawn from their behavior, nor do we learn anything more about Amir and Zaleha's pasts during the course of the film. They remain abstract figures, whose relationship and destiny are defined in terms of sexuality, gender and violence. The opening scenes highlight the process of social and economic exchange (the weddings, the husband's willingness to return Zaleha to Amir, Zaleha's transfer to and from the pimp), in which the woman is the (mute) traded object between men. The link between desire, sexuality, exchange and money is succinctly established and, in one of the film's many reversals, they in turn become Zaleha's means of exercising control over the kampung men, as well as highlighting the fate of kampung women in their own sexual and social relations with their men. Like Lulu in G. W. Pabst's PANDORA'S BOX (1929), Zaleha 'is that which allows both desire and money to circulate' (Elsaesser, 1983: 23).

On their first night back in Malaysia, Amir takes Zaleha to a hotel, where he continues to verbally abuse her. While he goes out to buy food, she makes a phone call that eventually brings the religious police to their door, charging them with khalwat. Amir, realizing that she has forced him into marriage, hits her across the face, to which she responds with a sardonic smile that is directed at the camera. This is a crucial moment, for it signals Zaleha's taking control of the narrative (until the final conflict) and the first step in her dominance over Amir, who is now trapped in the very marriage that he sought in the first place. Zaleha's chain-smoking and the provocative, but unselfconscious manner in which she reveals her bare legs and sits with her legs apart represent behaviors considered unacceptable for a Malay woman (Ché-Ross, 1996). To an extent, this is realistically justified as befitting the character of a prostitute, but there is also an element of voyeurism involved, made even more apparent when the camera gazes at her naked legs and back while she is having a bath before Amir's return. Interestingly, this is the first and last time that the film fetishizes her body so directly, partly justifying the claim that U-Wei Haji Shaari is 'almost camera-raping her' (Baharudin Latif, 1993a: 241). From now on, all 'looks' by and upon Zaleha are self-consciously proclaimed by the film and 'exceed' the parameters of Laura Mulvey's active male gaze/passive female recipient (Mulvey, 1975).[60]

Zaleha's arrival in Amir's kampung soon attracts the attention of its men, who watch her walking from the local shop alone and in the dark, with a sexual curiosity that the film notes but does not share. A more complex version of this collective 'look' occurs during a village meeting at which Amir is present. The local rubber plantation worker and 'village idiot,' Tapa, is called into the meeting where he is ridiculed, especially by Amir. Zaleha is walking along the road and is eventually seen by one of the men at the meeting, all of whom then fall silent and look at her, as if she was an apparition. The camera remains inside the meeting, only intermittently identifying Zaleha's presence in the background, but the scene pivots around her display of herself, underlined by a shot of a man on a bicycle stopping behind her and frankly staring at her. Amir himself is later captivated by the red outfit that Zaleha 'models' for Amir's sister-in-law, before abusing her and tearing her blouse in the process; his behavior is complicated by his earlier stroking of the red shoes in the bedroom, watched by an unseen Zaleha. The dynamics of looking, desire, fetishism and punishment set in motion by Zaleha are uncontainable by traditional explanations of voyeurism.

The relationship between Zaleha and Tapa is the most elemental in the film, totally based on her desire to be desired and his sexual wants. One night when Amir is away, Zaleha is sitting in front of an electric fan, fanning her thighs with a metal plate. There is a cut to an eye looking through a hole in the wall, so that the subsequent shot of Zaleha (and in retrospect, the previous shot of her as well) is marked as a point-of-view shot. The eye is initially not identified and it is not apparent that she knows she is being looked at. Soon a shot from the other side of the wall confirms that the eye belongs to Tapa and the alternate shots of Zaleha move from medium close-up to close-up to register her awareness of his gaze. The scene is based on the clichéd 'peeping tom' situation, but Tapa's scopophilia is heavily qualified and is abruptly terminated by the appearance of Amir's truck (a sort of coitus interruptus). Zaleha, on the other hand, exhibits considerable pleasure from being watched, reveling in her self-display. Tapa's voyeurism is unmasked in this scene and the sexual control is appropriated by the woman.

This scenario is repeated later in the film, when Tapa approaches the peephole again only to discover that Zaleha is not there. The camera remains with him as he finds another peephole and tries to climb up to it – his clumsy efforts highlight the hard work involved in being a 'peeping tom' and contrasts with the stretched-out figure of Zaleha watching television (presenting herself as a 'view') when Tapa eventually does succeed in looking through the hole. Zaleha is able to exercise power over Tapa in these scenes, despite the implied power of the voyeuristic gaze. In an even more melodramatic scene, Zaleha is sent out at night by Amir to buy salt, dressed in her torn red outfit and red high-heeled shoes. The shots of her walking through the jungle are as excessive as anything in Minnelli (e.g. the final fairground death in SOME CAME RUNNING) and Sirk (e.g. the Dorothy Malone 'death dance' in WRITTEN ON THE WIND). Tapa brings her the salt and says he wants her, but she tells him to wait. Their eventual sexual union employs most of the clichés of such illicit moments in melodramas. In the pouring rain, Tapa sees her standing among the rubber trees, inviting his attention, while Amir is changing a tire on a vegetable farm – his undoing/tightening of the wheel nuts is intercut with the sexual dance in the rubber plantation. The scene has been censored, but it ends with a shot of water and semen-colored latex dripping into a dish attached to a rubber tree. Once again, Zaleha controls the events and Amir's absence/presence suggests that her sexual advances are as much concerned with punishing her husband as with her own pleasure, which is primarily that of being desired.[61]

Zaleha's sexual aggressiveness has been labeled as an 'amorous amok' (Amir Muhammad, 1993: 26), quite an apt description, although her behavior has none of the 'deranged' frenzy of the traditional amuk. Zaleha is calm and assured in the tactics she employs to make men desire her. One of the first instances occurs during her outing in a nearby town, when she and a neighbor are eating lunch. Zaleha notices a man at a nearby table and looks at him directly and 'immodestly' (particularly for a Malay woman). The man returns her gaze, but Zaleha is totally in control, signified by a slow zoom shot into the man, intercut with the fixed, provocative look of Zaleha. A more ambivalent example takes place when Zaleha returns from bathing in the river. Before she arrives at the river, a young woman, Salina, is intently watching a man leaving the water – we later learn that he is Bakri, but at this stage neither of them are named. Zaleha and Salina leave the river together and both stop to look at Bakri sitting on his bicycle under a tree. All the shots of him remain a constant medium shot, while the shots of the two women move in from medium long shot to medium shot to medium close-up. At the end of this scene, the women walk off without a word having been spoken. They appropriate the active look in this scene and Bakri is almost a statue or a shrine that accepts their gaze as a Hindu god might. The darsan phenomenon is clearly present, but the effect is much diminished because of the women's overpowering control of the viewing situation. Furthermore, the internal dynamics within the shots of the women is paramount. In the scene's first shot, Salina and Zaleha are seen stopping and looking out of the frame. Zaleha is ahead of Salina, so it is unclear whether Zaleha is aware of Salina's smiling stare – she is certainly unaware of any relationship between Salina and Bakri. Her look at him is thus similar to her gaze at the man in the restaurant: open and confronting, but as she turns further to see Salina's more modest and yet direct stare, Zaleha puts on her sunglasses and walks away. The scene resembles Parvati's response to Devdas' arrival in her house in DEVDAS (Vasudevan, 1995: 315-316), but Bakri is constructed as a sexual rather than a divine image, countering the patriarchal tendency of the darsan perspective.

Zaleha actually encourages Salina to present herself more sexually and to engage in an illicit relationship with Bakri. It is all part of her unfocused 'liberation' of the kampung women. Kamariah was the neighbor, who, together with her children, accompanied Zaleha to the nearby town. After their meal, the man that Zaleha had stared at, a truck driver, invited the two women to an 'orang puteh' movie (a white man film, i.e. an American film) with him and his friend. Kamariah, her children and the other man are more interested in what Zaleha and the truck driver are doing in the back of the cinema than in the movie itself. It is unclear how this scene ends because it has been censored, but the outcome of their return to the kampung in the truck driver's vehicle is totally predictable. The kampung men are waiting on the road and violently assault the truck driver, while Kamariah's husband hits her and threatens to drive her from *his* house if this happens again. Zaleha remains standing in the truck's headlights as all the kampung people leave. Her influence on Kamariah has highlighted the oppression and abuse of women by men, but it has done little for Kamariah herself. Salina's fate is even harsher. Her encounter with Bakri in the jungle ends in sexual intercourse and is intercut with the slaughtering of a bull (by Tapa) for an upcoming festivity. Salina's father, pointing to the bull's testicles, jokes with some boys about circumcision and castration. Such loaded imagery makes the discovery of the lovers by a young boy inevitable. Salina and Bakri are taken to the surau (a small Muslim place of worship), where her father slaps her face and the pair are shamed in front of the community. This khalwat is very much instigated by Zaleha, but she is not there in the surau, preferring instead to visit Tapa, who is now dismembering the bull. Salina's furtive gestures towards independence are swiftly squashed and overlaid by a series of social and cultural interdictions that accentuate violence, subjugation, sexual control (castration and circumcision) and even death. Perhaps as with Kamariah's beating by her husband, Zaleha is stunned by this male aggression, but seems unable to confront it or even to be forewarned about its likely impact on her.

Following their arrival in her husband's kampung, Zaleha spends most of her time on her own, as her husband is frequently away buying vegetables. When Amir returns home after her trip to the nearby town, she taunts him into reprimanding her, but his response is mild compared to Kamariah's husband's. Only when Zaleha shows off her red dress does his desire and aggression result in him tearing her top and humiliating her in front of his brother and his brother's wife. Her response to his behavior is intriguing and represents the culmination of her control over him. She prepares 'nasi kangkang' (lit. squatted-over rice), a traditional Malay animistic practice, in which the steam from a bowl of cooked rice condenses on the private parts and drips back onto the rice, the effect being that the husband, after eating this rice, is totally under the spell of his wife. The nasi kangkang scene has been heavily censored and only fragments of Zaleha's crouching over the rice are visible, but its occurrence during a thunderstorm suggests a consequence and foreboding that is very familiar from the Malaysian and Indian melodramatic traditions. The film doesn't question the effectiveness of this Malay magic, which places Amir into a state of 'gila cinta' (love crazy). He obeys her totally, but his desire for her is cut short by her disinterest in him – Zaleha doesn't want him, she just wants him to want her. Unfortunately, the effect of the magic potion does not last and the inevitable retribution upon Zaleha is brutal and merciless.

After all his voyeuristic exploration of Zaleha's house, Tapa, now covered in blood from slaughtering the bull (and from killing the cloth merchant), forces his way in, wanting to take her away with him. Zaleha is terrified and, in the face of this aggressive masculinity, returns to the passive behavior she exhibited earlier in the film. She becomes an object to be fought over and ultimately to be destroyed. The arrival of the villagers around the house, the forced entry into the house by Amir and his brother, who proceeds to keep the villagers out and the ensuing fight between Amir and Tapa draws upon the Hang Tuah/Hang Jebat conflict. Amir, like Tuah, represents the conventional position of righteousness, whereas Tapa's uncomplicated desire and obsession is relatable to Jebat. Amir kills Tapa with the latter's machete (just as Tuah took the magical kris from Jebat in order to kill him). Neither Amir nor Tapa are characters of moral stature and their motivations are, of course, totally different from those of the legendary figures. The film visually identifies the raison d'etre of their conflict, by framing them on either side of Zaleha, who is crouched in the corner of the room in the background of the shot. She is now hysterical and totally powerless, unable to do more than remain defiant by yelling back at Amir that he means nothing to her. He kills her with the same machete and she slides down the post around which the action of the scene has been staged. The camera now returns to Amir's anguished face just as it started with his angry expression at the beginning of the film.

However, the film does not and could not end there, since it would imply an identification with Amir's plight that has so far been totally absent. The final enigmatic scene, like the opening scene, is about 'absent presences' and is constructed as a single panning shot that starts with a police car driving away from the kampung the next morning – its occupants are not visible and of no concern to the film. The rest of the shot focuses on a number of groups of boys: one group is hectored by an aggressive youth, another group is beating sides of beef hanging under the trees, while a third group is returning from a circumcision ceremony. The shot is accompanied by a mesmeric chant by a female singer, made up of separate phrases, such as 'money,' 'carrying a betelnut box on the head' (signifies virginity and traditional values), 'wife,' 'fire' and 'man.'[62] These words restate some of the major concerns of the film and this final scene's focus on the boys, particularly the circumcised boys (implying the rite of passage into manhood), suggests a powerful critique of masculinity by the film, evident in its abundant symbolic castrations. From this perspective, the film's original title represents that masculinity's conceptualization of woman as either or both wife and whore (the word 'jalang' is perhaps better translated as 'slut'). The final shot is remarkable for its abstractness and for the absence of the figure of woman as defined by Zaleha, who dominated the film to an extent unparalleled in Malaysian cinema. Her 'replacement' by the various groups of boys suggests that the vacuum she left is quickly being filled by these young men, who reproduce and reaffirm the ideology of this masculinity (the circumcision and the lecture). In that respect, the film's conclusion is very bleak, with only the extra-diegetic female singer able to provide a critical (female) perspective on the 'new world' being constructed before our eyes.

This discussion of PEREMPUAN, ISTERI &... has emphasized issues that have been significant in quite a number of the other films, but which have not received such overt attention. No other film has been so forthright in its condemnation of the kampung world and the different interpretations of the film are strongly connected to the particular agendas that groups or individuals bring with them. U-Wei Haji Shaari feels that Zaleha 'represents the potential strength and power of women,' while some women's groups regard it a negative portrayal of woman and others again argue that Zaleha remains a dependent woman, who is not in control of her life (Rashidah Abdullah, 1993). The film has been hailed by some as the 'ultimate Malay film' (Baharudin Latif, 1994c: 256) and its 'Malayness' is central to its objective in a way that does not apply to most of the other films discussed in this chapter. This 'assault' on kampung culture is particularly powerful, because it does not deviate from its relentless concentration on *Malay* society. The film's exemplary critical employment of the 'look' and the 'gaze,' conscious of traditional (western and Indian) and contemporary (especially art cinema) debates about this most contentious of theoretical paradigms, places it both within and also quite apart from the Malaysian cinematic tradition.[63] This accounts for what might well be regarded as the film's cultural and social 'offense': Zaleha's bold and unapologetic gaze at men, while never succumbing to their voyeuristic control over her. No other Malaysian film has been able to employ cinematic strategies so effectively and make them so central to the film's overall meaning. PEREMPUAN, ISTERI &... is that most unusual of cultural texts, able to hold the margin and the center in productive tension, thus opening up the relationship between non-Malay and Malay culture, international and Malaysian culture, cosmopolitan and kampung society, art film and commercial success (especially difficult in a country like Malaysia), woman and man, looking and 'to-be-looked-at' and finally, Malay and Malaysian cinema.

SEMBILU (Heartache/Love's Dilemma/Thorns, Yusof Haslam, 1994)

Of all the contemporary films discussed in this chapter, SEMBILU can most unambiguously be defined as an urban melodrama. This might suggest a rejection of the kampung world and to a certain extent that is the case. However, despite its superficial modernity (pop music, cars, motorcycles, automatic teller machines), the film's values are totally traditional, whether in terms of gender, ethnicity, family authority or morality. This concern with the traditional extends to the film's cultural and cinematic credentials, which are more reminiscent of the Malay films of the 1950's/60's than any of the other recent films so far discussed. Consequently, its popularity with young audiences throughout Malaysia is intriguing.

SEMBILU became the biggest grossing Malaysian-made film ever, only to be eclipsed by SEMBILU II the following year. Whereas PEREMPUAN, ISTERI &...'s popularity (and excellent financial return) came from the broad audience it attracted, SEMBILU clearly appealed to the young, music-oriented Malay viewer. In one respect, this is simply a return to the traditional audience of contemporary Malaysian films, but the film targeted its potential market very effectively by employing a number of clever marketing strategies. Firstly, Yusof Haslam engaged high-profile popular culture figures for the three starring roles: Awie and Ziana Zain are well-known singers, while Erra Fazira was a beauty queen and a popular singer (Fuziah Kartini Hassan Basri and Raja Ahmad Alauddin, 1995: 69); these attractive young people become the film's identification figures, while older actors/characters are the impediments to their emotional ful-

Figure 22: SEMBILU poster

fillment. Secondly, the director included their already successful songs in the film, much as Aziz Osman did with Search's music in FENOMENA. Thirdly, and most cannily, the plot is based on Awie's own love life (this is revealed in a credit title), while Ziana's infamous public image is also incorporated into the film (Ché-Ross, 1996); it is therefore not surprising that these two personalities retain their own names within the film's narrative, although there is no suggestion that Awie's love life involved Ziana. This third strategy promises the sort of exposé actually delivered by the fan magazine *in* the film, with its cover banner: 'Awie chooses Ziana as his replacement.' Is this perhaps the first 'documentary musical melodrama?'

The answer, of course, is no. Whatever the surface novelty of these tactics, they reside comfortably within the P. Ramlee mold of filmmaking and, before him, the Mandarin 'exploitation musical' films of Zhou Xuan (Teo, 1993: 32). It may also seem to have been a bold move on Yusof Haslam's part to bring the musician actors/characters that were on the periphery in films like FENOMENA and SELUBUNG to center stage, but this is exactly the strategy that P. Ramlee so successfully introduced to Malay cinema forty years earlier. Like the P. Ramlee musician-protagonist films (e.g. HUJAN PANAS, ANAK-KU SAZALI, IBU MERTUA-

KU), SEMBILU charts the growing popularity of the performer within the film, thus 'replaying' the career development of the already successful actor/musician. It is therefore not surprising that this film, like the P. Ramlee films, gives prominence to performance-based musical numbers, since the extra-diegetic performer must remain at least as visible as the diegetic character.

The film's formulaic use of the Indian popular cinema has been noted: 'glamorous stars, music, fighting scenes in the rain and storm, emotion-packed singing, and really black and white characters' (Fuziah Kartini Hassan Basri and Raja Ahmad Alauddin, 1995: 71). This description certainly sums up the film quite well, but it doesn't acknowledge the fact that much of that traditional Hindi melodrama influence is filtered through the Malay cinema of the 1950's and 1960's. SEMBILU's love triangle plot is very reminiscent of HUJAN PANAS and IBU MERTUA-KU. Like HUJAN PANAS, the male protagonist is trapped between two women, one of whom is quiet and rather submissive, while the other is aggressive and assertive. The hero seems unable to determine which he should choose and is ultimately forced into a decision because of circumstance (i.e. fate) – thus the appropriateness of one of the English titles: Love's Dilemma. IBU MERTUA-KU similarly involves a man desired by two women (rather than the other way around), and serves as a warning to the lovers in SEMBILU – the singer's first lover disregards her family's strong objections to the relationship. In IBU MERTUA-KU, the lovers dismiss this disapproval, but their marriage is inevitably doomed to failure. The end of SEMBILU does bring the original lovers together again, but the sequel ensures that they will always remain apart. All three films (continuing a trend in Malaysian cinema) construct a protagonist, who is reserved, passive, indecisive and supine – the Devdas-like figure already discussed and also the 'still center' around whom the emotional and physical conflicts rage. A newspaper review at the time of the film's release puts it a slightly different way: 'The hero unfortunately is shallow, too laid-back and non-committal with both girls (need we say typical again?)' (*New Straits Times*, 1994c: 20); what is here a criticism of current Malaysian cinema, is in fact the most recent manifestation of a distinct and long-standing tradition. However, like Amran in PENARIK BECA, the hero finally runs amuk and confronts the villain in a vicious and bloody fight. This final battle between the two males also highlights the impact of kung fu films on other filmmaking traditions (and that includes India and America); whereas the P. Ramlee fights are still silat-dominated, here the reference point is a crude version of the Chinese martial arts, accompanied by loud, obviously dubbed, sound effects, which are further manipulated as synthesized reverberations during some of the most violent exchanges with fist, boot and stick.

The film's narrative dynamic operates within the tradition of Malay musical melodrama. There is the obsessive doubling of characters and events, with two rivals for the hero's love, each of whom helps him to understand his problems during a long night-time walk in a park, another singer and his lover is contrasted with Awie and his first love, the two hero-villain confrontations, two brutal fights involving Awie, two thunderstorm-linked crises (thunderstorms generically connoting chaos and disorder) and two Ziana performances at the same location, each of which Awie attends only to leave halfway through. There are many other instances, but the resulting comparisons and contrasts suggest that same Manichean universe referred to at the beginning of the HUJAN PANAS analysis. SEMBILU's narrative drive is similarly weak; scenes following each other have little plot or thematic connection, often representing an alternation of events that run parallel to each other and occasionally converge, harmoniously or otherwise, mostly as a consequence of coincidence or fate. As previously pointed out in relation to PENARIK BECA, films like SEMBILU dispense with (lack?) transitional material that motivates character interaction, e.g. Wati and Alice talk in a park; Ziana and Joe talk in a car park; Wati and Awie talk in a park – the names don't matter, but these three successive scenes are a series of events that butt onto each other with almost no resonance.

Having 'buried' the film under the weight of its influences, I now want to comment on some of its singularities, although never cutting it adrift from its cultural context. The title literally means a splinter or a thorn and is suggestive of the minute, sharp pains of young love. While this is teen movie territory, the film eschews the typical comedy quotient of that genre for a more somber melodramatic emphasis on longing, suffering and loss. There is a 'childhood scene' of sorts, where, in monochrome, the headmaster tells Awie and Wati to stop seeing each other, punishing Awie with a number of strokes of the cane, despite him being the best singer in the school (the opportunity for a formative musical reference is not missed); characteristically, Awie later proposes that Wati concentrate on her studies, while she wonders why he is being so remote. The theme of adult intrusiveness on an innocent love affair is succinctly made and will be pursued in the film's present.

Awie has become a singer, while Wati is finishing a university degree, thus adding a social class difference (a kampung boy and a girl from an upper middle-class family) familiar from the Hindi and Malaysian cinemas of the 1950's. The main obstacle to their love is Wati's brother, Azman, who has become the de facto father of the household. He is, in the language of the film, 'gila talak' (lit. divorce crazed), significant to the extent that his objection to and hatred of Awie is based on his wife, Maria, leaving him for a singer, Roy. The Azman/Maria/Roy conflict takes up much of the first third of the film and ends in

Maria's death at the hands of Roy. Azman continues to hound his sister over Awie, but eventually he decides to concentrate on Awie himself: arranging for a bicycle gang to beat him up and later burn down his apartment – this finally leads to the showdown between Awie and Azman mentioned earlier. The Azman/Awie conflict contrasts the former's deviant, psychotic masculinity with Awie's unassertive behavior; Azman's aggression is actually primarily directed at women – he psychologically and physically abuses his ex-wife, his sister, her girlfriend and his secretary. His only unruffled relationship is with his mother, perhaps because she does accept his authority within the family. However, her slap across his face during the final Azman/Awie fight immediately stops Azman in his tracks – the effect is similar to the ending of MOTHER INDIA (1957), where the traditional mother-son relationship is ruptured by the mother in order to rebalance the moral universe. The other singer, Roy, is also contrasted with Awie; he is as brutal as Azman in his treatment of Maria, although she is characterized as immoral and a bad mother, quite deserving of the gruesome punishment she receives. Much like the P. Ramlee characters in the 1950's films, Awie's passive, deferring and somewhat uncertain masculinity is the film's positive rejoinder to all this male aggression and violence. Joe, Ziana's manager, is a more reserved figure than Azman and Roy, but his single-minded desire for and pursuit of Ziana is totally at odds with Awie's romantic vacillations.

The relationships between Awie, Wati and Ziana represent the most interesting aspects of the film. The Wati-Awie pairing is based on a long childhood friendship and a growing romantic attachment, largely initiated by Wati, despite her brother's objections. While Wati is university educated, she embodies the traditional Malay feminine virtues of modesty and acceptance of family authority; she rejects her family's attitude to Awie, but does not ultimately resist its judgment – on the other hand, she doesn't hesitate to accuse Awie of weakness and a lack of commitment. Wati's Chinese university friend, Alice, plays the stereotypical intermediary between the two lovers and organizes their reunion towards the end of the film. It takes place at the picturesque Cameron Highlands, functioning as a sanctuary away from all the conflict, like the Penang scenes in IBU MERTUA-KU and the Kashmir-located song and dance routines of countless Hindi films. Initially, Ziana's relationship with Awie is that of a fellow performer, somewhat jealous of his success and a little sycophantic. She invites him to the launch of her album at the Betelnut, a well-known Kuala Lumpur nightclub. Awie does come and after the performance has a (non-alcoholic) drink with Ziana, who now attempts to force herself upon him, much to the chagrin of Joe. Her song, an 'international' pop number like all the others in the film, is presented with minimal narrative interruption and has the appearance of a self-contained video clip. Ziana is an independent, aggressive woman, who treats her male manager with utter contempt. Her overtures towards Awie eventually pay off when Wati keeps being obstructed from seeing him by her brother. Despite the general tendency to label Ziana as a 'vamp' and a 'seductress' (*New Straits Times*, 1994c; Fuzia Kartini Hassan Basri and Raja Ahmad Alauddin, 1995: 69), she genuinely desires Awie; his capitulation to her as they embrace in her apartment is rather moving and betrays a vulnerability not previously noticed in her. Her earlier conversation with Wati in the park is virtually a debate about who 'owns' Awie and is the most pointed indication of Awie's irrelevance in deciding who is to be his beloved. The scene between the two women contrasts a rather dowdy Wati with the glamorous Ziana, who literally runs rings around Wati during their talk; the camera, recognizing the 'winner,' remains with her as Wati walks out of frame.

However, neither generic nor social determinants are in Ziana's favor. While Wati secretly meets Awie in the Cameron Highlands, Ziana enters his apartment and soon realizes her fate: Awie's filofax contains a photo of Wati, a love poem to her and a note of the date of their meeting – the only reference to Ziana is a short poem: 'I am only a presence in your life, although you are not the life I am looking for.' Awie returns home to find her slumped over his desk crying – his rather pathetic response is that love and relationships are too difficult for him. Ziana becomes the film's tragic heroine, exhibiting a much greater emotional depth than Wati (or Awie). This is encapsulated in a plaintive love ballad she sings at the Betelnut. Once again, the emphasis is on her performance, but this time it is narratively and emotionally connected to her plight. She is dressed in a high-collared, full-length gold gown – her absorption in the song, the blue light, the artificial fog, the clothes, her gestures and the glittering glycerin tears together epitomize a woman spurned, one who lost in love. Ziana's recognition of her fate is extremely moving, largely because of the excessiveness of the melodramatic mise-en-scene (reminiscent of Susan Kohner's tragic performance in Douglas Sirk's 1959 film, IMITATION OF LIFE). However, the next scene undercuts Ziana's acceptance of her fate, her independence and her strength. After reading Awie's note (asking for her forgiveness) in her dressing room – her mirror image framed by the make-up lights – she throws herself in Joe's arms and dissolves into tears. It becomes clear that she is just 'another dependent woman,' who seeks love where it is available and any suggestion of conniving opportunism on her part is not encouraged by the film (although the sequel does transform her into an amoral, scheming villain).

Ultimately, neither woman exhibits the self-sufficiency and strength of Hasnah in HUJAN PANAS, or the defiance of Zaleha in PEREMPUAN, ISTERI &.... Irrespective of their backgrounds and social status, Wati and Ziana are both, willingly or unwillingly, women who need and rely upon men. This represents an interesting contradiction in the film's gender relationships. Awie, unable to decide which of the two women he should choose, really doesn't need either of them. Not only is he often alone in the film, but that seems to represent his choice; even when with Wati or Ziana, he does little of the talking. Awie seems happiest when rehearsing and recording his songs. One of them is about Wati and is presented as an Indian film 'picturization,' with shots of the two of them together, although there are almost as many shots of each of them alone. Perhaps an extra-diegetic explanation might be appropriate here: Awie must continue to be desired by and available to all of his fans (in the sequel, Wati marries another, while Awie is last seen alone on his motorcycle) and his relationships with women in the film will always remain inconclusive.

Some commentators have criticized the film's moral and sexual lifestyle as inappropriate for Malaysia (Samsuddin Rahim, 1994), but I found the film highly 'moral' in asserting the 'proper' relations between men and women and between children and parents. Wati ultimately defers to her brother and mother and only tentatively holds Awie's hands in their presence at the end of the film. There is a lot of talk of immorality and khalwat, but this comes from Azman, who is hardly a role model. The film itself is not voyeuristic towards the characters – not even Ziana, who most closely approximates the 'duplicitous woman' of film noir, is presented as a sexual threat to masculinity or as a fetishized object of desire. Desire certainly dominates the film, but it is not expressed visually as in earlier Malaysian films, where the 'look' of the woman upon her beloved has so frequently been noted. Admittedly, the sequel is more prurient, with brutal murder and arranged khalwat scenes, which are in retrospect identified as dreams or simulations. Apart from these spurious references to khalwat, Islam is not a significant element in the film, contrary to its increasing presence in other contemporary Malaysian films.

The Malay kampung does not make an appearance in the film, except for a comment by Awie. However, the film is only intermittently urban, mostly associated with Awie's apartment and scenes of Azman stalking Roy and Awie. Unusual for a Malaysian film, the principal setting is suburban, but it is not presented as a harmonious environment, whether it be Wati's family home or Roy and Maria's house. The many park scenes, at the university, in the city and at the Cameron Highlands, signify a respite from the urban and suburban psychological and emotional conflicts, providing the characters with opportunities for uninterrupted discussions. These spaces are, to some extent, the film's kampung scenes, although without the cultural reverberation of that archetypal Malay world. But perhaps for young urban-born Malays, the kampung is slowly losing its significance. The reference to Malays rather than Malaysians is pointed, because this film, like most of the previous ones, persists with a Malay view of Malaysia, with the one non-Malay character – Alice – being little more than the ethnic off-sider familiar from much mainstream Malaysian cinema (and, of course, most other cinemas).

Conclusion

SEMBILU does not represent the 'end' of Malaysian cinema, rather a convenient destination, suggesting a continuity of traditional concerns and styles, even if these are now more affected by broader international trends than the 1950's Malaysian films were. The similarities between HUJAN PANAS and SEMBILU are greater than those between SEMBILU and PEREMPUAN, ISTERI &..., perhaps reflecting a developing distinction between popular cinema and a more self-conscious art cinema, arising from the different training of their directors. Yusof Haslam learned filmmaking from direct experience in the industry and credits the influence of P. Ramlee, Jamil Sulong, Jins Shamsuddin and Othman Hafsham (Fuziah Kartini Hassan Basri and Raja Ahmad Alauddin, 1995: 69), acknowledging the importance of the history of Malaysian cinema in all its heterogeneity. U-Wei Haji Shaari, like Shuhaimi Baba, trained at an overseas university and is undoubtedly familiar with a wide range of filmmaking traditions.[64] To wonder whose film is the more 'Malay(sian)' is, as I hope is evident from the arguments in this book, to ask the wrong question.

Conclusion

> 'These parallelisms... suppose the existence of a secret form
> of time, a pattern of repeated lines'
> (Jorge Luis Borges, 1979: 103).

> 'What is important, what has meaning, is the journey... [and]
> journeys are through history as well as through a landscape'
> (Theo Angelopoulos, quoted in Horton, 1997: 98).

The previous chapters have been a series of interrupted journeys or forays into and around Malaysian film culture, with each chapter approaching its subject increasingly more specifically, until a selection of films made in Malaysia were examined in detail in chapter 4 in order to illustrate the arguments presented throughout the book. The metaphor of the journey is important and relevant, because it suggests a movement through time and space. Movement has been the prime characteristic of the theoretical and cultural perspectives employed in the argument: the movement of ideas and the movement of peoples through place and history, defined as transtextuality and transmigration. The two are intimately linked by those 'lines of connectedness' frequently referred to in the book, and each chapter is structured as a series of 'border crossings' that highlight the cross-cultural nature of the enterprise. Journeys have also been central to the histories and stories of the cultures examined in this book: the journeys of the sojourners to the Archipelago, whether as elite or mass migrants; the fearful journeys across the kaala pani by Indian laborers; the journeys from the kampung to the city and back to the kampung; the journeys of the exiled Rama and Pandavas in the *Ramayana* and the *Mahabharata*; the journeys of the Chinese knight-errant men and women; the journeys of Hang Tuah. This chapter recaps and summarizes the complex and detailed arguments of the previous chapters, before presenting the major conclusions of the book.

The introduction considered the location of the analyst in relation to the book's argument, represented as literal and cultural journeys between Australia and Malaysia. The encounters with Malaysian cultural products attested to the difficulties and the creative possibilities of cross-cultural analysis, irrespective of the linguistic/cultural origin of the product. The films discussed indicate the heterogeneity and cultural complexity of film distribution and exhibition in Malaysia, where Malay, Chinese, Hong Kong, Indian and American films are all shown in 'mainstream' cinemas and the phenomenon of specialist or 'art' cinemas does not exist. However, the experience of watching these films in Malaysia did suggest a correlation between the linguistic/cultural origin of the films and the ethnic compositions of the audiences.

Chapter 1, *Border Crossings*, confronted the more theoretical issues of cross-cultural analysis and transtextuality, both of which are crucially connected to cultural interaction and hybridization, epitomized by Edward Said's essay, 'Traveling Theory,' which traced the movement and transformation of ideas through space and time. Consequently, anterior and posterior cultures/texts are connected by diasporic association, where, through processes such as translation and adaption, 'newness' is constructed. The case study of the transformation of the Western, as it encountered other cultural practices and narrative traditions, illustrated the ways in which generic characteristics adapted to local conditions and local genres. The journey is one of the Western's standard narrative devices and the case study adopted that device by traveling from the 'capital city,' the center of 20th century film culture – Hollywood – to its anterior culture, Europe, and then to one of the so-called margins of international culture: Asia. Along the way, aspects of the Western genre were absorbed, rejected and manipulated – changes that eventually affected the nature of the genre in Hollywood itself. These border-crossings also represent my personal historical journey through cinema, which gradually embraced European and then Asian films and reconceived the center/margin relationship (Hollywood versus the rest) as multi-directional 'global cultural flows' (Appadurai's term). The case study's eventual concentration on Japanese, Chinese (mainland and Hong Kong) and Indian films also highlights the fact that these represent the major influences on Malaysian culture. The chapter ended at the border, because the discussion of film in Malaysia first required historical and cultural contextualization.

Chapter 2, *Malaysian Society and Culture*, undertook a historical journey through the Malay Archipelago and the Malay Peninsula, but one that was continually interrupted by a series of 'digressions' to societies that impacted upon the region: India, the Arab world, China and the West. The construction of a national cultural identity based on criteria like origin, tradition and continuity, exemplified by the Melakan Golden Age, was challenged by the voluntary and forced 'lines of connectedness' that resulted from the commercial and cultural journeys that peoples made to and from the region. The relatively static spatial format of this chapter glosses the space-time characteristics of the Wayang and the Bangsawan, where predictability of place and of the conventions of spatial sequencing exist alongside a non-linear and non-causal temporal scheme, which encourages narrational strategies such as coincidence and digression. Wayang and Bangsawan were also the two major cultural forms discussed because they typify the complex interaction between diverse cultural traditions, and because they were major influences on Malaysian films.

Chapter 3, *Film in Malaysia*, resumed the journey interrupted at the end of chapter 1, by identifying influential cultural centers and tracking their interaction with local practices. Each of these centers is itself a conglomerate of cultural accretions, rather than a fixed set of attributes – the anterior text is always itself a posterior text. The most powerful influence is that of India, whose complex, multiple language/film culture was shaped by traditional and colonial forms (Parsee theater) and remains the single most important influence on Malaysian films up to the present. The Chinese cinema originated in Shanghai, the most European of Chinese cities early last century and the birthplace of Chinese modernism. The impact of Shanghai film culture extended to other parts of China, to Hong Kong, to Indonesia and to the Malay Peninsula. Hong Kong, originally an intermediary 'port of call,' emerged as the most important Chinese filmic influence on the Malay Archipelago (as well as on much of the Asian/African film world). In Indonesia, the presence of Chinese and Indian cultural and filmic traditions produced quite a different cinema, which itself stimulated the film industry in Malaya in the 1930's. Japan's occupation of the Peninsula during World War II affected the local industry in terms of production output and exhibition practices, but Japanese esthetic and filmic influences were confined to quite specific instances. Filmic interaction between Malaysia and its close neighbors has been minimal (the Philippines, some of whose directors worked in the Malay industry) or negligible (Thailand). On the other hand, the Arab influence has been significant, primarily through Islam; in filmic terms, the only reference is Egyptian cinema, a hegemonic industry in the Arab world (and in Africa). The European impact on Malaysian film was largely confined to the British colonial censorship system. While American film has been as pervasive in Malaysia as elsewhere, its overall popularity ran (until the late 1990's) a distant second to that of Hong Kong film and its cultural influence similarly ran a poor second to that of Indian cinema.

Consequently, Malaysian films have been and remain incorporative, adapting and reshaping filmic and other cultural material, so that its cinematic identity cannot be characterized as rigidly national in terms of uniqueness. Furthermore, it was argued that the relationship between these film cultures is better described as interdependent, because the diverse Malaysian audiences helped influence the genres, stars and narratives of films from places like Hong Kong, Bombay, Madras, Jakarta and Manila. Similarly, filmmakers from these production centers worked in Malaysian films, introducing their industrial, cultural and esthetic traditions, which were always adapted to local conditions. The most persistent of these factors was the almost total concentration on the Malay experience, resulting in the absence and therefore the invisibility of almost half of the population of the country, primarily the Chinese and Indian Malaysians.

After chapter 3's concentration on spatial 'lines of connectedness', chapter 4, *Malaysian Cinema*, returned to the more temporal journey of chapter 2, remaining locally focused, while maintaining the cross-cultural perspectives discussed in chapter 3. The chapter's title evokes the national cinema texts critiqued at the start of chapter 3, and chapter 4 actually employs their chronological structures, which tend to be narrativized as a scenario of 'origin, adversity, survival and triumph.' In that respect, this chapter 'flirts' with the national cinema discourse. However, the film analyses were very specific and detailed in attempting to tease out narrative, stylistic and thematic components, that demonstrated the problematic character of national cinema concepts such as coherence, homogeneity, uniqueness and national identity. Likewise, the analyses identified how trans-cultural interactions shaped the local film culture and how that local culture adopted and resisted aspects of cultural influences, or even rejected and erased them to create a particular local hybridity and heterogeneity. Each of the analyses demonstrated the multiple traditions and complex intertextuality of these films, thus stressing their cross-cultural condition, synchronically and diachronically.

HUJAN PANAS was perhaps the most 'Indian' film examined. As was the case with most Malaysian films in the 1950's, the director was Indian. The film adopts most of the Hindi melodrama conventions, even introducing the 'darsan look' in some of the early scenes. The protagonist resembles the Devdas/Majnun figure of Indian cinema, although with an intriguing local resolution that has features of the amuk phenomenon. Unlike the Indian equivalent, the mise-en-scene is unadorned, while the song/dance routines interrupt the narrative (as in Parsee theater and Bangsawan), but are strongly motivated by the performance-oriented plot (more typical of the Chinese musical melodramas, some of which similarly 'replayed' the successful musical career of their protagonists). Yet the film applies these diverse strategies to a homogenous Malay world, indifferent to the reality of a multi-ethnic society that constituted Malaya and Malaysia. Difference within the film's Malay community is limited to a tradition/modernity conflict between the two women (a typical Indian melodrama situation), although the gender relations, including the passive masculinity of the P. Ramlee figure, are more complex than in much Hindi cinema.

In retrospect, HUJAN PANAS represents a model of Malay cinema that has remained remarkably consistent over the past forty years. The Malay-directed PENARIK BECA continues this tradition, perhaps even emphasizing cross-cultural influences to a greater extent than the earlier film – P. Ramlee always amalgamated local and other influences in his films and his music. The film's musical numbers are more integrated into the film than was the case with HUJAN PANAS, but their extradiegetic 'reverberations' became a P. Ramlee trademark. Gender relations are linked to class and to westernization, issues harnessed to the kampung/city dichotomy that persists in the Malaysian cinema. The Hang Tuah/Hang Jebat-like conflict also became a recurrent theme in the ensuing films.

With HANG TUAH, this theme took center stage, although the adaption of this Malay foundational narrative by an imported Indian director/scriptwriter within the Indian melodrama tradition, introduced intertextual tensions that re-interpreted the anterior *Hikayat Hang Tuah* text. The film's emphasis on personal relations and on the margin, counter and critique the male power that dominated Melaka, the center of Malay culture. The heterogeneity of the work is demonstrated by the significant influence of both the Wayang and the *Ramayana*. The revisionist HANG JEBAT attempted to present Jebat's perspective, but the analysis demonstrated that his rebelliousness is quickly reduced to a (melodramatic) tragedy of a man in conflict with himself. In keeping with the P. Ramlee mode of filmmaking, Hussain Haniff draws upon Indian and Japanese cinematic references to tell this most Malay of stories. SEMERAH PADI is also considered to be strongly influenced by Japanese cinema, especially that of Kurosawa; however, the Indian presence is once again significant and both are harnessed to construct a narrative that characterizes itself as a foundational text alongside the *Hikayat Hang Tuah* and its filmic adaptions. The pre-Melakan setting of the film cannot mask the contemporary significance of this tale about the birth of a (new) nation.

IBU MERTUA-KU is undoubtedly the most heterogeneous of Malay films, incorporating most of the formal and thematic concerns so far discussed. Its close resemblance to DEEDAR, its Guru Dutt-inspired song 'picturizations' and the complex employment of darsan do not produce a clone of Indian popular cinema. All these elements contribute to an almost self-reflexive study of vision, attraction and desire that draws on previous Malay films, like HUJAN PANAS and ANTARA DUA DARJAT, to produce a film totally focused on the Malay experience and its internal fissures – not ethnicity, but class, gender and kampung/city tensions. MATINYA SEORANG PATRIOT replays many of these tensions, despite it having been made more than twenty years later. Westernization dominates the threats to kampung and (male) Malay identity, even though western art film techniques like image/sound displacements are eagerly included. On the other hand, Indian culture and cinema retains a powerful presence, including the *Mahabharata* and darsan, although the film attacks 'foreign' (especially Indian) influences on Malay culture.

FENOMENA and SELUBUNG are both 'return to source' narratives, drawing on Malaysia's East Coast kampung world for their discourses about Malay/Muslim identity. Both films return to the tradition of earlier Malay (and Indian) melodramas, where women are attracted to passive males, where 'childhood' scenes predestine adult behavior, and where songs are 'picturized' within the narrative. FENOMENA's rejection of modernity/westernization suggests that identity can only be found within the kampung, whereas SELUBUNG, adopting a more international perspective, proposes an urban Malay identity that must continue to be nurtured and sustained by the kampung tradition. The hybrid, cultural nature of Malaysian cinema is illustrated in FENOMENA by the animistic practice of 'Mandi Bunga' being combined with a forthright 'darsan look' by the heroine upon the Devdas-like hero. At the same time, the increasingly intrusive presence of pop musicians in these films recalls the musical melodramas of P. Ramlee.

Like IBU MERTUA-KU, PEREMPUAN, ISTERI &... stresses vision, attraction and desire, but does so to attack the culture that the P. Ramlee film and all previous Malay films have valorized: the kampung world. The film's single-minded focus on a Malay community becomes a critique of the homogeneity that has otherwise been such a 'blind spot' in Malaysian cinema. The masculinity that was a 'given' in earlier films is unmasked here through a rigorous analysis of the 'look,' including its Indian variant, the darsan phenomenon. In a contradictory way, the film's 'Malayness' is not evident in its style, which exhibits little of the cultural tradition that has informed Malaysian cinema. Therefore on both a thematic and formal level, this film confronts some of the central tensions within Malaysian society: Malay/Malaysia(n), city/kampung and male/female sexuality. The contrast with SEMBILU could not be greater, since the latter film represents a reworking and revitalization of the characteristic Malay cinema identified in the HUJAN PANAS comments above. The musician/performer, reminiscent of the P. Ramlee era, is again linked to a passive masculinity that attempts to locate itself in relation to tradition and modernity (as represented by the two women in the film).

The recycling of these diverse cultural materials suggests that the notion of a homogenous national cinema is constantly eroded by the heterogeneity of Malaysian film culture. National cinema discourse argues that difference is typically absorbed and assimilated, but the example of Malaysian cinema suggests that the tendency to homogenization is always and everywhere fragmented by newly introduced or pre-existing cultural material. The Malaysian films certainly raise issues about ethnicity, religion, gender, tradition/modernity, and social conditions that purport to 'speak the nation,' which could thus be construed as a set of defining characteristics of national (Malaysian) identity. However, as argued in chapter 2, the homogeneity of that identity is itself untenable. Paradoxically, the films imply the heterogeneity of Malaysian national identity by confining their attention to a single ethnicity: the Malays.

The ethnic singularity of the films therefore exposes the ethnic plurality of Malaysian society and even the cultural hybridity of Malay culture. In that respect, the Malay emphasis of the films (which exists irrespective of the ethnicity of the producer, director and scriptwriter) remains in constant tension with the cultural hybridity of the films themselves. In other words, the center (Malay culture) does not so much dominate and overpower the margin/the border as continue itself to be created by it through 'lines of connectedness' that are inevitable outcomes of cultural activity and cultural interaction, as characterized by that all-encompassing concept of transtextuality. The films therefore do not so much 'speak the nation' as 'speak of, around and beside the nation' and the perennial conflict between constructions of 'Malayness' and 'Malaysianness' may well be the most useful definition of this culture's identity.

The nature of Malaysian society and its colonial history might suggest that this cultural interaction is a special case, or at least only typical of 'postcolonial' societies. However, I would argue that such concerns with the margin and the border are endemic to all film cultures. As I demonstrated in the discussion of national cinema discourse, difference is typically erased in an attempt to locate the defining characteristics of national cultural identity. Most of the national cinema studies have been of societies that are considered culturally homogenous, where differences (ethnicity, religion, gender, sexuality, class, etc.) are pushed to the margins. In that respect, heterogeneity is often camouflaged to create the 'compulsion to oneness,' implicit in Stuart Hall's characterization of national identity. However, the 'lines of connectedness' between social and cultural topoi (whether local, regional, diasporic or international) continue to function both within and between communities, and cultural difference therefore lies at the heart of all nationally constituted cultures, although rarely as obviously as in Malaysia. This suggests that studies of national cinema need to be more conscious of the submerged or hidden heterogeneity within that culture, as well as between it and other cultures.

This 'inside-outside' pattern of cultural production also applies to the analytical process and to the analyst. My study of Malaysian films has inevitably missed or overlooked particular Malaysian cultural norms and nuances (although the very concept of a unitary Malaysianness has been discredited), just as Malaysian film analysts would have disregarded or ignored certain issues presented in this book, especially in chapters 3 and 4. Nevertheless, the analytical process adopted – the creative understanding approach suggested by Willemen, discussed in chapter 1 – tries to be as intertextual as the whole production/distribution/exhibition system and as the films themselves. This intertextuality has been tracked through the social and cultural histories identified in chapter 2 and has attempted to avoid, even reject, the analytical approach identified as projective appropriation usually labeled as American-European theory (Willemen, 1994: 212-213).

While aspects of this theoretical system have been considered (e.g. male control of 'the look'), its wholesale application to the films has been resisted or modified in the context of local historical/cultural conditions (e.g. the more passive male and the emphasis on darsan). It might have been tempting to embrace Mary Ann Doane's comments on the feminization of the male in the love story as appropriate to the P. Ramlee persona: '[There is] a very strong tendency within the genre of the love story to motivate an apparent overemphasis on music by situating its major male character – the object of female desire – in the role of the musician... the male undergoes a kind of feminization by contamination – in other words, he is to a certain degree emasculated by his very presence in a feminized genre... [if partially recouped] by making him into a respected artist, a musician' (Doane, 1987: 97). There is an uncanny applicability of these arguments to the male protagonist in Malaysian films, but such a reading must be resisted, because it counters the cultural context in which such characters exist. There is no feminization by contamination; women do position the male as an object of desire, but he is not emasculated as a result. His masculinity has not changed, it is just culturally different from the masculinity Doane is discussing. Furthermore, the genre of the Malaysian films is not primarily the love story – Doane's examples include LETTER FROM AN UNKNOWN WOMAN (1948) and INTERMEZZO (1939) – but the musical melodrama, where the male's occupation as musician is *generically* coded.

In conclusion, every culture is local, but no culture is autochthonous, contrary to the Malay concept of the bumiputera as 'sons of the soil.' If a culture is perceived as homogenous, it is only because of a failure to recognize its heterogeneity (a consequence of time) or to find it unacceptable (a consequence of cultural policy and power). Such heterogeneity arises from interaction, diasporic movement and transtextuality– but these processes are not unidirectional. They represent 'lines of connectedness' that exist on multiple levels. These lines may link a community to a homeland (the concern of much diasporic theory), but they may also become knotted up in the 'dominant' culture, e.g. Malay culture, to the point where they are so intertwined that they are inextricably contained within that dominant culture. However, difference will always remain visible and distinct – Salleh Ben Joned suggests a kebudayaan rojak (salad culture) for Malaysia (Salleh Ben Joned, 1994a: 56) – and never dissolves into an illusory homogeneity.

Notes

Notes to: Introduction

1. A Malay-English dictionary was used for the meanings of individual words (*Kamus Minerva*, 1992).
2. This is confirmed in a recent book on P. Ramlee, which also has a photo of a cinema called *Pagawam P. Ramlee* (Ahmad Sarji, 1999: 231-232).
3. There will be inconsistencies in the spelling of Bahasa Melayu words due to changes that were undertaken by the authorities in 1972, e.g. lapok=lapuk, boelan=bulan, Hamzah=Hamsah, Hussein=Hussain=Hussin; even now, words are spelled in different ways. All Bahasa Melayu words are presented in single quotes on their first appearance.
4. The first citation of a Malaysian film includes an English translation of the title; subsequent references will be confined to the Bahasa Melayu title. A similar arrangement applies to films in other languages where there aren't commonly used English titles. All films are dated on their first appearance in the text. All Malaysian films discussed at some length in the body of the text are listed in the filmography.
5. With the exception of some extracts from Jamil Sulong's *Kaca Permata* (which were translated by Raimy Ché-Ross) and some brief statements from Ahmad Sarji's book on P. Ramlee (which I translated), all written material consulted was published in English.
6. The absence of clearly delineated family and personal names in Malay requires the inclusion of the full name in all citations within the text.
7. There is a satisfying sense of symmetry about the fact that flying back to Australia at the conclusion of my research in May 2001 with Malaysian Airlines, their Malay in-flight movie was this same ALI BABA BUJANG LAPOK.
8. The relationship between cultural specificity and the search for universality in cross-cultural experience is discussed in my article: 'Experiencing India: A Personal History' (van der Heide, 1996a: 53-59).

Notes to: 1 Border Crossings

1. Malaysia lacks a tradition of serious film studies; there are, to my knowledge, only two academics in Malaysia, whose teaching and research activities are primarily devoted to film.
2. The aforementioned ALI BABA BUJANG LAPOK also has P. Ramlee in Western garb in the advertising poster, a reference to him swaggering around in gunfighter clothes for some time in the film – one of his underlings (they are the forty thieves) refers to him as John Wayne's brother.

3. The Chicano film, EL MARIACHI (1992), acknowledges and in turn parodies the Italian Western.
4. In an important study of Kurosawa, Mitsuhiro Yoshimoto provides a detailed and somewhat different examination of the jidai-geki category and its relationship to the samurai genre (Yoshimoto, 2000: 207-234).
5. The relationship between the Western and the jidai-geki category extends beyond just the employment of landscape and mise-en-scene attributes to include narrative conventions and gender roles (Yoshimoto, 2000: 231).
6. Christopher Frayling's recent biography of Leone spells out this 'debt' in some detail (Frayling, 2000: 118-126).
7. David Desser in the above-cited book on Kurosawa's samurai films actually argues that *Red Harvest* is a more important generic reference point for YOJIMBO than the Western is.
8. An interesting recent example of this is the literal quotation of a scene from YOJIMBO (a scene which I will go on to examine in some detail) in the 1992 American film THE BODYGUARD, a film that in turn stimulated the Hong Kong kung fu film, THE BODYGUARD FROM BEIJING (1994).
9. Nevertheless, Burch dismisses YOJIMBO as 'nothing more than a fusion of the latter-day chambara tradition with the Hollywood Western, which gave birth to that Cinecitta hybrid, the spaghetti Western' (318-319). Burch was never able to come to terms with the generic character of Japanese cinema.
10. Frayling painstakingly teases out the influences of each of these genres on the Italian Western.
11. There is a similarly constructed shot in VERA CRUZ (1954), where the Burt Lancaster character looks around the town's ramparts to see the massive number of peasants positioned there. VERA CRUZ was directed by Robert Aldrich, with whom Leone worked on SODOM AND GOMORRAH, and the film is a significant anterior text for the Italian Western, particularly Leone's, in its Mexican setting, its opportunistic bounty hunters/gunfighters who do not trust each other, the emphasis on money and gold, as well as the film's baroque style.
12. Phil Hardy here also mentions a number of hybrid Westerns such as RED SUN (1971), a French-Italian film set in the American West, in which Toshiro Mifune is a samurai who teams up with a gunfighter (Charles Bronson) to pursue the French villain, Alain Delon. Mifune, the doomed figure of so many samurai films, is here unable to deal with the 'superior' technology of Delon's fire power – quite the opposite to the way Bruce Lee handled such technologies in THE WAY OF THE DRAGON.
13. Unlike Fore, I would argue that Chow's mode of production is quite different from the Hollywood package-unit system.
14. The Chinese title of the film translates as 'Fierce Dragon Crosses River' (Zhang and Xiao, 1998: 287), accentuating the cultural/ethnic mission the protagonist is on.
15. Tony Williams notes that 'Hong Kong studios often bought the rights to Italian Western soundtracks featuring them within kung fu movies' (Williams, 2000: 152).
16. Quentin Tarantino and other young American filmmakers are themselves influenced by Hong Kong directors like Tsui Hark and John Woo, both of whom have also worked in America (Tsui Hark quite disastrously).
17. A 1993 Kazakh film is actually entitled THE WILD EAST.
18. The editor also notes the presence of a Chinese film journal called *Western Film*.

19. A 1983 dacoit film called WANTED: DEAD OR ALIVE has a very similar pre-credit sequence to FOR A FEW DOLLARS MORE, with a lone rider being shot by an unseen gunman, who is spatially located in the position of the film's spectator. However, the many songs in the film radically depart from the Italian Western's generic concerns, with one song set in the Kashmiri Mountains and on Dal Lake in Srinagar! The 1994 film, BANDIT QUEEN can also be read as a dacoit film with links to the Western, but these elements are submerged under its European art cinema mode of address; the film's director, Shekhar Kapur, actually made a Curry Western called JOSHILAY in 1989 (Rajadhyaksha and Willemen, 1999: 121). The Tamil 'mega-hit,' KAADALAN (Loverboy, 1994) has a musical number that is a pastiche of the Italian Western, reputedly 'in the tradition of the Tamil spaghetti westerns made by Jayasankar' (Chakravarty, quoted in Dhareshwar and Niranjana, 1996: 24).

Notes to: 2 Malaysian Society and Culture

1. The Indian novel *Samskara* by U. R. Anantha Murthy (Delhi, Oxford University Press, 1978) explores these meanings in relation to Hinduism in interesting and related ways. Samskara is a Sanskrit word that means, among other things, transformation and a rite of passage with its three attendant stages: separation, transition and re-incorporation (cf. the 'Afterword' to the novel by A. K. Ramanujan, p. 142). These 'changes of state' (spatial and temporal) are at the heart of transmigration and identity formation.
2. My own *Certificate of Naturalization as an Australian Citizen* uses the word 'Nationality' as my state prior to the granting of the certificate, but uses the term 'Naturalization' as the process by which I became an Australian citizen, so that I 'have *to all intents and purposes* the status of an Australian citizen' (quoted from the document, emphasis added), i.e. the status of a natural Australian citizen.
3. In fact, Dr. Mahathir did have some legitimate reasons for complaining about certain scenes in the series that equated Ragaan with Malaysia: a map that located Ragaan between Malaysia and Thailand (perhaps referring to the strongly Muslim state of Kelantan?), an Australian talks of driving from Thailand to Ragaan and then on from Ragaan to Singapore and, more pointedly, a scene where a Ragaani minister talks of 'shooting' Vietnamese boat people but later claims he said that he only wanted to 'shoo' them away – apparently Dr. Mahathir said something similar in the 1970's (Crouch quoted in Frost, 1994: 197).
4. I take my cue here from Partha Chatterjee, who argues that the nationalist histories of India promoted classical India in the national imaginary precisely because it was destroyed by 'the medieval darkness' of the 'Muslim period,' which thus became the first colonial power of India (Chatterjee, 1993: 102). This neatly allowed the nationalists to erase from the agenda the Aryan 'invasion' of the sub-continent some two and a half thousand years earlier.
5. The density of the arrow indicates the extent of the flow of power; the stability of the model is represented by the 'rectangularness' of the diagram (Wang, 1992: 228).

6. Singaravelu suggests that the granting of the title of Laksamana to a court official helped to position the Malay ruler as a reincarnation of the ideal king, Rama (Singaravelu, 1983: 277).
7. Amuk is a complex notion that has become locked into European perceptions of Malays. Jebat's behavior is probably the most famous example of amuk. It was also applied (by Dr. Mahathir Mohamad!) to the way that Malays behaved during the 1969 conflict (Winzeler, 1990: 97). Winzeler's psychological and cultural analysis of amuk is given a somewhat more political edge in Ugarte's review of books on the subject (Ugarte, 1992). A more detailed discussion of amuk is beyond the scope of this book.
8. Sears praises C. J. Koch's novel *The Year of Living Dangerously* for its account of Sukarno and the Wayang as well as the novel's Wayang structure.
9. 'Aku' means 'I'; the poem, written in 1943, rails against social conformity in favor of an almost anarchic individualism. References to the poem and the poet occur in some Malaysian films. P. Ramlee himself identified with the sentiments of the poem, as does the contemporary essayist, Salleh Ben Joned. While unstated, links appear to be developing between the rebellious Chairil Anwar and the newly heroic status of the rebellious Hang Jebat.
10. The first of the P. Ramlee BUJANG LAPOK films, BUJANG LAPOK (The Confirmed Bachelors, 1957), also deals with the migration of Malay youths to Singapore, setting the sense of community of the boarding house in the kampong world on the outskirts of the city against the attractions *and* the miseries of the urban center itself (the latter view of the city is illustrated by the subplot of a young woman cheating men into giving her money in order to support her frail mother, with whom she lives in a city slum).
11. Other such films are THE YEAR OF LIVING DANGEROUSLY (1982), UNDER FIRE (1982), THE KILLING FIELDS (1984), SALVADOR (1985), CRY FREEDOM (1987), GORILLAS IN THE MIST (1988) and NOT WITHOUT MY DAUGHTER (1991), and television programs like BANGKOK HILTON (1989) and CHILDREN OF THE DRAGON (1991).
12. I was in Malaysia on May 13, 2001. There was no significant reference to those events; all I noted was a brief comment in a newspaper article, which mentioned that the arrival of the Indian Prime Minister coincided with the anniversary of the riots (*New Sunday Times*, 2001: 10). Clearly, there was no interest or desire to revisit or commemorate that tragic occurrence, in spite of the fact that in March 2001 there had been a violent clash between Malays and Indians that resulted in at least six deaths – the worst inter-communal violence since 1969 (*Sydney Morning Herald*, 2001: 10).
13. Anwar Ibrahim was sentenced to 15 years in jail in 1999/2000 for corruption and sodomy – see the end of this chapter for some comments on the context in which this occurred.
14. Shannon Ahmad's novel was also made into a film by the Cambodian director Rithy Panh as RICE PEOPLE (1994), losing in the process, not surprisingly, its Islamic moorings.
15. In 1994, there was a program on Malaysian television called MENJELANG 2020, meaning 'Approaching 2020' or 'Towards 2020,' which dealt solely with science and technology.
16. A story about such an event at the Prime Minister's residence was shown on THE 7 O'CLOCK NEWS (TV3) on March 14, 1994.

17. An advertisement shown on television at Hari Raya Aidil Fitri in March 1994 and sponsored by Petronas, the state oil company, follows a Malay petroleum worker returning to his kampung from his oilrig; the imagery and mood suggest that the kampung is his true and ancestral home.
18. While these statistics are now quite old, conversations with academic and film director Raja Ahmad Alauddin (1993) confirm the continuity of this situation. The film director Aziz Osman also agrees, but believes that the second choice of Malay audiences might now be Hong Kong films rather than Indian films (1994). FINAS was unable to provide more current data.

Notes to: 3 Film in Malaysia

1. The subtitle of my article on Malaysian film (van der Heide, 1996b) and my 'take' on the quote by Hamzah Hussin at the head of this chapter.
2. The dust jacket refers to the book as 'The definitive history of cinema worldwide.'
3. The films in this paragraph are primarily given their English names, because that is how they are cited in the references.
4. O'Regan's book on Australian cinema (the third in the series edited by Susan Hayward) confronts the issue of the 'national' head on, and Part III of the book, 'Problematizing Australian Cinema,' looks through the cracks of national cinema to examine social formations, gender, nationhood and national cinema discourse (O'Regan, 1996).
5. The anthology, *Reframing Japanese Cinema* edited by Nolletti and Desser (1992), is a good starting point for the re-examination of Burch's views.
6. Susan Dermody's article on the presence and character of melodrama in Australian film provides a more flexible and complex discussion of the topic than this book does (Dermody, 1993).
7. 'Third cinema' is a term coined in the late 1960's as a radical challenge to the first cinema of Hollywood and the second auteurist art cinema (Solanas and Gettino, 1976).
8. Obviously, the Japanese realized the propaganda value of the new medium as quickly as anyone else; their victory over the Russians in 1905 was always regarded as a turning point – the first defeat of Europeans in Asia by Asians. The Japanese would use this achievement very successfully in their later attempts to convince countries like Indonesia and Malaya that their invasion of these countries was meant to overthrow western colonialism (Goto, 1996: 161-162).
9. Note the different names of the characters and of the films. Kakar refers to Laila and Majnun, the Indian films are all called LAILA MAJNU and the Malaysian films LAILA MAJNUN, although the advertisement for the 1933 film calls it LEILA MAJNUN.
10. The specific function of music in Egyptian cinema is detailed in Viola Shafik's book on Arab cinema (Shafik, 1998).
11. The 1994 Hong Kong Film Festival publication, *Cinema of Two Cities: Hong Kong – Shanghai* edited by Law Kar is an extremely informative start; later publications in this marvelous series further pursue this matter. A recent article by Tan See Kam elaborates the extent to which Hong Kong films have been influenced by 'sinicism –

the ideology of one China, one people and one culture,' an ideology that emerged in Shanghai in the 1930's (Tan, 2001).
12. The song 'Terang Bulan' (the Indonesian and Malayan films in which it appeared are lost, although I am not sure about the survival of the 1954 remake of TERANG BULAN DI MALAYA), was apparently never again performed in Malaysia (Rehman Rashid, 1993: 54).
13. Given the ethnic/religious conflicts in Indonesia over the last few years, this view may need some qualification now.
14. The nonsense films ('nansensu') are discussed in Barrett's article on Japanese comedy in *Reframing Japanese Cinema*.
15. The complex and antagonistic relationship between Sri Lankan cinema (Sinhala and Tamil) and Indian cinema (Hindi as well as Tamil) is beyond the scope of this book, although it represents a different perspective on the diasporic, 'cultural imperialism' and cross-cultural relationships than the Indian/Malaysian situation does. *Framework*, number 37 (1989) contains a number of articles on Sri Lankan cinema; Laleen Jayamanne's article 'Sri Lankan Family Melodrama: a Cinema of Primitive Attractions' counters the cultural imperialism argument.
16. The annual production figures are extracted from Jamil Sulong, Hamzah Hussein and Abdul Malik Mokhtar (1993). The Indian directors and their 1950's output are B. S. Rajhans (18), L. Krishnan (27), S. Ramanathan (17), K. M. Basker (16), B. N. Rao (14), V. Girimaji (2), K. R. S. Shastry (2), Phani Majumdar (7), Dhiresh Ghosh (3) and Kidar Sharma (1).
17. The production figures quoted in this paragraph have been compiled from a catalogue of Malay films produced by Jamil Sulong, Hamzah Hussein and Abdul Malik Mokhtar (1993).
18. Timothy White, at the 1995 Australian Defence Force Academy conference, responded to this issue raised in my paper at the conference (van der Heide, 1996b) by likening it to the absence of African-Americans from most mainstream Hollywood films.
19. An example of that tradition is, of course, L. Krishnan; Hamzah Hussin disagrees with this proposition, suggesting that it was derived from the British custom of using an initial rather than the full first name (Hamzah Hussin, 1994a).
20. With the recent resumption of film production in Singapore and its consequent attempt to define a film history for itself (an 'invention of tradition' or a 'foundational myth'?), there have been a number of events celebrating P. Ramlee's achievements in Singapore, events that have drawn the anger of Malaysian cultural gate-keepers (Uhde and Uhde, 2000: 11-12). The broader issue of national ownership is also discussed in the next footnote.
21. Cheah's article is of great interest beyond its re-examination of Cathay-Keris Studio and the work of Hussain Haniff. Without arguing the case, he discusses the filmmaking that took place in Singapore from 1933 to the late 1960's as *Singaporean* cinema. While acknowledging it as a Malay cinema, he incorporates it as part of the Singaporean national cinema, which is now undergoing a revival! Until this article, most references to film in Singapore have bemoaned the absence of a film production culture. Uhde and Uhde's recent book also emphasizes the Singaporean identity of the Malay film industry of the 1950's and 1960's (Uhde and Uhde, 2000).

While these competing claims to cultural ownership are fascinating, a discussion of the issue is beyond the scope of this book.
22. A. Samad Said mentions Indian film romances, whose recurrent theme was 'Tum Meri Laila Main Tumbara Majnu,' which he translates as 'You're my Romeo, I'm your Juliet' (p. 205), once again acceding to the tendency to westernize the original statement. My copy of A. Samad Said's book is an English translation from Bahasa Melayu and I don't know how he originally translated the Hindi phrase, but the English edition seems to me to be exactly the occasion for some cultural 'reorientation.'
23. Hanan also notes the Hollywood Western reference, but sees the films as 'an early and relatively unique example of culturally resistant Third World cinema' (Hanan, 1997: 60).
24. Hamzah Hussin was impressed by the Australian system of government grants and tax breaks for private companies, having read David Stratton's book *The Last Wave: The Australian Film Revival* (1980).
25. U-Wei Haji Shaari's PEREMPUAN, ISTERI &... has a feel for kampung life reminiscent of Indonesian kampung films.
26. These views were voiced in 1994 and, while they may now be qualified in light of the subsequent events in Indonesia, are still significant as longings and dreams.
27. David Bordwell makes an interesting case for the distinctive staging and especially the editing of action scenes in Hong Kong films in contrast to American (and, I believe, Malaysian) films; a contrast between a staccato-based (pause/burst/pause rhythm) expressive amplification of an event in Hong Kong film and an impression of action, based on 'constant and continual activity' in American cinema (Bordwell, 1997). These ideas are further developed in Bordwell's book on Hong Kong cinema, published in 2000.
28. BOAT PEOPLE has also been interpreted as an allegory of Mainland China's 'invasion' of Hong Kong.
29. Abbas goes on to argue that its appearance as a subject is intricately related to its 'disappearance,' in which 'the more you try to make the world hold still in a reflective gaze [its self-absorption], the more it moves under you' (Abbas, 1997: 26).
30. Anita Mui played a similar Shanghaiese chanteuse in Stanley Kwan's ghost story ROUGE (1989), which looks back with regret to a Hong Kong that has long disappeared and wonders about the possibility of commitment and proper conduct in making momentous decisions (Anita Mui searches present-day Hong Kong for the lover who failed to commit suicide with her in a proposed love-death pact fifty years earlier).
31. This is the context in which Bachchan became the model for Gibreel Farishta, one of the protagonists of Salman Rushdie's *The Satanic Verses*.

Notes to: 4 Malaysian Cinema

1. In chronological order they are (those in bold are treated in detail in this chapter): HUJAN PANAS (B. N. Rao, 1953, urban melodrama), PENARIK BECA (P. Ramlee, 1955,

urban melodrama), HANG TUAH (Phani Majumdar, 1956, historical melodrama), SEMERAH PADI (P. Ramlee, 1956, kampung melodrama), ANAK-KU SAZALI (Phani Majumdar, 1956, urban melodrama), BUJANG LAPOK (P. Ramlee, 1957, kampung/urban comedy), SUMPAH ORANG MINYAK (P. Ramlee, 1958, kampung horror melodrama), PENDEKAR BUJANG LAPUK (The Confirmed Bachelor Warriors, P. Ramlee, 1959, kampung comedy), ANTARA DUA DARJAT (P. Ramlee, 1960, kampung/urban melodrama), HANG JEBAT (Hussain Haniff, 1961, historical melodrama), ALI BABA BUJANG LAPOK, P. Ramlee, 1961, urban comedy), IBU MERTUA-KU (P. Ramlee, 1962, urban melodrama), LABU DAN LABI, (P. Ramlee, 1963, urban comedy), MADU TIGA (Three Wives, P. Ramlee, 1964, urban comedy), GERIMIS (P. Ramlee, 1968, urban melodrama), RANJAU SEPANJANG JALAN (Jamil Sulong, 1983, kampung melodrama), MATINYA SEORANG PATRIOT (Rahim Razali, 1984, kampung/urban melodrama), TSU FEH SOFIAH (Rahim Razali, 1985, kampung melodrama), ANAK SARAWAK (Son of Sarawak, Rahim Razali, 1988, kampung melodrama), FENOMENA (Aziz Osman, 1989, urban/kampung melodrama), HATI BUKAN KRISTAL (Raja Ahmad Alauddin, 1990, urban melodrama), BINTANG MALAM (Night Star, Adman Salleh, 1991, urban melodrama), FANTASI (Aziz Osman, 1992, urban/kampung fantasy/melodrama), XX RAY (Aziz Osman, 1992, science fiction comedy), SELUBUNG (Shuhaimi Baba, 1992, urban/kampung melodrama), ABANG 92 (Rahim Razali, 1993, urban melodrama), PEREMPUAN, ISTERI &... (U-Wei Haji Shaari, 1993, kampung melodrama), FEMINA (Aziz Osman, 1993, urban comedy), SEMBILU (Yusof Haslam, 1994, urban melodrama), RINGGIT KASORRGA (Shuhaimi Baba, 1994, urban/kampung melodrama). A further six more recent films were collected in 2001 to ascertain the current preoccupations of Malaysian cinema: XX RAY II (Aziz Osman, 1995, science fiction comedy), LAYAR LARA (Lara's Screen, Shuhaimi Baba, 1997, urban melodrama), MARIA MARIANA II (Yusof Haslam, 1998, urban melodrama), PUTERI IMPIAN II (Aziz Osman, 1998, urban comedy/melodrama), JOGHO (U-Wei bin HajiSaari, 1999, rural melodrama), IMPI MOON (Shuhaimi Baba, 2000, rural melodrama).

2. Video copies were provided by FINAS and the Media Department of the Universiti Kebangsaan Malaysia; pre-recorded videos were purchased from a number of retail outlets in Kuala Lumpur. The overall technical quality of the video copies studied was not very good and this applies not just to the older films. Nevertheless, they suffice for analytical purposes, enabling most formal aspects to be discussed, except for the quality of the cinematography and sometimes the clarity of the soundtrack. Films shot in widescreen are also not analyzable in those terms, because the television/video versions are mostly 'full-frame.' Most of the films lacked English subtitles and their dialogue was translated for me by a Bahasa Melayu speaker.

3. The full list, in the order of preference and in the English translations given in Baharudin Latif's article, is: WIFE, WOMAN AND... (PEREMPUAN, ISTERI &...), BETWIXT TWO CLASSES (ANTARA DUA DARJAT), MY MOTHER-IN-LAW (IBU MERTUA-KU), NO HARVEST SAVE A THORN (RANJAU SEPANJANG JALAN), PHENOMENON (FENOMENA), HANG JEBAT, VEIL OF LIFE (SELUBUNG), THE HEART IS NOT A CRYSTAL (HATI BUKAN KRISTAL), RED ROSE (MAWAR MERAH) and THE CONFIRMED BACHELORS (BUJANG LAPUK) (Baharudin Latif, 1995: 238). The same author's more recent list, 'Some Significant Malay Films' (Baharudin Latif, 2000: 144-145), only includes 12 (out of 25)

of my selected and updated films. This provides confirmation of the fact that any such lists are ephemeral and subject to constant revision.
4. The range of performance forms is too extensive to discuss here, but is treated in some detail in *The Cambridge Guide to Asian Theater* (Brandon, 1993: 117).
5. M. Madhava Prasad, in an extremely stimulating book on Hindi cinema, defines this mode of address as 'the feudal family romance' ('the dominant textual form of the popular Hindi cinema'), which arose with the coming of sound, reached its fruition in the 1950's and was partially transformed in the early 1970's (Prasad, 1998: 30-31).
6. The renouncer is the fourth and final stage of Hindu life and contrasts with the second stage of the householder, who is engaged with the world (Vasudevan, 1994: 95).
7. By contrast, in American melodrama women are the suffering figures; in the 'male melodramas' of Douglas Sirk and Vincente Minnelli, the anguish of the male protagonists typically relates to a crisis of masculinity.
8. In a similar vein, the image of the deity is the literal embodiment of the deity (Eck, 1985: 45). It is therefore not surprising that actors playing gods in Indian film and television programs easily acquire a god-like status, a 'boon' that a number of actors exploited when contemplating politics as a parallel career. The implication of such a direct relationship between the image and its referent in Hindu culture for a theory of difference in Indian cinema is most interesting, but is outside the scope of this argument.
9. Vasudevan suggests that Satyajit Ray's PATHER PANCHALI (Song of the Road, 1955) tends to highlight the 'Mulvey' look, with Apu's point-of-view being privileged (Vasudevan, 1994: 108). This is an interesting point in view of the debate about Satyajit Ray's 'westernized' film language, as discussed in van der Heide (1996a).
10. Amir is 'love-sick' for Aminah – the Malay term is 'gila cinta,' lit. love crazy, and his 'condition' is clearly related to the Majnun figure. Wazir Jahan Karim details the stages of emotional attachment in a fascinating article on courtship and marriage in Malay culture (Karim, 1990).
11. Aminah does marry Amir, because he is 'discovered' by a musical entrepreneur, but she eventually leaves him for another man, who takes her and her son away from Singapore.
12. Rao went on to direct seven more films for MFP (1953-56) and twelve for Cathay-Keris (1957-64), before returning to India.
13. The title is also written as PENAREK BECHA (as in the film's publicity material) or PENAREK BECA.
14. The recognition is manifested by one of the many musical 'stings' used by the film to convey a moment of melodramatic crisis.
15. This emphasis on P. Ramlee's multiplicity of creative skills is not fortuitous. Another explanation given for the P in his name is that it refers to a set of artistic persona, all of which he embodies: 'pelakon' (actor), 'pengarah' (director), 'penerbit' (producer), 'penulis' (writer), 'penyanyi' (singer), 'pencipta' (artist) and 'penyair' (poet) (Ché-Ross, 1996). Uhde and Uhde (2000: 10) produce a similar (but different) list. This extremely self-conscious 'arrival' of P. Ramlee the singer is preceded by a similar strategy to introduce P. Ramlee the actor into this first film directed by him. At the start of the film, Marzuki hails a rickshaw and is taken home. Only after having been paid does the rickshaw driver lift his head to reveal himself as P. Ramlee.

16. It is also somewhat reminiscent of the ending of METROPOLIS (Fritz Lang, 1926), where labor and capital suddenly accept each other, having been in total conflict throughout the whole film.
17. The Australian print of the film lacks the musical numbers, which makes the film seem more 'neo-realist' and more Satyajit Ray-like than it actually is.
18. Majumdar's first Indian film, STREET SINGER (1938), was regarded as a classic Bengali musical-melodrama and starred the legendary actor-singer Saigal, who three years earlier had played the role of Devdas in the 1935 version of the story; in the late 1940's Majumdar made a number of films that were praised for their social consciousness (Rajadhyaksha and Willemen, 1999: 142-143, 203, 277).
19. In order to overcome the variations in the spelling of the characters' names (e.g. Tun Tijah/Tun Teja), I will use the names from Sheppard's book.
20. Errington argues that the desire to be spoken about by others and to be remembered through the ages is a motivator in the *Hikayat Hang Tuah* – it also stops the Bendahara from having Tuah killed, despite the Sultan's order (Errington, 1979: 38). The emphasis on speaking and being remembered becomes a form of self-referentiality in the (written) oral tale, but is totally absent from Sheppard and from the film.
21. While not apparent in the film version, Hang Tuah has also been likened to Arjuna, one of the five Pandava brothers from the *Mahabharata*, because both acquired knowledge and awareness (Arjuna from Krishna, Tuah from various gurus), which enabled them to act with detachment and defeat their enemies (Errington, 1975: 97). The broad links between the Hang Tuah story and the *Mahabharata* have been mentioned in chapter 2.
22. This magical kris, now actually called Tameng Sari, is given by the King to Hang Tuah. When Tuah is later exiled from Melaka, this kris is given to Jebat by the Sultan and, in order for Tuah to eventually defeat Jebat in their final encounter, he has to find a way of regaining the kris – without it he couldn't possibly beat Jebat. The kris is a most significant Malay cultural signifier and it is not surprising that it became the visual symbol of the Cathay-Keris film studio (keris and kris are just different spellings).
23. Hamzah Hussin considers HANG TUAH to have been a failure, because it was too serious and respectful, despite Majumdar's ability as a director (Hamzah Hussin, 1994a); Ainon Haji Kuntom dismisses HANG TUAH as an uncritical approach to the legend (Ainon Haji Kuntom, 1973: 12).
24. Phani Majumdar directed a number of other films for MFP before returning to India in 1959, reputedly in response to the rise of Malay nationalism (Matsuoka Kanada, 1995: 48). The most significant of these was ANAK-KU SAZALI (My Son Sazali), made the same year as HANG TUAH, and starring P. Ramlee in a double role as the father (once again, a musician) and the son, who goes astray. The film is a generational melodrama in the Indian tradition, contrasting the idyllic innocence of childhood kampung life with the corrupting influences of the city. The musical numbers parallel this social transformation, by replacing the earlier live performances (culminating in an extended Bangsawan song/dance) with gramophone renditions of the father's successful songs (especially the optimistic title song, which the son plays to taunt and denigrate his father). The father eventually 'betrays' his criminal son to the police, amidst those perennial signs of disorder: thunder, lightning and waves

crashing against rocks. This sequence recalls the end of MOTHER INDIA, when the mother similarly denounces her evil son – an even more terrible 'duty,' because of the significance of the mother/son bond in Indian culture.
25. As translated in the film's subtitles.
26. The arrival of Islam in Sumatra is generally considered to have occurred in the early 14th century (Andaya and Andaya, 1982: 39).
27. Impalement involves inserting a stake into the rectum; death takes at least an hour. The Islamic punishment for adultery is stoning to death, which has never been undertaken in Malaysia (in an early episode of the Australian television series, EMBASSY, a local woman accused of adultery with an American is stoned to death; Dr Mahathir Mohamad, claiming that the program was set in Malaysia, took great offense to this scene) or 100 strokes of the rotan (a cane) – all 100 strokes must be applied even if the victim has already died (Ché-Ross, 1996).
28. Hamzah Hussin told me that the original story on which the film was based was written by Tunku Abdul Rahman, Malaysia's first Prime Minister (Hamzah Hussin, 1994a).
29. These words echo Jebat's warning to Hang Tuah in Usman Awang's 1961 play *Matinya Seorang Pahlawan (Jebat)* (The Death of a Warrior): 'But believe my words, Tuah/that in generations to come/... others will deplore your unquestioned allegiance' (Usman Awang, 1988: 193). This play presents Jebat as the unequivocal hero of the story and also stresses his relationship with the palace women and one called Dang Wangi in particular. I do not know whether the filmmaker was aware of this play, which is much more radical than Ali Aziz' version, before making the film.
30. Somewhat in contradiction to this wholesale slaughter, Errington mentions that in the Hikayat, Jebat asks Tuah to 'take care of his child by a palace concubine who is seven months pregnant' (Errington, 1975: 110). However, there is no suggestion that this was a love match. In the film, Jebat also asks Tuah to take care of his child.
31. Mohd Anis Md Nor also points out that filming the Zapin dance led to a greater freedom in its representation compared to its choreography in a Bangsawan performance, where social etiquette required the dancers to avoid having their backs to the Sultan in the play *and* to the audience in the theater (Mohd Anis Md Nor, 1993: 56).
32. In a similar fashion, the Indonesian 'Laila-Majnun' film, RORO MENDUT (Ami Priyoni, 1983), contains a song about the legend of Roro Mendut that occurs well before the completion of its telling by the film.
33. Hussain Haniff was the son of a painter of Bangsawan backdrops and Shaw Brothers movie posters, who had migrated to Singapore from what became Pakistan; the son became a highly regarded film editor for the Cathay-Keris Studio in the 1950's, before being given the chance to direct (*Wings of Gold*, 1994: 43). His directing career was brief but very prolific, making 13 films in five years; Hussain Haniff died in 1966 at the age of 32 – this fact alone seems to have hastened his status as a genius and the reputation of some of his films as masterpieces, especially his first directorial effort, HANG JEBAT (this no doubt led to the CITIZEN KANE comparison).
34. Another recent film about the legend, TUAH (1990) returns its interpretation to more traditional times (already evident in its title). It has an innovative plot, in which a contemporary 'good Samaritan' comes to believe he is Hang Tuah and feels compelled to return to 15th century Melaka to stop Hang Jebat's 'frenzied rebellion'

(*Buletin Finas*, 1989: 10); but the film's treatment of the Tuah/Jebat characters is quite conservative. In 1992, when in Kuala Lumpur, I saw an episode (number 15) of a television series called Tuah & Jebat; the story was at the stage where Jebat was successfully resisting all attempts by the Sultan and the Bendahara to oust him from the palace. The reaction of the Melakan people to Jebat's behavior was even more favorable than in Hang Jebat – they regarded him as a good and fair man, although taken back by his insistence on keeping the 700 women in the palace with him. Scenes of Jebat with some of these women in the throne room did convey something of the sensuality discussed above. In a 1994 conversation with Aziz Osman, he mentioned to me that for him the Tuah/Jebat relationship was an important one for Malaysians and that he intended to use the story in an upcoming film, although within a contemporary story (Aziz Osman, 1994). That film turned out to be XX Ray II, which is a science-fiction film, in which a group of people are accidentally transported back in time by a 'time machine gun.' They materialize in a large wooden building and can hear a crowd yelling. Suddenly, spear tips are forced upward through the floor. This would be enough information for a Malay audience to identify where (and 'when') they are – the Sultan's palace in Melaka. This is confirmed when Tuah somersaults (like a kung fu practitioner!) into the room. The film takes great liberties with the traditional story (including Tuah's task of saving the Sultan a second time from a usurper, now a female bomoh, played in high camp style by Ida Nerina), but not with the moral of the 'original' – the museum guide at the start of the film tells visitors the standard story and says that 'Hang Tuah exists and will always exist in the soul of the Malays.' It seems that in recent films at least, the rise of Jebat as the hero has faltered.

35. A further difference, one that typically distinguishes Malay melodrama from its Indian counterpart, is that all the main characters in Deedar sing, while in Ibu Mertua-ku only P. Ramlee sings – partly because the film is a performance-based musical, but also because P. Ramlee always dominated the song and dance routines in all his films.
36. Given the lyrics, it is not surprising that this song was often played after P. Ramlee's death (Ché-Ross, 1996). Ahmad Sarji's long entry on P. Ramlee, the actor-director, finishes with the song's title, reinforcing P. Ramlee's unassailable position in Malaysian culture (Ahmad Sarji, 1999: 232-254).
37. This is Ravi Vasudevan's judgment of a similar sequence in Guru Dutt's Pyaasa (Vasudevan, 1995: 317), in which Vijay's 'second love,' the prostitute Gulab, follows him up a staircase. Her desire is voiced by a nearby folk singer, who sings a devotional song about Radha's longing for Krishna. Unseen by Vijay, Gulab silently approaches and almost touches him only to hurriedly withdraw from his presence. Guru Dutt's next film, Kaagaz ke Phool, contains a similar scene, in which the 'second woman,' Shanti, conveys her impossible love and desire for Suresh by singing a song in his presence, but as interior monologue – therefore unheard rather than unseen.
38. P. Ramlee parodied the blinding scene in his next film, Labu dan Labi, where Labu's employer becomes so frustrated with him that he takes two forks and approaches Labu as if to blind him. Labu immediately falls to the floor simulating blindness and calling out the name of Kassim Selamat. Hamzah Hussin mentioned to me that 'Kassim Selamat' became a generally used term for a downtrodden man;

he also believes that IBU MERTUA-KU would most likely be censored today, because self-mutilation is contrary to the beliefs of Islam, beliefs that are more strongly enforced in the public domain now than they were in the 1950's and 1960's (Hamzah Hussin, 2001).

39. Unfortunately, P. Ramlee's 'Malaysian' films, made at the Merdeka Studio outside Kuala Lumpur from 1964-72, were never to return to this level of creativity nor did they achieve the critical or commercial recognition of the Singapore period. The general reasons for this were discussed in the previous chapter, but the facilities, equipment and technical support at Merdeka were far below the standard of those at MFP and Cathay-Keris. On the other hand, some of the stories were bolder. GERIMIS (1968) portrayed an interracial love story, much in the tradition of Cantonese melodramas like BLOOD STAINS THE VALLEY OF LOVE (sic) and LOVE ON A LONELY BRIDGE. The film's couple, a Tamil dancer and the Malay painter (P. Ramlee) develop marital problems, but it is never suggested that this might have anything to do with their different ethnic backgrounds, despite the strong pressures brought to bear on them by their respective parents. The film goes to great lengths to invent causes for their conflicts, to avoid discussing the subject that was then and remains today the central 'problematic' of Malaysian society, a reality to which Kee Thuan Chye's statement at the head of chapter 2 eloquently testifies.

40. The reference might well be to the opening sequences of THE GODFATHER (1972). I would add Nicolas Roeg's editing pyrotechnics in films like DON'T LOOK NOW (1971) as an influence.

41. An excellent coverage of the complex role of silat in traditional and contemporary Malay society is provided by Razha Rashid (1990).

42. Without condoning film censorship in any way, it is interesting to note that the Malaysian television version lacks most of the shots of the naked woman. This doesn't represent the censor's awareness of the film's contradiction at this point, but purely the censor's response to sexually 'explicit' material – the shot of Yohanis and Saiful embracing in a chair (referred to later) is also absent. On the other hand, the SBS version censored a shot of a wounded monkey. Both cases are examples of specific cultural taboos in action.

43. Perhaps not so subtle, since the shot of the poster is missing from the Malaysian television version.

44. These translations come from the SBS subtitles in the film.

45. Rahim Razali's 1988 film, ANAK SARAWAK has the Hindi cinema's archetypal lost-and-found plot, in which the good son and the bad son confront each other as 'the law' and 'the miscreant.'

46. Rahim Razali's next film, TSU FEH SOFIAH is centrally concerned with Islam and forms of fundamentalism in its story about the conversion of a Chinese/Malay woman to Islam (symbolized by the change in name inherent in the title and the reason for the English title). The film is also an important precursor to FENOMENA and SELUBUNG in its urbanized female protagonist's restorative relationship with the kampung world.

47. Such 'childhood scenes' were common in Indian cinema of the fifties and beyond, e.g. DEEDAR, AWARA and DEVDAS (1955), COOLIE and AGNEEPATH; they also occur in the Majumdar/P. Ramlee films, HANG TUAH and ANAK-KU SAZALI, as well as in

more recent Malaysian films like SELUBUNG, SEMBILU, MARIA MARIANA and MIMPI MOON.
48. This scene is also reminiscent of the ending of Mizoguchi's UGETSU MONOGATARI, where the child, watched by his father, prays at his mother's grave as her voice-over (from the beyond) speaks of the inevitable continuity of life.
49. The next film that Aziz Osman and producer/scriptwriter Zain Mahmood made together, FANTASI, was banned for some years for its more overt reincarnation theme, a Hindu/Buddhist concept alien and unacceptable to Islam. FANTASI actually quotes the 'Mandi Bunga' scene from FENOMENA, seen by the characters on television – it 'encourages' the reincarnated Dara to sensually massage her beloved.
50. For this reason, these 'liberal' films always refer to Terengganu when constructing a potent traditional East Coast Malay culture, since its presence in Kelantan is 'masked' by Islamic assertiveness. However, Terrengganu is now also governed by PAS.
51. Some critics attribute the film's achievements to Zain Mahmood, its producer/scriptwriter (Raja Ahmad Alauddin, 1994a; Samsuddin Rahim, 1994), suggesting that Aziz Osman's 'solo' efforts (XX RAY, FEMINA, etc.) lack the cultural and emotional complexity of the first two films.
52. In a challenging article about Malay attitudes concerning the war in Bosnia, Salleh Ben Joned makes a similar point: 'To them [Malay writers] the Bosnia that is under threat is not the pluralist democracy the world knows and values but an outpost of Islam in infidel Europe; that's why the Islamic world should rush to its help' (Salleh Ben Joned, 1994b: 30).
53. Aziz Osman's later films, such as XX RAY, FEMINA and PUTERI IMPIAN II, are no less 'international'; one doesn't need to travel to absorb cultural influences.
54. Shuhaimi Baba's widely acclaimed 1997 film, LAYAR LARA, continues to concentrate on the beautiful and the young, drawn from Malaysia's singers, models and actors, but they are here joined by a large group of veteran actors from the MFP and Cathay-Keris studio days. The film is about the making of a film and touches upon most of the typical highs and lows of the 'genre.' The plot revolves around a young actor who is only interested in having a good time, which results in her being sacked from the production. A long (and touching) scene with a film star of the studio era, who cannot differentiate between her film roles and her actual life, leads to a conversion of the young actor, now willing to totally humiliate herself to be re-employed. The film still has a television look about it, but some of the intimate scenes between characters are exceptionally well handled. It is dedicated to 'the film stars and veterans of Jalan Ampas and Cathay Kris studio,' but its engagement with that earlier film culture is rather minimal.
55. The practice of using Pan-Asian models and actors has irritated Malay politicians. In the late 1980's, the Malaysian Information Minister decreed that Pan-Asian and Caucasian actors were banned from film and television commercials. Pan-Asians, the product of mixed marriages, had come to represent 'an idealised blend of Malaysian looks,' but the government wanted to avoid the typecasting of the 'various races' (*Public Culture*, 1990: 142). However laudable the objection to typecasting was, the policy implied an equation between mixed marriages and westernization, which in the Malaysian context of the time, signaled disapproval. However, it is also

another rejection of heterogeneity, even though it was undertaken in the name of plurality (a somewhat different concept).

56. This analysis is based on the censored version as released on video. The three affected scenes are: Zaleha and the truck driver in the cinema, the 'nasi kangkang' scene, and Zaleha and Tapa in the rubber plantation.
57. Many Malaysians traveled to Singapore for the uncensored version, making it the most successful Malay film in Singapore's history (Cheah, 1993: 28).
58. Examples include ALL I DESIRE (1953), WRITTEN ON THE WIND (1957), MADAME BOVARY (1949), SOME CAME RUNNING (1959), PICNIC (1955) and PEYTON PLACE (1957). The MADAME BOVARY reference may appear out of place, but Flaubert's novel is probably the film's most significant anterior text, perhaps as filtered through the 1992 Indian film, MAYA MEMSAAB (Madame Maya), both of which confront a conservative society with the defiant force of female desire. The 'femme fatale' figure from film noir is also an important influence.
59. The unglamorous depiction of the kampung and the concentration on women's sexuality are somewhat reminiscent of A. Samad Said's 1961 novel, *Salina*, named after its prostitute heroine, although Salina is a more compliant woman than Zaleha. It is therefore appropriate that A. Samad Said is quoted on the film's poster as finding it a film 'full of hot embers... !'
60. Rey Chow discusses this issue with reference to the films of Zhang Yimou, and in particular the scene in JU DOU, where Ju Dou exposes her naked body to the gaze of the peeping Tianqing, thereby 'appropriat[ing] the "to-be-looked-at-ness" that conventionally constitutes femininity,' with voyeurism being replaced by exhibitionism (Chow, 1995: 167, 169), so that the control of the situation shifts from the man to the woman. It is a 'double mode of control on the level of the narrative,' where (reversing the active/passive locations in Elsaesser's statement, which refers to a male character) power is defined as passive but the mode in which this power is exercised and visualized is active (Elsaesser, 1990: 112). Both of these perspectives are relevant to Zaleha's position in the film and are further accompanied by an uncommonly assertive darsan effect first noted in FENOMENA.
61. There is an element of narcissism in Zaleha's behavior that is particularly evident in her relationship with the cloth merchant, Majid. Like Lheureux in Flaubert's *Madame Bovary*, he encourages her purchases of material, which she has made into stylish, tight-fitting clothes with the help of the local dressmaker. These clothes are quite provocative, drawing attention to her body (at one stage she says that if you've got it, flaunt it), but there is also an inference of self-desire, stimulated by her look at her adorned self. Like her counterpart, Emma Bovary, Zaleha's debt to the merchant escalates quickly; unlike Emma, she pays for her consumer goods with her body. The link between desire, consumption and money is never directly made in the film, but always implied through the constant exchange of money between characters.
62. Unfortunately, the film's credits are truncated on the video copy, so the end of the chant is missing.
63. Only the film's publicity stills and poster propose Zaleha as a sexual object 'to be looked at,' stretched out on a bed available for 'consumption,' in contrast to her visualization within the film itself (this image in the publicity material does not actually occur in the film).

64. Both U-Wei Haji Shaari (whose recent films are signed U-Wei bin HajiSaari) and Yusof Haslam released films in 1998 and they further extend the gap between popular and art films, a distinction quite new to Malaysian cinema. Yusof Haslam's MARIA MARIANA II is the sequel to his very successful 1996 film, MARIA MARIANA, and the two films together are very reminiscent of the sub-genre of 'sibling' Hindi films, which typically started with the siblings as children, who go their separate ways as adults, one into law enforcement and the other into crime. The Indian films (GANGA JUMNA (1961), DEEWAR (1975) and RAM LAKHAN (1989) are representative examples – the titles of the first and last films are also made up of the names of the siblings) were always about brothers, but the MARIA MARIANA films obviously change the gender, and also the extent to which the good/evil dichotomy is taken. Nevertheless, like the Indian films, the women's mother (generically, there is no father) is a significant force in accentuating family obligations. Maria joins the police force while Mariana takes a more hedonistic road. At the end of the first film, Maria, in saving her sister's life, appears to have been shot to death herself (FINAS, n. d.: 219). MARIA MARIANA II, not surprisingly, finds Maria alive and more active in the police drug squad than ever; Mariana is now working as a typist in an office, but her 'wild nature' is never dormant, here re-awakened by the arrival of Sazali, who turns out to be a drug dealer. There is a happy ending as sisters and mother are once again reunited. The casting is almost a duplicate of the SEMBILU films; the two sisters are played by the two actors whose characters fought over Awie in the earlier films, Awie plays a supporting role as Sazali, and the mothers in both series are played by the same actor. The songs are also similar, with Mariana (Ziana in the earlier films) singing her tearful ode to loss a number of times. The MARIA MARIANA films thus continue in the tradition of Malay musical melodramas, still strongly linked to Hindi popular cinema and as dependent on the presence of musical numbers and singers/models as ever. U-Wei's JOGHO is closer to the European art film than any Malaysian film I have seen. Like PEREMPUAN, ISTERI &..., the film is distant from its characters, observing their behavior in the neo-realist style, unwilling (and unable) to interfere in their inevitable slide towards tragedy. The self-conscious melodramatic turn of the earlier film is here replaced by an almost ethnographic examination of a community of Malays living in southern Thailand. The protagonist, Mamat, is a jogho, a bull trainer, who makes his money from betting on his bull winning a fight against another bull (a version of cock fighting, although, from the evidence of the film, not as dangerous for the animals). However, conflict occurs in the bullring and Mamat's brother is shot dead. This leads to a series of blood feuds between the two families and Mamat's incarceration at the end of the film. Unlike U-Wei's earlier film, which was set in the heart of Malay culture (the kampung), JOGHO is a 'border' text, evident on a literal level by characters constantly moving between southern Thailand (Patani) and Kelantan (the northeastern state of Malaysia) to keep out of the reach of the law (much as in the 1958 Orson Welles film, TOUCH OF EVIL); the border also signifies a confused cultural identity, in which these 'border people' or 'in-between people' are relics of a less nationalistically defined world. As Mamat says before he takes the blame for the final killing: 'I don't want Patani Malays to keep killing each other,' but that is exactly what happens and, it seems, will continue to happen. The film's theme is, like PEREMPUAN, ISTERI &..., emphatically Malay, but its telling is strictly within the parameters of the international art cinema.

Filmography

This filmography details the significant production personnel involved in the Malaysian films discussed at some length in the preceding chapters. The credits were taken from the films themselves; where part or all of the credits were missing, other documentation was consulted.

Hujan Panas (Hot Rain) (1953)
   Prod. Co.: Malay Film Productions; Dir.: B. N. Rau (Rao); Prod.: Run Run Shaw; Story and Arrangement: B. N. Rau (Rao); Script and Assistant Dir.: S. Hassan Sahab; Songs: P. Ramlee; Lyrics: Jamil Sulong; Choreo.: Edith Costello; Art Dir.: M. Haniff; Phot.: R. C. Purushotham; Audio.: Chan Chiew Tong; Ed.: H. R. Narayana, Wong Fun.
   Cast: P. Ramlee (Amir), Siput Sarawak (Aminah), Aini Hayati (Hasnah), Haji Mahadi (Hassan).

Penarik Beca (The Rickshaw Driver) (1955)
   Prod. Co.: Malay Film Productions; Dir.: P. Ramlee; Prod.: Runme Shaw; Story and Script: P. Ramlee; Songs: P. Ramlee; Lyrics: Jamil Sulong; Dialogues: S. Sudarmadji; Art Dir.: J. S. Anthony; Phot.: R. C. Purushotham; Audio.: Mok Chek Pok; Ed.: H. R. Narayana.
   Cast: P. Ramlee (Amran), Saadiah (Azizah), Kamil Salleh (Ghazali), Udo Omar (Marzuki), Habsah (Azizah's mother).

Hang Tuah (1956)
   Prod. Co.: Malay Film Productions; Dir.: Phani Majumdar; Prod.: Run Run Shaw; Associate Dir.: K. M. Basker; Assistant Dir.: Jamil Sulong; Script: Phani Majumdar, adapted from the story written by Mr. M. C. ff Sheppard, Malayan Civil Service; Dialogue: Buyong Adil, Jamil Sulong; Music: P. Ramlee; Lyrics: Jamil Sulong; Playback Singers: P. Ramlee, Normadiah, Lena; Choreo.: Devdatta Jetley; Silat Instructor: Malik Sutan Muda; Art Dir.: J. S. Anthony; Phot.: N. B. Vasudev; Audio.: Yap Poh Kai; Ed.: H. R. Narayana.
   Cast: P. Ramlee (Hang Tuah), Saadiah (Melur), Ahmad Mahmud (Hang Jebat), Zaitun (Tun Tijah), Haji Mahadi (Sultan), Daeng Idris (Bendahara), Yusof Latiff, Nurdin Ahmad, Siti Tg. Perak, Mariani, Sa'amah, Salbiah.

Semerah Padi (1956)
   Prod. Co.: Malay Film Productions; Dir.: P. Ramlee; Prod.: Run Run Shaw; Orig. Story: Omar Rojik; Script: P. Ramlee; Dialogue: S. Sudarmadji; Music: P. Ramlee; Lyrics: Jamil Sulong; Playback Singer: Saloma; Choreo.: Normadiah;

Silat Instructor: Malik Sutan Muda; Art Dir.: J. S. Anthony; Phot.: C. Ramachandran; Audio.: Mok Chek-po; Ed.: H. R. Narayana.

Cast: Nordin Ahmad (Teruna), Saadiah (Dara), P. Ramlee (Aduka), Daeng Idris (Headman), Normadiah (Galak), Salleh Kamil (Borek), A. Rahim (Jejaka).

ANAK-KU SAZALI (My Son Sazali) (1956)

Prod. Co.: Malay Film Productions; Dir.: Phani Majumdar; Prod.: Run Run Shaw; Script: Phani Majumdar; Music: P. Ramlee; Lyrics: Jamil Sulong; Playback Singers: Saloma, Normadiah; Choreo.: Normadiah; Art Dir.: J. S. Anthony; Phot.: M. Ramachandran; Audio.: C. L. Chong; Ed.: H. R. Narayana.

Cast: P. Ramlee (Hassan), Zaiton (Mahani/Ani), Rosnani (Rubiah/Bia), Nordin Ahmad (Mansur).

ANTARA DUA DARJAT (Between Two Classes) (1960)

Prod. Co.: Malay Film Productions; Dir.: P. Ramlee; Story and Script: Omar Rojik; Dialogue: P. Ramlee; Music: P. Ramlee; Lyrics: S. Sudarmaji; Art Dir.: A. V. Bapat; Phot.: A. Bakar Ali; Audio.: Kam Shin Boon; Ed.: H. R. Narayana.

Cast: P. Ramlee (Ghazali), Saadiah (Zaleha), Ahmad Nesfu (Zaleha's father, Tengku Karim), Rahimah Alias (Zaleha's mother), Zainon Fiji (Gazali's mother), S. Kadarisman (Mukri), Sudin (S. Shamsuddin), Aziz (Yusuf Latif), Hasan (Kuswadinata).

ALI BABA BUJANG LAPOK (Ali Baba Confirmed Bachelors) (1961)

Prod. Co.: Malay Film Productions; Dir.: P. Ramlee; Script: P. Ramlee; Music: P. Ramlee; Phot.: A. Bakar Ali; Audio.: Kamal Mustaffa; Ed.: H. R. Narayana.

Cast: P. Ramlee, S. Shamsuddin (Kasim Baba), Aziz Sattar (Ali Baba), Normadiah, K. Fatimah, Leng Hussain, Zaiton.

HANG JEBAT (1961)

Prod. Co.: Cathay-Keris Production; Dir.: Hussein Haniff; Script: Hussein Haniff and Ali Aziz from a play by Ali Aziz; Art Dir.: J. S. Anthony; Phot.: C. Ramachandran; Audio.: Chua Boon He; Ed.: Hussein Haniff.

Cast: Nordin Ahmad (Hang Jebat), Latiffah Omar (Dang Baru), Mahmud Jun (Patih Karma Wijaya), M. Amin, Siput Sarawak, Umi Kalthom.

IBU MERTUA-KU (My Mother-in-Law) (1962)

Prod. Co.: Malay Film Productions; Dir.: P. Ramlee; Story: Ahmad Nisfu; Script: P. Ramlee; Music: P. Ramlee; Playback Singers: P. Ramlee, Saloma; Art Dir.: A. V. Bapat; Phot.: A. Bakar Ali; Audio.: Kamal Mustaffa; Ed.: H. R. Narayana.

Cast: P. Ramlee (Kassim Selamat), Sarimah (Sabariah), Zaiton (Chombi), Ahmad Mahmood (Ismadi), Mak Dara (Mrs. Mansoor), Ahmad Nisfu (Mahyuddin Jailani), Zainon Fiji, Mohamad Hamid, K. Fatimah, Shariff Dol, Rahimah Alias, Md. Zain.

Labu Dan Labi (Labu and Labi) (1963)

Prod. Co.: Malay Film Productions; Dir.: P. Ramlee; Prod.: Vee Meng Shaw; Story: S. Kadarisman; Script: S. Sudarmadji; Dialogue: P. Ramlee; Music: P. Ramlee; Art Dir.: A. V. Bapat; Phot.: A. Bakar Ali; Audio.: Kamal Mustaffa; Ed.: H. R. Narayana.

Cast: P. Ramlee (Labi), Mohd. Zain (Labu), Mariani (Manisah), Udo Umar (Haji Bakhil), Shariff Dol, Rahimah Alias, Nyong Abdullah, Babjan, Saloma (as herself), Sarimah (as herself), Aziz Sattar (as himself).

Gerimis (Drizzles) (1968)

Prod. Co.: Merdeka Film Studio; Dir.: P. Ramlee; Script: A. R. Tompel; Dialogue: P. Ramlee; Music: P. Ramlee; Malay Lyrics: Jamil Sulong; Tamil Lyrics: R. E. Shanmugan; Art Dir.: Abd. Hamid Aziz; Phot.: Low Yew Wah; Audio.: Tan Chuan Hoon; Ed.: Johari Ibrahim.

Cast: P. Ramlee (Kamal), Chandra Shanmugan (Leela), A. R. Tompel, Ruminah Sidek (Tina), Idris Hashim, Noran Nordin, Khatijah Hashim (Tijah), V. I. Stanley, Hoon Thye Choong, Baby Sabaruddin, Saloma.

Matinya Seorang Patriot (Death of a Patriot) (1984)

Prod. Co.: Z.S.A. Holdings; Dir.: Rahim Razali; Ex. Prod.: Azmil Mustapha; Story and Script: Rahim Razali; Music: Adnan Abu Hassan; Martial Arts and Fights: Ku Ahhad Ku Mustapha; Art Dir.: Nasir Jani; Phot.: Zainal Othman; Audio.: Peter Lim, Zulkifli Salleh; Ed.: Mior Hashim Manap.

Cast: Eman Manan (Saiful), Noor Kumalasari (Yohanis), Zulkifli Zain (Safuan), Azmil, Saadiah (the mother), S. Roomai Noor (Yusuf), Mustaffa Maarof (Haji Shahban), Ahmad Tarmimi Siregar, A. V. Bapat.

Tsu Feh Sofiah (The Convert) (1985)

Prod. Co.: ASA XX; Dir.: Rahim Razali; Ex. Prod.: Mohd Suhaimi Abdullah; Prod.: Wan Rohani Zin; Script: Rahim Razali; Music: M. Nasir; Art Dir.: Mohd. Yusof Osman; Phot.: Moh. Nuri Harmaini; Audio.: Anuar Yusof; Ed.: Mior Hashim Manap.

Cast: Jacqueline Mitchell (Tsu Feh Sofiah), Rahim Razali (Cikgu Nik), Eman Manan (Alwi), Haji Arshad, Ahmad Tamimi Siregar, Abu Bakar Omar, Pyanhabib, Normah Damanhuri and the people of Langkawi.

FENOMENA (Phenomenon) (1989)
Prod. Co.: Teletrade; Dir.: Aziz M. Osman; Prod.: Zain Mahmood; Ex. Prod.: Zahari Zain, Alias Omar; Story and Script: Zain Mahmood; Music: M. Nasir; Art Dir.: Aziz M. Osman; Phot.: Baharuddin Hj. Azmi; Audio.: Musa Idris; Ed.: Ibrahim Ahmad.

Cast: Ramona Rahman (Isabella), M. Nasir (Azlan), Amy 'Search' (Amy), Abu Bakar Omar, Nor Amarina, Search.

FANTASI (Fantasy) (1992/1994)
Prod. Co.: Teletrade; Dir.: Aziz M. Osman; Prod.: Zain Mahmood; Script: Zain Mahmood from a story by Zain Mahmood and Aziz M. Osman; Music: Azman Abu Hassan; Special Effects: Micheal Gunther; Art. Dir.: Aziz M. Osman; Phot.: Jamal Maarif; Audio.: Musa Idris; Ed.: Ibrahim Ahmad.

Cast: Erma Fatimah (Nora), Faizal Hussein (Rahmat/Teruna), Mustafa Kamal (Silbi), Kuza (Dara), Melissa Saila (Azreen), Shah Rahman (Gamat).

SELUBUNG (Overcast/Veil of Life) (1992)
Prod. Co.: Identity Entertainers; Dir.: Shuhaimi Baba; Prod.: Abdullah Omar; Orig. Story: Nora Ariffin Fleming; Script: Shuhaimi Baba; Music: M. Nasir; Art Dir.: Zuraini Anuar; Phot.: Jamal Maarif; Audio.: Peter Lim; Ed.: Mariam Ibrahim, Meor Hashim Manaf, Raja Din.

Cast: Deanna Yusoff (Mas), M. Nasir (Kamal), Ida Nerina (E.J.), Liza Othman (Dr. Sardar), Jit Murad (Halim), Harith Iskandar (Musa), Hattan (Pintu), Sulina Kamarul (Lin), Zahim Albakri (Vince), Yasmin Yusoff (Zek), Amina J. Mokhtar (Hani), Mahmud Jun (Tok).

FEMINA (1993)
Prod. Co.: SV Productions; Dir.: Aziz M. Osman; Ex. Prod.: Din Glamour, Aziz M. Osman; Prod.: V. N. Raj; Script: Aziz M. Osman; Music: Azman Hj. Abu Hassan; Art Dir.: Aziz M. Osman, Badar; Phot.: Badaruddin Hj. Azmi; Ed.: Aziz M. Osman.

Cast: Erma Fatimah (Kartina), Eman Manan (Pyan), Susan Lankester (Anita), Din Glamour (Salim), Maria Faridah (Jasmin), Azman Abu Hassan (Norman), Sharifah Haslinda (Maya).

PEREMPUAN, ISTERI &... (Woman, Wife &...) (1993)
Prod. Co.: Berjaya Film Production; Dir.: U-Wei Haji Shaari; Prod.: Pansha; Script: U-Wei Haji Shaari; Music: Azmeer; Art Dir.: Johari Abd. Hamid; Phot.: Omar Ismail; Audio.: Zulkifli Salleh; Ed.: Rassul Salim.

Cast: Sofia Jane Hisham (Zaleha), Nasir Bilan Khan (Amir), Yusof Mohammad (Halim), Fetty Zul (Kamariah), Normah Damanhuri (Asiah), M.

Rajoli (Som Chai), Jamaluddin Kadir (Jalil), Hamdah Wahab (Rokiah), Zaidi Omar (Tapa).

RINGGIT KASORRGA (Playground) (1994)
Prod. Co.: Pesona Pictures; Dir.: Shuhaimi Baba; Prod.: Shuhaimi Baba; Script: Shuhaimi Baba; Music: Razman Mohd Noor; Art Dir.: Zuraini Anuar; Phot.: Badaruddin Hj. Azmi; Audio.: Peter Lim; Ed.: Kamaruddin Abu.
Cast: Deanna Yusoff (Nina), Tiara Jacquelina (Meera), Hans Isaac (Khal), Zaidi Omar (Dato' Shah), Hani Mohsin (Mat).

SEMBILU (Heartache) (1994)
Prod. Co.: Skop Productions; Dir.: Yusof Haslam; Prod.: Yusof Haslam; Script: Yusof Haslam; Music: Awie; Art Dir.: Musa Mohamad, Badar; Phot.: Badarudin Hj. Azmi; Audio.: P. H. Lim, Musa Idris; Ed.: Salehan Shamsudin.
Cast: Awie (Awie), Erra Fazira (Wati), Mustapha Kamal (Azman), Ziana Zain (Ziana), Alice Voon (Alice), Roy Azman (Roy), Noraini Hashim (the mother), Aida Rahim.

SEMBILU II (1995)
Prod. Co.: Skop Productions; Dir.: Yusof Haslam; Prod.: Yusof Haslam; Script: Yusof Haslam, from the continuation of Awie's love life; Art Dir.: Musa Mohamad; Phot.: Badarudin Hj. Azmi; Audio.: P. H. Lim, Musa Idris; Ed.: Salehan Shamsudin.
Cast: Awie (Awie), Erra Fazira (Wati), Ziana Zain (Ziana), Mustapha Kamal (Azman), Alice Voon (Alice), Noraini Hashim (the mother).

XX RAY II (1995)
Prod. Co.: Nizarman and Grand Brilliance; Dir.: Aziz M. Osman; Prod.: Ruhani Abd Rahman; Script: Aziz M. Osman; Music: Jailani Salehan; Art Dir.: Hamir Shoib; Photo.: Badaruddin Hj. Azmi; Audio.: Azman Abu Hassan; Ed.: Aziz M. Osman.
Cast: Aziz M. Osman (Amin), Jalaluddin Hassan (Hang Tuah), Lidyawati (Shima), Ida Nerina (Sri Bayu), Azmil Mustapha (Sultan Mansur Shah), Osman Kering.

LAYAR LARA (Lara's Screen) (1997)
Prod. Co.: Pesona Pictures; Dir.: Shuhaimi Baba; Script: Shuhaimi Baba; Music: Maman, Mohar; Art Dir.: Zuraini Anuar; Phot.: Keong Low; Audio.: Peter Lim; Ed.: Kamaruddin Abu.

Cast: Ida Nerina (Ena Manjalara), Azean Irdawaty (Auntie Zai), Sidi Oraza (Malik), Man Bai (Daud), Maman (Shark), Kavita Sidhu (Zizi), and guest stars Salmah Mahmud, Siput Sarawak, Aziz Jaafar, Mahmud Jun, Aziz Satar.

Maria Mariana II (1998)

Prod. Co.: Skop Productions and Grand Brilliance; Dir.: Yusof Haslam; Prod.: Yusof Haslam; Script: Yusof Haslam; Music: Johari Teh; Art Dir.: Musa Mohamad, Faizal Yusof; Photo.: Omar Ismail; Audio.: Hasmy Kamal, P. H. Lim; Ed.: Salehan Shamsudin.

Cast: Erra Fazira (Maria), Ziana Zain (Mariana), Awie (Sazali), Rosyam Nor (Remy), Ning Baizura (Rozy), Noraini Hashim (Puan Zalnab), Zulkifli Ismail (Dr. Faris), Roy Azman (Ray), Shaharon Anuar (A. S. P. Anuar).

Jogho (1998)

Prod. Co.: Gambar Tanah Licin and NHK; Dir.: U-Wei bin HajiSaari; Script: U-Wei bin HajiSaari; Music: Embie C. Noer; Art Dir.: Fadhil Idris; Phot.: Khalid Zakaria; Ed.: Kamarudin Abu.

Cast: Khalid Salleh (Mamat), Normah Damanhuri (Minah), Sabri Yunus (Jali), Baharudin Haji Omar (Abang Lazim), Wan Hanafi Su (Pak Isa), Adlin Aman Ramli (Sani), Liza Rafar (Faizah).

Bibliography

A. Kadir Jasin (2001). 'Of Quotas and the Hornets' Nest,' *New Sunday Times*, May 13, 2001, p. 11.

A. Samad Said (1991). *Salina*. Kuala Lumpur, Dewan Bahasa dan Pustaka.

A. Samad Said (1994). *Between Art and Reality: Selected Essays*. Kuala Lumpur, Dewan Bahasa dan Pustaka.

A. Wahab Ali (1991). *The Emergence of the Novel in Modern Indonesian and Malaysian Literature: a Comparative Study*. Kuala Lumpur, Dewan Bahasa dan Pustaka.

Abbas, Ackbar (1997). *Hong Kong: Culture and the Politics of Disappearance*. Minneapolis, University of Minnesota Press.

Abdul Ghafar bin Baba (1989). 'Message,' in Baharudin Latif (ed). *Cintai Filem Malaysia/Love Malaysian Films*. Hulu Kelang, National Film Development Corporation Malaysia, p. vii.

Abdul Rahman (1993). Personal communication. November 11, 1993.

Abeyesekera, Sunila (1997). 'Looking Back, Moving Forward: 50 Years of Cinema in Sri Lanka,' *Cinemaya*. 35, pp. 4-10.

Ackerman, Susan E. and Raymond L. M. Lee (1988). *Heaven in Transition: Non-Muslim Religious Innovation and Ethnic Identity in Malaysia*. Honolulu, University of Hawaii Press.

Ahmad Sarji (1999). *P. Ramlee: Erti Yang Sakti*. Subang Jaya, Pelanduk Publications.

Ainon Haji Kuntom (1973). *Malay Film Industry in Singapore and Malaysia*. Penang, Universiti Sains Malaysia.

Aishah Ali (1981). 'A Glorious Chapter in the Malay Film Industry,' *The New Straits Times Annual '81*. Kuala Lumpur, New Straits Times, pp. 36-41.

Akerman, Susan E. and Raymond L. M. Lee (1988). 'Theory, National Policy and the Management of Minority Cultures,' *Southeast Journal of Social Science*. 16: 2, pp. 132-142.

Amir Muhammad (1993). 'Scorching Look at Sexual Hypocrisy,' *New Straits Times*. August 28, 1993, p. 26.

Andaya, Barbara Watson and Leonard Y. Andaya (1982). *A History of Malaysia*. London, Macmillan.

Anderson, Benedict (1991). *Imagined Communities: Reflections on the Origin and Spread of Nationalism* (Revised edition). London, Verso.

Anderson, Benedict (1992). 'The New World Disorder,' in Suzy Baldwin (ed). *24 Hours* (Special supplement). February, pp. 40-46.

Anderson, J. L. (1962). 'When the Twain Meet: Hollywood's Remake of THE SEVEN SAMURAI,' *Film Quarterly*. 15: 3, pp. 55-58.

Anderson, J. L. (1992). 'Spoken Silents in the Japanese Cinema; or, Talking to Pictures: Essaying the *Katsuben*, Contextualizing the Texts,' in Arthur Nolletti, Jr. and David Desser (eds). *Reframing Japanese Cinema: Authorship, Genre, History*. Bloomington, Indiana University Press, pp. 259-311.

Ang, Ien (1992). 'Hegemony-in-Trouble: Nostalgia and the Ideology of the Impossible in European Cinema,' in Duncan Petrie (ed). *Screening Europe: Image and Identity in Contemporary European Cinema*. London, British Film Institute, pp. 21-31.

Appadurai, Arjun (1990). 'Disjuncture and Difference in the Global Cultural Economy,' *Public Culture*. 2: 2, pp. 1-24.

Armes, Roy (1987). *Third World Film Making and the West*. Berkeley, University of California Press.

Aveling, Harry (1996). 'Claiming Islam: the Religious Dimensions of Shannon Ahmad's Novel *Al-Syiqaq*,' in Bruce Bennett, Jeff Doyle and Satendra Nandan (eds). *Crossing Cultures: Essays on Literature and Culture of the Asia-Pacific*. London, Skoob Books, pp. 215-224.

Aziz Osman (1994). Personal communication. March 4, 1994.

Baharudin Latif (1975). 'Malaysia,' in Peter Cowie (ed). *International Film Guide 1976*. London, Tantivy Press, pp. 265-267.

Baharudin Latif (1977). 'Malaysia,' in Peter Cowie (ed). *International Film Guide 1978*. London, Tantivy Press, p. 222.

Baharudin Latif (1981). 'Malaysia,' in Peter Cowie (ed). *International Film Guide 1982*. London, Tantivy Press, pp. 199-200.

Baharudin Latif (1989a). 'The Beginning,' in Baharudin Latif (ed). *Cintai Filem Malaysia/Love Malaysian Films*. Hulu Kelang, National Film Development Corporation Malaysia, pp. 45-48.

Baharudin Latif (1989b). 'The Revival,' in Baharudin Latif (ed). *Cintai Filem Malaysia/Love Malaysian Films*. Hulu Kelang, National Film Development Corporation Malaysia, pp. 49-52.

Baharudin Latif (1989c). 'P. Ramlee: the Living Legend,' in Baharudin Latif (ed). *Cintai Filem Malaysia/Love Malaysian Films*. Hulu Kelang, National Film Development Corporation Malaysia, pp. 63-65.

Baharudin Latif (1989d). 'Malaysia/Indonesia Relations on Film Exhibition,' in Baharudin Latif (ed). *Cintai Filem Malaysia/Love Malaysian Films*. Hulu Kelang, National Film Development Corporation Malaysia, pp. 245-247.

Baharudin Latif (1990). 'New Directors: Encouraging Phenomenon,' *Buletin Finas*. 10, pp. 2-4.

Baharudin Latif (1992). *A History of Malaysian Cinema*. Unpublished Paper.

Baharudin Latif (1993a). 'Malaysia,' in Peter Cowie (ed). *International Film Guide 1994*. London, Hamlyn, pp. 239-242.

Baharudin Latif (1993b). Personal communication. January 2, 1993.
Baharudin Latif (1994a). Personal communication. March 8, 1994.
Baharudin Latif (1994b). Personal communication. August 23, 1994.
Baharudin Latif (1994c). 'Malaysia,' in Peter Cowie (ed). *International Film Guide 1995*. London, Hamlyn, pp. 255-258.
Baharudin Latif (1995). 'Malaysia,' in Peter Cowie (ed). *International Film Guide 1996*. London, Hamlyn, pp. 237-241.
Baharudin Latif (2000). 'A Brief History of Malaysian Film,' in David Hanan (ed). *Film in Southeast Asia: Views from the Region*. SEAPAVAA/Vietnam Film Institute, pp. 120-145.
Baharudin Latif (ed) (1989). *Cintai Filem Malaysia/Love Malaysian Films*. Hulu Kelang, National Film Development Corporation Malaysia.
Bakhtin, M. M. (1986). *Speech Genres and Other Late Essays*. Austin, University of Texas Press.
Bakhtin, Mikhail (1981). 'Forms of Time and Chronotope in the Novel,' in *The Dialogic Imagination: Four Essays*. Austin, University of Texas Press, pp. 84-258.
Banks, David J. (1987). *From Class to Culture: Social Conscience in Malay Novels since Independence*. Monograph 29/Yale University Southeast Asian Studies, Yale Center for International and Area Studies.
Barker, Mark (2001). 'Foreign Media in the Firing Line,' *Sydney Morning Herald*. March 19, 2001, p. 10.
Barnouw, Erik and S. Krishnaswamy (1980). *The Indian Film* (Second edition). New York, Oxford University Press.
Barrett, Gregory (1992). 'Comic Targets and Comic Styles: an Introduction to Japanese Film Comedy,' in Arthur Nolletti, Jr. and David Desser (eds). *Reframing Japanese Cinema: Authorship, Genre, History*. Bloomington, Indiana University Press, pp. 210-226.
Barthes, Roland (1981). 'Theory of the Text,' in Robert Young (ed). *Untying the Text: a Post-structuralist Reader*. Boston, Routledge & Kegan Paul, pp. 31-47.
Barthes, Roland (1982). *Empire of Signs*. New York, Hill and Wang.
Basu, Siddhartha, Sanjay Kak and Pradip Krishen (1980). 'Cinema and Society: a Search for Meaning in a New Genre,' *India International Centre Quarterly*. 8: 1, pp. 57-76.
Becker, A. L. (1979). 'Text-building, Epistemology, and Aesthetics in Javanese Shadow Theatre,' in A. L. Becker and Aram A. Yengoyan (eds). *The Imagination of Reality: Essays in Southeast Asian Coherence Systems*. Norwood, N. J., Ablex, pp. 211-243.
Bhabha, Homi K. (1994). *The Location of Culture*. London, Routledge.

Blackburn, Stuart H. (1989). 'The *Mahabharata*,' in Stuart H. Blackburn, Peter J. Claus, Joyce B. Flueckiger and Susan S. Wadley (eds). *Oral Epics in India.* Berkeley, University of California Press, pp. 236-238.

Bordwell, David (1985). *Narration in the Fiction Film.* London, Methuen.

Bordwell, David (1997). 'Aesthetics in Action: Kung Fu, Gunplay, and Cinematic Expressivity,' in Law Kar (ed). *Fifty Years of Electric Shadows.* Hong Kong, Hong Kong International Film Festival, pp. 81-89.

Bordwell, David (2000). *Planet Hong Kong: Popular Culture and the Art of Entertainment.* Cambridge, Harvard University Press.

Bordwell, David, Janet Staiger and Kristin Thompson (1985). *Classical Hollywood Cinema: Film Style and Mode of Production to 1960.* London, Routledge & Kegan Paul.

Borges, Jorge Luis (1970). 'Theme of the Traitor and the Hero,' in *Labyrinths.* Harmondsworth, Penguin, pp. 102-105.

Brand, Michael (1995). *The Vision of Kings: Art and Experience in India.* Canberra, National Gallery of Australia.

Brandon, James R. (1993). *The Cambridge Guide to Asian Theatre.* Cambridge, Cambridge University Press.

Brennan, Timothy (1990). 'The National Longing for Form,' in Homi K. Bhabha (ed). *Narration and Nation.* London, Routledge, pp. 44-70.

Buchsbaum, Jonathan (1996). '"My Nationality is Cinematography": Renoir and the National Question,' *Persistence of Vision.* 12/13, pp. 29-48.

Buletin Finas (1989). 'Tuah,' *Buletin Finas.* 9, p. 10.

Burch, Noel (1979). *To the Distant Observer: Form and Meaning in the Japanese Cinema.* London, Scolar Press.

Buscombe, Edward (1993a). *The BFI Companion to the Western* (Second edition). London, British Film Institute.

Buscombe, Edward (1993b). 'The Magnificent Seven,' in John King, Ana M. Lopez and Manuel Alvarado (eds). *Mediating Two Worlds: Cinematic Encounters in the Americas.* London, British Film Institute, pp. 15-24.

Caughie, John (1981). 'Introduction,' in John Caughie (ed). *Theories of Authorship.* London, Routledge & Kegan Paul/British Film Institute, pp. 199-207.

Cawelti, John (n.d.). *The Six-gun Mystique.* Bowling Green, Ohio, Bowling Green University Popular Press.

Cawelti, John G. (1974). 'Reflections on the New Western Films,' in Jack Nachbar (ed). *Focus on the Western.* Englewood Cliffs, N. J., Prentice-Hall. pp. 113-117.

Chambers, Iain (1994). *Migrancy, Culture, Identity.* London, Routledge.

Chandra, Anupama (1994). 'It's a Mad, Bad World,' *India Today.* July 31, 1994, pp. 88-89.

Chatterjee, Partha (1993). *The Nation and its Fragments: Colonial and Postcolonial Histories*. Princeton, New Jersey, Princeton University Press.

Chatterjee, Partha (1995). 'A Bit of Song and Dance,' in Aruna Vasudev (ed). *Frames of Mind: Reflections on Indian Cinema*. New Delhi, UBSPD, pp. 197-218.

Ché-Ross, Raimy (1996). Personal communication. August 1996.

Cheah, Philip (1993). 'PEREMPUAN, ISTERI DAN... ?', *Cinemaya*. 21, pp. 28-29.

Cheah, Philip (1997). 'Singapore Rediscovered,' *Cinemaya*. 35, pp. 54-56.

Cheah, Philip and Aruna Vasudev (1995). 'Teller of Tales: U-Wei bin Hajisaari in Conversation,' *Cinemaya*. 30, pp. 14-17.

Cheng Yu (1984). 'Anatomy of a Legend,' in Li Cheuk-to (ed). *A Study of Hong Kong Cinema in the Seventies*. Hong Kong, Hong Kong International Film Festival, pp. 23-25.

Chin, Helen (1989). 'Made in Malaysia Chinese Movies,' in Baharudin Latif (ed). *Cintai Filem Malaysia/Love Malaysian Films*. Hulu Kelang, National Film Development Corporation Malaysia, pp. 197-200.

Chopyack, James (1987). 'The Role of Music in Mass Media, Public Education and the Formation of a Malaysian National Culture,' *Ethnomusicology*. 31: 3, pp. 431-454.

Chow, Rey (1995). *Primitive Passions: Visuality, Sexuality, Ethnography, and Contemporary Chinese Cinema*. New York, Columbia University Press.

Christie, Ian (1994). *The Last Machine: Early Cinema and the Birth of the Modern World*. London, British Film Institute.

Cintai Filem Malaysia (1989). 'Merdeka Studio,' in Baharudin Latif (ed). *Cintai Filem Malaysia/Love Malaysian Films*. Hulu Kelang, National Film Development Corporation Malaysia, pp. 29-30.

Clark, Paul (1987). *Chinese Cinema: Culture and Politics since 1949*. Cambridge, Cambridge University Press.

Clifford, James (1988). *The Predicament of Culture: Twentieth-Century Ethnography, Literature, and Art*. Cambridge, Harvard University Press.

Co, Teddie (1990). 'Ramon A. Estella: Troubadour Filmmaker,' *Cinemaya*. 9, pp. 46-51.

Conomos, John (1992). 'Cultural Difference & Ethnicity in Australian Cinema,' *Cinema Papers*. 90, pp. 10-15.

Cook, David (1981). *A History of Narrative Film*. New York, W. W. Norton.

Crapanzano, Vincent (1986). 'Hermes' Dilemma: the Masking of Subversion in Ethnographic Description,' in James Clifford and George E. Marcus (eds). *Writing Culture: the Poetics and Politics of Ethnography*. Berkeley, University of California Press, pp. 51-76.

Crick, Malcolm (1991). 'Tourists, Locals and Anthropologists: Quizzical Reflections on "Otherness" in Tourist Encounters and in Tourism Research,' *Australian Cultural History*. 10, pp. 6-18.

Cumbow, Robert C. (1987). *Once Upon a Time: the Films of Sergio Leone*. Metuchen, N. J., The Scarecrow Press.

Das Gupta, Chidananda (1991). *The Painted Face: Studies in India's Popular Cinema*. New Delhi, Roli Books.

De Cruz, Errol (1981). 'Malaysia's very own Mogul,' *The Star*. June 12, 1981, p. 20.

De Swaan, Abram (1991). 'Notes on the Emerging Global Language System: Regional, National and Supranational,' *Media, Culture and Society*. 13, pp. 309-323.

Dermody, Susan (1993). 'The Register of Nightmare: Melodrama as it (dis)appears in Australian Film,' in Wimal Dissanayake (ed). *Melodrama and Asian Cinema*. Cambridge, Cambridge University Press, pp. 232-253.

Dermody, Susan and Elizabeth Jacka (1988). *The Screening of Australia. Volume 2: Anatomy of a National Cinema*. Sydney, Currency Press.

Derrida, Jacques (1992). *The Other Heading: Reflections on Today's Europe*. Bloomington, Indiana University Press.

Desser, David (1983). *The Samurai Films of Akira Kurosawa*. Ann Arbor, UMI Research Press.

Dhareshwar, Vivek and Tejaswini Niranjana (1996). 'KAADALAN and the Politics of Resignification,' *Journal of Arts and Ideas*. 29, pp. 5-26.

Diawara, Manthia (1992). *African Cinema: Politics and Culture*. Bloomington, Indiana University Press.

Dissanayake, Wimal and Malti Sahai (1992). SHOLAY: *a Cultural Reading*. New Delhi, Wiley Eastern Limited.

Doane, Mary Ann (1987). *The Desire to Desire: the Woman's Film of the 1940's*. Bloomington, Indiana University Press.

Eck, Diana L. (1985). *Darsan: Seeing the Divine Image in India* (Second revised edition). Chambersburg, PA, Anima Books.

Elley, Derek (1998). 'Hong Kong,' in Peter Cowie (ed). *Variety International Film Guide 1999*. London, Faber, pp. 160-164.

Elsaesser, Thomas (1983). 'Lulu and the Meter Man,' *Screen*. 24: 4-5, pp. 4-36.

Elsaesser, Thomas (1987). 'Tales of Sound and Fury: Observations on the Family Melodrama,' in Christine Gledhill (ed). *Home is Where the Heart is: Studies in Melodrama and the Woman's Film*. London, British Film Institute, pp. 43-69.

Elsaesser, Thomas (1990). 'Transparent Duplicities: THE THREEPENNY OPERA (1931),' in Eric Rentschler (ed). *The Films of G. W. Pabst: an Extraterritorial Cinema.* New Brunswick, Rutgers University Press, pp. 103-115.
Errington, Shelly (1975). *A Study of Genre: Meaning and Form in the Malay Hikayat Hang Tuah.* Ann Arbor, U. M. I.
Errington, Shelly (1979). 'Some Comments on Style in the Meanings of the Past,' in Anthony Reid and David Marr (eds). *Perceptions of the Past in Southeast Asia.* Singapore, Heinemann, pp. 26-42.

Fatimah Abu Bakar (1995). 'Tuah-Jebat Anti-Climax,' *New Straits Times.* October 21, 1995, p. 3.
Felheim, Marvin (1972). 'Reader's Forum,' *Journal of Popular Film.* 1: 3, pp. 325-326.
Fernandez-Armesto, Felipe (1995). *Millennium: a History of our Last Thousand Years.* London, Bantam.
FINAS (n.d.). *Filem Malaysia 1975-1999.* Kuala Lumpur, FINAS.
Fore, Steve (1994). 'Golden Harvest Films and the Hong Kong Movie Industry in the Realm of Globalization,' *The Velvet Light Trap.* 34, pp. 40-58.
Frayling, Christopher (1981). *Spaghetti Westerns: Cowboys and Europeans from Karl May to Sergio Leone.* London, Routledge & Kegan Paul.
Frayling, Christopher (2000). *Sergio Leone: Something To Do With Death.* London, Faber.
Frost, Stephen (1994). 'EMBASSY and the New Orthodoxy in Australian-Southeast Asian Relations,' *Southeast Asian Journal of Social Science.* 22, pp. 189-208.
Fu, Poshek (1997). 'The Turbulent Sixties: Modernity, Youth Culture, and Cantonese Film in Hong Kong,' in Law Kar (ed). *Fifty Years of Electric Shadows.* Hong Kong, Hong Kong International Film Festival, pp. 40-46.
Fuziah Kartini Hassan Basri and Raja Ahmad Alauddin (1995). 'The Search for a Malaysian Cinema: between U-Wei, Shuhaimi, Yusof and LPFM,' *Asian Cinema.* 7: 2, pp. 58-73.

Gabriel, Teshome (1986). 'Colonialism and "Law and Order" Criticism,' *Screen.* 27: 3-4, pp. 140-147.
Gabriel, Teshome (1989). 'Towards a Critical Theory of Third World Films,' in Jim Pines and Paul Willemen (eds). *Questions of Third Cinema.* London, British Film Institute, pp. 30-52.
Garga, B. D. (1995). 'The Turbulent Thirties,' in Aruna Vasudev (ed). *Frames of Mind: Reflections on Indian Cinema.* New Delhi, UBSPD, pp. 17-28.
Geetz, Clifford (1973). *The Interpretation of Cultures.* New York, Basic Books.
Gellner, Ernest (1983). *Nation and Nationalism.* Oxford, Basil Blackwell.

Goto Ken'chi (1996). 'Indonesia under the "Greater East Asia Co-Prosperity Sphere",' in Donald Denoon et al. (eds). *Multicultural Japan: Paleolithic to Postmodern*. Cambridge, Cambridge University Press, pp. 160-173.

Grenfell, Newell (1979). *Switch On: Switch Off: Mass Media Audiences in Malaysia*. Kuala Lumpur, Oxford University Press.

Hall, Stuart (1988). 'New Ethnicities,' in Kobena Mercer (ed). *Black Film Black Cinema*. London, Institute of Contemporary Arts, pp. 27-31.

Hall, Stuart (1990). 'The Emergence of Cultural Studies and the Crisis of the Humanities,' *October*. 53, pp. 11-23.

Hall, Stuart (1992). 'The Question of Cultural Identity,' in Stuart Hall, David Held and Tony McGrew (eds). *Modernity and its Futures*. Cambridge, Polity Press in association with Blackwell Publication and The Open University, pp. 274-316.

Hamilton, Annette (1990). 'Fear and Desire: Aborigines, Asians and the National Imaginary,' *Australian Cultural History*. 9, pp. 14-35.

Hamzah Hussin (1994a). Personal communication. August 24, 1994.

Hamzah Hussin (1994b). Personal communication. August 26, 1994.

Hamzah Hussin (2001). Personal communication. May 9, 2001.

Hanan, David (1992). 'Usmar Ismail: Pioneer and Nationalist,' *Cinemaya*. 16, pp. 30-39.

Hanan, David (1997). 'Five Classic Indonesian Masters,' *Cinemaya*. 35, pp. 58-61.

Hannerz, Ulf (1989). 'Notes on the Global Ecumene,' *Public Culture*. 1: 2, pp. 66-75.

Hardy, Phil (1983). *The Western: the Aurum Film Encyclopedia*. London, Aurum Press.

Hayward, Susan (1993). *French National Cinema*. London, Routledge.

Heider, Karl (1991). *Indonesian Cinema: National Culture on Screen*. Honolulu, University of Hawaii Press.

Higson, Andrew (1989). 'The Concept of National Cinema,' *Screen*. 30: 4, pp. 36-46.

Hirano, Kyoko (1992). *Mr. Smith goes to Tokyo: Japanese Cinema under the American Occupation, 1945-1952*. Washington, Smithsonian Institution Press.

Hobsbawm, Eric (1983). 'Introduction: Inventing Tradition,' in Eric Hobsbawm and Terence Ranger (eds). *The Invention of Tradition*. Cambridge, Cambridge University Press, pp. 1-14.

hooks, bell (1991). *Yearning: Race, Gender, and Cultural Politics*. London, Turnaround.

Horton, Andrew (1997). '"What do our Souls Seek?": an Interview with Theo Angelopoulos,' in Andrew Horton (ed). *The Last Modernist: the Films of Theo Angelopoulos*. Trowbridge, Flicks Books, pp. 96-110.
Hussin Mutalib (1990). *Islam and Ethnicity in Malay Politics*. Singapore, Oxford University Press.

Ibrahim Saad (1983). 'National Culture and Social Transformation in Contemporary Malaysia,' *Southeast Asian Journal of Social Science*. 11: 2, pp. 59-69.
Infante, Eddie (1991). *Inside Philippine Movies, 1970-1990: Essays for Students of Philippine Cinema*. Manila, Ateneo de Manila University Press.
Iskandar, T. (1970). 'Some Historical Sources used by the Author of *Hikayat Hang Tuah*,' *Journal of the Malaysian Branch of the Royal Asiatic Society*. 43: 1, pp. 35-47.

Jacka, Elizabeth (1988). 'Australian Cinema: an Anachronism in the '80s?', in Susan Dermody and Elizabeth Jacka (eds). *The Imaginary Industry: Australian Film in the Late '80s*. North Ryde, Australian Film, Television and Radio School, pp. 117-130.
Jacka, Elizabeth (1993). 'Film,' in Stuart Cunningham and Graeme Turner (eds). *The Media in Australia: Industries, Texts, Audiences*. Sydney, Allen & Unwin, pp. 72-85.
Jain, Madhu (1990). 'The Curry Eastern Takeaway,' *Public Culture*. 2: 2, pp. 121-128.
Jain, Ravindra K. (1993). *Indian Communities Abroad: Themes and Literature*. New Delhi, Manohar.
Jameson, Richard (1973). 'Something to do with Death: a Fistful of Sergio Leone,' *Film Comment*. 9: 2, pp. 8-16.
Jamil Sulong (1989). 'Bangsawan's Influence in Malay Films,' in Baharudin Latif (ed). *Cintai Filem Malaysia/Love Malaysian Films*. Hulu Kelang, National Film Development Corporation Malaysia, pp. 56-60.
Jamil Sulong (1990). *Kaca Permata: Memoir Seorang Pengarah*. Kuala Lumpur, Dewan Bahasa dan Pustaka.
Jamil Sulong (1994). Personal communication. March 9, 1994.
Jamil Sulong, Hamzah Hussein and Abdul Malik Mokhtar (eds) (1993). *Daftar Filem Melayu* (A Catalogue of Malay Films). Hulu Kelang, FINAS.
Jarvie, I. C. (1977). *Window on Hong Kong: a Sociological Study of the Hong Kong Film Industry and its Audience*. Hong Kong, University of Hong Kong.
Jayamanne, Laleen (1992). 'Sri Lankan Family Melodrama: a Cinema of Primitive Attractions,' *Screen*. 33: 2, pp. 145-153.
Johan Jaaffar (1984). 'Hold it! Cut! Let P. Ramlee Rest in Peace,' *New Straits Times*. March 25, 1984, p. 12.

Kakar, Sudhir (1990). *Intimate Relations: Exploring Indian Sexuality.* New Delhi, Penguin.
Kakar, Sudhir and John M. Ross (1992). *Tales of Love, Sex and Danger.* Delhi, Oxford University Press.
Kamaruddin M. Said (1992). 'The Signifier and Heroes in the *Hikayat Hang Tuah*: a Reinterpretation,' *Malay Literature.* 5: 2, pp. 156-179.
Kamus Minerva (1992). *Kamus Minerva: Malay-English, English-Malay Dictionary.* Seremban, Minerva Publications.
Karim, Wazir Jahan (1990). 'Prelude to Madness: the Language of Emotion in Courtship and Early Marriage,' in Wazir Jahan Karim (ed). *Emotions of Culture: A Malay Perspective.* Singapore, Oxford University Press, pp. 21-63.
Karim, Wazir Jahan (1992). *Women and Culture: Between Malay Adat and Islam.* Boulder, Westview Press.
Karnad, Girish (1989). 'Theatre in India,' *Daedalus.* 118: 4, pp. 331-352.
Karthigesu, Ranggasamy (1988). 'Television as a Tool for Nation-building in the Third World: a Post-Colonial Pattern, using Malaysia as a Case-study,' in Phillip Drummond and Richard Paterson (eds). *Television and its Audience: International Research Perspectives.* London, British Film Institute, pp. 306-326.
Kassim Ahmad (1966). *Characterisation in Hikayat Hang Tuah.* Kuala Lumpur, Dewan Bahasa dan Pustaka.
Kassim Ahmad (1968). 'A Common Story,' in Lloyd Fernando (ed). *Twenty-Two Malaysian Stories.* Singapore, Heinemann Asia, pp. 24-29.
Katz, Ephraim (1994). *The Macmillan International Film Encyclopedia* (New edition). London, Macmillan.
Kaur, Amarjit (1993). *Historical Dictionary of Malaysia* (Asian Historical Dictionaries No. 13). Metuchen, New Jersey, The Scarecrow Press.
Kee Hua Chee (1992). 'P. Ramlee: Malaysia's All-Time Mega Star,' *Wings of Gold: the Inflight Magazine of Malaysia Airlines.* May 1992, pp. 16-33.
Kee Thuan Chye (1992). *Just in So Many Words: Views, Reviews & Other Things.* Singapore, Heinemann.
Kee Thuan Chye (1993). 'Dilemma of a Dog Barking at a Mountain: Pragmatist-Idealist Dialectic and the Writer in Malaysia,' in C. Y. Loh and I. K. Ong (eds). *Skoob Pacifica Anthology No. 1: S.E. Asia Writes Back!* London, Skoob Books, pp. 141-148.
Kessler, Clive (1992). 'Archaism and Modernity: Contemporary Malay Political Culture,' in Joel S. Kahn and Francis Loh Kok Wah (eds). *Fragmented Vision: Culture and Politics in Contemporary Malaysia.* North Sydney, Allen & Unwin, pp. 133-157.
Kessler, Clive (2001). 'Mahathir's Endgame,' *Show Cause.* 5, pp. 21-22.

Kitses, Jim (1969). *Horizons West*. London, Thames and Hudson/British Film Institute.

Krishnan, L. (1994a). Personal communication. March 8, 1994.

Krishnan, L. (1994b). Personal communication. August 26, 1994.

Lal, P. (1980). 'Introduction,' in *The Mahabharata of Vyasa*. New Delhi, Vikas Publishing House, pp. 3-60.

Law Kar (1992a). 'Programme Notes,' in Law Kar (ed). *Overseas Chinese Figures in Cinema*. Hong Kong, Hong Kong International Film Festival, pp. 95-118.

Law Kar (1992b). 'Appendix 1: Biographical Notes,' in Law Kar (ed). *Overseas Chinese Figures in Cinema*. Hong Kong, Hong Kong International Film Festival, pp. 119-123.

Law Kar (ed) (1986). *Cantonese Melodrama, 1950-1969*. Hong Kong, Hong Kong International Film Festival.

Law Wai-ming (1994). 'Old Images of Two Cities: the Position of Mandarin Cinema in 1950's Hong Kong,' in Law Kar (ed). *Cinema of Two Cities: Hong Kong – Shanghai*. Hong Kong, Hong Kong International Film Festival, pp. 37-38.

Lawson, Sylvia (1979). 'Towards Decolonization: some Problems and Issues for Film History in Australia,' *Film Reader*. 4, pp. 63-71.

Lee, Alan (1979). 'Cathay Sells Shares to Bumiputra,' *The Star*. December 28, 1979, p. 21.

Lee, Raymond L. M. (1990). 'Secularization and Religious Change: Malaysia as a Testing Ground,' *Sarjana*. 6, pp. 69-79.

Lent, John A. (1990). *The Asian Film Industry*. London, Christopher Helm.

Leung, Grace L. K. and Joseph M. Chan (1997). 'The Hong Kong Cinema and its Overseas Market: a Historical Review, 1950-1995,' in Law Kar (ed). *Fifty Years of Electric Shadows*. Hong Kong, Hong Kong International Film Festival, pp. 143-151.

Leyda, Jay (1972). *Dianying – Electric Shadows: an Account of Films and the Film Audience in China*. Cambridge, Mass., MIT Press.

Li Cheuk-to (1987). 'Introduction,' in Li Cheuk-to (ed). *Cantonese Opera Film Retrospective*. Hong Kong, Hong Kong International Film Festival, p. 9.

Li Cheuk-to (1989). 'Programme Notes,' in Li Cheuk-to (ed). *Phantoms of the Hong Kong Cinema*. Hong Kong, Hong Kong International Film Festival, pp. 86-99.

Lim, Elaine (1993). 'Malaysian Locales for Big-Budget HK Series,' *New Straits Times*. November 16, 1993, p. 27.

Lim, Rebecca (1989). 'Malaysian-Indonesian Coproductions,' in Baharudin Latif (ed). *Cintai Filem Malaysia/Love Malaysian Films*. Hulu Kelang, National Film Development Corporation Malaysia, pp. 211-213.

Liu, James J. Y. (1967). *The Chinese Knight-Errant*. London, Routledge & Kegan Paul.

Lockard, Craig A. (1991). 'Reflections of Change: Sociopolitical Commentary and Criticism in Malaysian Popular Music since 1950,' *Crossroads*. 6: 1, pp. 1-106.

Lockard, Craig A. (1995). '"Hey, We Equatorial People": Popular Music and Contemporary Society in Malaysia,' in John A. Lent (ed). *Asian Popular Culture*. Boulder, Westview Press, p. 11-28.

Mabbett, I. W. (1977). 'The "Indianization" of Southeast Asia: Reflections on the Historical Sources,' *Journal of Southeast Asian Studies*. 8: 2, pp. 143-161.

Mahirin Binti Hassan (1978). 'P. Ramlee – a Son of Penang,' *Malaysia in History*. 21: 2, pp. 75-79.

Malcomson, Scott L. (1985). 'The Pure Land Beyond the Seas: Barthes, Burch and the Uses of Japan,' *Screen*. 26: 3-4, pp. 23-33.

Malkmus, Lizbeth and Roy Armes (1991). *Arab and African Film Making*. London, Zed Books.

Maniam, K. S. (1983). *The Cord*. Kuala Lumpur, Aspatra Quest Publishers.

Mansor bin Puteh (1989-90). 'Malaysia: Uncharted Course,' *Cinemaya*. 6, pp. 32-33.

Mansor bin Puteh (1990). 'Inching Ahead,' *Cinemaya*. 7, pp. 4-6.

Masud, Iqbal (1995). 'The Great Four of the Golden Fifties,' in Aruna Vasudev (ed). *Frames of Mind: Reflections on Indian Cinema*. New Delhi, UBSPD, pp. 29-42.

Matheson, Virginia (1985). 'Literature as Social Criticism: the Writings of the Generation of the 1950's (ASAS 50).' Unpublished Paper prepared for the Malaysian Society Colloquium on Malaysian Social and Economic History.

Matsuoka Kanda, Tamaki (1995). 'Indian Film Directors in Malaya,' in Aruna Vasudev (ed). *Frames of Mind: Reflections on Indian Cinema*. New Delhi, UBSPD, pp. 43-50.

Matusky, Patricia (1993). *Malaysian Shadow Play and Music: Continuity of an Oral Tradition*. Kuala Lumpur, Oxford University Press.

Mazlan Nordin (1993). 'Deeds of Two Malay Warriors Continue to Stir Public Interest,' *New Straits Times*. October 1, 1993, p. 12.

McCormack, Gavan (1996). 'Introduction,' in Donald Denoon et al. (eds). *Multicultural Japan: Paleolithic to Postmodern*. Cambridge, Cambridge University Press, pp. 1-15.

McFarlane, Brian and Geoff Mayer (1992). *New Australian Cinema: Sources and Parallels in American and British Film*. Cambridge, Cambridge University Press.

Milner, A. C. (1993). 'Islamic Debate in the Public Sphere,' in Anthony Reid (ed). *The Making of an Islamic Political Discourse in Southeast Asia*. Clayton, Victoria, Centre for Southeast Asian Studies, Monash University, pp. 109-126.

Mishra, Vijay (1985). 'Towards a Theoretical Critique of Bombay Cinema,' *Screen*. 26: 3-4, pp. 133-146.

Mishra, Vijay (1995). 'The Diasporic Imaginary: Theorizing (the Indian) Diaspora,' Unpublished Paper, presented at the Humanities Research Centre, Australian National University, February 1995.

Mohd Anis Md Nor (1993). *Zapin: Folk Dance of the Malay World*. Singapore, Oxford University Press.

Mohd. Hamdan Hj. Adnan (1988). 'Malaysian Films: Survival or Revival,' *Media Asia*. 15: 3, pp. 155-164.

Mohd Hamdan bin Haji Adnan (1991). 'Development and Anti-Development Messages in Film, Television and Advertising,' *Media Asia*. 18: 2, pp. 63-72.

Mohd. Kamsah Sirat (1992). 'Indonesian Films in Singapore,' in Salim Said and J. E. Siahaan (eds). *Indonesian Film Panorama*. Jakarta, Permanent Committee of the Indonesian Film Festival, pp. 88-91.

Mohd. Taib Osman (1984). *Bunga Rampai: Aspects of Malay Culture*. Kuala Lumpur, Dewan Bahasa dan Pustaka.

Morley, David and Kevin Robins (1989). 'Spaces of Identity: Communications Technologies and the Reconfiguration of Europe,' *Screen*. 30: 4, pp. 10-34.

Mudrooroo (1994). *Aboriginal Mythology*. London, HarperCollins.

Muhammad Haji Salleh (1991). *Yang Empunya Cerita: the Mind of the Malay Author*. Kuala Lumpur, Dewan Bahasa dan Pustaka.

Muhammad Yusoff Hashim (1992). *The Malay Sultanate of Malacca*. Kuala Lumpur, Dewan Bahasa dan Pustaka.

Mulvey, Laura (1975). 'Visual Pleasure and Narrative Cinema,' *Screen*. 16: 3, pp. 6-18.

Murray, Scott (ed) (1994). *Australian Cinema*. St. Leonards, Allen & Unwin/Australian Film Commission.

Nagata, Judith (1980). 'Religious Ideology and Social Change: the Islamic Revival in Malaysia,' *Pacific Affairs*. 53: 3, pp. 405-439.

Nandan, Satendra (1995). Personal communication. 1995.

Nanney, Nancy K. (1988). 'Evolution of a Hero: the Hang Tuah/Hang Jebat Tale in Malay Drama,' *Asian Theatre Journal*. 5: 2, pp. 164-174.

New Straits Times (1986). 'In Search for a Healthier Film Industry,' *New Straits Times*. January 18, 1986, p. 4.

New Straits Times (1994a). 'Dr M: Be Wary of Western Media Influence,' *New Straits Times*. March 14, 1994, p. 1.

New Straits Times (1994b). 'Malay's share of Economy "still small",' *New Straits Times*. August 26, 1994.

New Straits Times (1994c). 'SEMBILU,' *New Straits Times*. August 27, 1994, p. 20.

New Sunday Times (2001). 'The NST Diary,' *New Sunday Times*, May 13, 2001, p. 10.

Ng Ho (1981). 'Jiang Hu Revisited: towards a Reconstruction of the Martial Arts World,' in Leong Mo-ling (ed). *A Study of the Hong Kong Swordplay Film (1945-1980)*. Hong Kong, Hong Kong International Film Festival, pp. 73-86.

Ng Ho (1983). 'Anecdotes from Two Decades of Hong Kong Cinema: 1947-1967,' in Shu Kei (ed). *A Comparative Study of Post-War Mandarin and Cantonese Cinema: the Films of Zhu Shilin, Qin Jian and other Directors*. Hong Kong, Hong Kong International Film Festival, pp. 139-144.

Nolletti, Arthur, Jr. and David Desser (eds) (1992). *Reframing Japanese Cinema: Authorship, Genre, History*. Bloomington, Indiana University Press.

Noriega, Chon A. (1992). 'Introduction,' in Chon A. Noriega (ed). *Chicanos and Film: Representation and Resistance*. Minneapolis, University of Minnesota Press, pp. xi-xxvi.

Nowell-Smith, Geoffrey (1987). 'Minnelli and Melodrama,' in Christine Gledhill (ed). *Home is Where the Heart is: Studies in Melodrama and the Woman's Film*. London, British Film Institute, pp. 70-74.

Nowell-Smith, Geoffrey (ed) (1996). *The Oxford History of World Cinema*. Oxford, Oxford University Press.

O'Regan, Tom (1992). 'Too Popular By Far: on Hollywood's International Popularity,' *Continuum*. 5: 2, pp. 302-351.

O'Regan, Tom (1996). *Australian National Cinema*. London, Routledge.

Ong, Aihwa (1990). 'State versus Islam: Malay Families, Women's Bodies, and the Body Politic in Malaysia,' *American Ethnologist*. 17: 2, pp. 258-276.

Ooi, Vicki (1980). 'Jacobean Drama and the Martial Arts Films of King Hu: a Study in Power and Corruption,' *Australian Journal of Screen Theory*. 7, pp. 103-123.

Pandian, M. S. S. (1992). *The Image Trap: M. G. Ramachandran in Film and Politics*. New Delhi, Sage Publications.

Papastergiadis, Nikos (1990). 'Ashis Nandy: Dialogue and the Diaspora – a Conversation,' *Third Text*. 11, pp. 99-108.

Pattison, Barrie (1994). 'The 39th Asia-Pacific Film Festival,' *Cinema Papers*. 102, pp. 22-23.

Prasad, M. Madhava (1998). *Ideology of the Hindi Film: A Historical Construction*. New Delhi, Oxford University Press.

Proudfoot, Ian (1994). Seminar. Faculty of Asian Studies, Australian National University, October 14, 1994.
Public Culture (1990). 'Seeking the Right Look,' *Public Culture*. 2: 2, pp. 142-143.

Quinn, George (1987). 'The Campaign against Melodrama in the Theatre State: Elite Institutions and the Aesthetics of Prose Narrative in Indonesia and Malaysia,' *Review of Indonesian and Malaysian Affairs*. 21: 1, pp. 44-53.

Rai, Amit (1994). 'An American Raj in Filmistan: Images of Elvis in Indian Films,' *Screen*. 35: 1, pp. 51-77.
Raja Ahmad Alauddin (1992). 'A Brief History of the Development of Indonesian Films in Malaysia,' in Salim Said and J. E. Siahaan (eds). *Indonesian Film Panorama*. Jakarta, Permanent Committee of the Indonesian Film Festival, pp. 83-87.
Raja Ahmad Alauddin (1993). Personal communication. November 12, 1993.
Raja Ahmad Alauddin (1994a). Personal communication. March 11, 1994.
Raja Ahmad Alauddin (1994b). Personal communication. August 20, 1994.
Rajadhyaksha, Ashish (1996), 'India: Filming the Nation,' in Geoffrey Nowell-Smith (ed). *The Oxford History of World Cinema*. Oxford, Oxford University Press, pp. 678-689.
Rajadhyaksha, Ashish and Paul Willemen (1994). *Encyclopaedia of Indian Cinema*. London, British Film Institute/New Delhi, Oxford University Press.
Rajadhyaksha, Ashish and Paul Willemen (1999). *Encyclopaedia of Indian Cinema* (Revised edition). London, British Film Institute/New Delhi, Oxford University Press.
Rashidah Abdullah (1993). 'Question of Choice Left Unexplored,' *New Straits Times*. September 13, 1993, p. 34.
Rayns, Tony (1992). 'Folk Tales, Past and Present,' *China Screen*. 1, p. 36.
Razha Rashid (1990). 'Martial Arts and the Malay Superman,' in Wazir Jahan Karim (ed). *Emotions of Culture: A Malay Perspective*. Singapore, Oxford University Press, pp. 64-95.
Rehman Rashid (1993). *A Malaysian Journey*. Petaling Jaya, Rehman Rashid.
Reid, Anthony (1988). *South East Asia in the Age of Commerce, 1450-1680, Volume 1: The Lands below the Winds*. New Haven, Yale University Press.
Review of Indonesian and Malaysian Affairs (1981). 'The Cinema and Colonial Rule in Southeast Asia: a Documentary Anecdote,' *Review of Indonesian and Malaysian Affairs*. 15: 1, pp. 151-155.
Richards, Jeffrey (1983). '"Patriotism with Profit": British Imperial Cinema in the 1930's,' in James Curran and Vincent Porter (eds). *British Cinema History*. London, Weidenfeld and Nicolson, pp. 245-256.

Richie, Donald (1984). *The Films of Akira Kurosawa* (Revised edition). Berkeley, University of California Press.

Richie, Donald (1991). 'Narrative Traditions: East and West,' *Cinemaya*. 13, pp. 14-16.

Richman, Paula (1991a). 'Introduction: the Diversity of the Ramayana Tradition,' in Paula Richman (ed). *Many Ramayanas: the Diversity of a Narrative Tradition in South Asia*. Berkeley, University of California Press, pp. 3-21.

Richman, Paula (1991b). 'E. V. Ramasami's Reading of the *Ramayana*,' in Paula Richman (ed). *Many Ramayanas: the Diversity of a Narrative Tradition in South Asia*. Berkeley, University of California Press, pp. 175-201.

Rodriguez, Hector (1997). 'Hong Kong Popular Culture as an Interpretive Arena: the Huang Feihong Film Series,' *Screen*, 38: 1, pp. 1-24.

Rohani Mat Saman (1989). 'Women Producers,' in Baharudin Latif (ed). *Cintai Filem Malaysia/Love Malaysian Films*. Hulu Kelang, National Film Development Corporation Malaysia, pp. 102-105.

Romney, Jonathan (1992). 'Hall of Mirrors,' *Sight and Sound*. 1: 10, p. 14-17.

Rosen, Philip (1984). 'History, Textuality, Nation: Kracauer, Burch, and Some Problems in the Study of National Cinema,' *Iris*. 2: 2, pp. 69-84.

Ruhani Abdul Rahman (1994). Personal communication. March 9, 1994.

Ruhani Abdul Rahman (2001). Personal communication. May 3, 2001.

Rushdie, Salman (1989). *The Satanic Verses*. New York, Viking.

Rushdie, Salman (1991). *Imaginary Homelands*. London, Granta Books.

Sahai, Malti (1987). 'Raj Kapoor and the Indianization of Charlie Chaplin,' *East-West Film Journal*. 2: 1, pp. 62-76.

Said, Edward (1978). *Orientalism*. Harmondsworth, Penguin.

Said, Edward (1984). *The World, the Text, and the Critic*. London, Faber and Faber.

Said, Edward (1993). *Culture and Imperialism*. London, Chatto and Windus.

Saiful Azhar Abdullah (1994). 'PM: Let's prove an Islamic nation can progress,' *New Straits Times*. February 25, 1994, p. 1.

Salim Said (1991). *Shadows on the Silver Screen: a Social History of Indonesian Film*. Jakarta, The Lontar Foundation.

Salim Said (1992). 'The Rise of the Indonesian Film Industry,' *East-West Film Journal*. 6: 2, pp. 99-115.

Salleh Ben Joned (1994a). *As I Please: Selected Writings 1975-1994*. London, Skoob Books.

Salleh Ben Joned (1994b). 'Malay Writers and Bosnia,' *New Straits Times*. August 31, 1994, pp. 30, 38.

Sam Ho (1996). 'Licensed to Kick Men: the Jane Bond Films,' in Law Kar (ed). *The Restless Breed: Cantonese Stars of the Sixties*. Hong Kong, Hong Kong International Film Festival, pp. 40-46.

Samsuddin Rahim (1994). Personal communication. August 29, 1994.

Sarkar, H. B. (1983). 'The *Ramayana* in Southeast Asia: a General Survey,' in K. R. Srinivasa Iyengar (ed). *Asian Variations in Ramayana*. New Delhi, Sahitya Akademi, pp. 206-220.

Sarris, Andrew (1968). *The American Cinema: Directors and Directions 1929-1968*. New York, E. P. Dutton.

Schatz, Thomas (1983). *Old Hollywood/New Hollywood: Ritual, Art, and Industry*. Ann Arbor, UMI Research Press.

Sears, Laurie J. (1996). *Shadows of Empire: Colonial Discourse and Javanese Tales*. Durham, Duke University Press.

Sek Kei (1996). 'The War between the Cantonese and Mandarin Cinemas in the Sixties and how the Beautiful Women lost to the Action Men,' in Law Kar (ed). *The Restless Breed: Cantonese Stars of the Sixties*. Hong Kong, Hong Kong International Film Festival, pp. 30-33.

Sen, Krishna (1994). *Indonesian Cinema: Framing the New Order*. London, Zed Books.

Shafik, Viola (1998). *Arab Cinema: History and Cultural Identity*. Cairo, The American University in Cairo Press.

Shaharuddin b. Maaruf (1984). *Concept of a Hero in Malay Society*. Singapore, Eastern Universities Press.

Shamsul Akmar (2001). 'Need To Find Common Ground,' *New Sunday Times*, May 13, 2001, p. 4.

Sharma, Ashwani (1993). 'Blood, Sweat and Tears: Amitabh Bachchan, Urban Demi-God,' in Pat Kirkham and Janet Thumim (eds). *You Tarzan: Masculinity, Movies and Men*. New York, St. Martin's Press, pp. 167-180.

Sheppard, M. C. ff (1962). *The Adventures of Hang Tuah* (Fifth edition). Singapore, Eastern Universities Press.

Shohat, Ella (1989a). *Israeli Cinema: East/West and the Politics of Representation*. Austin, University of Texas Press.

Shohat, Ella (1989b). 'Anomalies of the National: Representing Israel/Palestine,' *Wide Angle*. 11: 3, pp. 33-41.

Shohat, Ella and Robert Stam (1994). *Unthinking Eurocentrism: Multiculturalism and the Media*. London, Routledge.

Silver, Alain (1975). 'Samurai,' *Film Comment*. 11: 5, pp. 10-15.

Singaravelu, S. (1981). 'The Rama Story in Malay Tradition,' *Journal of the Malaysian Branch of the Royal Asiatic Society*. 54: 2, pp. 131-147.

Singaravelu, S. (1983). 'The Literary Version of the Rama Story in Malay,' in K. R. Srinivasa Iyengar (ed). *Asian Variations in Ramayana*. New Delhi, Sahitya Akademi, pp. 276-295.

Smith, Paul (1993). *Clint Eastwood: a Cultural Production*. Minneapolis, University of Minnesota Press.

Solanas, Fernando and Octavio Gettino (1976). 'Towards a Third Cinema,' in Bill Nichols (ed). *Movies and Methods*. Berkeley, University of California Press, pp. 44-64.

Solehah Ishak (1987). *Histrionics of Development: a Study of Three Contemporary Malay Playwrights*. Kuala Lumpur, Dewan Bahasa dan Pustaka.

Solehah Ishak (1992). 'State Problems and Staged Solutions,' *Malay Literature*. 5: 1, pp. 80-95.

Somboon, C. (1984). 'Striving for Perfection,' *The Star*. May 17, 1984, p. 11.

Stam, Robert (1989). *Subversive Pleasures: Bakhtin, Cultural Criticism, and Film*. Baltimore, The Johns Hopkins University Press.

Stam, Robert (1992). *Reflexivity in Film and Literature: from Don Quixote to Jean-Luc Godard*. New York, Columbia University Press.

Stevenson, Rex (1974). 'Cinemas and Censorship in Colonial Malaya,' *Journal of Southeast Asian Studies*. 5: 2, pp. 209-224.

Suara FINAS (1992). 'The Rich and the Film Industry,' *Suara FINAS*. 11, p. 24.

Sweeney, Amin (1972). *The Ramayana and the Malay Shadow-Play*. Kuala Lumpur, The National University of Malaysia Press.

Sweeney, Amin (1989). 'The Malay Novelist: Social Analyst or Informant? Or Neither?', *Review of Indonesian and Malaysian Affairs*. 23, pp. 96-124.

Sweeney, Amin (1991) 'Literacy and the Epic in the Malay World,' in Joyce Burkhalter Flueckiger and Laurie J. Sears (eds). *Boundaries of the Text: Epic Performances in South and Southeast Asia*. Ann Arbor, Center for South and Southeast Asian Studies, University of Michigan, pp. 17-29.

Sweeney, Amin (1994). *Malay Word Music: a Celebration of Oral Creativity*. Kuala Lumpur, Dewan Bahasa dan Pustaka.

Tan Chunfa (1994). 'The Influx of Shanghai Filmmakers into Hong Kong and Hong Kong Cinema,' in Law Kar (ed). *Cinema of Two Cities: Hong Kong – Shanghai*. Hong Kong, Hong Kong International Film Festival, pp. 74-82.

Tan See Kam (2001). 'Chinese Diasporic Imaginations in Hong Kong Films: Sinicist Belligerence and Melancholia,' *Screen*. 42: 1, pp. 1-20.

Tan Sooi Beng (1989-90). 'The Performing Arts in Malaysia: State and Society,' *Asian Music*. 21: 1, pp. 137-171.

Tan Sooi Beng (1992). 'Counterpoints in the Performing Arts of Malaysia,' in Joel S. Kahn and Francis Loh Kok Wah (eds). *Fragmented Vision: Culture and*

Politics in Contemporary Malaysia. North Sydney, Allen & Unwin, pp. 282-305.

Tan Sooi Beng (1993). *Bangsawan: a Social and Stylistic History of Popular Malay Opera*. Singapore, Oxford University Press.

Taylor, Clyde (1987). 'Eurocentrics vs New Thought at Edinburgh,' *Framework*. 34, pp. 140-148.

Taylor, John Russell (1983). *Strangers in Paradise: The Hollywood Emigres, 1933-1950*. London, Faber.

Teo, Stephen (1993). 'Oh, Karaoke! – Mandarin Pop and Musicals,' in Law Kar (ed). *Mandarin Films and Popular Songs: 40's-60's*. Hong Kong, Hong Kong International Film Festival, pp. 32-36.

Teo, Stephen (1994). 'The Shanghai Hangover – the Early Years of Mandarin Cinema in Hong Kong,' in Law Kar (ed). *Cinema of Two Cities: Hong Kong – Shanghai*. Hong Kong, Hong Kong International Film Festival, pp. 17-24.

Teo, Stephen (1997a). 'Hong Kong's Electric Shadow Show: from Survival to Discovery,' in Law Kar (ed). *Fifty Years of Electric Shadows*. Hong Kong, Hong Kong International Film Festival, pp. 18-24.

Teo, Stephen (1997b). 'LOVE ON A LONELY BRIDGE,' in Law Kar (ed). *Fifty Years of Electric Shadows*. Hong Kong, Hong Kong International Film Festival, p. 186.

Teo, Stephen (2000a). 'BLOOD & TEARS OF THE OVERSEAS CHINESE,' in Law Kar (ed). *Border Crossings in Hong Kong Cinema*. Hong Kong, Hong Kong International Film Festival, p. 162.

Teo, Stephen (2000b). 'Hong Kong Journal,' *Film Comment*. 36: 6, pp. 11-13.

The SBS World Guide (1994). Melbourne, The Text Publishing Company.

Thomas, Rosie (1987). 'India: Mythologies and Modern India,' in William Luhr (ed). *World Cinema since 1945*. New York, Ungar, pp. 301-329.

Thomas, Rosie (1995). 'Melodrama and the Negotiation of Morality in Mainstream Hindi Film,' in Carol A. Breckenridge (ed). *Consuming Modernity: Public Culture in a South Asian World*. Minneapolis, University of Minnesota Press, pp. 157-182.

Thomaz, Luis Filipe Ferreira Reis (1993). 'The Malay Sultanate of Melaka,' in Anthony Reid (ed). *Southeast Asia in the Early Modern Era: Trade, Power, and Belief*. Ithaca, Cornell University Press, pp. 69-90.

Thompson, Kristin (1985). *Exporting Entertainment: America in the World Market, 1907-1934*. London, British Film Institute.

Trinh T. Minh-ha (1989). 'Outside In Inside Out,' in Jim Pines and Paul Willemen (eds). *Questions of Third Cinema*. London, British Film Institute, pp. 133-149.

Ugarte, Eduardo (1992). 'Running Amok: the "Demoniacal Impulse",' *Asian Studies Review.* 16: 1, pp. 182-189.

Uhde, Jan and Yvonne Ng Uhde (2000). *Latent Images: Film in Singapore.* Singapore, Oxford University Press.

Ungku Maimunah Mohd. Tahir (1989). 'The Notion of "Dakwah" and its Perceptions in Malaysia's Islamic Literature of the 1970's and '80's,' *Journal of Southeast Asian Studies.* 20: 2, pp. 288-297.

Usman Awang (1988). '*The Death of a Warrior* (translated by Rahmah Hj. Bujang from the original Malay drama, *Matinya Seorang Pahlawan (Jebat)*,' *Asian Theatre Journal.* 5: 2, pp. 175-197.

van der Heide, Bill (1995). 'Boundary Riding: Cross-Cultural Analysis, National Cinema and Genre,' *Social Semiotics.* 5: 2, pp. 213-237.

van der Heide, Bill (1996a). 'Experiencing India: A Personal History,' *Media International Australia.* 50, pp. 53-59.

van der Heide, Bill (1996b). 'Malaysian Movies: the Shaw Brothers meet the Pandava Brothers in the Land below the Wind,' in Bruce Bennett, Jeff Doyle and Satendra Nandan (eds). *Crossing Cultures: Essays on Literature and Culture of the Asia-Pacific.* London, Skoob Books, pp. 101-110.

van der Heide, William (2001). 'SEMERAH PADI: A Proposal for a New Nation,' *Asian Cinema.* 12: 1, pp. 3-13.

Vasey, Ruth (1992). 'Foreign Parts: Hollywood's Global Distribution and the Representation of Ethnicity,' *American Quarterly.* 44: 4, pp. 617-642.

Vasudev, Aruna (1995). 'Cannes,' *Cinemaya.* 28-29, pp. 75-77.

Vasudevan, Ravi (1992). 'Glancing off Reality: Contemporary Cinema and Mass Culture,' *Cinemaya.* 16, pp. 4-9.

Vasudevan, Ravi (1994). 'Dislocations: the Cinematic Imagining of a New Society in 1950's India,' *The Oxford Literary Review.* 16, pp. 93-124.

Vasudevan, Ravi S. (1995). 'Addressing the Spectator of a "Third World" National Cinema: the Bombay "Social" Film of the 1940's and 1950's,' *Screen.* 36: 4, 305-324.

Vasudevan, Ravi (2000a). 'Shifting Codes, Dissolving Identities: The Hindi Social Film of the 1950's as Popular Culture,' in Ravi Vasudevan (ed). *Making Meaning in Indian Cinema.* New Delhi, Oxford University Press, pp. 99-121.

Vasudevan, Ravi (2000b). 'National Pasts and Futures: Indian Cinema,' *Screen.* 41: 1, pp. 119-125.

Vatikiotis, Michael (1994). 'Morality Plays,' *Asiaweek.* March 10, 1994, pp. 40-41.

Vincendeau, Ginette (ed) (1995). *Encyclopaedia of European Cinema.* London, Cassell/British Film Institute.

von der Mehden, Fred R. (1993). *Two Worlds of Islam: Interaction between Southeast Asia and the Middle East*. Gainsville, University Press of Florida.
von Vorys, Karl (1975). *Democracy without Consensus: Communalism and Political Stability in Malaysia*. Princeton, Princeton University Press.

Wang Gungwu (1992). *Community and Nation: China, Southeast Asia and Australia* (New edition). St. Leonards, Allen & Unwin.
White, Timothy (1995). 'Malaysian Cinema and the Japanese Occupation.' Unpublished Paper presented at the Crossing Cultures Symposium on Literatures and Cultures of the Asia-Pacific Region, November 7, 1995, Australian Defence Force Academy, Canberra.
Willemen, Paul (1994). 'The National,' in *Looks and Frictions: Essays in Cultural Studies and Film Theory*. London, British Film Institute, pp. 206-219.
Williams, Tony (2000). 'The Crisis Cinema of John Woo,' in Poshek Fu and David Desser (eds). *The Cinema of Hong Kong: History, Arts, Identity*. Cambridge, Cambridge University Press, pp. 137-157.
Wings of Gold (1994). 'The Visionary Hussain Hanif,' *Wings of Gold*. August 1994, pp. 42-43.
Winzeler, Robert (1990). 'Amok: Historical, Psychological, and Cultural Perspectives,' in Wazir Jahan Karim (ed). *Emotions of Culture: a Malay Perspective*. Singapore, Oxford University Press, pp. 96-122.
Wright, Will (1975). *Sixguns and Society: a Structural Study of the Western*. Berkeley, University of California Press.

Yoshimoto, Mitsuhiro (2000). *Kurosawa: Film Studies and Japanese Cinema*. Durham, Duke University Press.
Yu Mo-wan (1981). 'Swords, Chivalry and Palm Power: a Brief Survey of the Cantonese Martial Arts Cinema, 1938-1970,' in Leong Mo-ling (ed). *A Study of the Hong Kong Swordplay Film (1945-1980)*. Hong Kong, Hong Kong International Film Festival, pp. 99-106.

Zainal Alam Kadir (1996). 'Why Our Films Don't Sell,' *New Straits Times*. January 31, 1996, p. 3.
Zhang, Yingjin (1994). 'Rethinking Cross-Cultural Analysis: the Questions of Authority, Power, and Difference in Western Studies of Chinese Films,' *Bulletin of Concerned Asian Scholars*. 26: 4, pp. 44-53.
Zhu Hong (ed) (1988). *The Chinese Western: Short Fiction from Today's China*. New York, Ballantine Books.
Zieman (1997). 'P. Ramlee's Legend Continues to Live,' *New Straits Times*. May 29, 1997, p. 5.

Zizek, Slavoj (1992). *Looking Awry: An Introduction to Jacques Lacan through Popular Culture*. Cambridge, Massachusetts, The MIT Press.

Index

92 Legendary La Rose Noire 157

A. R. Tompel 134
A. Samad Said 85, 141, 176
Abang 92 106
Abdel Wahab, Mohamed 127
Adam's Rib 18
adat 67, 94-95
Adventures Of Hang Tuah, The 100, 176
Agneepath 158
Ahmad Sarji 139
Aku Mahu Hidup 146
Alam Ara 125
Ali Aziz 97, 192
Ali Baba Bujang Lapok 12-13
American cinema 39-41, 111-112, 120-123, 243
American western 36-37
Ami Priyoni 155
Amok 153
amuk 74, 90, 168, 179, 193-194, 197, 207, 229, 235, 244
Anak-ku Sazali 168, 234
Anand, Dev 147
Andaya, Barbara and Leonard 90
Andaz 164, 174
Anderson, Benedict 60, 63, 79
Ang, Ien 111
Angelopoulos, Theo 241
Antara Dua Darjat 174, 200, 211, 245
Antara Senyum Dan Tangis 137
Antonioni, Michelangelo 46
Anwar Ibrahim 93, 102
Apocalypse Now 30
Appadurai, Arjun 55, 242
Arjuna 68, 206
Armes, Roy 105
Au Revoir, Mon Amour 157
Australian cinema 113-115, 123

Awara 126, 164-165, 171-172, 174-175, 200
Aziz Osman 18-19, 154, 156, 198, 212, 218, 224, 234, 260

Bachchan, Amitabh 52, 148-149, 158
bahasa Melayu 12, 90, 99-100, 102
Bakhtin, Mikhail 29, 31-32, 35, 108
Bakti 133
Balink, Albert 128
bangsa 100, 187, 189
bangsawan 11, 81-85, 96-97, 119, 124, 127, 129, 131, 136-138, 143, 169, 172, 177, 191, 194, 242, 244
Baharudin Latif 155, 218, 224
Barthes, Roland 32
Battle Of Algiers 45
Battleship Potemkin 197
Becker, A. L. 77
Bell, Heskell 120
Ben Hur 45
bendahara 73, 98, 179, 193-194
Benjamin, Walter 35
bersanding 67, 188
Better Tomorrow III, A 156
Better Tomorrow, A series 50
Bhabha, Homi 33, 35
Bhagavad Gita 68
Bible, The 59, 67
Big Boss, The 49, 146-147, 149, 156
Big Jake 54
bi-laterality 67, 95, 170
Birth Of A Nation, The 123
Bitter Moon 226
Black Rose, The 157
Blood & Tears Of The Overseas Chinese 131
Blood Money 47
Blood Stains The Valley Of Love 142
Boat People 156

Bobby 147-148
Boetticher, Budd 42
bomoh 67, 94, 213
Bordwell, David 19, 165
Bordwell, David, Janet Staiger and Kristin Thompson 111
Borges, Jorge Luis 241
Borhan, Deddy M. 150
Borzage, Frank 202
Brennan, Timothy 63
British cinema 119-122
BUCHANAN RIDES ALONE 42
Buchsbaum, Jonathan 110
BUJANG LAPOK 252
BUJANG LAPOK series 13, 131
BULLET FOR THE GENERAL, A 45
bumiputera 62, 94, 100, 102, 117, 150, 166, 211, 248
Burch, Noel 112
Buscombe, Edward 39
bushido 38, 47

Cantonese martial arts film 48, 148
Cantonese melodrama 143, 148, 169, 199
Cantonese opera film 48, 143, 169
Cathay 117, 119, 150
Cathay-Keris 117, 119, 133-136, 145-146, 151
Cawelti, John 42, 48, 54
censorship 119-122, 153-154, 243
CENTER STAGE 157
Chairil Anwar 86, 174
Chambers, Iain 55
Chan, Jackie 149, 157
Chaplin, Charlie 139
Chatterjee, Partha 61
Chen Kaige 50
Cherita Mahraja Wana 69, 75
Chinese cinema 50-51, 123, 243
CHINESE GHOST STORY series 49
Chisty, K. R. S. 124, 132
CHISUM 54

CHOCOLAT 109
chop suey western 47-51
Chow, Raymond 149
CHUNGKING EXPRESS 15-16
CITIZEN KANE 197
colonial Malaysia 77-86
COLOSSUS OF RHODES, THE 45
Common Story, A 86
CONTEMPT 45
COOLIE 158
Coppola, Francis Ford 206
Cord, The 78
creative understanding 29, 30, 247
cross-cultural analysis 22-23, 29-32, 108, 241, 247
Cumbow, Robert C. 42, 46
curry western 51-54

dakwah 93-94, 99-100
dalang 12, 72, 74-77, 99, 184, 210
darsan 67, 165, 167, 181, 185, 187, 203, 210, 216, 226, 229-230, 244-246, 248
dayang 73, 179, 193-195
de Man, Paul 33
DEEDAR 164, 199, 245
DEEWAR 148, 158
Denis, Claire 109
Dermody, Susan 114
Derrida, Jacques 58
Desser, David 38
Devdas 164, 168, 170-171, 175, 178, 188, 199, 201, 215, 235, 244, 246
DEVDAS (1935) 164, 190
DEVDAS (1936) 137
DEVDAS (1955) 164-166, 230
Devdas 138, 164
diaspora 33-34, 242, 248
DIRTY HARRY 52
Doane, Mary Ann 248
DRAGON: THE BRUCE LEE STORY 48
DRAGON GATE INN 47-48
Draupadi 68, 208
Dutt, Guru 163-164, 168, 245

Eastwood, Clint 45, 54
Egyptian cinema 126, 243
Eisenstein, Sergei 197
El Atrache, Farid 127, 139
EMBASSY 64
Eros Djarot 155
Estella, Ramon 136
ethnicity 62-63
exploitation musical 143, 169, 174, 182, 234
extra turns 84, 137

FANTASI 18, 153, 156
FEMINA 16-21
FENOMENA 212-218, 220, 222-224, 234, 245
Fernandez-Armesto, Felipe 57
Filipino cinema 243
FINAS 18, 147, 150-154
FIST OF FURY 49, 146, 149
FISTFUL OF DOLLARS, A 42-44
FOR A FEW DOLLARS MORE 44, 50, 52
foundational myth 62, 70
foundational narrative 71-74, 183-184, 191
French cinema 109-110, 123
FROM RUSSIA WITH LOVE 148

Gabriel, Teshome 115
Gellner, Ernest 60
gendai-geki 38
Generation of '50 85-86
Genette, Gérard 29, 32
genre 27-28, 35, 44
GERIMIS 162
Ghatak, Ritwik 166
Ghosh, Dhiresh 134
Godard, Jean-Luc 45-46, 110
GREAT TRAIN ROBBERY, THE 123
Grenfell, Newell 105
Griffith, D. W. 123
GUMASTAVIN PENN 169

Hall, Stuart 58, 61, 64, 70, 247
hamburger western 36-37, 39
Hamilton, Annette 115
Hamzah Hussin 91, 105, 119, 131-132, 136, 139-140, 146, 150, 208, 226
Hanan, David 144
Hang Jebat 73-74, 85-86, 97-98, 176, 178-183, 189, 191-198, 206-207, 209, 211, 226, 231, 245
HANG JEBAT 97, 100, 140, 183, 191-198, 245
Hang Jebat Menderhaka 97, 100, 192
Hang Tuah 72-74, 85-86, 97-98, 100, 176, 177-183, 186, 189, 191-198, 206-207, 209, 226, 231, 241, 245
HANG TUAH 73, 97, 100, 134, 176-184, 186-187, 189, 191, 193, 195-197, 211, 218, 245
HARIMAU TJAMPA 145, 191
HATI BUKAN KRISTAL 145
Hayward, Susan 109
He Ping 50
HELEN OF TROY 45
heterogeneity 21, 63-64, 68, 103, 241, 246, 248
heteroglossia 108-109
HIGH AND LOW 39
HIGH NOON 37, 51, 144
HIGH PLAINS DRIFTER 54
Higson, Andrew 107
Hikayat Hang Tuah 69, 72-74, 76, 84, 91, 97, 177, 183, 193, 195, 197, 206, 245
Hikayat Pandawa Jaya 69
Hikayat Pandawa Lima 69, 73
Hikayat Seri Rama 55, 69
Hindi film 51-54, 136-137, 141, 159, 162-165, 169, 199, 224, 235, 237
Ho Ah Loke 118, 135, 140
homogeneity 63, 97, 103, 246, 248
Hondo, Med 109
Hong Kong cinema 47-50, 141-144, 148-149, 156-158, 243
horror film 144

Hu, King 48
HUANG FEIHONG series 48-49, 142, 144, 157
Hui, Ann 156
HUJAN PANAS 134, 166-170, 181, 196, 201, 204, 234-236, 238, 240, 244-246
Hulu Melaka 101
Hussain Haniff 140, 151, 191, 197, 245
hybridity 29, 63, 138, 247

I WAS A MALE WAR BRIDE 18
IBU MERTUA-KU 83, 166, 172, 198-204, 213, 215, 235, 237, 245-246
IBU TIRI 131
identity 58-66
IDIOT, THE 39, 202
Iliad, The 37, 67, 72, 126
IMAN 174
IMITATION OF LIFE 238
IMPI MOON 155
IN THE MOOD FOR LOVE 158
Indian cinema 51-54, 123, 125, 141, 147, 158-159, 162-166, 243
Indonesian cinema 123, 127-129, 132, 144-145, 147, 155-156, 191
Infante, Eddie 136
INTERMEZZO 248
intertextuality 29, 33, 247
invention of tradition 62, 96
IRISAN-IRISAN HATI 155
Islam 69, 76, 81, 88, 93-95, 99-100, 153, 186-189, 211, 213, 217, 220-222, 239
Israeli cinema 113
Italian cinema 41-47

Jacka, Elizabeth 114
JALSAGHAR 81
Jamil Sulong 127, 131, 136, 146, 189, 240
Jane Bond films 148
Japanese cinema 38-44, 112-113, 131, 243
JEDDA 114
jidai-geki 38

Jins Shamsuddin 149-150, 240
JOGHO 264
Johan Jaaffar 97, 140
JU DOU 226

KAAGAZ KE PHOOL 164
kaala pani 78, 241
Kakar, Sudhir 126, 147-148
KAKI BAKAR 106
Kalsoum, Oud 127
Kamaruddin M. Said 98
kampung 20, 67, 86, 102, 176, 184-191, 204, 206-209, 213-215, 217, 220, 222, 225-233, 239, 241, 245-246
Kapoor, Raj 14, 126, 139, 147-148, 156, 163-164, 166, 168, 171, 210
Kapoor, Shammi 147
Karim, Wazir Jahan 67
Karna 148
Kassim Ahmad 86, 97-98, 183, 195
kebangsaan 100
kebudayaan rojak 100, 248
Kee Thuan Chye 57, 99, 154
KELUARGA SI CHOMAT 150
kerajaan 69-70, 79-80, 186, 193
Kessler, Clive 70, 98, 102
khalwat 211, 227, 230, 239
Khan, Mehboob 163
KILL AND PRAY 45
KILLER, THE 50
knight-errant 47, 49, 148, 241
komedi stambul 127-128
Kotaku Oh Kotaku 97
kris 96, 175-176, 178, 180-181, 193, 196-197, 231
Krishna 68, 147, 206
Krishna-lover 147
Krishnan, L. 133-134, 136-137, 140-141
KUCH KUCH HOTA HAI 159
Kumar, Dilip 14, 156, 164, 199
kung fu film 47, 49, 147, 149, 235
Kurosawa Akira 39-44, 131, 189-190, 197, 202, 245

Kwan, Stanley 157

LABU DAN LABI 26-27
Laila 126, 148, 164, 185
LAILA MAJENEUN 126
LAILA MAJNU 125
LAILA MAJNUN 124-129, 132
laksamana 74, 178, 194, 196
Laksmana 68
Lawson, Sylvia 113
LAYAR LARA 262
Lee, Bruce 48-49, 146-147, 149
Leone, Sergio 42-47, 51, 54
LETTER FROM AN UNKNOWN WOMAN 248
LIFE IS CHEAP . . . BUT TOILET PAPER IS EXPENSIVE 50
LIFE ON A STRING 50
LILY VAN JAVA 128
lines of connectedness 22, 26-27, 101-103, 111, 125, 159-160, 162, 241, 244, 247-248
LOETOENG KASAROENG 127
Loke Wan Tho 118, 135, 142
Longford, Raymond 123
LOVE IN PENANG 142, 199
LOVE ON A LONELY BRIDGE 142
LOVERS, THE 157
Low Wai 146, 149
LOWER DEPTHS, THE 39
LOYAL 47 RONIN, THE 38
Lumière, Louis 123

MAD MAX: BEYOND THUNDERDOME 114-115
MAGNIFICENT SEVEN, THE 39-41, 44-45, 50, 52
Mahabharata 34, 51, 54, 67-68, 72-74, 123, 125-126, 148, 196, 206-208, 241, 245
Mahadi J. Murat 161
Mahathir Mohamad 22, 64, 94, 101-102, 153, 208
Majapahit 73, 180

Majnun 126, 148, 164, 170-171, 175, 178, 185, 201, 244
Majnun-lover 126, 138, 147, 164
Majumdar, Phani 134, 176
Malay Film Productions 117, 119, 133-136, 145-146
Malay identity 65-66, 95
Malay nationalism 79-81, 84, 86, 97
Malayan identity 65-66
Malaysian cinema 23, 85, 96, 100, 105-106, 132-141, 145-147, 149-156, 159-160, 161-240, 246
Malaysian film culture 23, 25-26, 103, 116-160
Malaysian identity 65-66, 103
Mandarin martial arts film 48, 149
Mandarin melodrama 143, 148
Maniam, K. S. 78, 99
MARIA MARIANA 155, 264
MARIA MARIANA II 155, 264
martial arts film 47-51, 144, 156
mass migration 78
MATA SHAITAN 151
Matinya Seorang Pahlawan 97, 100, 211
MATINYA SEORANG PATRIOT 101, 106, 198, 205-211, 217, 245
MAWAR MERAH 151
Mayer, Geoff 114
MCA 90, 101
McFarlane, Brian 114
MEGHE DHAKA TARA 166
MEKANIK 118, 154
Melakan sultanate 70-74, 89, 101, 178-182, 194, 242
Méliès, Georges 123
melodrama 82, 130, 142, 151, 162-166, 168-169, 172, 190, 199-200, 213, 229, 233, 236, 244
MENANTU DURHAKA 129
Merdeka Studio 117, 134-135, 140, 146
MIC 90, 101
Minnelli, Vincente 226, 229
Miu Hang-nee 131

Mizoguchi Kenji 38, 131, 173, 190
Morricone, Ennio 46
MOTHER INDIA 237
Muhammad Haji Salleh 72
Muhammad Yusoff Hashim 71, 91
Mulvey, Laura 165, 203, 228
MUTIARA 131

Nandy, Ashis 34
Nanyang films 142, 199
narrative of a nation 61, 71, 86, 103, 186
national cinema 21-23, 27-28, 106-116, 118, 123-124, 159, 161, 244, 246-247
National Cultural Policy see NCP
national culture 60-65, 79, 106
National Film Development Corporation Malaysia see FINAS
national identity 23, 60-65, 103, 106, 247
nationalism 60, 64, 79, 101
naturalization 60
NCP 93, 95-101, 103, 124, 210
NEP 92-95, 102, 149
New Economic Policy see NEP
newness 33-34, 186, 189, 242
NIGHT CRIES 114-115
NO REGRETS FOR OUR YOUTH 39
noodle western 38-41
NORA ZAIN AGEN WANITA 001 146, 149
NORTHERN CRESCENT 59
NOW, VOYAGER 212

Odyssey, The 37, 45, 67, 72
Omar Rojik 190
ON OUR SELECTION 114
ONCE UPON A TIME IN CHINA II 26
ONCE UPON A TIME IN CHINA series 49, 144, 157
ONCE UPON A TIME IN THE WEST 43, 45-47, 49, 53
orang asli 62, 179
ORANG MINYAK 137
O'Regan, Tom 112
Othman Hafsham 151, 154, 240

Ozu Yasujiro 131, 173, 200

P. Ramlee 11, 13, 26, 76, 85, 127, 131, 134, 136, 138-141, 143-146, 150, 166-167, 169, 170-176, 179, 182-183, 185, 188, 190-191, 198-204, 211, 216, 218, 221, 223, 227, 234-235, 237, 240, 244-246, 248
Pabst, G. W. 227
Pahlawan Melayu 85
Pandavas 68, 148, 206, 208, 241
PANDORA'S BOX 227
panggung 11
Parsee theater 81-84, 124-126, 165, 169, 244
pawagam 11
Peckinpah, Sam 54
PENARIK BECA 170-176, 190, 201, 204, 211, 235-236, 244
PEREMPUAN, ISTERI &... 106, 118, 145, 154, 165, 198, 216, 224, 225-233, 238, 240, 246
Phalke, D. G. 123
playback singer 138
Polanski, Roman 226
polyphony 108
Porter, E. S. 123
postcolonial Malaysia 87-101
pre-colonial Malaysia 66-77
PROJECT A 157
projective appropriation 29, 248
PUTERA BERTOPENG 137
PUTERI IMPIAN 155
PUTERI IMPIAN II 155
PYAASA 164-167, 169, 200

Qur'an, The 67, 81, 211, 220

Rahim Razali 100, 198, 205-206, 212
RAHSIA HATIKU 146
Raja Ahmad Alauddin 139, 153, 155, 226
RAJA BERSIONG 146

RAJA HARISHCHANDRA 123, 125
Rajhans, B. S. 124, 129, 132-133, 138, 169
Rama 68, 74-75, 163-164, 181, 194, 196, 241
Ramachandran, M. G. 139
Ramanathan, S. 133
Ramayana 34, 51, 54-55, 61, 67-69, 72, 74, 76, 163-164, 180, 241, 245
RAMBO III 157
Ramli Ibrahim 98-99
RAN 39
RANJAU SEPANJANG JALAN 100, 106, 150
Ranjau Sepanjang Jalan 99-100
Rao, B. N. 126, 134, 166, 169
RASHOMON 190, 197
Ratnam, Mani 158
Ravana 68, 75, 163-164, 180-181, 194, 196
Ray, Satyajit 81, 166, 171
REBECCA 212
RED SORGHUM 50
Renoir, Jean 110
Richie, Donald 116
RINGGIT KASORRGA 145, 153, 209, 224
ROJA 158
ronin 38, 42
Roomai Noor 136
RORO MENDUT 155
Rosen, Philip 107
Rosnani Jamil 151
Roy, Bimal 163-164, 171
Ruiz, Raul 25
rukunegara 92
Rushdie, Salman 33-34

Said, Edward 30, 34-35, 242
Salim Said 144
Salina 85, 176
Salleh Ben Joned 98-100, 195, 248
samurai film 38-41
sandiwara 84, 131
SANJURO 39
Sarris, Andrew 111

Satanic Verses, The 33
SCHINDLER'S LIST 153
Scorsese, Martin 46
SEARCHERS, THE 46
Sejarah Melayu 62, 72-73, 76, 91, 177, 183
SELAMAT TINGGAL KEKASIHKU 137
SELUBUNG 218-224, 226, 234, 245
SEMBILU 155, 157, 166, 218, 233-240, 246
SEMBILU II 155, 233
SEMERAH PADI 100, 145, 172, 183-191, 211, 227, 245
SENARIO LAGI 155
SENARIO THE MOVIE 155
SENTIMENTAL BLOKE, THE 114, 123
SERUAN MERDEKA 132
SEVEN SAMURAI 37, 39-41, 53, 185
Shaharuddin b. Maaruf 98
Shakespeare, William 82-84
SHANE 37
SHANGHAI BLUES 157
Shanghai cinema 123, 127-130, 157, 243
Shannon Ahmad 99
Shao brothers *see* Shaw Brothers
Shaw Brothers 47-48, 83, 117, 119, 129-136, 141-142, 146, 149-150, 176
Sheppard, M. C. 100, 176
Shohat, Ella 113
SHOLAY 52-54, 148
SHREE 420 166, 210
Shuhaimi Baba 151, 155, 218, 221, 224, 240
Siegel, Don 54
silat 94, 156, 180, 206, 209, 235
Singapore 80, 85-87, 176, 204
Singaporean cinema 254
SINGAPURA DI WAKTU MALAM 133
Siput Sarawak 151
Sirk, Douglas 168, 202, 226, 229, 238
Sita 68, 163-164, 180-181, 194, 196
Sjumandjaja 126
Slamet Rahardjo Djarot 155
SMILE OF THE LAMB, THE 113
socials 51-52, 163, 172

SODOM AND GOMORRAH 45
sojourner 78-79, 112, 241
Solehah Ishak 90
SOLEIL O 109
SOME CAME RUNNING 166, 229
SONG OF A SONGSTRESS 143
SONG OF MALAYA 142
spaghetti western 28, 41-47, 147
SPEED 157
Spielberg, Steven 19, 153
Sri Lankan cinema 133
Stam, Robert 32
STORY OF THE KELLY GANG, THE 123
STREET ANGEL 130, 139, 143, 157
stunt film 51-54
SUAMI, ISTERI DAN...? 154
sultanate 70, 87, 88, 94, 101
SUMPAH ORANG MINYAK 144, 200
Sweeney, Amin 55, 76
sword and sandal epic 45, 49
sword film 38, 41-44
sword-fighting film 47
SWORDSMAN IN DOUBLE-FLAG TOWN, THE 50-51

Tamil film 141, 158-159, 169, 224
TAMU AGUNG 144
Tan and Wong Film Company 129
Tan Sooi Beng 82
Teguy Karya 155
Teo, Stephen 143
TERANG BOELAN 128-129
TERANG BULAN DI MALAYA 131
TERMINATOR II 157
TERPAKSA MENIKAH 127
Thai cinema 243
THERE'S ALWAYS TOMORROW 166
THRONE OF BLOOD 39, 197
TIGA BURONAN 144
TITANIC 157
TJAMBUK API 145
TJOET NJA' DHIEN 155
TO LIVE 14

TONI 110
tonil 127-128
TOPENG SHAITAN 131
Torah, The 67
TOUCH OF ZEN, A 48
transmigration 57
transtextuality 29, 32-36, 247-248
Trinh T. Minh-ha 30
TSU FEH SOFIAH 212-213
Tsui Hark 26, 49, 156-157
TURTLE BEACH 89-91
TWO ACRES OF LAND 176

UGETSU MONOGATARI 190
UMNO 90-91, 93, 102
UNFORGIVEN 54
United Malay National Organisation *see* UMNO
Usman Awang 97, 100, 211
Usmar Ismail 144-145
U-Wei bin HajiSaari *see* U-Wei Haji Shaari
U-Wei Haji Shaari 155, 198, 225-226, 228, 232, 240, 264

vampire film 144
Vasudevan, Ravi 141, 165
ventriloquist identification 29, 30
Vincendeau, Ginette 110
Visconti, Luchino 47
von Vorys, Karl 89

Wang Gungwu 70, 79, 93
Wang, Wayne 50
WAY OF THE DRAGON, THE 48-49, 149
wayang 11, 74-77, 84, 94, 155, 172, 178, 180, 184, 194, 210, 242, 245
wayang Parsee 82
WEDDING IN GALILEE 113, 222
Welles, Orson 197
western 26, 36-55, 145, 242
WHEN BEAUTY FADES FROM THE TWELVE LADIES' BOWER 143

WILD BUNCH, THE 54
Willemen, Paul 29, 108, 247
WIND FROM THE EAST 45
Wong Kar-wai 15, 158
Woo, John 50
WORLD OF SUZIE WONG, THE 210
WRITTEN ON THE WIND 168, 229
Wu Tianming 50

XX RAY 118, 154, 156
XX RAY II 154, 198, 260

YELLOW EARTH 50
YOJIMBO 39, 41-44, 48

Yusof Haslam 154, 166, 233-234, 240, 264

ZAKHMI AURAT 53
ZANJEER 52, 148
zapin 96, 124, 136, 190, 196
ZATOICHI series 48, 113
Zhang Che 149
Zhang Yimou 14, 50
Zhang, Yingjin 31
Zhou Xuan 139, 143, 169, 234
Zizek, Slavoj 62
ZU: WARRIORS FROM THE MAGIC MOUNTAIN 49